Narrative Theory and the Cognitive Sciences

CSLI Lecture Notes
Number 158

Narrative Theory and the Cognitive Sciences

edited by
David Herman

CSLI
PUBLICATIONS
Center for the Study of
Language and Information
Stanford, California

Copyright © 2003
CSLI Publications
Center for the Study of Language and Information
Leland Stanford Junior University
Printed in the United States
07 06 05 04 03   5 4 3 2 1

Library of Congress Cataloging-in-Publication Data

Narrative theory and the cognitive sciences /
edited by David Herman.
p.   cm. – (CSLI lecture notes ; no. 158)

ISBN 1-57586-467-3 (alk. paper)
ISBN 1-57586-468-1 (pbk. : alk. paper)

1. Discourse analysis, Narrative.
2. Narration (Rhetoric) 3. Cognitive science.
I. Herman, David, 1962 - II. Title. III. Series.
P302.N315   2003
401′.41–dc22   2003017134
CIP

∞ The acid-free paper used in this book meets the minimum requirements of
the American National Standard for Information Sciences—Permanence of
Paper for Printed Library Materials, ANSI Z39.48-1984.

CSLI was founded in 1983 by researchers from Stanford University, SRI
International, and Xerox PARC to further the research and development of
integrated theories of language, information, and computation. CSLI headquarters
and CSLI Publications are located on the campus of Stanford University.

CSLI Publications reports new developments in the study of language, information,
and computation. In addition to lecture notes, our publications include
monographs, working papers, revised dissertations, and conference proceedings. Our
aim is to make new results, ideas, and approaches available as quickly as possible.
Please visit our web site at
http://cslipublications.stanford.edu/
for comments on this and other titles, as well as for changes and corrections by the
author and publisher.

Contents

Contributors

H. PORTER ABBOTT: English Department, University of California at Santa Barbara, Santa Barbara, CA 93106, USA.
pabbott@english.ucsb.edu

GIOVANNA EGIDI: Department of Psychology, SUNY at Stony Brook, Stony Brook, NY 11794, USA.
gegidi@ic.sunysb.edu

CATHERINE EMMOTT: Department of English Language, 12 University Gardens, University of Glasgow, Glasgow G12 8QQ, UK.
C.Emmott@englang.arts.gla.ac.uk

MONIKA FLUDERNIK: English Department, University of Freiburg, D-79085 Freiburg, Germany.
monika.fludernik@anglistik.uni-freiburg.de

WILLIAM FRAWLEY: Dean, Columbian College of Arts and Science, George Washington University, Washington, DC 20052, USA.
frawley@gwu.edu

RICHARD J. GERRIG: Department of Psychology, SUNY at Stony Brook, Stony Brook, NY 11794, USA.
rgerrig@notes.cc.sunysb.edu

DAVID HERMAN: Department of English, North Carolina State University, Raleigh, NC 27695, USA.
dherman@unity.ncsu.edu

MANFRED JAHN: English Department, University of Cologne, Albertus-Magnus-Platz, D-50923 Cologne, Germany.
manfred.jahn@uni-koeln.de

KITTY KLEIN: Department of Psychology, North Carolina State University, Raleigh, NC 27695, USA.
kitty_klein@ncsu.edu

URI MARGOLIN: Department of Comparative Literature, University of Alberta, Edmonton, Alberta T6G 2E5, Canada.
uri.margolin@ualberta.ca

JOHN T. MURRAY, PSY. D: 704 Brush Hill Road, Milton, MA 02186, USA.

ALAN PALMER: 14 Dorset Road, London, SW8 1EJ, UK.
a@palmer-lon.fsnet.co.uk

MARIE-LAURE RYAN: 6705 Red Ridge Trail, Bellvue, CO 80512, USA.
marilaur@msn.com

RAOUL N. SMITH: College of Computer Science, Northeastern University, Boston, MA 02115, USA.
rnsmith@ccs.neu.edu

MARK TURNER: Center for Advanced Study in the Behavioral Sciences, 75 Alta Road, Stanford CA 94305, USA.
turner@casbs.stanford.edu

Preface

This volume provides strong support for a claim made by James Wertsch in his exposition of Vygotsky's sociocultural approach to intelligent behavior: 'the notion of mental function can properly be applied to social as well as individual forms of activity.'[1] The book demonstrates how a group participating in a collective endeavor—in this case, an inquiry into the common ground between theories of narrative and research in the cognitive sciences—forms a system or gestalt that is 'smarter' than any of the individuals making up that system. The thinking whole, in short, is more than the sum of its thinking parts. My chief hope is that *Narrative Theory and the Cognitive Sciences* will in turn stimulate more interdisciplinary scholarship on stories viewed as both a record and an enabling cause of intelligent activity. If that comes to pass, then the volume will have helped give rise to an even larger, collectively more perspicacious group of researchers engaged in the endeavor only begun here.

In working on this volume, I have been fortunate enough to have the assistance of many people whose help made the book possible. At the risk of omitting other names that ought to be included, I single out the following colleagues, contributors, and friends for their assistance, good will, and patient support during recent months: Bill Frawley, Deborah Hooker, Manfred Jahn, Uri Margolin, Brian McHale, Alan Palmer, Alan Richardson, Ellen Spolsky, Mary Helen Thuente, Walt Wolfram, and Lisa Zunshine. At the Publications of the Center for the Study of Language and Information, I thank Chris Sosa for her expert guidance on editorial matters during every phase of the project. As always, my deepest thanks go to Susan Moss and to Tinker, for the unfolding story and what it continues to teach me.

---

[1] J. Wertsch, *Voices of the Mind: A Sociocultural Approach to Mediated Action* (Cambridge, MA: Harvard University Press), p. 27.

Acknowledgments

H. Porter Abbott, "Unnarratable Knowledge: The Difficulty of Understanding Evolution by Natural Selection."
The illustration that appears in this chapter is reprinted with the permission of The Free Press, a Division of Simon & Schuster Adult Publishing Group, from *At the Water's Edge: Macroevolution and the Transformation of Life* by Carl Zimmer. Copyright © 1998 by Carl Zimmer.

Catherine Emmott, "Constructing Social Space: Sociocognitive Factors in the Interpretation of Character Relations."
The excerpts that appear in this chapter are reprinted with permission from:
(i) HarperCollins Publishers Ltd. and Plume, an imprint of Penguin Group (USA) Inc. for extracts from *Girl with a Pearl Earring* by Tracy Chevalier, copyright © 1999 by Tracy Chevalier.
(ii) HarperCollins Publishers Ltd. and Jonathan Clowes Ltd., London, on behalf of Doris Lessing for extracts from *The Four-Gated City* by Doris Lessing, copyright © 1969 by Doris Lessing.
(iii) HarperCollins Publishers Ltd. and HarperCollins Publishers Inc. for extracts from "The Real Thing" in *London Observed: Stories and Sketches* by Doris Lessing, copyright © 1987, 1988, 1989, 1990, 1991, 1992 by Doris Lessing.

Alan Palmer, "The Mind Beyond the Skin."
This chapter is to appear in *Fictional Minds* by Alan Palmer to be published in spring 2004 by the University of Nebraska Press. © 2004 University of Nebraska Press. Used with permission.
The excerpts that appear in this chapter are from *Vile Bodies* by Evelyn Waugh. Copyright © 1930 by Evelyn Waugh; opyright renewed 1958 by Evelyn Waugh. Used with permission from Little, Brown and Company, (Inc.)

1

Introduction

DAVID HERMAN

1 Interdisciplinary Narrative Theory: A Sketch

Although they are united by their common concern with the forms and functions of narrative, and also by their shared focus on the relations between stories and intelligent behavior, the twelve new essays gathered in this volume are notable for the diversity of their data sets, descriptive techniques, and explanatory aims.[1] The contributors' samples range from stories constructed for cognitive-psychological experiments, to narratives told by patients in psychotherapy, to stories collected during sociolinguistic interviews, to news stories, to stories written for children, to narratives from several artistic genres, including various kinds of fiction, Neoclassical French drama, a movie screenplay, and Wagnerian opera. The authors' methods of inquiry are equally diverse, ranging from reflection on what goals a theory of narrative should set itself and how it should go about reaching those goals, to quantitatively based evaluation of competing research hypotheses concerning stories, to case studies of individual narratives, to consideration of how stories form part of the basic mental equipment of 'cognitively modern humans', in Mark Turner's phrase. Some of the essays, indeed, use several of these methods (and others) at once.

---

[1] I here use the terms *intelligence, intelligent behavior*, and *cognition* more or less synonymously, adopting Barbara Rogoff's (1990) definition of *intelligence* as the socially supported ability to solve problems grounded in particular domains of activity. However, I do not mean to suggest that all the contributors to the volume would subscribe to this same definition.

Narrative Theory and the Cognitive Sciences.
David Herman (ed.).
Copyright © 2003, CSLI Publications.

The extraordinary variety of the contributors' tutor texts and research foci testifies to the pervasiveness and polyfunctionality of narrative itself. As accounts of what happened to particular people in particular circumstances and with specific consequences, stories are found in every culture and subculture and can be viewed as a basic human strategy for coming to terms with time, process, and change. At issue is a strategy for sensemaking that contrasts with, but is in no way inferior to, 'scientific' modes of explanation that characterize phenomena as mere instances of general covering laws.[2]

In the narratological literature, narrative is broadly defined as a sequentially organized representation of a sequence of events (Chatman 1990; Genette 1980 [1972]; Prince 1982; Rimmon-Kenan 1983).[3] In this context, events can be understood as time- and place-specific transitions from some source state S (e.g., a battle is imminent) to a target state S' (the battle has been won or lost). As Prince (1973) noted, however, event-sequences are a necessary but not a sufficient condition for stories. What distinguishes (1) from (2)—what makes (2) a narrative instead of a mere agglomeration of unrelated elements, as in (1)—is the structure into which states and events are slotted in the second case but not the first.

(1) The battle was over. The battle was imminent. The fight took place.

(2) The battle was imminent. Then the fight took place. As a result, the battle was over.

---

[2] Relevant in this context is Jerome Bruner's (1986) distinction between 'narrative' and 'paradigmatic' (or logico-classificatory) modes of thinking. Bruner's argument that narrative thinking constitutes a mode of cognition on a par with paradigmatic thinking has helped spawn the research tradition sometimes referred to broadly as 'narrative psychology' (cf. Sarbin 1986). However, as Hoshmand (2000) points out in her overview article, work conducted under the auspices of narrative psychology actually includes a number of more or less interrelated endeavors: epistemological reflection on narrative as a paradigm for knowledge viewed as socially constructed; a mode of meta-psychological or meta-theoretical inquiry using narrative as a base metaphor for theory construction and theoretical integration; a method for substantive psychological inquiry complementing quantitative methods and drawing on 'narrative ways of knowing', i.e. those associated with ethnographic, grounded-theory, and phenomenological styles of investigation; and the application of concepts from narrative theory by clinical practitioners and psychological researchers (cf. Howard 1991). Narrative pychologists engaged in any of these endeavors will, I believe, find at least portions of the present volume useful. Conversely, all the contributors to the volume investigate issues proximate to, or in some cases overlapping with, those explored in one or more of the just-mentioned subdomains of narrative psychology.

[3] Compare the definition offered by Margolin in his contribution to this volume: '...narrative is essentially a verbal representation of things in time, and more specifically of changes of state caused by physical events.'

In (1) two states and an event are presented additively, but in (2) the target state is an inversion of the source state, and moreover the inversion in question is caused by the event that intervenes between the source and target states. The difference between narrative and non-narrative sequences thus derives from the higher-order, supersentential structure that can be discerned in (2) but not (1). Inversely, humans' 'narrative competence' stems from their ability to produce and understand representations of event-sequences in which such higher-order structure obtains—even if, in the case of verbal narrative, that structure is not explicitly signalled via temporal adverbs (*then*), causal connectives (*as a result*), or other linguistic means.

For his part, Todorov (1968) imposed an even more restrictive condition on how states and events have to be distributed for an event-sequence to qualify as a story. For Todorov, narratives prototypically follow a trajectory leading from an initial state of equilibrium, through a phase of disequilibrium, to an endpoint at which equilibrium is restored (on a different footing) because of intermediary events—though not every narrative will trace the entirety of this path (cf. Bremond 1973; Kafalenos 1995). Todorov thereby sought to capture the intuition that stories characteristically involve some sort of conflict, or the thwarting of participants' intended actions by unplanned events, which may or may not be the effect of other participants' intended actions. From this perspective, to be categorized as a narrative, an event-sequence must involve some kind of noteworthy (hence 'tellable') disruption of an initial state of equilibrium by an unanticipated and often untoward event or chain of events (cf. Propp 1968 [1928]). Bruner (1991) advances a similar claim when he suggests that stories embody a dialectic of 'canonicity and breach'. As Bruner puts it, 'to be worth telling, a tale must be about how an implicit canonical script has been breached , violated, or deviated from in a manner to do violence to…[its] "legitimacy"' (1991: 11).

In contrast with some of the earlier narratological research, the contributions to the present volume seek less to specify necessary and sufficient conditions for story than to explore the semiotic, cognitive, and sociointeractional environments in which narrative acquires salience and to which stories in turn lend structure. Indeed, as I argue in my own contribution, narratives are found virtually everywhere because the construction of stories lends crucial support to so many practices and types of activity. Stories enable people to communicate about past, imagined, or otherwise non-proximate situations and events (Goffman 1974, 1981). Further, by construing themselves and their cohorts as 'characters' in an unfolding narrative, people are able to make inferences about their own and others' minds (Herman under review). Stories can also be used to build an account of who was responsible for what during a criminal trial or a family argument

(Ochs et al. 1992; Ochs and Capps 2001). Just as crucially, narrative helps people fashion the vicissitudes of personal experience into a more or less coherent life story (Linde 1993).

Theorists' recognition of the vital role played by stories in our everyday lives is both a cause and a byproduct of the development (one might say explosion) of new approaches to narrative analysis in recent years. Likewise, the publication of *Narrative Theory and the Cognitive Sciences* can be seen as part of what might be called a broader 'narrative turn' that has been unfolding over the past several decades, with narrative becoming a central concern in a wide range of disciplinary fields and research contexts.[4] On the one hand, as the chapters by Gerrig and Egidi, by Klein, and by Frawley, Murray, and Smith all demonstrate, scholars working in the confederated disciplines of the cognitive sciences have shown an increasing willingness to take on ever more complex and richly situated narratives (see also Johnstone 1990; Ochs and Capps 2001; and the diverse approaches sketched by the essays included in Bamberg 1997). Researchers in these disciplines have begun to embrace the challenge of characterizing how readers or listeners process extended natural-language narratives, as opposed to the short, artificially constructed narratives designed by early cognitive theorists—those stories being a discourse-level analog of the 'sentoids' inhabiting the pages of linguistics textbooks but only very distantly related to the kinds of sentences actually used by people in naturally occurring communicative contexts.[5]

On the other hand, humanists studying various forms of verbal art, and in particular narratives, have become increasingly open to and knowledgeable about developments in the cognitive sciences. As Richardson and Steen (2002) point out in their introduction to a recent special journal issue devoted to 'Literature and the Cognitive Revolution', '[a] number of literary theorists and critics...have steadily been producing work that finds its inspiration, its methodology, and its guiding paradigms through a dialogue with one or more fields within cognitive science: artificial intelligence,

---

[4] Here and throughout, in referring to *the cognitive sciences* (in the plural) I have in mind Wilson and Keil's (1999) taxonomic scheme, in which six 'confederated disciplines' can be grouped together under the umbrella field at issue: philosophy; psychology; the neurosciences; computational intelligence; linguistics and language; and culture, cognition, and evolution. Collectively, the essays in the present volume can be construed as making a case for the inclusion of narrative theory on this roster, at the very least as an autonomous module within linguistics and language. Along the same lines, Herman (2001) suggests how incorporation of concepts and methods from narrative theory would give an even fuller picture of the research landscapes mapped in *The MIT Encyclopedia of the Cognitive Sciences* (Wilson and Keil 1999).

[5] For further comments on the consequences of using artificially constructed narratives in cognitive research, see Emmott's contribution to this volume.

cognitive psychology, post-Chomskian linguistics, philosophy of mind, neuroscience, and evolutionary biology' (1). Richardson and Steen mention a range of cognitively inflected programs for research adopted by humanists since at least the 1980s, including groundbreaking work by Spolsky (1993; cf. Schauber and Spolsky 1986), Tsur (1982), and Turner (1991). As for cognitively oriented humanistic research on narrative in particular, many of the lines of inquiry developed in the present volume originated in earlier work by the contributors themselves. Relevant precedents include Abbott (2000a, 2000b; see also the essays assembled in Abbott 2001), Emmott (1997), Fludernik (1996), Jahn (1997, 1999), Ryan (1991), and Turner (1991, 1996).

By meeting each other half way, then, theorists working on either side (or somewhere in the middle) of the divide between C. P. Snow's (1993) 'two cultures' have set the stage for this volume. To provide additional context for this meeting of minds concerned with (real as well as fictional) minds, it is necessary to move back in time a few decades. The cross-disciplinary narrative turn exemplified by the essays collected here was given impetus by the confluence of a number of research initiatives, three of which can be singled out as especially important in the context of the present volume. The three initiatives in question, which happened more or less concurrently, are the rise of structuralist theories of narrative in France in the mid to late 1960s; the advent of the sociolinguistic study of personal-experience narratives, in research pioneered by William Labov and Joshua Waletzky in the late 1960s and early 1970s and then extended and refined by discourse analysts, ethnographers, sociolinguists, and others in the decades since (see Bamberg 1997 for an overview); and the focus on narrative by cognitive psychologists and artificial intelligence researchers concerned with story grammars and with scripts and schemata beginning in the 1970s.

Section 2 briefly sketches these research initiatives and suggests how an integrative, interdisciplinary framework for narrative analysis—an approach that weaves together strands of research that began as separate areas of inquiry—can help circumvent problems that arise when stories are studied in an over-compartmentalized way. In other words, the ongoing *rapprochement* of narrative theory and the cognitive sciences can be seen as the result of an effort to create a kind of gestalt, a unified program for research, that is greater than the sum of its parts. Section 3 discusses how the essays gathered here are integrative in another sense as well, bridging two broad approaches to the study of narrative and intelligence. One approach focuses on the representations and processes required to make sense of stories; the other focuses on stories as themselves a means for sense-making. Finally, section 4 provides an overview of the volume as a whole, giving a thumbnail sketch of each contribution and discussing how the four Parts of the book relate to one another.

2 Toward an Integrative Theory of Stories: Synthesizing Structuralist, Contextualist, and Cognitive Approaches

2.1 The Structuralist Paradigm

Tzvetan Todorov coined the French term 'la narratologie' ('narratology') in 1969 to designate what he and other Francophone structuralists (e.g., Roland Barthes 1977 [1966], Gérard Genette 1980 [1972], and A. J. Greimas 1983 [1966]) conceived of as a science of narrative modeled after the 'pilot-science' of Saussure's structural linguistics (Todorov 1969; de Saussure 1959). By analogy with Saussurean structuralism, the early narratologists sought to account for the underlying code (*la langue*) enabling (i.e., supporting the design and interpretation of) particular narrative 'messages' (*la parole*).[6] Far from being a handmaiden to interpretation, a nomenclature or technique used to identify *what* a given narrative means, narratology was to be a framework for studying systematically *how* narrative means—for giving an account of the semiotic system thanks to which stories can be created and recognized *as* stories (Prince 1982; Herman 1999). For structuralist narrative theorists, the scope of this semiotic system was subject to investigation rather than assumed as pre-given. In Barthes's (1977 [1966]) account, the system clearly encompassed many more stories than those belonging to the domain of literary narrative. Thus, noting that narratives can be presented in a variety of formats and genres, Barthes (1977 [1966]) argued explicitly for an approach to the analysis of stories that transcended disciplinary boundaries—an approach in which stories can be viewed as supporting a variety of cognitive and communicative activities, from spontaneous conversations and courtroom testimony to visual art, dance, and mythic and literary traditions.

Emphasizing the need for a systematic investigation of narrative in whatever setting, medium, or genre it obtains, structuralist narratology thus prepared the ground for interdisciplinary research on stories. Indeed—as the

---

[6] David Lodge (1999) provides an excellent brief account of the larger structuralist project in which the early narratologists participated: 'Structuralism is, or was, a movement in what Continental Europeans call 'the human sciences', which sought to explain and understand cultural phenomena (from poems to menus, from primitive myths to modern advertisements) as manifestations of underlying systems of signification, of which the exemplary model is verbal language itself, especially as elucidated by the Swiss linguist Ferdinand de Saussure' (xi).

present volume suggests—Barthes's call for a cross-disciplinary inquiry into narrative has been answered in the years following the heyday of structuralism.[7] However, the early narratologists were hamstrung by their own structuralist methodology; their conception of the 'pilot-science' of linguistics was already out of phase with then-current (not to mention emergent) developments in language theory and related fields of study. In two respects, in particular, the stucturalists' models would have benefitted from greater awareness of research being conducted by other scholars. In fact, much contemporary work in interdisciplinary narrative theory can be seen as an attempt to reconcile the emphasis on narrative as a structure or semiotic system with two complementary emphases that had also begun to emerge by the 1960s and 1970s—i.e., the contextualist and cognitive emphases.

2.2 The Contextualist Paradigm

In the first place, theorists concerned with the social contexts of language use began to outline the rudiments of a 'linguistics of parole' that Saussure himself had envisioned but never implemented in setting out the foundations of structuralist linguistics (Harris 2001). From this perspective, 'messages' or utterances (including the extended utterances that take narrative shape) should be viewed not as manifestations of a code that preexists all communicative acts, but rather as an interactional achievement, negotiated by participants using an inherently variable linguistic code in situated contexts. This contextualist approach to language-in-use fostered the creation of subfields such as linguistic pragmatics (Austin 1962, Grice 1989), discourse analysis, and sociolinguistics (including conversation analysis and quantitative approaches to linguistic variation). It was in this environment that Labov and Waletzky wrote their groundbreaking 1967 essay on 'Narrative Analysis: Oral Versions of Personal Experience', which spawned a variety of sociolinguistic approaches to narrative analysis, some of them quite different from Labov's and Waletzky's own (again, Bamberg 1997 provides a useful overview).

To be sure, the model developed by Labov and Waletzky (1967) (and further specified in a follow-up article published in 1972 by Labov) continued to focus on matters of narrative structure. But its chief aim was to forge an approach to studying stories-in-use that could accommodate both

---

[7] Narrative now falls within the purview of many social-scientific, humanistic, and other (sub)disciplines, including sociolinguistics; discourse analysis; communication studies; literary theory; human-computer interaction; philosophy; cognitive, social, and clinical psychology; film studies; ethnography; sociology; media studies; historiography; legal studies; the study of institutions and organizations; and others.

structural and contextual factors. The model established what remains a much-relied-upon vocabulary for labelling the structural components of personal-experience narratives (abstract, orientation, complicating action, evaluation, result, coda). It also identified clause- and sentence-level structures tending to surface in each of these components, suggesting that story-recipients monitor the discourse for signs enabling them to 'chunk' what is said into units-in-a-narrative-pattern. For example, clauses with past-tense verbs in the indicative mood are likely to occur in (i.e., be a reliable indicator of) the complicating action of the narrative, whereas storytellers' evaluations depart from this baseline syntax, their marked status serving to indicate the point of the narrative, the reason for its telling. As my previous sentence suggests, Labov's model laid the groundwork for further inquiry into *both* the linguistic (or structural) *and* the interactional (or contextual) profile of narratives told during face-to-face encounters. Conversational narratives do consist of identifiable clause-, sentence-, and discourse-level features; yet they are also anchored in contexts where their tellers have to have a (recognizable) point or else be ignored, shouted down, or worse (see Goodwin 1990: 239-57).

Although approaches that have built on Labov's and Waletzky's foundational work adopt different strategies for striking a balance between structural features and contextual functions of stories, the effort to strike that balance remains a constant. Students of narrative working in the conversation-analytic tradition, for example, find evidence about communicative contexts in the disposition or sequencing of structural elements themselves (Jefferson 1978, 1988; Sacks 1972; Schegloff 1997). By contrast, for theorists drawing on Goffman's interactionalist model to study narrative (Goffman 1981; Goodwin 1990; Herman 1999; Schiffrin 1987), the sociocommunicative logic of stories derives from the way particular moves required for the (joint) elaboration of a narrative are meshed into an overarching, emergent participation framework. By virtue of this framework or supraindividual whole, storytellers and interlocutors take on various footings, positions, and hence identities over the course of the presentation of a story. Note that in all of these versions of the contextualist paradigm, narrative can be seen to facilitate intelligent behavior. Stories support the (social) process by which the meaning of events is determined and evaluated, enable the distribution of knowledge of events via storytelling acts more or less widely separated from those events in time and space, and assist with the regulation of communicative behaviors, such that the actions of participants in knowledge-yielding and -conveying talk can be coordinated.[8]

---

[8] For more detailed arguments along these lines, see my contribution to the volume.

2.3 The Cognitive Paradigm

In addition to being constrained by their impoverished notion of the communicative functions of stories in contexts of use, the early structuralist models were limited by their failure to specify the exact status of the code—the structure—regulating the production and understanding of particular narratives. Here the narratologists did not explore fully enough the implications of the Saussurean notion of *la langue*, or linguistic system, which they themselves characterized as an analog for the system governing the use and interpretation of particular narrative texts or discourses. For Saussure, the linguistic system was at once a mental construct and a social fact (de Saussure 1959; see also Culler 1986; Harris 1987, 2001). He held that linguistic competence is a function of the cognitive equipment that speakers acquire when they internalize or 'assimilate' (de Saussure 1959: 14) the linguistic system associated with a language—i.e., the principles governing the language's phonological, morphological, and syntactic patterns, together with the semantic and pragmatic properties attaching to expressions formed by way of those principles. But the linguistic system itself does not exist except as instantiated in the (minds of members of the) speech community that uses the language.[9] Thus, the system of a language is at once cognitively based and socially constituted, being a mental resource for individuals yet rooted in the social life of communities of speakers. For this reason, facts about the linguistic system should not be confused with the facts about the idiolects used by particular speakers, although idiolectal variants can, if assimilated into the social life of the language, very well actuate broader changes, i.e., create new facts about *la langue*.

Although structuralist narratologists did not exploit these aspects of the very Saussurean framework on which they founded their enterprise, story analysts working in other fields have accentuated the cognitive dimensions of the narrative 'code' and also (as discussed in my next subsection) the social underpinnings of that code. In the 1970s and 1980s both cognitive psychologists and artificial-intelligence researchers developed hypotheses about the mental equipment associated with mastery of the system of narrative. On the one hand, researchers such as David E. Rumelhart (1975) and Jean Matter Mandler (1984) postulated the existence of what they characterized as cognitively based story grammars or narrative rule systems. Such

---

[9] Thus Saussure speaks of *la langue* as 'a grammatical system that has a potential existence in each brain, or, more specifically, in the brains of a group of individuals. For language is not complete in any speaker; it exists perfectly only within a collectivity' (1959: 13-14).

grammars were cast as formal representations of the cognitive mechanisms used to parse stories into sets of units (e.g., settings and episodes) and principles for sequencing and embedding those units (for a fuller discussion, see Herman 2002: 10-13). As Mandler put it, '[t]he contention of all story grammars is that stories have an underlying, or base, structure that remains relatively invariant in spite of gross differences in content from story to story. This structure consists of a numbered of ordered constituents' (1984: 22).

Research informing the story-grammar approach has been redirected and reinflected in recent years, yielding frameworks like those developed by Stein (2002) and Stein, Trabasso, and Albro (2001). In this more recent research, formal representations of causal networks have replaced 'grammatical' models (see Trabasso and Sperry 1985; Trabasso and van den Broek 1985), enabling computer-based implementations of causal structures and processes only hinted at in the earlier work.[10] Nonetheless, the research at issue continues to focus on the cognitive equipment, the intelligent activity, of users and interpreters of narrative viewed as a system for communication and cognition, with the latter term defined broadly to include emotional knowledge.

Roughly contemporaneously with the work on story grammars, research in artificial intelligence had also begun to focus attention on the cognitive basis for creating and understanding stories. 1977 saw the publication of Schank and Abelson's *Scripts, Plans, Goals, and Understanding: An Inquiry into Human Knowledge Structures* (Schank and Abelson 1977), a foundational study of how stereotypical knowledge reduces the complexity and duration of many processing tasks. One such task, central to Schank's and Abelson's study, is the interpretation of narratives. Indeed, the concept of 'script', i.e., a knowledge representation in terms of which an expected sequence of events is stored in the memory, was designed to explain how people are able to build up complex interpretations of stories on the basis of very few textual or discourse cues.

Experiential repertoires, stored in the form of scripts, enable readers or listeners of stories to 'fill in the blanks' and assume that if (for example) a narrator mentions a masked character running out a of bank with a satchel of money, then that character has in all likelihood robbed the bank in question. From this perspective, what makes a story a story, and for that matter how 'narrative-like' a given story seems, can be explained in terms of the relation between the explicit cues included in a text or a discourse and the scripts on which readers or listeners rely in processing those cues (see Her-

---

[10] Work in this tradition falls within the domain of what Gerrig and Egidi refer to in their chapter as explanation-based theories of narrative processing.

man 2002: 85-113). More recent research on knowledge representations suggests the limits as well as the possibilities of the original script concept (Davis 1990; Hayes 1999). Yet work in artificial—or, in Wilson's and Keil's (1999) terms, 'computational'—intelligence continues to underscore the necessity of viewing narrative itself as a relational construct. More specifically, stories should be construed as the pairing or blending of (certain kinds of) semiotic structures with (certain kinds of) cognitive resources.

2.4 Integration and Synergism

However, returning to one of the basic insights of Saussure's theory of language, and extending the contextualist paradigm in new directions, narrative theorists are now giving particular emphasis to the claim that semiotic structures and cognitive resources need to be triangulated with a third component—namely, social conditions and processes—to create a truly integrative approach to stories. At issue, to repeat, is a program for research that incorporates the structuralist, contextualist, and cognitive approaches but affords new insights through their very combination, thanks to the synergy thereby created. Especially relevant, in this context, is Vygotsky's 'socio-historical' approach to mental functioning (Vygotsky 1978; Frawley 1997; Wertsch 1985, 1991, 1998).[11] Vygotsky emphasized the sociointeractional bases of cognition, arguing that intelligence is mediated by sign-systems and other psychological (as well as material) tools or artifacts. An essential resource for thought, systems of signs are, as Saussure recognized, socially constituted and propagated, being embedded in social groups and instantiated in social encounters (acts of *la parole*). Viewed in this Vygotskian-Saussurean light, the project of integrating narrative theory and the cognitive sciences can be seen as an effort to understand how people weave tapestries of story by relying on abilities they possess as simultaneously language-using, thinking, and social beings. Or, to put the same point another way, a cross-disciplinary approach to stories—an approach of the sort cumulatively elaborated by the contributors to this volume—may help reveal the extent to which intelligence itself is rooted in narrative ways of knowing, interacting, and communicating.

---

[11] The chapter by Frawley, Murray, and Smith, along with my own contribution, draws on Vygotsky's ideas to characterize narrative as a sociosemiotic resource for cognition.

3 Two Strategies for Studying Narrative and Intelligence

In addition to facilitating a synthesis of the structuralist, contextualist, and cognitive paradigms described in my previous section, the essays collected here can be described as integrative in another way, as well. Taken together, the essays attempt to bridge two strategies for studying the interrelations between stories and intelligence—and thus for linking narrative theory and the cognitive sciences. On the one hand, analysts of narrative have studied mental representations and cognitive processes instrumental to people's ability to make sense of stories. Relevant representations include mental models of characters, episodes, and story settings; relevant processes include the storage of situations and events in short- and long-term memory and the interpretation of referring expressions (e.g. pronouns) used in narrative discourse. On the other hand, analysts have studied narrative as itself an instrument for sense-making, a semiotic and communicative resource that enables humans to make their way in a sometimes confusing, often difficult world. Contributors to the present volume engage with central questions arising from both of these perspectives, with some chapters focusing on the types of mental activity required to understand narratively organized texts and others focusing on the ways in which thinking can be described as organized by narrative means. The volume is its own best argument, I believe, for the advantages of construing stories as both a major target of and an important basis for cognition.

3.1 Making Sense of Stories

Understanding long, detailed, and formally sophisticated literary narratives is for many people a natural, seemingly automatic process. Early on, however, artificial intelligence researchers showed that quite complex linguistic and cognitive operations are required to generate or comprehend even the most minimal stories. Hence creating a computer system with 'narrative intelligence'—e.g., building an interface that would make users feel as though their interactions with the system were part of an emergent story (Herman and Young 2000; Mateas and Senger 1999)—poses considerable challenges. More broadly, to account for recipients' ability to interpret narratively organized discourse, a number of contributors hypothesize that generic cognitive capacities as well as specialized processing mechanisms come into play—from short-term and long-term memory stores (Gerrig and Egidi), to mental representations of places and movements in storyworlds (Ryan), to the conceptual blending of autonomous narratives into 'double-scope stories' (Turner), to inferences about the mental functioning of and social relationships between characters represented in stories (Emmott, Margolin, Palmer). Along the same lines, a number of the contributors discuss interactions between top-down (script- or frame-driven) and bottom-up (data-driven) processing strategies in contexts of narrative understanding. As the chapters by Emmott, Fludernik, Margolin, and Palmer suggest, scripts and frames guide readers' interpretations of particular situations, participants, and events; but in turn, as the world presented in a narrative unfolds, the text can force readers or listeners to modify or shift the interpretive models on which they have hitherto relied (see Jahn 1997, 1999). A similar dynamic is evident in the process of cognitive mapping discussed by Ryan.

Moreover, from a standpoint informed by discourse analysis and cognitive linguistics, narrative can be viewed as a discourse environment in which producers as well as interpreters of stories use many different linguistic resources—or coding strategies—to establish and maintain reference to discourse entities that interact with one another in narrative-specific ways (Emmott 1997). Indeed, narrative subsumes the full range of coding strategies bound up with language use generally, because stories encompass states, events, places, objects, and participants, who can in turn build up mental representations of (and talk about) states, events, places, objects, themselves, and other participants. To account for the range of processing mechanisms involved, cognitively inclined narrative theorists have thus suggested that listeners and readers trying to make sense of conversational and literary narratives draw on a core set of principles and parameters—what Emmott characterizes as 'contextual frames', Fludernik (1996) as TELLING, VIEWING, ACTING, EXPERIENCING, and REFLECTING frames, and Herman (2002, forthcoming) as micro- and macrodesign principles associated with 'story logic'. The chapters by Emmott and Fludernik revisit issues of narrative comprehension from this 'discourse perspective', as does Jahn's discussion of the cognitive logic by which external stories are internalized during the interpretive process.

3.2 Stories as Sense-Making

But narrative can also be viewed as an instrument for the exercise or even enhancement of cognitive abilities, and not just a target for cognition. From this perspective, narrative functions as a basic resource for intelligent activity across a variety of settings, as well as a strategy for regaining psychological well-being after traumatic or stressful events. Thus, Klein's essay reports findings from social-psychological research that indicates a positive correlation between narrative construction and health, whereas the chapter by Frawley, Murray, and Smith discusses beneficial, client-empowering uses of stories in therapeutic settings. For its part, Turner's chapter suggests that humans navigate their environment and make sense of incomprehensibly large-scale processes and events by constructing, remembering, and blending more or less analogous stories. Abbott, meanwhile, notes how humans' predisposition to understand the world in narrative terms poses obstacles to the acceptance (or even comprehension) of scientific theories that resist or disallow being conceptualized in story-like ways. Jahn's chapter characterizes the internalization of external stories and the externalization of internal ones as a complex data structure enabling people to link perceptual, cognitive, communicative, and other forms of activity. And my own chapter details a number of other ways in which stories can be viewed as 'tools for thinking'.

In short, collectively revealing narrative to be a crossroads where multiple perspectives on intelligent behavior can be productively combined, the essays in the volume suggest the importance of fostering more interchange between narrative theorists and those working in disciplines traditionally affiliated with the cognitive sciences. The volume itself should afford new opportunities for just this sort of dialogue.

4 An Overview of the Volume

The following subsections provide a synopsis of the volume as whole. Expanding on my comments in the previous section, I furnish a thumbnail sketch of each essay and also describe how it fits within the overarching structure of the book. In this way, I attempt to give a fuller sense of the contents of the volume and also of how the four Parts of the book are related to one another.

4.1 Approaches to Narrative and Cognition

The essays contained in Part I of the volume provide a sense of the interdisciplinary scope of contemporary narrative theory. Specifically, these contributions examine narrative from the perspectives afforded by cognitive psychology, social psychology, linguistics, and therapeutic practice. Richard Gerrig's and Giovanna Egidi's lead-off essay, 'Cognitive Psychological Foundations of Narrative Experiences', furnishes context for the volume as a whole, exploring the relevance for narrative theory of recent work cognitive psychology. Gerrig and Egidi investigate the basic cognitive mechanisms that allow authors to achieve a wide range of narrative effects; the authors' chief concern is, in other words, 'the backbone of literary experiences'. Decomposing the mechanisms at issue into *processes* and *representations*, the authors point out that some cognitive psychologists seek to give an exhaustive account of processes functioning at each moment of a reader's encounter with (the representations evoked by) a narrative. Other theorists, meanwhile, set themselves a more modest goal, trying to account for just those processes that are automatic.

Focusing on memory processes in particular, Gerrig and Egidi review evidence suggesting that readers in fact achieve continuity across the span of narratives automatically, rather than using explicit memory searches to reconstruct a coherent story. More specifically, readers' narrative experiences seem to reflect (or to be built on the foundation of) what a number of researchers have characterized as a process of resonance, i.e., 'a fast, passive, and easy process by which cues in working memory interact in parallel with, and allow access to, information in long-term memory'. Resonance thus affects both the moment-by-moment processing of narrative texts and the long-term representations by means of which narratives are stored in the memory. Furthermore, even though it enables the 'disentangling' of representations, resonance is not directed to the goal of facilitating narrative experiences. It is, rather, an emergent property of a cognitive process that has no special relationship to narrative comprehension. The remainder of Gerrig's and Egidi's chapter draws on narratives constructed by experimenters as well as literary examples to bolster the case that cognitive psychological research is deeply relevant for narrative theory. Positioning their account against the backdrop provided by two broad research trends—the minimalist theory (or memory-based text processing) and the constructionist theory (or explanation-based processing)—Gerrig and Egidi explore how readers of narratives monitor their goals, and also how readers update their models of emergent storyworlds.

Whereas Gerrig and Egidi's essay thus focuses on processes enabling readers to make sense of stories, the next two chapters in Part I examine narrative as a major tool for sense-making. In 'Narrative Construction, Cognitive Processing and Health', Kitty Klein synthesizes findings from social, clinical, and developmental psychology suggesting that an individual's construction of a narrative account of a stressful or traumatic experience is predictive of improvements in mental function and in physical and psychological health. Klein's essay begins with a useful survey of attempts to operationalize and quantify concepts pertaining to narrative, reviewing various coding schemes employed by psychologists studying stories. These schemes run the gamut from simple word counts; to counts based on lexical categories (e.g., words expressing causal relations between events, or 'cognitive-mechanism' words such as the verbs *know*, *understand*, *realized*, and *remembered*); to schemes based on judges' ratings, including those in which judges code individual utterances and those in which they deploy holistic scoring systems for 'narrative coherence'. Klein's cost-benefit analysis shows the advantages and disadvantages of the various strategies for operationalization. Whereas counts based on numbers of words or lexical categories can easily be automated, they can also produce misleading results because phrase-, clause-, sentence-, and discourse-level environments are factored out of the analysis. (For example, as Klein shows later on in her essay, causal relations between events in a story can be implied without being explicitly marked at the lexical level, via words and phrases such as *because* or *as a result*.) For their part, schemes based on judges' ratings are subject to other limitations, including the amount of training required for judges and problems with the reliability and validity of judges' assessments. Considerations of this sort suggest the difficulty faced by any researcher who attempts a meta-analysis of the findings from studies in which different coding systems were used.

Be that as it may, and despite the difficulty of developing quantitative measures for narrative-related concepts, narrative remains a significant research focus in social-psychological inquiry. Klein's own essay focuses on memories of stressful life experiences as a domain in which the construction of narratives can be shown to play an importantly beneficial role. The essay builds on previous research suggesting that narratives improve cognitive functioning by enabling people to encapsulate painful experiences that would otherwise impede working memory. Thanks to such narrative encapsulation, the working-memory capacity that would otherwise be used to inhibit (or, worse, relive) intrusive memories of the negative experience can instead be freed up for other cognitive tasks. Testing this and related hypotheses, Klein and her colleagues conducted expressive-writing experiments in which participants were asked to write about a serious event that had recently had a negative impact on their lives. Some participants were explicitly encouraged to construct a narrative about the event in question. To date, findings indicate that increases in the narrative coherence of participants' accounts were responsible for the observed health benefits of the expressive-writing tasks in which they engaged. Klein's essay thus reveals what may be a direct correlation between narrative construction and health, opening up new opportunities for collaborative research by psychologists and narrative theorists.

William Frawley's, John T. Murray's and Raoul N. Smith's study of 'Semantics and Narrative in Therapeutic Discourse' likewise focuses on stories as a sense-making strategy. Characterizing therapy as a mode of personal theory-construction, the authors note that 'sense-making stories' emerge from the overall therapeutic encounter, i.e., within a 'multivalent framework', instead of being carried out by any particular individual. (In this respect, Frawley, Murray, and Smith adopt the sociointeractional or group-based approach to intelligence pioneered by Vygotsky and incorporated into my own essay, as well, in Part II of the volume.) Contrasting psychotherapy with other kinds of doctor-patient interactions, the authors argue that whereas standard doctor-patient conversations retain asymmetric power relations at a deep level, pscyhotherapeutic interventions are co-constructed: 'therapeutic knowledge is constituted by insight in the moment of speaking, rather than uncovered in factual discovery'. Focusing on structural factors of therapeutic narrative, Frawley, Murray, and Smith begin by discussing how sense-making stories are jointly elaborated by clients and psychotherapists; how those stories function to create domains of plausibility in terms of which clients can form new explanations of events in their lives; and how the stories told in therapy are essentially reflexive: '[t]he goal of the narrative in therapy *is the narrative*'.

The authors also draw on tools from semantic theory and from research in linguistic pragmatics to characterize the narratives co-constructed during therapy. On the one hand, the theory of lexical relations and semantic networks help uncover how a therapist and client jointly work toward a new narrative—a story in which the client possesses greater agency (as the *source* of situations and events) than in the narrative that had hitherto been the dominant framework for the client's sense of self. On the other hand, ideas from pragmatics enable Frawley, Murray, and Smith to throw light on other aspects of the narratives emerging in and by means of therapy, including collaborative uses of metaphors and the strategic deployment of semantic scales (e.g., 'On a scale of 1 to 5, with 5 the highest, can you tell me how much progress you have been making in the therapy?').

4.2 Narrative as Cognitive Endowment

The essays in Part II concern themselves with narrative viewed as a basic cognitive endowment, continuing the investigation into stories as an instrument for sense-making across many domains of knowledge and types of activity. Mark Turner's 'Double-scope Stories' includes a wide-ranging discussion of many forms of narrative. This chapter draws on Gilles Fauconnier's and Turner's theory of 'conceptual blending' (Fauconnier and Turner 2002) to explore what the author characterizes as an essentially human ability: namely, the capacity to engage in 'elaborate mental blending of two [or more] separate stories'. H. Porter Abbott's 'Unnarratable Knowledge', meanwhile, uses a case-study approach to show how humans' in-built 'weakness for narrative clarity' can sometimes be at odds with scientific theory-building. My own essay on 'Story as a Tool for Thinking' concludes Part II. The essay draws on a number of research traditions to argue that narrative functions as a highly adaptable, multi-situational resource for thought—a mode of cognitive and communicative practice supporting a variety of problem-solving activities.

Turner's essay suggests that the capacity to create, store, reactivate, and blend narratives is an ability that is unique to cognitively modern humans. Not only can humans escape the 'high command' of the present moment, the actual story they are living out, by daydreaming or inhabiting an imagined narrative scenario. More than this—in a move that Turner likens to 'plucking forbidden fruit'—people can connect two stories that should by rights be kept distinct, blending them to form a third story. Thus, humans can blend a present situation with an imagined or remembered scenario, or they can blend two competing narrative construals of the present moment. In Turner's account, blends of this sort derive from 'a basic human mental operation, with constitutive and governing principles. It played a crucial role, probably *the* crucial role, in the descent of our species over the last fifty or one hundred thousand years.' Examining a number of double-scope stories, where there is particularly elaborate blending of two or more autonomous narratives, Turner identifies several recurrent features: mapping between elements of the two stories, selective projection (whereby different elements of each story are projected into the blended story), and emergent structure, i.e., meanings that result from the integration of the two stories but that do not attach to either story taken in isolation. The essay discusses examples of double-scope stories across many genres and periods, including Racine's *Phèdre*, the story of the crucifixion, the medieval work *The Dream of the Rood*, the story of Seabiscuit, a racehorse which was blended with that of the American people during the Great Depression, and stories written for children.

For its part, Abbott's contribution argues that the resistance to (or noncomprehension of) Darwin's theory of evolution by natural selection is a testament to our in-built 'cognitive predisposition toward narrative models of understanding.' Abbott points out that, as originally conceptualized by Darwin, the notions 'natural selection' and 'species' could not be construed as entities with agency, or for that matter enties that might figure in any coherent narrative of evolution. Interpreters of Darwin have thus been faced with the difficulty of 'constructing an explanatory narrative that shows agency but that has to make do with an apparent lack of entities and even an apparent lack of events, without which, of course, there can be no narrative.' However, because natural selection is a theory about change over time, it is also difficult *not* to describe the theory in narrative terms.

The essay goes on to explore a number of narrativizing strategies more or less explicitly acknowledged as such by commentators attempting to make sense of or else circumvent the implications of Darwin's theory, whose two-tiered model of species-level and individual-level phenomena presented a severe 'challenge to narrative imagining.' There is no easily narrativizable link between Darwin's two levels, because natural selection is not a force of change or agent of propagation, but instead a pattern—i.e., the pattern afforded by 'the continually changing aggregate result of survivals and deaths, of propagation and the absence of progeny.' Theories competing with Darwin's thus tapped into the human predisposition toward narrative-based explanations in their bid to gain acceptance by the public. Adherents to 'saltationism' or abrupt species changes offered an explanatory narrative at the species level, whereas proponents of the (meliorist) Lamarckian theory of evolution by acquired characteristics located the explanatory narrative at the level of individuals. Creationists, meanwhile, have exploited the principle of narrative salience in a different way, 'stressing the linearity of the masterplot and the singularity of its causal agent.' By contrast, Abbott argues that to grasp the course of evolution as one governed by a Darwinian principle of natural selection, an overarching narrative model has to abandoned—even if narrative imagining remains applicable at the granular level of the events that make evolution possible.

Finally, my own contribution continues to explore the nature of narrative as a basic cognitive endowment. More specifically, the essay outlines an approach to studying narrative as a 'cognitive artifact', i.e., something used by humans for the purpose of aiding, enhancing, or improving cognition. Cognitive artifacts encompass material as well mental objects—calendars and spreadsheets as well as proverbs and mnemonic techniques. All such artifacts can be used for the purposes for which they were initially designed or else for novel, unanticipated purposes. Narrative occupies multiple locations within this artifactual system. For one thing, the notion 'story' denotes both an abstract cognitive structure and the material trace of that structure left in writing, speech, sign-language, three-dimensional visual images, or some other representational medium. Further, although stories have a structure by which they are anchored to a specific, targeted purpose—to convey information to interlocutors, viewers, or readers about a specific sequence of events—they can be used more or less opportunistically for any number of other purposes. Stories can be used to give support for positions presented in arguments; as a resource for comparing and contrasting features of past and present situations; and as a strategy for generating and assessing counterfactual, what-if scenarios.

Having sketched out this broad perspective on stories as a tool for thinking, which can be traced back to Vygotsky's ideas about the socio-interactional roots of human intelligence (Vygotsky 1978), I use this framework to investigate a narrative told during a sociolinguistic interview. Focusing on how narrative supports five (overlapping) problem-solving activities—'chunking' experience, imputing causal relations between events, managing 'typification' problems, sequencing behaviors, and distributing intelligence—I argue that the story under study affords crucial representational tools that make problems in each of these five categories more tractable. Along the way I explore implications of my approach for narrative theory and the cognitive sciences.

4.3 New Directions for Cognitive Narratology

Both Part III and Part IV of the volume contain essays making major contributions to the emergent field of scholarship sometimes referred to as cognitive narratology. The chapters assembled in Part III outline new directions for research in this field; those gathered in Part IV focus on the study of fictional minds, or representations of the mental functioning of fictional characters, in particular.

As an interdisciplinary program for research (see, e.g., Emmott 1997; Fludernik 1996; Herman 2001, 2002; Jahn 1997, 1999; Palmer 2002; Schneider 2001; van Peer and Chatman 2001), cognitive narratology blends concepts and methods from narratology with ideas originating from psychology, artificial intelligence, the philosophy of mind, and other approaches to issues of cognition. Work in this hybridized domain of inquiry seeks to construct a cognitive basis for—or motivation of—categories and principles developed by theorists concerned with narrative structure and narrative interpretation. Conversely, cognitive narratologists assume that greater familiarity with techniques for analyzing naturally occurring narrative discourse—whether spoken or written, quotidian or literary—can benefit scholars working within the disciplines traditionally grouped among the cognitive sciences. Cognitive narratology has thus helped sow the ground in which the present volume takes root, providing theoretical support for the cross-disciplinary research presented in many of these twelve chapters. More generally, cognitive narratology has fostered the expectation that there is indeed a positive, reciprocal influence, a basic synergy, between research on intelligent behavior and detailed analysis of narratives of all sorts.

Reinforcing that expectation is the first essay in Part III, Manfred Jahn's '"Awake! Open your eyes!" The Cognitive Logic of External and Internal Stories'. As Jahn points out, whereas researchers in the cognitive sciences have often emphasized the psychological and cultural importance of 'internal' narratives (stories associated with memory, dreams, introspection, etc.), narratologists have traditionally focused on external or physically tangible narratives as their proper object of study. Arguing that a 'cycle of narrative' connects external and internal stories, Jahn's essay underscores how study of narrative's many functions and forms requires a synthesis of narrative theory and the cognitive sciences. Jahn conceptualizes external and internal stories as data structures connected by flows of information which enable *procedures* of internalization and externalization, the former involving sub-procedures of 'bounding', 'distilling', 'emplotting', and 'indexing' (i.e., storage in long-term memory) and the latter submodularizing into lower-level procedures of 'adapation', 'addressee orientation', and 'translation' (e.g., mapping visual representations into linguistic means of expression). Noting that his model creates a causal chain linking the reception and pro-duction of stories, Jahn also remarks that whereas 'this explicit linkage closes the door to a "mentalist" model in which "the thinker" appears to be a solitary manipulator of self-contained mental representations, it opens the door to a system which accepts cognizers as participants in an essentially social process.' The author then discusses three test cases revolving around memory retrieval, adapative storytelling, feedback loops, and forgetting. These cases include a represented scene of storytelling in Billy Wilder's film *The Apartment*, Samuel Taylor Coleridge's autobiographical account of how his poem 'Kubla Kahn' came to be composed, and the story told by Siegfried in a scene from Act III of Richard Wagner's opera *Götterdämme-rung*.

Meanwhile, as Ryan points out in her essay, the notion of the map has been widely associated with cognitive processes, both in literary theory and cognitive science proper. The concept of 'cognitive map', in particular, was introduced by Edward Tolman in 1948 to describe rats' ability to navigate a maze to reach food when the familiar path has been blocked; but the idea has since been extended by scholars such as Richard Bjornson (1981) and Fredric Jameson (1988) to encompass the process by which readers con-struct (or, in the case of postmodern works, fail to construct) global mental representations of the social, spatial, and other worlds evoked in literary texts. Opting for a narrower and more literal definition of cognitive maps, Ryan's contribution focuses on how readers construct mental models of the spatial relations beween characters, objects, places, and regions mentioned in or implied by the discourse of a narrative.

Specifically, the author uses Gabriel García Márquez's 1982 novel *Chronicle of a Death Foretold* to explore how the phenomenon of being immersed in a fictional world—of experiencing it as real and present—is crucially dependent on the reader's ability to construct a mental model of the geography of the fictional world. Conducting an empirical investiga-tion of how actual readers form such cognitive maps, Ryan asked a group of high school students to draw a map of the world of García's Márquez's novel. Ryan then evaluated the maps by numerically scoring them in terms of three criteria: inventory, spatial relations, and mapping style. The crite-rion of inventory concerns what kinds of objects were included in the stu-dents' drawings, where the objects came from (i.e., the text itself or other sources), and what the selection of objects indicates about the map maker's conceptualization of the plot. The criterion of spatial relations concerns where the objects were positioned relative to one another on the maps. Lastly, the criterion of mapping style concerns whether the maps were drawn as pure plans (i.e., from a vertical pespective with conventional rather than iconic symbols), iconic plans, mixed plan-picture (with a picture defined as a representation drawn from a horizontal point of view and attempting to reproduce the visual perception of an observer), predominantly pictorial representation, or pure picture. As Ryan notes, even if it is incomplete or not wholly faithful to the text, the mental map of a textual world can fulfill its purpose of enabling a particular reader's immersion in the narrative.

Fludernik's contribution is the last chapter in Part III. Her essay begins with a concise, useful summary of the major tenets of her influential 1996 study *Towards a 'Natural' Narratology*—one of the foundational texts of the field of cognitive narratology—and then goes on to consider some criticisms that have been levelled against the model set out in her earlier study. Fludernik's book laid important groundwork for cognitive narratology by formulating a theoretical model based on conversational or 'natural' narrative and drawing on a number of tools (the idea of schemata, prototype theory, and so on) from the cognitive sciences. Offering a reappraisal of her earlier study in light of comments and criticisms by other scholars, the author focuses special attention on two sources of concern: the universality of the cognitive parameters identified in the book and, relatedly, how those parameters pertain to the diachronic development of new narrative forms.

Taking the second issue first, the author argues that, even though cognitive parameters are always liable to recontextualization in new forms, a diachronic approach can in fact be accommodated within a cognitivist perspective. At issue are four parameters situated at four levels of narrative transmission, including (i) basic-level schemata readers use to interpret an action or a goal; (ii) schemata defining material material within a perspectival paradigm, or what Fludernik characterizes as the ACTION, TELLING, EXPERIENCING, VIEWING, and REFLECTING frames; (iii) generic frames such as those associated with 'satire' or 'dramatic monologue'; and (iv) higher-level schemata on which readers rely to constitute narrativity, i.e., to understand a given text *as* a narrative. Rather than privileging naturally occurring storytelling situations, as some of her critics have claimed, Fludernik argues that in the historical development of narrational forms natural 'base frames' are extended into new domains, such that the ACTION, TELLING, and VIEWING frames are transferred to new contexts in which they no longer realistically apply. As for the issue of universality,

Fludernik discusses how this issue can in fact be broken down into several questions, depending on which level of narrative transmission is the main concern.

4.4 Fictional Minds

Taken together, the three essays in Part IV—Uri Margolin's 'Cognitive Science, The Thinking Mind, and Literary Narrative', Catherine Emmott's 'Constructing Social Space: Sociocognitive Factors in the Interpretation of Character Relations', and Alan Palmer's 'The Mind beyond the Skin'—articulate a powerfully integrative approach to the analysis of fictional minds. In parallel with the overall aims of cognitive narratology, the essays draw on tools from the cognitive sciences to develop new descriptive and explanatory techniques for the study of fictional mental functioning, while also suggesting ways in which more careful scrutiny of fictional minds can help illuminate the 'real minds' (to use Palmer's phrase) on which specialists in the cognitive sciences have traditionally focused.

Margolin's chapter provides an overview of the major issues involved in the study of fictional minds. For Margolin, the cognitive sciences can be defined in broad terms as a cluster of disciplines engaged in systematic inquiry into the acquisition, internal representation, storage and retrieval, and symbolic or behavioral use of information. Further, '[i]t goes without saying that the totality of an individual's mental life, be it actual or created by a literary text, also includes affects and desires or volitions and that the cognitive component is intimately interrelated with both.' Equipped with this broad understanding of cognitive mental functioning (a term that he borrows from Alan Palmer), Margolin then shows how a focus on such mental functioning can help theorists rethink the four levels of narrative communication identified by structuralist narratologists: actual author vis-à-vis actual reader; implied author vis-à-vis implied reader; narrator and narratee; and characters or storyworld participants vis-à-vis themselves and one another, such participants being interacting individuals who perceive the world around them, build mental representations of it, construct in their minds theories about their co-agents, and so on. However, in accordance with cognitive narratology's assumption that there is a reciprocal, mutually beneficial relation between studying real and studying fictional minds, Margolin's claim is not merely that cognitive-science discriminations and models can advance current attempts to theorize about authoring and interpreting (characters' mental activities within) narratives. What is more, 'the fictional presentation of cognitive mechanisms in action, especially of their breakdown or failure, is itself a powerful cognitive tool which may make us aware of actual cognitive mechanisms, and, more specifically, of our own mental functioning.'

For her part, Emmott zooms in on the social dimensions of cognitive mental functioning discussed in preliminary terms in Margolin's overview chapter. Emmott argues that although cognitive research has increased our understanding of narrative processing, workers in this field have tended to neglect social relations between characters in narratives. The reasons for this oversight can be traced back to the origins of cognitive approaches, whose early incarnations 'examined small fragments of artificially constructed materials that often do not contain developed characters and consist of event sequences that are too short for there to be any complex social relations.' Accordingly, drawing on more extended, naturally occurring textual examples, Emmott proposes to adapt a number of cognitive theories for the purpose of showing how readers of narratives construct and interpret the 'social spaces' inhabited by fictional minds. Using the term *social space* as a metaphor both for social relations among characters and for cases where these relations cross spatio-temporal boundaries in the world of the narrative, Emmott examines a number of key issues in this connection.

To start, the author revisits cognitive status models developed in linguistic work on reference in discourse, arguing that such models need to take into account stylistically unusual references to characters—modes of referring that sometimes reflect social perspectives central to the themes of narratives. Further, Emmott draws on her own theory of contextual frames (Emmott 1997) to explore how narrative understanding involves assumptions about the co-presence of characters in physical contexts together with inferences about the social consequences of such proximity. The author also re-examines the possibilities and limits of classical schema theory to consider how backgrounded minor characters sometimes emerge into the forefront of readers' attention as representatives of social institutions or public attitudes. The final part of her essay explores, in more general terms, the links between social relations and degrees of physical proximity between characters, focusing for example on cases in which 'physical space is sub-divided to reflect social power and exclusion.'

Rounding out the collection is Alan Palmer's 'The Mind Beyond the Skin'. Complementing Margolin's and Emmott's broad-based studies of fictional minds in many kinds of narratives, Palmer's essay uses a single text (Evelyn Waugh's 1930 novel *Vile Bodies*) to identify a few of the areas of fictional mental functioning that have hitherto been neglected within narrative theory. In particular, the essay suggests that narratology has been concerned for too long primarily with the privacy of consciousness, and that an emphasis on the social nature of thought, and in particular the various ways in which the mind extends beyond the skin, is now required. Palmer thus shares with Margolin an interest in how the study of real minds helps illuminate the mental functioning of characters (and vice versa), and with Emmott an interest in the specifically social dimensions of those fictional minds and their environments.

Palmer begins with an account of how readers use cognitive frames and scripts to interpret texts, and more specifically how they apply the key frame of the continuing consciousness of storyworld individuals. The existing or pre-stored knowledge that enables us to construct other real minds prepares us, as readers, for the work of constructing fictional mental functioning. Because fictional beings are necessarily incomplete, frames, scripts, and preference rules are required to supply the defaults that fill the gaps in the discourse and provide the presuppositions that enable the reader to construct continuing consciousnesses from the text. Such gap-filling is particularly important in the case of a 'behaviorist' narrative such as *Vile Bodies*, where the reading process has to be very creative in constructing fictional minds from less information than is available in other types of narrative. Palmer's essay attempts to expand our notion of fictional minds by exploring two major subframes of the main consciousness frame: the relationship between thought and action; and group or shared thinking. Within the first, Palmer discusses what he calls the decoding of action statements, the thought-action continuum, and cases of 'indicative description', which detail characters' actions but also indicate the states of mind accompanying them. The second subframe, shared, joint, or group thinking, relates to what psycholinguists call intermental thinking or intersubjectivity, as opposed to intramental or individual thinking. Here, Palmer discusses norm establishment and maintenance, group conflict, and intermental assent and dissent. Revealing the extent to which information about fictional minds is accessible even in contexts of so-called behaviorist narrative, the essay develops an approach whose degree of applicability to other kinds of texts remains to be explored.

References

Abbott, H. P. 2000a. The Evolutionary Origins of Storied Mind: Modeling the Prehistory of Narrative Consciousness and its Discontents. *Narrative* 8: 247-56.

Abbott, H.P. 2000b. What Do We Mean When We Say 'Narrative Literature'? Looking for Answers across Disciplinary Borders. *Style* 34: 260-73.

Abbott, H.P., ed. 2001. On the Origins of Fiction: Interdisciplinary Perspectives. Special issue of *SubStance* 94/95: 1-278.

Austin, J. L. 1962. *How to Do Things with Words*. Oxford: Oxford University Press.

Bamberg, M., ed. 1997. Oral Versions of Personal Experience: Three Decades of Narrative Analysis. Special issue of the *Journal of Narrative and Life History* 7: 1-415.

Barthes, R. 1977 [1966]. Introduction to the Structuralist Analysis of Narratives. *Image Music Text*, trans. Stephen Heath, 79-124. New York: Hill and Wang.

Bjornson, R. 1981. Cognitive Mapping and the Understanding of Literature. *SubStance* 30: 51-62.

Bremond, C. 1973. *Logique du récit*. Paris: Seuil.

Bruner, J. 1986. *Actual Minds, Possible Worlds*. Cambridge, MA: Harvard University Press.

Bruner, J. 1991. The Narrative Construction of Reality. *Critical Inquiry* 18: 1-21.

Chatman, S. 1990. *Coming to Terms: The Rhetoric of Narrative in Fiction and Film*. Ithaca: Cornell UP.

Culler, J. 1986. *Ferdinand de Saussure*. Revised ed. Ithaca: Cornell University Press.

Davis, E. 1990. *Representations of Common-Sense Knowledge*. Stanford: Morgan Kaufmann.

Emmott, C. 1997. *Narrative Comprehension: A Discourse Perspective*. Oxford: Oxford University Press.

Fauconnier, G., and M. Turner. 2002. *The Way We Think: Conceptual Blending and the Mind's Hidden Complexities*. NY: Basic Books.

Fludernik, M. 1996. *Towards a 'Natural' Narratology*. London: Routledge.

Frawley, W. 1997. *Vygotsky and Cognitive Science: Language and the Unification of the Social and Computational Mind*. Cambridge, MA: Harvard University Press.

Genette, G. 1980 [1972]. *Narrative Discourse: An Essay in Method*, trans. J. E. Lewin. Ithaca: Cornell University Press.

Goffman, E. 1974. *Frame Analysis: An Essay on the Organization of Experience*. New York: Harper and Row.

Goffman, E. 1981. *Forms of Talk*. Philadelphia: University of Pennsylvania Press.

Goodwin, M. H. 1990. *He-Said-She-Said: Talk as Social Organization Among Black Children*. Bloomington: Indiana University Press.

Greimas, A. J. 1983. *Structural Semantics: An Attempt at a Method*, trans. D. McDowell, R. Schleifer, A. Velie. Lincoln: University of Nebraska Press.

Grice, P. 1989. *Studies in the Way of Words*. Cambridge, MA: Harvard University Press.

Harris, R. 1987. *Reading Saussure*. London: Duckworth.

Harris, R. 2001. *Saussure and His Interpreters*. New York: New York University Press.

Hayes, P. 1999. Knowledge Representation. *The MIT Encyclopedia of the Cognitive Sciences*, eds. R. A. Wilson and F. C. Keil, 432-34. Cambridge, MA: MIT Press.

Herman, D. 1999. Towards a Socionarratology: New Ways of Analyzing Natural-language Narratives. *Narratologies: New Perspectives on Narrative Analysis*, ed. D. Herman, 218-46. Columbus: Ohio State University Press.

Herman, D. 2001. Narrative Theory and the Cognitive Sciences. *Narrative Inquiry* 11: 1-34.

Herman, D. 2002. *Story Logic: Problems and Possibilities of Narrative*. Lincoln: University of Nebraska Press.

Herman, D. Forthcoming. Toward a Transmedial Narratology. *Narrative across Media: The Languages of Storytelling*, ed. M.-L. Ryan. Lincoln: University of Nebraska Press.

Herman, D. Under review. Framed Narratives and Distributed Cognition.

Herman, D., and R. M. Young. 2000. Narrative Structure in Intelligent Tutoring Systems. Presentation delivered at the Society for the Study of Narrative Literature; Atlanta, GA.

Hoshmand, L. T. 2000. Narrative Psychology. *Encyclopedia of Psychology*, ed. A. E. Kazdin, 382-87. Oxford: Oxford University Press.

Howard, G. S. 1991. Culture Tales: A Narrative Approach to Thinking, Cross-cultural Psychology, and Psychotherapy. *American Psychologist* 46: 187-97.

Jahn, M. 1997. Frames, Preferences, and the Reading of Third-Person Narratives: Towards a Cognitive Narratology. *Poetics Today* 18: 441-68.

Jahn, M. 1999. 'Speak, friend, and enter': Garden Paths, Artificial Intelligence, and Cognitive Narratology. *Narratologies: New Perspectives on Narrative Analysis*, ed. D. Herman, 167-94. Columbus: Ohio State University Press.

Jameson, F. 1988. Cognitive Mapping. *Marxism and the Intrepretation of Culture*, eds. N. Cory and L. Grossberg, 347-60. Urbana: University of Illinois Press, 1988.

Jefferson, G. 1978. Sequential Aspects of Storytelling in Conversation. Studies in the Organization of Conversational Interaction, ed. J. Schenkein, 219-48. New York: Academic.

Jefferson, G. 1988. On the Sequential Organization of Troubles—Talk in Ordinary Conversation. *Social Problems* 35: 418-41.

Johnstone, B. 1990. *Stories, Community, and Place: Narratives from Middle America*. Bloomington: Indiana University Press.

Kafalenos, E. (1995) Lingering along the Narrative Path: Extended Functions in Kafka and Henry James. *Narrative* 3: 117-38.

Labov, W. 1972. The Transformation of Experience in Narrative Syntax. *Language in the Inner City*, 354-96. Philadelphia: University of Pennsylvania Press.

Labov, W., and J. Waletzky. 1967. Narrative Analysis: Oral Versions of Personal Experience. *Essays on the Verbal and Visual Arts: Proceedings of the 1966 Annual Spring Meeting of the Ethnological Society*, ed. J. Helm, 12-44. Seattle: University of Washington Press. Reprinted in Bamberg (1997: 3-38).

Linde, C. 1993. *Life Stories: The Creation of Coherence.* Oxford: Oxford University Press.

Lodge, D. 1999. Foreword. *Modern Criticism and Theory*, 2nd ed., ed. D. Lodge with N. Wood, xi – xiv. Essex: Longman.

Mandler, J. M. 1984. *Stories, Scripts, and Scenes: Aspects of Schema Theory.* Hillsdale, NJ: Lawrence Erlbaum.

Mateas, M., and P. Sengers, eds. 1999. *Narrative Intelligence: Papers from the 1999 AAAI Fall Symposium.* Technical Report FS-99-01. Menlo Park, CA: American Association for Artificial Intelligence Press.

Ochs, E., and L. Capps. 2001. *Living Narrative: Creating Lives in Everyday Storytelling.* Cambridge, MA: Harvard University Press.

Ochs, E., C. Taylor, D. Rudolph, and R. Smith. 1992. Storytelling as Theory-Building Activity. *Discourse Processes* 15: 37-72.

Palmer, A. 2002. The Construction of Fictional Minds. *Narrative* 10: 28-46.

Prince, G. 1973. *A Grammar of Stories.* The Hague: Mouton.

Prince, G. 1982. *Narratology: The Form and Functioning of Narrative.* Berlin: Mouton.

Propp, V. 1968 [1928]. *Morphology of the Folktale*, trans. L. Scott; revised by L. A. Wagner. Austin: University of Texas Press.

Richardson, A., and F. Steen. 2002. Literature and the Cognitive Revolution: An Introduction. *Poetics Today* 23: 1-8.

Rimmon-Kenan, S. 1983. *Narrative Fiction: Contemporary Poetics.* London: Methuen.

Rogoff, B. 1990. *Apprenticeship in Thinking: Cognitive Development in Social Context.* New York: Oxford University Press.

Rumelhart, D. E. 1975. Notes on a Schema for Stories. *Representation and Understanding: Studies in Cognitive Science*, eds. D. G. Bobrow and A. Collins, 211-36.

Ryan, M.-L. 1991. *Possible Worlds, Artificial Intelligence and Narrative Theory.* Bloomington: Indiana University Press.

Sacks, H. 1972. On the Analyzability of Stories by Children. *Directions in Sociolinguistics: The Ethnography of Communication*, eds. J. J. Gumperz and D. Hymes, 325-45. New York: Holt, Rinehart, and Winston.

Sarbin, T. R., ed. 1986. *Narrative Psychology: The Storied Nature of Human Conduct*. New York: Praeger.

Saussure, F. de. 1959. *Course in General Linguistics*, eds. C. Bally and A. Sechehaye (in collaboration with A. Riedlinger), trans. W. Baskin. New York: The Philosophical Library.

Schank, R. C., and R. P. Abelson. 1977. *Scripts, Plans, Goals, and Understanding*. Hillsdale, NJ: Lawrence Erlbaum Associates.

Schauber, E., and E. Spolsky. 1986. *The Bounds of Interpretation: Linguistic Theory and Literary Text*. Stanford: Stanford University Press.

Schegloff, E. 1997. 'Narrative Analysis' Thirty Years Later. *Journal of Narrative and Life History* 7: 97-106.

Schiffrin, D. 1987. *Discourse Markers*. Cambridge: Cambridge University Press.

Schneider, R. 2001. Toward Cognitive Theory of Literary Character: The Dynamics of Mental-Model Construction. *Style* 35: 607-40.

Snow, C. P. 1993. *The Two Cultures and the Scientific Revolution*, ed. Stefan Collini. London: Cambridge University Press.

Spolsky, E. 1993. *Gaps in Nature: Literary Interpretation and the Modular Mind*. Albany: State University of New York Press.

Stein, N. L. 2002. Memories for Emotional, Stressful, and Traumatic Events. *The Development of Representation, Thinking and Memory: Essays in Honor of Jean Mandler*, eds. N. L. Stein, P. Bauer, and M. Rabinowitz, 247-65. Mahwah, NJ: Lawrence Erlbaum Associates.

Stein, N.L., Trabasso, T. and Albro, E. R. 2001. Understanding and Organizing Emotional Experience: Autobiographical Accounts of Traumatic Events. *English Studies of America* 19: 111-30.

Todorov, T. 1968. La Grammaire du récit. *Langages* 12: 94-102.

Todorov, T. 1969. *Grammaire du 'Décaméron'*. The Hague: Mouton.

Trabasso, T., and L. L. Sperry. 1985. Causal Relatedness and the Representation of Narrative Events. *Journal of Memory and Language* 24: 595-611.

Trabasso, T., and P. van den Broek. 1985. Causal Thinking and the Representation of Narrative Events. *Journal of Memory and Language* 24: 612-30.

Tsur, R. 1992. *Toward a Theory of Cognitive Poetics*. Amsterdam: North-Holland.

Turner, M. 1991. *Reading Minds: The Study of English in the Age of Cognitive Science*. Princeton: Princeton University Press.

Turner, M. 1996. *The Literary Mind*. Oxford: Oxford University Press.

Van Peer, W., and S. Chatman, eds. 2001. *New Perspectives on Narrative Perspective*. Albany: State University of New York Press.

Vygotsky, L. S. 1978. *Mind in Society: The Development of Higher Psychological Processes*, eds. M. Cole, V. John-Steiner, S. Scribner, and E. Souberman. Cambridge, MA: Harvard University Press.

Wertsch, J. 1985. *Vygotsky and the Social Formation of Mind.* Cambridge, MA: Harvard University Press.

Wertsch, J. 1991. *Voices of the Mind: A Sociocultural Approach to Mediated Action.* Cambridge, MA: Harvard University Press.

Wertsch, J. 1998. *Mind As Action.* New York: Oxford University Press.

Wilson, R. A., and F. C. Keil, eds. 1999. *The MIT Encyclopedia of the Cognitive Sciences.* Cambridge, MA: MIT Press.

Part I

Approaches to
Narrative and Cognition

2

Cognitive Psychological Foundations of Narrative Experiences

RICHARD J. GERRIG AND GIOVANNA EGIDI

1 Introduction

Consider the opening paragraphs of Eudora Welty's short story, 'No Place for You, My Love' (1955: 3):

> They were strangers to each other, both fairly well strangers to the place, now seated side by side at luncheon—a party combined in a free-and-easy way when the friends he and she were with recognized each other across Galatoire's. The time was a Sunday in summer—those hours of afternoon that seem Time Out in New Orleans.
>
> The moment he saw her little blunt, fair face, he thought that here was a woman who was having an affair. It was one of those odd meetings when such an impact is felt that it has to be translated at once into some sort of speculation.

To create a mental representation of this scene, readers must engage in a number of activities that have, as a rule, been the province of cognitive psychology and cognitive science. Consider, for example, the role that memory processes must play for readers to perceive the full richness of Welty's words. Readers may retrieve from memory their own past knowledge of restaurants to make sense of the general framing of the scene. They may retrieve their knowledge of marital infidelity to understand how it might be

Narrative Theory and The Cognitive Sciences.
David Herman (ed.).
Copyright © 2003, CSLI Publications.

marked on a woman's face. They may retrieve memories of social interactions to create a context for what might constitute an 'odd meeting' when great 'impact is felt'.

Cognitive scientists study memory processes, as well as other processes and representations, that provide the backbone of literary experiences. We would surely judge readers' experiences to be incomplete if all they did was construct a minimal instantiation of the situation. In that sense, many nuances of literary appreciation are beyond the scope of extant cognitive science theories. Still, researchers in cognitive science have made important strides in specifying the types of processes and representations that provide the point of departure for those more nuanced literary experiences. In this chapter, we review some fundamental advances in the cognitive psychology of narrative experiences. We begin with a brief account of the goals of theories in this domain. We then devote the bulk of the chapter to an exploration of the relationship between literary experiences and cognitive processes.

2 The Goals of Cognitive Psychological Research

We have already alluded to the constructs that play major roles in cognitive psychological theories: Processes and representations. *Processes* are the mental operations that enable readers to make the leap from symbols on a page to elaborate models of narrative worlds. Some of those processes are devoted to decoding letters and words and attaching meanings to those words. In this chapter, however, we will focus on those processes beyond the word that enable readers to experience narrative worlds. *Representations* are the products of those mental processes that get stored, for some duration, in memory. Researchers have suggested that readers create representations at a number of levels (e.g., Johnson-Laird 1983; van Dijk and Kintsch 1983; Zwaan and Radvansky 1998). Some representations remain fairly close to the details of a text. Others are more elaborate, based on incorporations from sources of information beyond the text.

We can characterize the goals of cognitive psychological theories with respect to processes and representations[1]:

---

[1] It is important to note that we are defining what we take to be the goals of theories that have emerged specifically from the cognitive psychology of narrative rather than from other areas of cognitive science or psychology itself. Researchers in other traditions, such as social psychology and artificial intelligence, have devoted effort to topics that remain outside the province of cognitive psychological theories. For example, as we shall describe later in the chapter, cognitive psychological theories focus on how readers update their representations. However, those theories have not generally considered the relationship between representation and action or representation and belief. That is, most theories within cognitive

1. A comprehensive theory should give an exhaustive account of the processes that function at each moment while a reader experiences a narrative.

2. A comprehensive theory should give an exhaustive account of the different representations that evolve during moment-by-moment reading.

3. A comprehensive theory should give an account of the final representation of a narrative that resides in long-term memory once the experience has ended.

For many researchers, the first goal has a somewhat more restricted form. Rather than trying to provide an exhaustive account of all processes, the theories focus only on those processes that are *automatic*. Automatic processes are those processes that, given appropriate starting conditions, operate in all circumstances. Thus, an exhaustive account of that set of processes provides the true backbone of narrative experiences. As two prominent researchers put it, 'Automatic inferences are those that are encoded in the absence of special goals or strategies on the part of the reader, and they are constructed in the first few hundred milliseconds of processing. They therefore merit attention because they form the basic representation of a text from which other, more purposeful inferences are constructed' (McKoon and Ratcliff 1992: 441). As we shall discuss shortly, theories of the boundaries on automatic properties have been controversial. However, we wish to fill out this section on the goals of cognitive psychological theories by providing a case study of research that addresses all three goals.

Consider this brief excerpt from Felice Picano's novel *The Book of Lies* (1998: 281):

> The house phone rang and Conchita came to tell me it was Von Slyke.
>
> 'I was about to call you,' I told him. 'I just finished the cataloguing. I want to photocopy everything.'

Several pages later, without being mentioned in the interim, Conchita returns (Picano 1998: 286):

> I was just biting down on that good-news/bad-news when Conchita appeared in the library doorway.
>
> 'Did he say when they're coming back?' she asked.
>
> That surprised me a little. I thought she already knew.
>
> 'Not for a while. They're going to Majorca today. Was there something you wanted to tell Mr Von Slyke.'

psychology treat narrative representations as being compartmentalized with respect to real-world beliefs.

In the second excerpt, Conchita uses a 'he' that ought to be difficult for readers to understand. Its referent resides five pages earlier in the novel. Those five pages range over a diversity of topics so that Mr Von Slyke (the referent of 'he') is ultimately quite backgrounded. Still, when Conchita utters 'he', it seems that Mr Von Slyke comes effortlessly to mind.

These excerpts from *The Book of Lies* exemplify one structure that is common in contemporary works of literature: the narrative unfolds in an episodic fashion with different characters and themes disappearing and reappearing over time. Some texts interweave lengthy episodes; others include brief flashbacks within on-going action. For instance, the narration can present a continuous stream of detailed action in a scene, in which the fictional time of the action can also be the time it takes the average reader to read the passage. However, the action can also be summarized in few pages in which days, months, or years are reported without details; or it can be omitted altogether, resulting in a speed-up. The flow of narration can also be interrupted by descriptive pauses in which no action is reported and the story time stops (Genette 1980 [1972]; Herman 2002). No matter how detailed a description is, it cannot represent every single detail of the place where the action unfolds. Rather, narratives refer to a small selection of details and let readers complete their work by imagining the rest (Iser 1978). The resulting discontinuity that characterizes narratives requires an active role on part of the reader.

As cognitive psychologists, we wish to understand how it is that readers are able to make coherent sense of the variety of narratives authors provide. In particular, we can ask whether readers must generally expend effort to disentangle narratives. That is, must readers use explicit memory searches to reconstruct a narrative that is fully coherent in time and place? Or, is it instead the case that readers possess cognitive processes that allow narratives to be disentangled automatically? We review a program of research that supports an automatic route by which readers achieve continuity across the span of narratives. That program of research also traces the relationship between the moment-by-moment experience of a narrative and the long-term memory representations that result.

Consider once more the excerpt from *The Book of Lies*. If readers are to disentangle this text without conscious intervention, we need it to be the case that the first interaction with Conchita becomes accessible again as they are reading the second conversation. Cognitive psychologists designate the type of memory in which the immediate products of processing reside as *working memory*. With respect to that construct, the claim is that we wish for the first Conchita interaction to become accessible once more in working memory at the same time readers experience the second. Research suggests that a particular memory process, *resonance*, produces exactly such an effect (Gerrig and McKoon 1998, 2001; Lea, Mason, Albrecht, Birch, and Myers 1998; McKoon, Gerrig, and Greene 1996; Myers and O'Brien 1998; O'Brien, Rizzella, Albrecht, and Halleran 1998). Resonance is a fast, passive, and easy process by which cues in working memory interact in parallel with, and allow access to, information in long-term memory (Gillund and Shiffrin 1984; Hintzman 1988; Murdock 1982; Myers and O'Brien 1998; Ratcliff 1978; McKoon and Ratcliff 1992; Tulving 1974). In this case, the reader's conceptual representations of Conchita should serve as cues that resonate through the representation of the text to heighten the accessibility in working memory of representations of concepts associated with her. Thus, resonance ought to produce the type of disentangling we seek.

Experimental evidence supports the role of resonance in on-going experiences of texts. Consider the story given in Table 1. Although this story pales by comparison to the literary example, it shares the same conceptual structure. The first few lines of the story introduce two characters. In the middle portion, those characters are parted and then, in the reunion portion, they regain one another's company. The prediction, based on the assumption that resonance is at work, is that the accessibility of information from the introductory portion of the story will wax and wane as a function of the cues provided by other portions of the story.

Introduction: Jane was dreading her dinner with her cousin, Marilyn. She complained loudly to her roommate Gloria. 'Every time I go to dinner at my cousin's I get sick.' Gloria asked, 'Why did you agree to go?' Jane said, 'Because I'm too wimpy to say no.' Jane went off to have dinner.

(Participants read either the Outsider present or Outsider absent middle portions of the text.)

Outsider present: When she arrived, Marilyn was just finishing the cooking. 'You're in luck,' she said, 'we're having fried squid.' Jane knew she was in for a wonderful evening. The two of them sat down to dinner. After dinner, they talked for a while, and then Jane left.

Outsider absent: Gloria decided to cook something nice for herself for dinner. 'As long as I'm home alone,' she thought, 'I'll eat well.' Gloria searched her refrigerator for ingredients. She found enough eggs to make a quiche. After dinner, she put the dishes in the dishwasher.

Conclusion: Gloria was still up when Jane arrived home about midnight. (Reunion sentence.) Gloria asked Jane, 'Did she make the evening unbearable?' (Pronoun sentence.) Jane chuckled and said, 'I just want to get some sleep.'

Table 1: An Example Story from McKoon et al. (1996)

Consider the *outsider present* version of the story (i.e., imagine one read the story with that middle portion) with respect to the concept *cousin*. The cousin is introduced in the discourse between Gloria and Marilyn. In the outsider present version, the action stays with the cousin. Thus, we would expect the concept *cousin* to be relatively accessible throughout this version of the story. By comparison, we would expect that *cousin* would, relatively speaking, fade away in the *outsider absent* version of the story. However, if resonance is at work, we would expect *cousin* to achieve comparable accessibility in both versions as soon as readers begin to experience the reunion portion of the story.

To test this prediction, McKoon, Gerrig, and Greene (1996) asked readers to perform a relatively straightforward task. Participants in the experiments read a series of stories (comparable in structure to the example given in Table 1) one sentence at a time on a computer screen. At the end of some sentence, a single test word appeared on the screen. The participants were required to indicate, as quickly and as accurately as possible, whether that test word had appeared in the story. This task provides an index of the accessibility of particular concepts from the story. We would expect, for example, that readers' ability to say that 'cousin' had appeared in the story would vary as a function of whether that concept was present or absent in the middle portions of the stories. In fact, at the end of those middle portions 'cousin' was consistently less accessible for the outsider absent than for the outsider present versions. However, by the end of the reunion sentence, the accessibility of 'cousin' was equivalent across the two versions. The same pattern was obtained for other concepts from the introductory portions of the stories, such as 'dreading' for the Table 1 example. This latter result is important because it reinforces the hypothesis that this is an automatic, rather than a goal-driven process. These results support the contention that resonance provides automatic disentangling of these temporally discontinuous episodes.

The experiments and task we have just described focus on the moment-by-moment processing of the texts. McKoon et al. (1996) conducted another set of studies that examined the consequences of resonance for more long-term representations. The experiments used the same stories, but participants were asked to carry out a different mix of tasks. As before, they read the stories one sentence at a time on a computer screen. After every four stories, participants were asked to perform a second task. They were presented with word lists and asked to indicate for each word whether the word appeared in one of the stories they had just read. In some cases, words from the same story (e.g., 'dreading' and 'squid') were adjacent to each other in the lists. In this task, performance is facilitated—or *primed*—when words that have a prior association come one after the other. To the extent that an association had formed between the two words during the moment-by-moment processing of the story, we would expect participants' performance to be primed by the preceding word.

Consider once again the contrast between the outsider present and outsider absent versions of the stories. For the outsider present versions of the stories, concepts from the end of the story should be closely associated with concepts from the beginning of the story: Concepts from the beginning of the story are sustained through the middle all the way to the end. For the outsider absent versions of the story, the middle portion fails to sustain the main thread of the story. Therefore, to the extent that concepts from the beginning of the story are associated with concepts from the end, it must be because resonance has functioned to bring those concepts together in the context of the reunion and pronoun sentences. If this model is correct, we would expect to see a priming relationship between beginning and end concepts for both types of stories (i.e., outsider present and outsider absent). However, we would expect to find a priming relationship between middle and end concepts only for the outsider present stories. McKoon et al.'s (1996) data showed exactly that pattern of associations. The results confirm that resonance gives rise both to short-term disentangling of the stories' episodes during moment-by-moment processing as well as long-term disentangling in the stories' ultimate representations in memory.

One must always exercise caution generalizing from the modest texts of psychology experiments to the immodest texts of literary craftspeople. Still, the accumulation of evidence from the research on this topic suggests rather strongly that resonance provides an automatic means through which the various components of texts are pieced together into a coherent whole. This does not, of course, mean that authors' inventions might not create circumstances in which readers have to expend purposeful effort to piece together the elements of narrative worlds. In fact, the resonance model specifies the circumstances in which that might be necessary: any time cues are insufficient for a passive search of memory to 'find' the appropriate prior stretches of text. Within broad limits, however, authors can interweave their themes with the knowledge that readers' cognitive processes prepare them to sort matters out with no conscious awareness.

One final observation, to which we will return in various guises throughout this chapter, is that this useful outcome—a disentangled representation—is an emergent property of a process that has no special relationship to text processing. That is, resonance is not, in any sense, directed to the goal of facilitating narrative experiences. Rather, it is a general cognitive process the existence of which has, presumably, allowed authors to expand the range of texts they can produce while having benefits to the readers outweigh costs.

In the next section, we provide examples of questions that are easily motivated on the basis of literary analyses. We then review the theories and experiments researchers in cognitive science have generated to shed light on those topics. In each case, we describe an individual program of research in some detail. We wish readers to see for themselves the basis of cognitive psychological generalizations.

3 Theories of Narrative Experience

Let us return to Welty's story 'No Place for You, My Love'. As we noted, the story begins at a luncheon in a New Orleans restaurant. Later in the story, the main characters visit a very different sort of restaurant, 'Baba's Place', well south of New Orleans. The woman—the one with the 'little blunt, fair face'—declines to order (Welty 1955: 18): 'Nothing for me, thank you,' she said. 'I'm not sure I could eat, after all.' She changes her mind and requests 'some water', but that request is not honored (19-20):

> Baba was smiling. He had set an opened, frosted brown bottle before her on the counter, and a thick sandwich, and stood looking at her. Baba made her eat some supper, for what she was.

To understand both restaurant scenes, readers retrieve information from memory. There's no need for Welty to explain the rituals surrounding restaurant visits. She can provide the fragments that are critical to her story, with the strong expectation that readers will fill in the rest.

One of the earliest areas of cognitive psychological research was concerned with the ways in which readers use memory structures to enhance their narrative experiences. The restaurant *script* is, in fact, is the prototypical example of the type of structure readers possess. A script is a memory structure that specifies the list of actions people perform in repeated situations such as visits to restaurants, lectures, and grocery stores (Abelson 1981; Schank and Abelson 1977). When reading stories that take place in scripted situations, people evoke this type of memory structure to guide their comprehension (Bower, Black, and Turner 1979). Scripts are a special case of a more general type of memory structure called *schemas*. Schemas gather together experiences—of people, places, things, and so on—into units that function during narrative experiences (and also, of course, in other domains of life) (Bartlett 1932; Brewer and Nakamura 1984; Whitney, Budd, Bramucci, and Crane 1995). For even the brief sentences from Welty, we can enumerate a large number of schemas that might come into play: Schemas about human emotions, about beer, about sandwiches, and so on.

Readers' use of schemas provides at least two benefits to authors. First, as we have noted, schemas allow them to delineate a scene with quick gestures. Once, for example, a restaurant scene has been minimally set, waiters, clattering trays, and wandering violinists can be addressed with little cognitive cost. Second, schemas allow authors to call quiet attention to departures from the norm. It is not, for example, an ordinary event to be served food in a restaurant that one has not ordered. Readers' use of the restaurant script enables them to notice this departure from the ordinary.

There are some respects, however, in which the construct of the schema is insufficiently limited, with respect to moment-by-moment text processing: It cannot be the case—nor would it be adaptive were it the case—that all the information a reader possesses about a particular topic becomes part of an ongoing representation of the text. For example, although it would presumably be true that each human character mentioned in a narrative would have a brain, a heart, two lungs, and so on, we would be surprised to learn that that information becomes part of the text representation each time someone read a sentence like 'Baba was smiling.' Text representations reflect a mixture of the actual words of a text and inferences that readers encode based on those words. As we've just illustrated, schemas allow readers to draw more inferences than would be functional. As such, a major topic of cognitive psychological research has been to establish the range of inferences that readers automatically encode. In fact, for many years, this was the most prominent goal of much text processing research.

Even so, much of the early research wasn't guided by any particularly strong theoretical perspective. That is, researchers often made individual claims about the automaticity of different classes of inferences without relating them to an overarching theory. Finally, in the 1990's, two theories emerged that provided contrasting views of the set of automatic inferences: the *minimalist theory* (which has evolved into *memory-based text processing*) and the *constructionist theory* (which has evolved into *explanation-based processing*). As the name implies, the minimalist hypothesis suggested that a rather minimal set of inferences are encoded by all readers at all times. Specifically, McKoon and Ratcliff (1992: 441) argued that only 'two classes of inferences, those based on easily available information and those required for local coherence, are encoded during reading, unless a reader adopts special goals or strategies.' As an example of an inference required for local coherence recall the pair of sentences, 'Baba was smiling. He had set an opened, frosted brown bottle before her on the counter, and a thick sandwich, and stood looking at her.' To understand this pair of sentences, readers must draw the inference that 'He' refers to 'Baba'. The class of inferences 'based on easily available information' has proved more elusive because, in the original formulation, the phrase 'easily available' was underspecified. The memory-based approach to text processing (e.g., McKoon et al. 1996; O'Brien, Lorch, and Myers 1998) addresses this concern by identifying the memory processes that make information 'easily available'. In our discussion of the way readers disentangle texts, we already gave an example of a memory-based approach to a particular text process. As we noted then, an important component of the philosophy that guides the memory-based approach is that it encompasses general cognitive processes: At least with respect to automatic inferences, it does not promulgate a particular model of what readers must or should do.

The constructionist theory, by contrast, imparts specific goals to the reader (Graesser, Singer, and Trabasso 1994; Singer, Graesser, and Trabasso 1994; cf. Emmott 1997). That is, the constructionist theory suggests that the cognitive processes that underlie narrative experiences operate to provide people with a particular type of reading experience. The constructionist theory is guided by the principle of 'search (or effort) after meaning' (Graesser et al. 1994: 371) which generates three assumptions (371-72):

1. *The reader goal assumption.* The reader constructs a meaning representation that addresses the reader's goals [...]

2. *The coherence assumption.* The reader attempts to construct a meaning representation that is coherent at both local and global levels [...]

3. *The explanation assumption.* The reader attempts to explain why actions, events, and states are mentioned in the text.

Because of the emphasis on explanation, researchers in this tradition also use the label *explanation-based theory* (the term we prefer). Proponents of memory-based processing would no doubt agree that readers often attempt to explain why actions are mentioned in a text. The issue that separates the two theories is whether readers carry out such activities as a *necessary* part of text processing.

As with the memory-based approach, the explanation-based approach has given rise to specific applications. We noted that researchers have characterized different levels at which readers represent texts. One type of representation that has gained empirical support is the *situation model*—a representation of 'the state of affairs described in a text' (Zwaan and Radvansky 1998: 162). Within the explanation-based tradition, Zwaan, Langston, and

Graesser (1995; see also Zwaan, Magliano, and Graesser 1995) have articulated the *event-indexing model* which provides an account of the dimensions of situation models (292): 'When processing the first story event, the reader constructs five indices. Each story event is indexed on the time frame in which it occurs, the spatial region in which it occurs, the protagonist (or protagonists) it involves, its causal status with regard to the prior event (or events), and its relatedness to a protagonist's goals. Then the reader monitors whether incoming story events require updating an index on any of these situational dimensions'. Although the event-indexing model may be accurate, it clearly commits readers' cognitive resources to a very specific range of activities. This, again, is the most important contrast with the memory-based processing approach to narrative experiences which envisions a much narrower range of processes that readers *must* perform.

Because the explanation-based account and its corollaries make broader claims than does memory-based processing, it has proven easier to find exceptions to its predictions (e.g., Albrecht and O'Brien 1993; O'Brien et al. 1998; Rapp and Gerrig 2002). However, rather than focusing on limitations of either theory, we wish to describe topics that illustrate ways in which research in cognitive psychology can reveal the 'backbone' of narrative experiences. Even so, our goal with respect to our choices of topics is to give some sense of the extent to which a particular type of reader or of reading is institutionalized in our cognitive processes.

3.1 Readers' Monitoring of Goals

Early in 'No Place for You, My Love', the protagonist establishes the explicit goal that will provide structure for the rest of the story (Welty 1955: 5):

> 'I have a car here, just down the street,' he said to her as the luncheon party was rising to leave, all the others wanting to get back to their houses and sleep. 'If it's all right with— Have you ever driven down south of here?'
>
> Out on Bourbon Street, in the bath of July, she asked at his shoulder, 'South of New Orleans? I didn't know there was any south to *here*. Does it just go on and on?' She laughed, and adjusted the exasperating hat to her head in a different way. It was more than frivolous, it was conspicuous, with some sort of glitter or flitter tied in a band around the straw and hanging down.
>
> 'That's what I'm going to show you.'
>
> 'Oh—you've been there?'
>
> 'No!'

As the story unfolds, small goals arise that are nested within this larger goal: The man and woman wish to avoid insects ('There were thousands, millions of mosquitoes and gnats—a universe of them, and on the increase'; Welty 1955: 8), they wish to make a ferry ('Now skidding down the levee's flank, they were the last-minute car, the last possible car that would squeeze on'; Welty, 1955: 8-9), and so on. To experience 'No Place for You, My Love', readers must be cognizant of the relationship between these local circumstances and the more general goal of reaching the southernmost point of the road.

Readers' experiences of goals have been a major focus of cognitive psychological research on text processing. For example, as we noted earlier, the explanation-based theory suggests that much of readers' effort is devoted to recovering explanations for why actions and events occur; goals provide much of the impetus for actions and events. Trabasso and his colleagues (e.g., Trabasso and Sperry 1985; Trabasso and van den Broek 1985; Trabasso, van den Broek, and Suh 1989) provided evidence that one product of readers' narrative experiences are *causal networks* that represent the relationships between the causes and consequences of events in a story. Some story events form the main *causal chain* of the story whereas others, with respect to causality, are dead ends. When asked to recall stories, readers find it relatively more difficult to produce details that are not along that main causal chain. We would, for example, expect that readers of Welty's story would be unlikely to recall the lovely details about the woman's hat.

In our brief goal analysis of 'No Place for You, My Love', we suggested that local goals are nested within the overarching imperative to 'go south'. This structure represents one of the many complex interweavings of goals provided by literary works. Researchers in the explanation-based tradition have examined the consequences of goal hierarchies for moment-by-moment processing. The most important claim is that readers keep goal information activated in working memory as they proceed in reading, until all the actions toward the achievement of that goal have been performed and the goal is fulfilled (Lutz and Radvansky 1997). On this theory, readers devote greatest attention to the most recent unfulfilled goal. Magliano and Radvansky (2001) sought to demonstrate the way in which the accessibility of goals changes in readers' text representations as a function of the status of other goals.

Consider the story presented in Table 2. This story, which is representative of the stories used in Magliano and Radvansky's (2001) experiment, presents an initial goal (i.e., 'Betty wanted to move to the same city as her mother') that remains unfulfilled at the end of the first episode. According to the explanation-based theory, that goal should retain some prominence in working memory. However, the story's second episode introduces a second goal (i.e., 'She really wanted to give her mother a present') that should divert some of the reader's attention. By the end of the second episode, the status of that second goal differed as a function of versions of the story. In the *failed goal* version, the character had not been able to discharge the Episode 2 goal. In the *completed goal* and *dead-end goal versions*, the Episode 2 goal has been discharged.

Episode 1: Once there was a woman named Betty. Betty's mother had been sick lately. Betty wanted to move to the same city as her mother **(goal 1)**. She went to the personnel office at her company. The office manager said he could not authorize her request. He told her that she needed to discuss the matter with the regional vice president.

Episode 2: The next day Betty realized that her mother's birthday was coming soon.

(Participants read the Failed Goal, Completed goal, *or* Dead-end goal *middle portions of the text.)*

Failed goal: She really wanted to give her mother a present **(goal 2)**. She went to the department store. She found that everything was too expensive. She could not buy anything for her mother. She was very sad.

Completed goal: She really wanted to give her mother a present **(goal 2)**. She went to the department store. She found a pretty purse. She was very happy.

Dead-end goal: She bought the present she wanted to give her mother **(goal 2)**. Then, she went to the department store. She found a pretty purse. She was very happy.

Episode 3: Several days later, Betty saw her friend knitting. Betty was also good at knitting. She decided to knit a sweater. She selected a pattern from a magazine. She followed the instructions in the article. Finally, Betty finished a beautiful sweater.

Episode 4: She pressed the sweater. She folded it carefully.

Probe Question: Did Betty want to move close to her mother?

She sent it to her mother (failed goal version). (or)

She put it in the closet for the next time she went out. (completed and dead-end version)

She was very happy.

(Note that the Probe Question interrupted Episode 4.)

Table 2: An Example Story from Magliano and Radvansky (2001)

Recall that, according to the explanation-based theory, the more recent Episode 2 goal should be relatively more prominent in readers' representations until it is satisfied. Once that is the case, Episode 1 goal should regain accessibility. To provide evidence for these predictions, Magliano and Radvansky (2001) asked the participants in their experiment to respond 'yes' or 'no' to questions about the content of the text. As indicated in Table 2, those probe questions appeared toward the end of the stories.

There were two probe questions for each experimental story. The first probe always tested participants' ability to confirm the first goal (e.g., Did Betty want to move close to her mother?). Because of its renewed accessibility, participants should find it easier to confirm the Episode 1 goal when the Episode 2 goal has been satisfied. The data supported that prediction: Participants took reliably less time to confirm the Episode 1 goal when the Episode 2 goal was completed or was a dead end than when the character had failed to complete it.

Based on this experiment, we cannot know whether these adjustments with respect to the accessibility of goals are automatic or require reader effort: the probe sentence occurs too far downstream from the proposed locus of the effect (i.e., right after the Episode 2 goal is satisfied) to conclude that the reemergence of the Episode 1 goal is effortless. However, even if the monitoring of goals requires readers' strategic intervention, this experiment still informs us that readers are ready and willing to undertake that intervention. Although readers no doubt extract more from 'No Place for You, My Love' than a causal network, it seems likely that they maintain some awareness of the overarching goal to 'go South'. The results of Magliano and Radvansky's (2001) experiment suggest, however, that readers' awareness of that goal evolves in a predictable fashion as they read the story.

3.2 Readers' Assessment of the Future and the Past

When the male protagonist of 'No Place for You, My Love' proposes 'Have you ever driven down south of here?', this is a good moment for readers to pause and reflect on the likely consequences: Readers, that is, might allow themselves to make predictions about what the story's future will bring. Meanwhile, as the story unfolds, readers must construct a coherent representation that reflects both the current situation and what they have learned earlier. In various ways, researchers in cognitive psychology have explored how readers meld past, present, and future as they undergo narrative experiences (Gerrig 1993).

As we just noted, readers always have the privilege of taking a moment's pause to imagine what might come next. For that reason, cognitive psychological research has focused on the circumstances in which readers are likely to make predictive inferences without strategic intervention. For example, in 'No Place for You, My Love', readers learn that, as the protagonists follow their road south, 'More and more crayfish and other shell creatures littered their path, scuttling or dragging' (Welty 1955: 8). Do readers automatically encode the inference that some of those crayfish and their peers will not survive the car's passage? (If they do, the next sentence confirms the inference: 'These little samples, little jokes of creation, persisted and sometimes perished, the more of them the deeper down the road went.')

The study of predictive inferences was inaugurated by McKoon and Ratcliff (1986) with brief and sometimes dramatic texts: 'The director and the cameraman were ready to shoot closeups when suddenly the actress fell from the 14th story.' McKoon and Ratcliff's research led to the conclusion that readers were encoding predictive inferences, but that the inferences were not highly specific. That is, rather than encoding specifically that the actress would die, readers appeared to be encoding the more general prediction that 'something bad will happen.' Other researchers have extended McKoon and Ratcliff's agenda by using less truncated texts, in which the inference arises more generally from the circumstances.

Consider, for example, the story in Table 3. Here, Cook, Limber, and O'Brien (2001) have provided a text that varies the overall contextual support for a predictive inference.

Introduction: Jimmy was the new kid on the block. Although his parents urged him to go meet the other kids in the neighborhood, he was shy and hadn't made any new friends. One Saturday morning, his mom asked him to go to the store for her. While he was walking back home, Jimmy ran into some of the kids from the neighborhood. They asked him if he wanted to play with them.

(*Participants read either the* Low Context *or* High Context *middle portions of the text.*)

Low Context: Jimmy was delighted and ran across the street to play with them. They taught him a fun game that involved throwing Nerf balls at a target to get points.

High Context: Jimmy was delighted and ran across the street to play with them. They taught him a fun game that involved throwing rocks at a target to get points.

Continuation Section: Jimmy and his friends were having a great time. Jimmy even won the game once or twice. He stepped up to take his turn and aimed at the target. He missed, though, and he accidentally hit the door of a new car.

Table 3: An example story from Cook et al. (2001)

In the *high context* version, the mention that the game was played with rocks supports the inference, downstream, that Jimmy's accident would cause a dent. This inference would not, presumably, occur when the object hitting the door was a Nerf ball, as in the *low context* version. The extent to which readers, in fact, made the inference was assessed using a word naming procedure. In this procedure participants are asked to name a word as quickly as they can. The amount of time it takes them to name a word is an index of the word's accessibility in memory. In Cook et al.'s experiment, words that encoded the appropriate inference (such as 'dent') were presented after the end of each passage. Participants named the inference words consistently faster in the presence of high contextual constraints. What makes this result interesting is that the inference is not carried by one sentence of the stories. Rather, readers must piece together a model of the situation to encode the inference.

In subsequent experiments, Cook et al. (2001) examined the extent to which readers' predictive inferences become a part of their long-term memory. To address this topic, Cook et al. contrasted circumstances in which an outcome was implied (as in the earlier study) with those in which it was explicitly stated. Now, in the *explicit* version of Jimmy's story, a sentence read 'He missed, though, and he accidentally hit the car door of a new car and dented it' whereas the *implicit* version retained 'He missed, though, and he accidentally hit the car door of a new car.' Next, participants read a paragraph of text that created distance from the moment at which they would have encoded the inference:

> Jimmy was late for dinner so he said goodbye to his new friends and ran home. He couldn't wait to go play with them again the next day. He happily told his mom that he had finally met some of the other kids in the neighborhood and had a great time. He told her about the game they played.

Finally, participants encountered a critical sentence:

> He told her about denting the car door.

If the representations at which readers arrived were identical when the inference was either explicit or implicit, we would expect participants to have equal difficulty understanding 'He told her about denting the car door'. In fact, participants found the sentence harder to integrate when the inference had only been implicit. From this series of experiments we learn about some of the transient states that underlie readers' narrative experiences. We cannot know, just by generating intuitions from texts, what the cognitive psychological reality will be.

Let us now turn to the ways in which readers' understanding of the current moment in a text is informed by what has come before. Picano's novel *The Book of Lies* provides a dramatic example of a revelation—toward the book's very end—that colors enormously everything that preceded it. (Spoiler alert: Do not read the remainder of this paragraph, should you wish to preserve the secret.) The novel concerns, in large part, the efforts of Ross Ohrenstedt to produce new knowledge about a group of writers known as the 'Purple Circle'. (The Purple Circle is a fictionalization of the real-world 'Violet Quill', a group of prominent gay male writers, of which Picano was a member.) At the end, when Ross believes he has succeeded, he has an awkward moment with his patron, Damon Von Slyke (Picano 1998: 399):

> 'Good! Now if you'll answer one more question. You're not gay either, are you? Not gay. Not even bisexual, are you?'

> 'You have to understand, Mr Von Slyke... I knew if I was going to write about the Purple Circle and be taken seriously by anyone, including yourselves, that I'd be totally suspect unless I fit in, unless I...'

> '*Thank* you!' he interrupted. 'I've heard enough. I see now that you aren't at all gay.'

Throughout the novel, the reader has been led to believe that Ross is gay. With this revelation, it seems impossible not to do a mental review of the 'evidence' in the book—to see the ways in which readers allowed themselves to be misled.

When we discussed the ways in which readers disentangle narratives, we illustrated how the first impetus for such a mental review will be provided by automatic processes. These are exactly the type of circumstances in which we would expect cues to resonate through memory to provide heightened accessibility to previous episodes in which the evidence for Ross's sexuality figured prominently. This is one automatic way in which present and past merge in the experience of narratives. However, another topic of research interest has been the extent to which the present—as it is revealed—overwrites the past. In Ross's case, does the reader's knowledge of his true sexuality forever overshadow past misdirection?

This question of updating provides an interesting contrast between the explanation-based and memory-based approaches to text processing. According to the explanation-based approach, readers should fully update their models of characters (recall the *event-indexing model* we described earlier) when they acquire new information. Once the character model has been updated, old information should be left in the background never (automatically) to be consulted again. Thus, if the explanation-based model is correct, once readers have updated their Ross model with respect to his sexuality, they should never again consider the possibility that it could be otherwise. By contrast, the memory-based model suggests that cues resonating through long-term memory representations should continue to evoke the earlier information no matter what the current state of knowledge.

Research by O'Brien et al. (1998; see also Albrecht and O'Brien 1993) supports the predictions of the memory-based approach. Consider the story given in Table 4.

Introduction: Today, Mary was meeting a friend for lunch. She arrived early at the restaurant and decided to get a table. After she sat down, she started looking at the menu.

(*Participants read the* **Consistent Elaboration, Inconsistent Elaboration**, *or* **Qualified Elaboration** *middle portions of the text.*)

Consistent Elaboration: This was Mary's favorite restaurant because it had fantastic junk food. Mary enjoyed eating anything that was quick and easy to fix. In fact, she ate at McDonald's at least three times a week. Mary never worried about her diet and saw no reason to eat nutritious foods.

Inconsistent Elaboration: This was Mary's favorite restaurant because it had fantastic health food. Mary, a health nut, had been a strict vegetarian for ten years. Her favorite food was cauliflower. Mary was so serious about her diet that she refused to eat anything which was fried or cooked in grease.

Qualified Elaboration: As she was waiting, Mary recalled that this had been her favorite restaurant because it had fantastic health food. Mary recalled that she had been a health nut and a strict vegetarian for about ten years but she wasn't anymore. Back then, her favorite food had been cauliflower. At that time, Mary had been so serious about her diet that she refused to eat anything which was fried or cooked in grease.

Filler: After about ten minutes, Mary's friend arrived. It had been a few months since they had seen each other. Because of this they had a lot to talk about and chatted for over a half hour. Finally, Mary signaled the waiter to come take their orders. Mary checked the menu one more time. She had a hard time deciding what to have for lunch.

Target sentences: Mary ordered a cheeseburger and fries.

She handed the menu back to the waiter.

Closing: Her friend didn't have as much trouble deciding what she wanted. She ordered, and they began to chat again. They didn't realize there was so much for them to catch up on.

Table 4: An example story from O'Brien et al. (1998)

Let's begin with the target sentence toward the end, 'Mary ordered a cheeseburger and fries'. The earlier material in the story makes this act of Mary's easier or harder to assimilate. Suppose, for example, participants read the version of the story that includes the *consistent elaboration*. In that case, they are told that Mary is a great fan of McDonald's. Mary's eating habits remain consistent throughout the story; readers should find it relatively easy to integrate the notion that she ordered a cheeseburger and fries. By contrast, the *inconsistent elaboration* presents a problem. In the version of the story that includes that portion of the text, Mary is identified as a strict vegetarian. We would expect that readers would be bewildered when they learn that she has ordered a cheeseburger and fries. In fact, as indexed by the increased time it takes them to indicate that they'd understood the sentence, readers are somewhat bewildered by that version.

The critical case, however, is what O'Brien et al. (1998) called the *qualified elaboration*. In this version, Mary's history is completely spelled out. She *was* a vegetarian, but she has fallen away from the faith. According to explanation-based theories, readers should only carry forward a model of Mary in which she is an omnivore. That knowledge should make it relatively easy for readers to integrate Mary's lunch order into their overall text representation. By contrast, the memory-based view asserts that resonance will make Mary's whole history accessible once again. As such, her past vegetarianism should function during integration—with the effect of slowing assimilation of the cheeseburger and fries. In fact, participants who read stories with the qualified elaboration still took more time to indicate their understanding of the target sentence than did those who read the versions with consistent elaborations.

As with the other research we have described, we believe these results have interesting implications for the way that authors might conceptualize how readers experience narratives. O'Brien et al.'s experiments suggest that, as readers update their models, they are still—automatically—compelled to revisit the past. As such, the past and the present crowd together to give a nuanced sense of how a character has developed. With respect to Ross Ohrenstedt, this means that readers will continue to confront the issue of his sexuality despite the concluding revelation of the novel. In addition, we see from these experiments that ordinary memory processes—processes that do not incorporate any model of what readers should or must do—provide this integration of present and past.

4 Conclusions

In this chapter, we have reviewed cognitive psychological research on narrative experiences with an eye toward demonstrating the immediate relevance of that research for the study of literary and other texts. We have used examples from Welty's story 'No Place for You, My Love' and Picano's novel *The Book of Lies* because they aspired to a certain level of literariness but were otherwise quite ordinary. That is, we intend our examples to have been representative of the sorts of experiences many readers are likely to have. Similarly, we hope that the applications we have illustrated have relevance beyond the brief invented stories that, for methodological reasons, dominate research on text processing.

Even so, every time we experience a work of literature we are reminded how much more progress cognitive psychological research must make to meet the goals we identified in our opening section. We will offer one example here. When we discussed the structure of 'No Place for You, My Love', we noted an official goal that brings overarching unity to the story: 'Have you ever driven down south of [New Orleans]?' In light of the 'go south' goal, we were able to make some suggestions about what readers are likely to be thinking (i.e., what will be most accessible in their representations) at various points in the story. Still, there's clearly more going on in this story than the official imperative to 'go south'. The man and the woman, after all, were 'strangers to each other'. Why would the man propose the trip and why would the woman accept the proposal? (Midway through the story, the woman says, 'I believe there must be something wrong with me, that I came on this excursion to begin with'; Welty 1955: 17.) Cognitive psychological research on goals has only focused on the explicit goals that are, almost always, stated directly in the texts. At present, the relevant theories have no way of conceptualizing how it is that readers find their way to a retrospective understanding of the implicit reasons why characters make the choices that they make. Thus, although cognitive scientists have developed some genuine insights about how people read, engagement with literary texts helps underscore the cognitive complexity of narrative comprehension, suggesting the need for perpetually broadening the research agenda.[2]

---

[2] We would like to thank David Herman for helpful comments on earlier drafts of this chapter. This material is based upon work supported by the National Science Foundation under Grant No. ITR0082602. Any opinions, findings, and conclusions or recommendations expressed in this material are those of the authors and do not necessarily reflect the views of the National Science Foundation. Please address correspondence to Richard J. Gerrig, De-

References

Abelson, R. P. 1981. Psychological Status of the Script Concept. *American Psychologist* 36: 715-29.

Albrecht, J. E., and E. J. O'Brien. 1993. Updating a Mental Model: Maintaining Both Local and Global Coherence. *Journal of Experimental Psychology: Learning, Memory, and Cognition* 19: 1061-70.

Bartlett, F. C. 1932. *Remembering*. Cambridge: Cambridge University Press.

Bower, G. H., J. B. Black, and T. J. Turner. 1979. Scripts in Memory for Text. *Cognitive Psychology* 11: 177-220.

Brewer, W. F., and G. V. Nakamura. 1984. The Nature and Function of Schemas. *Handbook of Social Cognition*, ed. R. S. Wyer and T. K. Srull, vol. 1, 119-60. Hillsdale, NJ: Erlbaum.

Cook, A. E., J. E. Limber, and E. J. O'Brien. 2001. Situation-based Context and the Availability of Predictive Inferences. *Journal of Memory and Language* 44: 220-34.

Emmott, C. 1997. *Narrative Comprehension*. Oxford: Oxford University Press.

Genette, G. 1980 [1972]. *Narrative Discourse,* trans. J. E. Lewin. Ithaca: Cornell University Press.

Gerrig, R. J. 1993. *Experiencing Narrative Worlds*. New Haven, CT: Yale University Press.

Gerrig, R. J., and G. McKoon. 1998. The Readiness Is All: The Functionality of Memory-based Text Processing. *Discourse Processes* 26: 67-86.

Gerrig, R. J., and G. McKoon. 2001. Memory Processes and Experiential Continuity. *Psychological Science* 12: 81-85.

Gillund, G., and R. M. Shiffrin. 1984. A Retrieval Model for Both Recognition and Recall. *Psychological Review* 91: 1-67.

Graesser, A. C., M. Singer, and T. Trabasso. 1994. Constructing Inferences During Narrative Text Comprehension. *Psychological Review* 101: 371-95.

Herman, D. 2002. *Story Logic: Problems and Possibilities of Narrative.* Lincoln, NE: University of Nebraska Press.

Hintzman, D. 1988. Judgments of Frequency and Recognition Memory in a Multiple-trace Memory Model. *Psychological Review* 95: 528-51.

Iser, Wolfgang. 1978. *The Act of Reading: A Theory of Aesthetic Response.* Baltimore, MD: Johns Hopkins University Press.

Johnson-Laird, P. N. 1983. *Mental Models*. Cambridge, MA: Harvard University Press.

---

partment of Psychology, Stony Brook University, Stony Brook, NY 11794-2500, USA; rgerrig@notes.cc.sunysb.edu

Lea, R. B., R. A. Mason, J. E. Albrecht, S. L. Birch, and J. L. Myers. 1998. Who Knows What About Whom: What Role Does Common Ground Play in Accessing Distant Information? *Journal of Memory and Language* 39: 70-84.

Lutz, M. F., and G. A. Radvansky. 1997. The Fate of Completed Goal Information in Narrative Comprehension. *Journal of Memory and Language* 36: 293-310.

Magliano, J. P., and G. A. Radvansky. 2001. Goal Coordination in Narrative Comprehension. *Psychonomic Bulletin & Review* 8: 372-76.

McKoon, G., R. J. Gerrig, and S. B. Greene. 1996. Pronoun Resolution Without Pronouns: Some Consequences of Memory-based Text Processing. *Journal of Experimental Psychology: Learning, Memory, and Cognition* 22: 919-32.

McKoon, G., and R. Ratcliff. 1986. Inferences About Predictable Events. *Journal of Experimental Psychology: Learning, Memory, and Cognition* 12: 82-91.

McKoon, G., and R. Ratcliff. 1992. Inference During Reading. *Psychological Review* 99: 440-66.

Murdock, B. B. 1983. A Distributed Memory Model for Serial-order Information. *Psychological Review* 90: 316-38.

Myers, J. L., and E. J. O'Brien. 1998. Accessing the Discourse Representation During Reading. *Discourse Processes* 26: 131-57.

O'Brien, E. J., R. F. Lorch, Jr., and J. L. Myers, eds. 1998. Memory-based Text Processing [Special issue]. *Discourse Processes* 26 (2 and 3).

O'Brien, E. J., M. L. Rizzella, J. E. Albrecht, and J. G. Halleran. 1998. Updating a Situation Model: A Memory-based Text Processing View. *Journal of Experimental Psychology: Learning, Memory, and Cognition* 24: 1200-10.

Picano, F. 1998. *The Book of Lies*. Los Angeles: Alyson Books.

Rapp, D. N., and R. J. Gerrig. 2002. Readers' Reality-driven and Plot-driven Analyses in Narrative Comprehension. *Memory & Cognition* 30.5: 779-88.

Ratcliff, R. 1978. A Theory of Memory Retrieval. *Psychological Review* 85: 59-108.

Schank, R. C., and R. P. Abelson. 1977. *Scripts, Plans, Goals, and Understanding*. Hillsdale, NJ: Erlbaum.

Singer, M., A. C. Graesser, and T. Trabasso. 1994. Minimal or Global Inferences During Reading. *Journal of Memory and Language* 33: 421-41.

Trabasso, T., and L. Sperry. 1985. Causal Relatedness and Importance of Story Events. *Journal of Memory and Language* 24: 595-611.

Trabasso, T., and P. van den Broek. 1985. Causal Thinking and the Representation of Narrative Events. *Journal of Memory and Language* 24: 612-30.

Trabasso, T., P. van den Broek, and S. Y. Suh. 1989. Logical Necessity and Transitivity of Causal Relations in Stories. *Discourse Processes* 12: 1-25.

Tulving, E. 1974. Cue-dependent Forgetting. *American Scientist* 62: 74-82.

Van Dijk, T. A., and W. Kintsch. 1983. *Strategies of Discourse Comprehension.* New York: Academic Press.

Welty, E. 1955. *The Bride of Innisfallen and Other Stories by Eudora Welty.* New York: Harcourt, Brace and Company.

Whitney, P., D. Budd, R. S. Bramucci, and R. S. Crane. 1995. On Babies, Bath Water, and Schemata: A Reconsideration of Top-Down Processes in Comprehension. *Discourse Processes* 20: 135-66.

Zwaan, R. A., M. C. Langston, and A. C. Graesser. 1995. The Construction of Situation Models in Narrative Comprehension: An Event-indexing Model. *Psychological Science* 6: 292-7.

Zwaan, R. A., J. P. Magliano, and A C. Graesser. 1995. Dimensions of Situation Model Construction in Narrative Comprehension. *Journal of Experimental Psychology: Learning, Memory, and Cognition* 21: 386-97.

Zwaan, R. A., and G. A. Radvansky. 1998. Situation Models in Language Comprehension and Memory. *Psychological Bulletin* 123: 162-85.

3

Narrative Construction, Cognitive Processing, and Health

KITTY KLEIN

1 Introduction

In this chapter, I will present an overview of the psychological evidence that narrative accounts of traumatic events aid the healing process. I begin with a discussion of how psychologists have tried to quantify the narrative concept. I then present the theoretical rationale for how narrative development could affect health and well being. Next I present results from correlational and experimental studies relevant to the proposition that constructing a coherent narrative about a stressful event contributes to better physical and psychological outcomes. I conclude with a plea for more cross-disciplinary effort to increase our understanding of the role of narrative in people's recovery from trauma.

Psychologists have long been interested in how people tell stories about their experiences and how these stories reflect their memories of those experiences. Life stories are continually developing as people attempt to integrate new experiences (Cohler 1982). There has also been a great deal of attention devoted to how children come to see events as causally connected and how their ability to link events into narrative wholes develops (Bamberg 1997; Trabasso and Stein 1997). Researchers have also dwelt on the themes or contents of narratives and how these themes reflect fundamental

Narrative Theory and the Cognitive Sciences.
David Herman (ed.).
Copyright © 2003, CSLI Publications.

dichotomies of the human experience (Hermans 1999; Meichenbaum and Fitzpatrick 1993). In contrast to research that focuses on the story, its structure, or its contents as the end point, my purpose in this chapter is to discuss how people use autobiographical stories to understand particular events in their lives and how this understanding contributes to emotional and physical well being. My emphasis will be on narrative accounts of traumatic or stressful events and how psychologists have used these narratives as both reflections of treatment progress and as an intervention to affect health. I will cover three broad topics: how psychologists code or measure narrative, how narrative development presumably influences recovery from stressful events, and how narrative development affects health and cognition.

2 The Measurement of Psychological Constructs

For the past 100 years, psychologists have agreed on the need to have an operational definition of the constructs they study. An operational definition is a description in quantifiable terms of what to measure and the steps to follow in order to measure it consistently. Having an operational definition is particularly important in a discipline in which so many variables are essentially latent constructs; i.e., they cannot be observed directly but must be inferred from overt manifestations. These manifestations may involve something directly observable and fairly straightforward, as when investigators use reaction time to index some aspect of a cognitive or sensory process. Often, the measurement is more indirect, as when researchers rely on subjects' self-reports about internal states or about perceptions of other people or events, or when they employ coders or experts to evaluate and classify a behavior.

For example, consider the syndrome known as post-traumatic stress disorder (PTSD). I select PTSD as an example because it is a disorder whose symptoms may be abated by the development of a coherent narrative about the precipitating event (Foa, Molnar, and Cashman 1995). Some aspects of PTSD can be operationalized as directly observable physiological conditions, e.g. smaller hippocampal volume (Bremner 2001) or lower concentrations of urinary cortisol (Yehuda et al. 1995). PTSD can also be measured using self-reports of symptoms assessed via a series of questions on a standardized instrument, e. g., the PTSD Symptom Scale–Self-report (PSS-SR: Foa, Riggs, Dancu, and Rothbaum 1993). PTSD can further be operationalized as a clinician's diagnosis based on the American Psychiatric Association Association's DSM-IV criteria. All of these definitions specify the rules or operations needed to measure PTSD, e.g. an MRI brain scan or urinary cortisol analysis, a checklist of symptoms, or the Structured Clinical Interview for DSM-IV (First, Spitzer, Gibbon, and Williams 1995). Typically, there is some overlap between different systems for measuring a variable, and new procedures are usually benchmarked against a standard.

2.1 The Measurement of Narrative

There are several reasons why developing operational definitions for narrative has proven a difficult task. First, psychological researchers have identified a subset of other variables within the narrative domain, e. g. 'narrative structure', 'narrative cohesion', and 'narrative density'. Different researchers have operationalized these terms very differently. Second, in order for the definition to be useful in quantitative research applications, it should produce a value that quantifies text features on the basis of intensity or amount. Different investigators have employed different underlying models of how to apply numbers to text characteristics. For example, some definitions, particularly those based on lexical aspects of narrative, may treat percentage of words in various categories. Thus, any narrative text can be described as having a certain percentage of words of various types, e.g. pronouns. Other definitions involve a summative approach, in which the presence of each attribute requires the presence of less restrictive attributes as well. An example of this system is Stein's (1988) story-structure coding system. Incomplete episodes are stories in which the events are causally structured into episodes (settings, initiating events, internal responses, attempts, consequences, and reactions) but one or more of these categories is omitted. The next higher level is the complete episode. Complete-episode stories are the same as incomplete- episode stories but include all basic episodic categories. Thus, a text that qualifies as a complete-episode story cannot also qualify as an incomplete episode.

Another way of assigning numbers to features of narrative is to use a compensatory system, in which a text is evaluated on a number of criteria and a summary score computed. A midrange summary score does not indicate whether the narrative was rated 'medium' on all the attributes or scored very high on some and very low on others.

Use of these different scoring rules ultimately reflects a difference in how the concept of narrative is defined. Not surprisingly, therefore, the use of multiple operational definitions in empirical research on how narrative promotes health has not always produced consistent findings. The variety of definitions has also made it difficult to link the psychological study of narrative with disciplines that have traditionally focused on narrative.

2.2 Narrative Coding Schemes Employed By Psychologists

As noted above, psychologists have employed different systems for coding narrative. These systems may be loosely categorized as involving directly observable features of stories (e. g. word counts), self-reports of narrative features, or ratings by judges. The latter category includes coding utterances for the presence/absence of narrative features and the application of more elaborate holistic scoring methods to the entire text.

2.2.1 Directly Observable: Word Counts

Coding systems in this category can be roughly subdivided into simple word counts and lexically based word counts. In the simple word count group are measures like the number of characters per word, number of words per sentence, and total number of sentences, which are the criteria Zoellner, Alvarez-Conrad, and Foa (2002) use to define narrative structure in their patients' descriptions of being assaulted.

Reading ease and grade level are two systems based on simple word and character counts. Zoellner et al. (2002) and Amir, Stafford, Freshman, and Foa (1998) defined narrative organization using two reading indices. The first one, the Flesch Reading Ease score (Flesch 1949), is based on the number of syllables per word and the number of words per sentence. Higher scores mean that more people can readily understand the passage. The second one, the Bormuth grade level analysis, uses word length in characters and sentence length to determine grade-school levels. Thus compared to a score of 8, a score of 10 would indicate a higher grade level, and by inference more narrative organization

Meanwhile, Barclay (1996) defines 'narrative density' as the frequency of propositions found within a narrative, with a higher number indicating higher density. Barclay proposes that too many propositions make narrative confusing and that too few lead to misunderstandings.

The flaws in these simple word count definitions are numerous and recognized by their promoters. Zoellner et al. (2002) argue that their word- and sentence-length measures reflect the rudimentary state of existing measures for examining narrative and point out that lack of sensitivity in applying these measures may lead to null results. However, as I will demonstrate later, these simple counts may not be as barren as their critics claim.

2.2.2 Directly Observable: Lexical Coding

Lexically based systems for assessing narrative go beyond simple word, sentence, or propositional counts to counts (actually percentages) of particular kinds of words. Arguably the best known system for this kind of analysis is Pennebaker and Francis's (1999) Linguistic Inquiry and Word Count (LIWC). LIWC is a computerized program that scans text files for predetermined categories of words. These categories can be grammatical (e. g. pronouns) or content-based, for example, words denoting negative emotions. LIWC has been used extensively in analysis of essays produced in experiments investigating the effects of emotional disclosure through structured writing. Pennebaker and Francis have argued that the use of insight-related and causal words reflects an individual's attempt to find meaning for an experience. They define 'narrative coherence' as a high incidence of words related to cause and insight.

Barclay (1996) employed a similar but non-computerized scoring system to measure 'narrative organization' in individuals' memories of their youth. Narrative organization is the percentage of words in a narrative that refer to temporal structure and location and are causal-conditional or evaluative. Higher percentages of these words, particularly the use of evaluative and causal-conditional terms, indicate more 'coherent' organization of the narrative. In contrast to Pennebaker, causal-conditional words have no special status in Barclay's definition of narrative.

Zoellner, Alvarez-Conrad, and Foa (2002) further divided narratives told by assault victims into pre-threat, threat, and post-threat sections. Each section was then coded for the number of utterances that contained content regarding negative feelings and sensations.

These lexically based systems, although perhaps an improvement on simple counts, are also limited in their ability to capture key features of narrative. Pennebaker and Francis (1999) note that the LIWC procedure fails to capture irony or metaphor and can misclassify words because it does not take context into consideration.

Despite their limitations, both simple and lexically based word count systems have one advantage over most other definitions: they can be automated. Automation confers several advantages. Text analysis via computer is very rapid, usually requiring only a fraction of a second. Assuming that independent judges and dictionary definitions have verified the word classifications that the program uses, the researcher need not take additional steps to ensure inter-judge reliability. Additionally, biases that may contaminate self-reports, such as those stemming from subjects' perceptions of what is socially desirable, are not present. Thus, not every researcher adopts Olson and Salter's (1993) position that 'Word frequency data is surely the most remote sort of data from which to infer interpretive patterns' (344).

2.2.3 Self-reports

Although psychologists use self-report measures for a huge number of psychological constructs, there are few, if any, examples of asking writers or speakers to describe the narrative qualities of their essay or speech. Self-reports of 'how well-structured' an essay was have been obtained (Klein and Boals 2001), but these self-reports are not typically used to define narrative.

2.2.4 Judges' Ratings

A number of researchers use judges to rate narrative attributes. There are two basic schemes. One involves the dissection of the text into utterances or propositions; the other, judgments of the text as a whole.

2.2.4.1 Coding Utterances

The first, more reductionist scheme for using judges involves identifying propositions or utterances and then making judgments about various aspects of these units. Aspects judged include grammatical, lexical, and content features.

Foa, Molnar, and Cashman (1995), for example, coded utterance units as repetitions of other utterances; thoughts, which were further categorized as desperate, disorganized or organized; negative feelings; sensations; actions; dialogues; speech fillers; and details. These categories were then recoded into primary categories of fragmentation (repetitions, unfinished thoughts and fillers); degrees of organization; internal events (thoughts, feelings, sensations); and external events (dialogues, details, and actions).

Likewise, Pratt, Boyes, Robins, and Manchester (1989) define 'narrative cohesion' as reference cohesion of pronouns and articles. They examined noun phrases, coding for two problems: ambiguity and additions. The number of each of four types of conjunctions—additives, temporals, causals, and adversatives—was also counted.

Among the problems with these systems, identified by Van Minnen, Wessel, Dijkstra, and Roelofs (2002), are that the categories reflect different kinds of psycholinguistic levels, that these levels are not mutually exclusive, and that multiple levels may be present in the same sentence.

2.2.4.2 Holistic Scoring Systems

These systems involve application of a fairly elaborate set of criteria that are applied to the text as a whole. Features, such as differentiated components or causal connectors, are not counted as such; rather, the text must have a pattern of perspectives and connections of various types. 'Narrative complexity', according to Suedfeld and Pennebaker (1997), mirrors the characteristics of an individual's cognitive processing that occurred at the time of writing. Integrative complexity is the extent to which the narrator can recognize more than one dimension of the situation (differentiation) and also recognize the relations among differentiated perspectives (integration). Integrative complexity of an entire text is scored on a 1-7 scale with 1 indicating a single perspective with no integration and 7 indicating integration of differentiated components in a superordinate scheme.

Katz (1999) has developed another holistic scoring system that is used to code text for narrative coherence in a manner that appears closer to traditional views of narrative (Becker 1999). In this system, narrative coherence requires a character or set of characters, a scene, a beginning that sets up an expectation of what will follow, a middle, and an end in which the expectation is fulfilled. Texts receive scores from 1 (incoherent) to 5 (exceptionally coherent) based on how many criteria they meet.

Wong and Watt (1991) coded older people's reminiscences using a scoring system that mixed thematic content and structure. For example, reminiscences could be categorized as 'transmissive', i.e. told in order to pass on a cultural heritage. One of the categories, 'narrative' was defined as a reminiscence that described but did not interpret the past. Wong and Watt applied their system to each paragraph of the reminiscence, giving each text a score for each of their six categories.

The advantage of these scoring systems is that they provide a far more sensitive and complex analysis of text than do the more mechanistic systems. They also have their disadvantages. Judges must be trained to use the system, typically an investment of 10-15 hours. Further, there is always the danger that judges' acumen will be compromised by fatigue or that their standards may change across a scoring session.

Although operationalizing the concept 'narrative' has thus proven difficult, researchers continue to explore the functions of stories vis-à-vis people's physical and mental health. The sections that follow focus on stressful life experiences as a domain in which narratives arguably play an importantly beneficial role. As suggested by the studies I review, gaining a fuller understanding of the interrelations between narrative construction and health remains a pressing task for psychologists and narrative theorists alike.

3   Memories Of Stressful Events

There is widespread agreement that highly negative experiences are difficult to assimilate into one's understanding of oneself and the world. One reason for this difficulty is the absence of a knowledge base that can be used to understand and interpret the stressful event.

According to Barsalou (1988), memories of previous events provide the basis for making sense of later ones. Understanding an event requires the retrieval of relevant generic knowledge that lets people understand what has occurred so far, predict what may happen next, and determine appropriate responses to the event. Eventually, memory for a particular experience becomes integrated with generic knowledge and with the specific episodes needed to understand it. Because stressful events by definition violate people's expectations, there will rarely be generic knowledge structures available (Creamer, Burgess, and Pattison 1992; Janoff-Bulman 1992), making the integration of the experience difficult if not impossible (Horowitz 1975). The inability to anticipate the unfolding of the experience reflects the absence of a clear schema or script to guide the interpretation of the event (Stein and Liwag 1997). It is this expectancy violation that produces the emotional reaction associated with stressful experiences. Even when culturally shared scripts are available, as for the impending death of a loved one, bereaved partners often experience overwhelming sadness because the script did not prepare them for their own reactions to their loss (Stein, Liwag, and Wade 1996).

A second reason why stressful memories are so difficult to assimilate and understand is that they are more disorganized, incoherent, incomplete, and less vivid compared to autobiographical memories of less stressful events (Brewin 2001). Furthermore, clinical observations have led to the proposal (Foa and Kozak 1986; Foa, Steketee, and Rothbaum 1989) that cognitions representing stressful events are numerous and are linked to many other concepts in large, poorly organized memory networks. As such, memory access to them can occur through many different links but these large structures remain difficult to access in their entirety.

Over time, most people do develop event schemas for their stressful experiences, presumably by first recognizing the relationships between episodes, then abstracting shared features based on similarity, and finally forming an abstract or hypothetical structure of the event (Abelson 1981) that replaces the initial unconnected representations of single episodes. Foa and Riggs (1994) argue that recovery from a traumatic event requires organizing and streamlining the traumatic memory. Fivush (1998) has suggested that with repeated trauma, scripts develop that focus on commonalities, with an accompanying loss of specific details. This process can be very slow. In

Tait and Silver's (1989) study, 37% of the sample still searched for a meaningful perspective to understand negative life events that had occurred on average 23 years earlier.

The fragmented and disorganized memories of stressful episodes that have not, or cannot, be integrated into one's self-schema tend to be hyperaccessible. By this, I mean that they are called easily into consciousness by external or internal stimuli. An external stimulus would be meeting someone who resembles a deceased friend; an internal stimulus would be thinking about an activity in which the friend participated that subsequently leads to memories of the friend. These memories are involuntary; that is, they are not the products of a deliberate attempt to recall the event or the person.

Involuntary memories of stressful events are called intrusive memories. Intrusive memories are particularly insidious because they essentially reinstate the emotional and cognitive aspects of the stressful experience (Baum 1990). The unwanted intrusion of intensely negative memories can have a disruptive effect 'on the current operation of the whole cognitive system' (Conway and Pleydell-Pearce 2000: 271.)

Intrusive memories have been of particular interest to clinical psychologists because of their presence in many psychiatric disorders. Most studies of intrusive autobiographical memories are of clinical samples (Reynolds and Brewin 1998). In nonpatient samples, people exposed to naturalistic stressful events, such as earthquakes, experience decreases in intrusive memories two weeks after the events (Harber and Pennebaker 1992). In clinical samples continuing intrusive memories are usually associated with more severe and long-lasting symptoms (Greenberg 1995), but this relationship is not always found in nonclinical participants (Lepore 1997).

The intrusiveness of involuntary memories is generally determined by self-reports, using Horowitz's Impact of Event Scale (IES, from Horowitz, Wilner, and Alvarez 1979). The IES items ask how often, during the past seven days, participants had undesired memory intrusions.

Horowitz (1975) has proposed that memories associated with past stressful events continue to intrude until they can be integrated with preexisting schematized knowledge. How narrative construction might promote this integration is of considerable interest to clinicians and cognitive psychologists.

4 How Construction of a Coherent Narrative Could Reduce Intrusive Memories

One explanation is that composing a story reduces the size and complexity of the original experience into a smaller unit that 'lets memory work less hard' (Schank and Abelson 1995: 42). In the course of narrative creation, memories of negative events become embedded in the story, weakening the accessibility of these bad experiences and lessening the likelihood that internal or external stimuli will activate them. A more radical explanation advanced by Pennebaker and Seagal (1999) is that the act of converting emotions and images into words actually changes the nature of the memory of the stressful event. Integrating thoughts and feelings into a coherent narrative allows the memory to be transferred from a state of hyperaccessibility to what Wegner and Smart (1997) call a state of nonactivation, where it is unlikely to erupt into consciousness. As I have noted elsewhere (Klein 2002), the assumption is that narrative creation should decrease the accessibility of stress-related cognitions through its ability to transform the mental representation of the event.

The assumption that narrative construction can actually alter memory differentiates this view from more traditional conceptions of narrative. Narrative has often been viewed as the product of a universal human need to communicate with others and to make sense of the world (Miller 1995). For psychologists interested in health improvements following the construction of narratives, the emphasis is on how developing a narrative produces a new version of the original memory as opposed to helping a person understand what 'really' happened. There is growing consensus that memories are not carbon copies of the original experience, but instead are reconstructed in accordance with currently active goals of the rememberer (Conway and Pleydell-Pearce 2000). One of the marvelous features of narrative is that it can transform memories of unspeakably awful experiences into streamlined representations that lose their ability to derail cognition.

5 Narrative Development and Health

Despite the interest in how narrative might transform stressful memories or provide new schema, there are few reports of direct assessments of memory change following narrative creation. Instead, features of or changes in narratives about stressful or traumatic events are used as proxies for changes in the underlying memory representations of the events. The studies I review here come from two different research designs. One, the correlational approach, involves observing changes or differences in narratives about traumatic experiences and associated changes in psychological or physical health. With a few exceptions, this approach has been used to examine personal narratives involving experiences in which the narrator's very life was threatened. Outcome measures generally target psychological health.

The second approach is experimental. It requires randomly assigning some individuals the task of creating narratives about stressful experiences and then comparing their health changes to individuals randomly assigned the task of writing non-narrative essays. Although some of these experiences will have been life-threatening, in the experimental work done in my laboratory, the great majority of the essays investigated deal with grief and loss, loneliness, and family and interpersonal conflicts. Outcome measures in the experimental studies include psychological well being and cognitive function, but the primary focus of this work has been on improvements in physical health following completion of the writing tasks.

5.1 Narrative and Mental Health: Correlational Evidence

There are numerous anecdotal reports from clinical psychologists that patients able to produce narrative accounts of stressful events experience more positive therapy outcomes (Harvey, Orbuch, Chwalisz, and Garwood 1991) and are better able to cope with further stress (van der Kolk and Fisler 1995; Meichenbaum and Fitzpatrick 1993). There are also several recent reports of empirical tests of this association. Unfortunately, results of several of these studies should be viewed with caution. Some used samples too small to have adequate power to detect effects, performed numerous correlational analyses without adjusting for the increases in error that occur in multiple statistical tests, or failed to include an appropriate control group.

Foa, Molnar, and Cashman (1995) studied narratives of rape victims before and after they received ten biweekly cognitive behavioral therapy treatments that required them to relive the rape. The narrative coding system involved analyzing utterances for the extent to which the utterances were coherently interrelated; included thoughts and feelings; included actions or dialogues; or were examples of fragmentation. With the exception of fragmentation, there were changes across all measures as the treatment progressed. Following treatment, the percentage of utterances in the first two categories increased from the percentage observed pretreatment. The percentage of utterances representing actions or dialogues decreased. All participants demonstrated an improvement on measures of psychopathology and several of these measures correlated with changes in the fragmentation and disorganization scores of the narratives.

Van Minnen, Wessel, Dijkstra, and Roelofs (2002) used the same narrative coding scheme as Foa et al. (1995). Because all of Foa et al.'s patients improved, van Minnen et al.'s (2002) question was whether narratives by individuals who did not benefit from therapy would differ from narratives by patients who improved. Their sample consisted of students with a variety of trauma histories. As in Foa et al. (1995), narratives from the first and last of nine weekly therapy sessions were compared. All participants showed a decrease in disorganized thoughts and references to external events in the pre- to post-treatment narratives. All narratives showed an increase in internal event references. Improved participants showed greater decreases in disorganized thoughts, but this was the only feature of narrative structure in terms of which improved and non-improved patients differed. As the authors note, one difficulty in interpreting such correlational data is that because most of the narrative changes occurred in both groups, they may be a mere byproduct of the multiple recountings of the experience during treatment, rather than reflecting a change in the memory for the traumatic event that signals recovery from the trauma.

Alvarez-Conrad, Zoellner, and Foa (2001) applied Pennebaker and Francis' (1999) LIWC lexical coding system to rape victims' descriptions of their assault two weeks after therapy had begun. Their hypotheses, that more frequent use of emotional and cognitive words, and fewer references to death, would predict decreased PTSD symptoms post-treatment, improved physical health, and better functioning, were not strongly supported. PTSD symptom severity was correlated with references to death in the narratives and anxiety symptoms were lower for women whose narratives contained more cognitive words. By and large, however, the relationships were weak or inconsistent across sections (pre-threat, threat, and post-threat) of the description.

Zoellner, Alvarez-Conrad, and Foa (2002) divided the same sample of twenty-eight assault victims into two groups, based on the amount of peritraumatic dissociation the patient displayed. Peritraumatic dissociation refers to alterations in the experience of time, both slowing and rapidly accelerating, out-of-body experiences, and feelings of unreality that occur during traumatic events. The authors predicted that narratives describing the assault given by patients higher in peritraumatic dissociation would be more disorganized and fragmented compared to patients lower in dissociation. Narrative disorganization was indexed using word counts and reading-level scores. Contrary to the hypothesis, individuals reporting higher levels of dissociative symptoms produced narratives with more characters per word and higher reading-level scores. Given that all the members of the small sample met the DSM-IV criteria for chronic PTSD and the nature of the methods used to determine narrative disorganization, it is hard to know what to make of their results.

Amir, Stafford, Freshman, and Foa (1998) studied rape narratives produced shortly after the attack. Narrative articulation was defined as reading level of the transcriptions. Victims whose narratives were low in articulation were more likely to develop more severe PTSD symptoms three months later. While the authors conclude that less developed trauma narratives hinder recovery from trauma, it is also possible that the women most traumatized by the attack produced less developed narratives and for the same reason were more at risk for PTSD.

Wong and Watt (1991) report a correlational study of narrative and health that did not use PTSD patients. Wong and Watt interviewed elderly people, asking for their life stories. Each paragraph in the reminiscences was coded using a holistic scoring system. They also obtained self-reports of physical health and psychological well being that were used to divide the sample into 'successful' and 'nonsuccessful agers'. Successful agers' reminiscences contained more integrative and instrumental themes and fewer paragraphs with obsessive themes compared to unsuccessful agers. Scores on their narrative scale, which they defined as a simple description of a life, did not distinguish between the successful and nonsuccessful groups.

5.2   Narrative and Physical Health: Experimental Evidence

In addition to the correlational studies described above, there is a large and growing literature in which participants are randomly asked to create a narrative about a stressful event or to describe, in as dry a fashion as possible, a commonplace nonemotional event. To the extent that these experiments also include appropriate controls, they have the advantage of allowing a causal interpretation of the results. Thus, if an experimenter manipulates the presence/absence of the narrative treatment condition, the treatment can be construed as the cause of differences in the outcome measures. Most of the experiments utilize Pennebaker's (1989) 'expressive writing' paradigm. Other names for the same paradigm are 'structured writing' and 'emotional writing'. In typical experiments, expressive writers are instructed to describe their feelings and thoughts about a stressful experience and attempt to 'tie it all together'. Both long hand and computer entry have been used to record the essays. The same instructions have been used in verbal disclosure experiments. Following are a typical set of instructions for the experimental group.

> In the next session of this experiment, your task is to write about your
> very deepest thoughts and feelings regarding a negative event that has
> had a serious impact on your life. In your writing, try to let yourself
> go and write continuously about your emotions and thoughts related

to these events. Describe the facts and feelings of your experiences. Write about the experience in as much detail as you can. Do your best to 'tie it all together' at the end of the writing. You do not have to save what you have entered once you have finished, but it would benefit our study greatly if you would. The important thing is that you really let yourself go and dig down to your very deepest thoughts and feelings about the negative event.

Depending on the experiment, the negative event may be the 'most traumatic and upsetting experience of your entire life' (Pennebaker, Kiecolt-Glaser, and Glaser 1988; Richards, Beal, Seagal, and Pennebaker 2000); 'a traumatic event or traumatic loss' (King and Miner 2000); 'the most stressful experience you have ever undergone' (Smyth, Stone, Hurewitz and Kaell 1999); 'coming to college' (Klein and Boals 2001; Pennebaker and Francis 1996); 'being laid off' (Spera, Buhrfeind, and Pennebaker 1994); the 'breakup of your relationship' (Lepore and Greenberg in press), 'the death of your spouse' (Segal, Bogaards, Becker and Chatman 1999); any trauma or upheaval (Kelley, Lumley, and Leisen 1997); 'an event that has been highly stressful, traumatic or about which you have felt very guilty' (Klein and Boals 2001; Lutgendorf, Antoni, Kumar, and Schneiderman 1994); or an upcoming standardized examination (Lepore 1997).

Control group participants are asked to write/talk about a trivial topic, for example, time management or a description of their room. Typical instructions are:

In the next sessions of this experiment, your task is to write for 20 minutes about how you spent your time yesterday. List everything you did, as completely as you can remember from the time you got up in the morning until you went to bed. Include as much detail as you can. Do not include your thoughts and feelings about any of the events; just describe them as completely and unemotionally as you can. You do not have to save what you have entered once you have finished, but it would benefit our study greatly if you would. The important thing is that you really let yourself go and dig down to your very deepest thoughts and feelings about the negative event.

Regardless of experimental topic, the beneficial effects of two to four 20-minute sessions of expressive writing/talking are remarkable. These benefits include physical health, psychological well being, and cognitive function. Compared to individuals asked to write about trivial topics, experimental participants who write about their deepest thoughts and feelings show reductions in physician visits for some months after writing (Pennebaker and Beall 1986; Pennebaker, Kiecolt-Glaser, and Glaser 1988; Pennebaker and Francis 1996; Gidron et al. 2002). Rheumatoid arthritis patients exhibited better physical function following a verbal disclosure intervention (Kelley, Lumley, and Leisen 1997) and improved physicians' ratings following expressive writing (Smyth, Stone, Hurewitz, and Kaell 1999).

There is also evidence that expressive writing reduces blood pressure (Crow, Pennebaker, and King, in a study cited by Davidson et al. 2002; Fonareva 2002; Pennebaker, Kiecolt-Glaser, and Glaser 1988) and improves immune function (Booth, Petrie, and Pennebaker 1997; Pennebaker, Kiecolt-Glaser, and Glaser 1988; Petrie, Booth, Pennebaker, Davison, and Thomas 1995).

Expressive writing or structured verbal disclosure can also produce increases in psychological well being, including reductions in self-reports of intrusive memories (Klein and Boals 2001; Segal and Murray 1994; Segal, Bogaards, Becker, and Chatman 1999); decreases in hopelessness and depression in the bereaved elderly (Segal et al. 1999); decreases in students' grief after a friend's suicide (Kovac and Range 2000); and improved mood in rheumatoid arthritis patients (Kelley, Lumley, and Leisen 1997).

Expressive writing also affects achievement outcomes. Laid-off middle managers in Spera et al.'s (1994) research who were assigned to an expressive writing condition found new jobs more quickly than a control group of managers who simply listed the steps they had taken to find a Job.   In a number of experiments with students (Cameron and Nicholls 1998; Pennebaker, Colder, and Sharp 1990; Pennebaker and Francis 1996; Klein and Boals 2001), writing about coming to college produced grade-point-average improvements.

Finally, there are data suggesting that expressive writing can produce working memory (WM) improvements (Klein and Boals 2001).   WM capacity is the 'capacity for controlled, sustained attention in the face of interference or distraction' (Engle, Kane, and Tuholski 1999: 104) and is assessed with cognitive tasks that require a participant to remember information (e. g. a list of words) while performing another task (e. g. solving simple arithmetic equations).   Because most cognitive psychologists have considered WM capacity to be a highly stable individual difference, and because WM capacity is strongly predictive of performance on a variety of real-world tasks, e. g. SAT scores, reading comprehension, and measures of fluid intelligence, (Engle, Tuholski, Laughlin, and Conway 1999), the findings that expressive writing can produce WM capacity increases adds a new dimension to the mind-body link.

Although expressive writing interventions have been effective for college students, maximum security prisoners, arthritic and asthmatic patients, currently employed and laid-off employees, and survivors of the Holocaust, there is some data that it is not infallibly effective.   Gidron et al. (1996) found that writing did not benefit a sample of PTSD patients, presumably because they could not organize their traumatic experiences. It has also failed to produce the desired effects for the recently bereaved (Stroebe, Stroebe, Zech, Schut, and van den Bout 2002) or for students who have experienced the suicide or homicide of a close friend (Range, Kovac, and Marion 2000).

5.3 Evidence That Increases in Narrative Coherence Are Responsible for Observed Benefits of Expressive Writing

Summarizing across experiments, the effect of writing is an average 23 percent improvement in physical and psychological health in people asked to write about a stressful event compared to individuals writing about the control topic (Smyth 1998). Not surprisingly, a number of theories have been advanced for these positive effects. Early theorizing about expressive writing attributed its effects to a cathartic release of thoughts and feelings associated with these experiences (e. g. Pennebaker 1989). According to this view, not disclosing thoughts and feelings about a stressful event requires inhibitory work that is reflected in autonomic and central nervous system arousal (Smyth and Pennebaker 1999). This arousal is presumably a chronic low-level stressor that takes its toll on mental and physical health. Disclosure through writing relieves the need for inhibiting thoughts and feelings and results in health benefits. However, the data from a number of experiments do not support this position. Greenberg and Stone (1992) found equal benefits from expressive writing regardless of whether individuals had disclosed their thoughts and feelings about the trauma to others. Self-reports of how inhibited a person feels after writing are also not related to benefits. There is, as well, an accumulating body of research demonstrating that catharsis without cognitive processing has little therapeutic value (Lewis and Bucher 1992).

Current explanations focus on the cognitive changes produced by expressive writing (Pennebaker 1997). In a reanalysis of six expressive writing experiments, Pennebaker and Seagal (1999) found that the most significant predictors of improved health were increases in causal words (e.g. *because, reason*) and insight words (e.g. *understand, realize*) across essays. Increases in these words reflect participants' attempts to understand the events and emotions described in their essays. Participants whose initial essays contained high frequencies of words denoting cause and insight and who do not increase those frequencies experienced no benefits from writing. Pennebaker and Seagal argue that it is the increases in causal and insight words across the three or four writing sessions that reflect writers' development of a coherent story. As noted earlier, Pennebaker uses these word categories to define narrative coherence.

There is some independent experimental support for the importance of such causal and insight words with respect to the narrative repackaging of traumatic experience. In Klein and Boals' (2001) experiments on WM capacity, writers who demonstrated the largest increases in the use of causal and insight words showed the greatest improvements on the post-experimental WM test. Recall, however, that in Alvarez-Conrad et al.'s (2001) study of rape victims, increases in these word categories were unrelated to psychopathology following treatment.

Despite the findings that increases in cause and insight words predict health and working memory benefits, there remains the question of how increases in narrative coherence could have such effects. The pathways by which writing might operate include numerous indirect effects, including better health behaviors and compliance with medical regimens. Stone, Smyth, Kaell, and Hurewitz (2000) examined six factors that could potentially mediate the effects of writing on physical health. None of the variables tested—changes in affect, social relationships, stress, substance use, medication, or sleep quality—were responsible for the effects of writing. In their WM experiment, Klein and Boals (2001) found that levels of intrusive/avoidant thoughts about stressful experiences were correlated with WM capacity and that the effects of expressive writing on WM capacity were mediated by a reduction in these thoughts. Because intrusive memories essentially reinstate emotional and cognitive aspects of the stressful experience (Baum 1990), they may have the capability to elicit changes in endocrine responses, specifically cortisol, that could affect both physical and psychological health as well as memory processes. Future research needs to investigate further the possibility that reductions in intrusive thoughts following the writing intervention prompt lowered cortisol concentrations, in turn leading to improvements in health and cognitive function.

6   Do Different Narrative Coding Schemes Produce Comparable Results?

Given the variety of schemes psychologists use to code narrative and the inconsistencies between experiments that manipulate narrative formation and therapy studies in which patients create or do not create a narrative, it might be instructive to apply these schemes to the same set of texts. I now present some exploratory data that allow us to begin these comparisons. I approached this question using three different analytical procedures. The first involved examining simple correlations between types of coding systems; the second involved comparing the results of coding systems applied to texts presumed to differ in narrative coherence; and the third involved the manipulation of instructions to compose a narrative account of a stressful event.

6.1 Relationship between Simple Word Counts, Lexical Coding Analyses, and Holistic Scoring

Using the third of the three essays from sixty-nine expressive writers in Klein and Boals' second experiment (Klein and Boals 2001), I conducted a simple word count, analyzed sentence length, and also applied Katz's (1999) holistic scoring system for narrative coherence. Two coders were trained on the Katz system. Agreement between coders was .80. Thirty-three of the essays were about positive experiences and thirty-six were about negative experiences. The results indicated statistically reliable correlations between the holistic scores and both the number of words and the number of words per sentence. The percentage of insight words was not related to either counting system or the holistic system. The percentage of causal words was not related to the number of words in the essay but was strongly associated with the number of words per sentence. What was surprising in the analysis was that there was a modest negative correlation between the percentage of insight words in the essay and the holistic narrative coherence score. In other words, higher coherence was associated with fewer insight words.

I conducted additional analyses on the essays written about the negative experiences to see if the measures of readability and grade level that Zoellner et al. (2002) and Amir et al. (1998) had applied to rape narratives would be differentially related to either the lexical coding scheme or the holistic scoring of narrative coherence. Neither measure was correlated with the percentage of cause or insight words or with the holistic score.

Boals, Klein, and Banas (2001) have further explored the counterintuitive finding that narrative coherence was inversely associated with coherence defined as the percentage of insight words. Because there was a high correlation between the percentages of causal and insight words, the categories were combined into a single measure, cognitive mechanisms. As was the case for the insight words alone, higher narrative coherence using the Katz system was associated with lower frequencies of cognitive mechanism words.

Given the number of investigators who have defined narrative coherence as the proportion of cognitive mechanism words in a narrative, Boals et al. (2001) thought it prudent to replicate their findings using texts that were clearly narrative vs. those that were not. They conducted a LIWC analysis on lyrics from thirteen popular songs that told a story about a past event (Narrative Songs) and thirteen popular songs that did not (Non-narrative Songs). Frank Sinatra's 'It Was a Very Good Year' is an example of a narrative song. The Beatles' 'All You Need Is Love' is an example of a non-narrative song. Non-narrative songs contained a larger percentage of cognitive mechanism words than narrative songs. Results also revealed that non-narrative songs contained more than twice the percentage of insight words found in narrative songs. Thus, in two different analyses, more frequent use of cause and insight words was associated with less narrative coherence.

In yet another attempt to explore the relationship between these coding schemes, Klein, Boals, and Schwartzel (2002) randomly assigned thirty-eight participants the task of writing about a negative experience; participants were asked to follow the standard expressive writing instructions or else to write about the experience using a version of the instructions that encouraged narrative formation. The latter group was asked

> to use a 'story-like' format to convey your thoughts. In doing so, your 'story' should have a clear *beginning* (which sets the stage for what is to follow), *middle* (which explains the events and your interpretation as to why they occurred), and an *ending* (which will describe the outcome of the event and will tie it all together).

Again, we applied Katz's holistic scoring system and Pennebaker and Francis's LIWC lexical coding system to count cause and insight words. Not surprisingly, the essays written under the narrative instructions received higher narrative coherence scores. Consistent with the inverse relationships noted in the nonexperimental studies described above, there was a significant negative relationship between the two measures. Finally, participants instructed to write a narrative used fewer cause and insight words compared to writers given standard expressive writing instructions.

Further evidence that a lexical coding analysis and a holistic scoring system may not produce identical results comes from a study by Suedfeld and Pennebaker (1997). They re-analyzed the essays from an earlier expressive writing study to evaluate their integrative complexity. In contrast to the LIWC analysis in which higher frequencies of cognitive mechanism words are associated with better health, participants whose essays were near average had fewer physician visits. Participants whose essays indicated high degrees of integrative complexity fared no better than did participants whose narratives were low in integrative complexity.

As noted in the introduction to this chapter, convergence between operational procedures should occur if these procedures are effectively measuring the same construct. Clearly, the procedures for measuring narrative coherence, structure, and organization do not yield similar conclusions when performed on the same set of texts. In the next section, I suggest that the lexical coding systems might better be described as measures of causal coherence, that causal coherence must be established before a narrative can be developed, and that once an adequate narrative structure is in place, auto-biographical stories no longer require causal words as markers of causal connections.

7   Causal Coherence

Fletcher, Brigs, and Linzie (1997) have argued that the perception of causal relations is essential to understanding any complex and dynamic system, be it a narrative, a physical device, or the stock market.   Identification of causal relations is particularly important for narrative (van den Broek, Rohleder, and Narváez 1996), because to understand the text the reader must make numerous inferences to establish the relations between various parts of the narrative.   These causal relations may be based on motives of the pro-tagonist, physical relations between events, relations between events that cause changes in an internal state of the character, or enabling relations be-tween two events.   Van den Broek et al. define causal coherence in terms of these causal relations.   Bower and Rinck (1997) go on to argue that narra-tive is judged coherent to the extent that these causal relations can be found. To detect a causal relation, the reader must connect inferences from immedi-ately preceding text still in working memory, information from earlier text, now located in long term memory (LTM), and background knowledge that was not in the text but that is also in long term memory.   This process takes time, with inferences about more proximal events requiring less time and more distal links longer time.   LTM searches are slow, particularly for background knowledge that has not been recently accessed, and must be continually interrupted to maintain the antecedent event in working mem-ory.   In contrast to the numerous operational definitions of narrative coher-ence, degrees of causal coherence are typically assessed by measuring read-ing times (e.g. Bower and Rinck, 1997; van den Broek 1989; van den Broek et al. 1996). Fletcher et al. (1997) showed that following a causal coherence break that required a search of LTM, the cost in reading time av-erages 12 milliseconds per word compared to the same narrative presented without the break.

7.1   Causal Coherence And Use Of Causal Words

A child as young as four years is able to infer causes, reasons, and conse-quences and can answer questions asking about characters' intentions and goals (Trabasso and Stein 1997).   There appears to be no research addressing the role that cause or insight words may play in developing this competency. However, an inspection of Stein and Albro's (1999) transcripts of stories told by 3-5 year olds reveals that in less developed stories containing only reactive sequences, the child uses 'because' to cement what to an older storyteller would be an obvious causal connection. For example: 'One day there was a big storm, that came and washed away everything that the fox owned, including the nice juicy fish he loved. The fox was so sad *because* his food was lost'. In the most developed stories that present goal-based episodes, obstacles, and endings, few, if any, causal words appear.

In terms of the difficulties of establishing causal relations, someone undergoing a severely stressful experience may be likened to a child trying to understand a series of events and how these events reflect antecedent conditions and predict consequences. When confronted with an unexpected aversive event, such as being diagnosed with a severe illness, most people's initial reaction is to try to understand how (insight) or why (cause) the event occurred. For many events, antecedent conditions will be very difficult to find. Like the small child, the older individual may resort to making causal connections explicit, through the use of cause and insight words. Initially, an increase in these words may indeed indicate an attempt to understand and explain the event. However, at some point, a true narrative develops in which the structure of the narrative itself provides all the information for making causal inferences, reducing the need to make them explicit. Development of the narrative structure thus obviates the need for explicit causal connectors, resulting in a negative relationship between the frequency of cause words and holistic judgments of narrative.

To test this prediction, Heather Hall and I asked 59 students to read four essays from an earlier expressive writing study that differed markedly in their ratings using the LIWC lexical code and the Katz holistic scoring system. The target essays represented the four combinations of high LIWC scores for cause and insight, low LIWC scores for cause and insight, and high or low narrative coherence ratings. We timed how long it took participants to read each essay. After each essay, we asked them whether or not the narrative included a setting, temporal order, action, and ending, whether the author expressed a goal, and if yes, whether the author evaluated the extent to which the goals were met. Reading times per word were faster for target essays containing more cause and insight words, suggesting that explicit causal coherence shortened readers' forays into LTM. Reading times did not vary as a function of narrative coherence. However, regardless of the LIWC scores, target essays that had received higher narrative coherence scores were rated by more participants as having a temporal order, setting, and action. The essays did not differ in the ratings of whether or not they had an ending. More participants rated essays with high LIWC scores as presenting an evaluation of whether or not the goal was met.

8   Summary And Conclusions

In this chapter, I have reviewed the evidence that creating a narrative about a stressful or traumatic event improves people's health, cognitive function, and psychological well being. I have also described the variety of operational definitions that psychologists have used to assess narrative and the extent to which these definitions produce similar findings. Finally, many psychologists believe that in addition to helping people understand stressful events, narrative changes the memory representations of these events, making them less likely to erupt into consciousness. Narrative's power to diminish intrusive memories appears to have much to do with its positive effects on health, emotion, and cognition. Collaboration between narrative theorists and psychologists interested in cognition and health in the aftermath of stressful events could prove a fruitful endeavor that would add much to our understanding of people and the stories they tell about their lives.

References

Abelson, R. P. 1981. Psychological Status of the Script Concept. *American Psychologist* 36: 715-29.

Alvarez-Conrad, J., L. A. Zoellner, and E. B. Foa. 2001. Linguistic Predictors of Trauma Pathology and Physical Health. *Applied Cognitive Psychology* 15: 159-70.

Amir, N., J. Stafford, M. S. Freshman, and E. B. Foa. 1998. Relationship Between Trauma Narratives and Trauma Pathology. *Journal of Traumatic Stress* 11: 385-92

Bamberg, M., and J. Reilly. 1996. Emotion, Narrative, and Affect: How Children Discover the Relationship Between What to Say and How to Say It. *Social Interaction, Social Context, and Language: Essays in Honor of Susan Ervin-Tripp,* eds. D. I. Slobin and J. Gerhardt, 329-41. Mahwah, NJ: Lawrence Erlbaum Associates.

Bamberg, M. 1997. A Constructivist Approach to Narrative Development. *Narrative Development: Six Approaches,* ed. M. Bamberg, 89-132. Mahwah, NJ: Lawrence Erlbaum Associates

Barclay, C. R. 1996. Autobiographical Remembering: Narrative Constraints on Objectified Selves. *Remembering our Past*, ed. D. Rubin, 94-128. Cambridge: Cambridge University Press.

Barsalou, L. W. 1988. The Content and Organization of Autobiographical Memories. *Remembering Reconsidered: Ecological and Traditional approaches To the Study of Memory*, eds. U. Neisser and E. Winograd, 193-243. New York: Cambridge University Press.

Baum, A. 1990. Stress, Intrusive Imagery and Chronic Distress. *Health Psychology* 9: 653-75.

Becker, B. 1999. Narratives of Pain in Later Life and Conventions of Storytelling. *Journal of Aging Studies* 13: 73-87.

Boals, A., K. Klein, and A. Banas. 2001. The Relationship of Expressive Writing, Narrative Type, and Health. Poster Presented at Southeastern Psychological Association Meetings, Atlanta GA.

Booth, R. J., K. J. Petrie, and J. W. Pennebaker. 1997. Changes in Circulating Lymphocyte Numbers Following Emotional Disclosure: Evidence of Buffering? *Stress Medicine* 13: 23-29.

Bower, G. H., and M. Rinck. 1997. Goals as Generations of Activation in Narrative Understanding. *Narrative Development: Six approaches.* ed. M. Bamberg, 111-34. Mahwah, N.J: L. Erlbaum Associates.

Bremner, J. D. 2001. Hypotheses and Controversies Related to Effects of Stress on the Hippocampus: An Argument for Stress-induced Damage to the Hippocampus in Patients with Posttraumatic Stress Disorder. *Hippocampus* 11: 75-81.

Brewin, C. R. 2001. A Cognitive Neuroscience Account of Posttraumatic Stress Disorder and Its Treatment. *Behaviour Research and Therapy* 39: 373-93.

Cameron, L. D., and G. Nicholls. 1998. Expression of Stressful Experiences Through Writing: Effects of a Self-regulation Manipulation for Pessimists and Optimists. *Health Psychology* 17: 84-92.

Cohler, B. J. 1982. Personal Narrative and Life Course. *Life-span Development and Behavior*, eds. P. B. Baltes and O. G. Brim, 205-41. New York: Academic Press.

Conway, M. A., and C. W. Pleydell-Pearce. 2000. The Constructon of Autobiographical Memories in the Self-memory System. *Psychological Review* 107: 261-88.

Creamer, M. 1995. A Cognitive Processing Formulation of Posttrauma Reactions. *Beyond Trauma: Cultural and Societal Dynamics,* eds. R. J. Kleber, C. R. Figley, and B. P. R. Gersons, 55-74. New York: Plenum Press.

Creamer, M., P. Burgess, and P. Pattison. 1992. Reaction to Trauma: A Cognitive Processing Model. *Journal of Abnormal Psychology* 101: 452-59

Davidson, K., A. R. Schwartz, D. Sheffield, R. S. McCord, S. J. Lepore, and W. Gerin. 2002. Expressive Writing and Blood Pressure. *The Writing Cure:*

How Expressive Writing Promotes Health and Emotional Well-being, eds. S. Lepore and J. Smyth, 17-30. American Psychological Association: Washington, D.C.

Engle, R., M. J. Kane, and S. W. Tuholski. 1999. Individual Differences in Working Memory Capacity and What They Tell Us about Controlled Attention, General Fluid Intelligence and Functions of the Prefrontal Cortex. *Models of Working Memory: Mechanisms of Active Maintenance and Executive Control,* eds. A. Miyake and P. Shah, 102-31. Cambridge, UK: Cambridge University Press.

Engle, R. W., S. W.Tuholski, J. E. Laughlin, and R. A. Conway. 1999. Working Memory, Short-term Memory, and General Fluid Intelligence: A Latent-Variable Approach. *Journal of Experimental Psychology: General* 128: 309-31.

First, M. B., R. L. Spitzer, M.. Gibbon, and J. B. Williams. 1995. *Sturctured Clinical Interview for DSM-IV Axis I Disorders-Patient Edition SCID-I/P, Version 2.* New York: Biometrics Research Department, New York State Psychiatric Institute.

Fivush, R. 1998. Children's Recollections of Traumatic and Non-traumatic Events. *Development and Psychopathology.* 10: 699-716.

Flesch, R. 1949. *The Art of Readable Writing.* New York: Harper and Brothers.

Fletcher, C. R., A. Briggs, and B. Linzie. 1997. Understanding the Causal Structure of Narrative Events. *Developmental Spans in Event Comprehension and Representation: Bridging Fictional and Actual Events,* eds P. W. van den Broek, P. J. Bauer, and T. Bourg, 343-60. Mahwah, NJ : Lawrence Erlbaum Associates.

Foa, E. B. and M. J. Kozak. 1986. Emotional Processing of Fear: Exposure to Corrective Information. *Psychological Bulletin* 99: 20-35.

Foa, E. B., G. Steketee, and B. O. Rothbaum. 1989. Behavioral/Cognitive Conceptualizations of Post-traumatic Stress Disorder. *Behavior Therapy* 20: 155-76.

Foa, E. B., D. S. Riggs, C. V. Dancu, and B. O. Rothbaum. 1993. Reliability and Validity of a Brief Instrument for Assessing Posttraumatic Disorder. *Journal of Traumatic Stress* 6: 459-73.

Foa, E. B., and D. S. Riggs. 1994. Posttraumatic Stress Disorder and Rape. *Posttraumatic Stress Disorder: A Clinical Review,* ed. R. S. Pynoos, 133-63. Baltimore, MD: The Sidran Press.

Foa, E. B., C. Molnar, and L. Cashman. 1995. Change in Rape Narratives During Exposure Therapy for Posttraumatic Stress Disorder. *Journal of Traumatic Stress* 8: 675-90.

Fonareva, I. G. 2002. The Effects of Two Stress-Reducing Techniques, Expressive Writing and Yogic Breathing, on Different Aspects of Functioning. Unpublished Honors Thesis, North Carolina State University.

Gidron, Y., T. Peri, J. F. Connolly, and A. Y. Shalev. 1996. Written Disclosure in Posttraumatic Stress Disorder: Is It Beneficial for the Patient? *Journal of Nervous and Mental Disease* 184: 505-7.

Gidron, Y., E. Duncan, A. Lazar, A. Biderman, H. Tandeter, and P. Shvartzman. 2002. Effects of Guided Written Disclosure of Stressful Experiences on Clinic Visits and Symptoms in Frequent Clinic Attenders. *Family Practice* 19: 161-66.

Greenberg, M. A. 1995. Cognitive Processing of Traumas: The Role of Intrusive Thoughts and Reappraisals. *Journal of Applied Social Psychology* 25: 1262-96

Greenberg, M. A., and A. A. Stone. 1992. Emotional Disclosure about Traumas and Its Relation to Health: Effects of Previous Disclosure and Trauma Severity. *Journal of Personality and Social Psychology* 63: 75-84.

Harber, K. D., and J. W. Pennebaker. 1992. Overcoming Traumatic Memories. *The Handbook of Emotion and Memory*, ed. S. A. Christianson, 359-85. Hillsdale, NJ: Lawrence Erlbaum Associates.

Harvey, J. H., T. L. Orbuch, K. D. Chwalisz, and G. Garwood. 1991. Coping with Sexual Assault: The Roles of Account-Making and Confiding. *Journal of Traumatic Stress* 4: 515-31

Hermans, H. J. M. 1999. Self-narrative in the Life Course: A Contextual Approach. *Narrative Comprehension, Causality and Coherence: Essays in Honor of Tom Trabasso*, eds. S. R. Goldman, A. C. Graesser, P. van den Broek, 223-64. Mahwah, NJ: Lawrence Erlbaum Associates.

Horowitz, M. J. 1975. Intrusive and Repetitive Thoughts after Experimental Stress: A Summary. *Archives of General Psychiatry* 32: 1457-63.

Horowitz, M. J., N. Wilner, and W. Alvarez. 1979. Impact of Event Scale: A Measure of Subjective Stress. *Psychosomatic Medicine* 41: 209-18.

Janoff-Bulman, R. 1992. *Shattered Assumptions*. NY: The Free Press.

Katz, S. 1999. Holistic Scoring for Coherence. Unpublished manuscript. North Carolina State University.

Kelley, J. E., M. A. Lumley and J. C. Leisen. 1997. Health Effects of Emotional Disclosure in Rheumatoid Arthritis Patients. *Health Psychology* 16: 331-40.

King, L. A., and K. N. Miner. 2000. Writing About the Perceived Benefits of Traumatic Events: Implications for Physical Health. *Personality and Social Psychological Bulletin* 26: 220-30.

Klein, K., and A. Boals. 2001. Expressive Writing Can Increase Working Memory Capacity. *Journal of Experimental Psychology: General* 130: 520-33.

Klein, K. 2002. Stress, Expressive Writing and Working Memory. *The Writing Cure: How Expressive Writing Promotes Health and Emotional Well-being*, ed. S. Lepore and J. Smyth, 135-56. Washington, D. C.: American Psychological Association.

Klein, K., A. Boals, and N. K. Schwartzel. 2002. Effects of Expressive Writing Instructions on the Use of Cognitive and Emotional Words. Manuscript in Preparation.

Kovac, S. H., and L. M. Range. 2000. Writing Projects: Lessening Undergraduates' Unique Suicidal Bereavement. *Suicide and Life-Threatening Behavior* 30: 50-60.

Lepore, S. J. 1997. Expressive Writing Moderates the Relation Between Intrusive Thoughts and Depressive Symptoms. *Journal of Personality and Social Psychology* 73: 1030-37.

Lepore, S. J., and M. A. Greenberg. 2002. Mending Broken Hearts: Effects of Expressive Writing on Mood, Cognitive Processing, Social Adjustment and Health Following a Relationship Breakup. *Psychology and Health* 17: 547-60

Lewis, W. A., and A. M. Bucher. 1992. Anger, Catharsis, the Reformulated Frustration-Aggression Hypothesis and Health Consequences. *Psychotherapy* 29: 385-92.

Lutgendorf, S. K., M. H. Antoni, M. Kumar, and N. Schneiderman. 1994. Changes in Cognitive Coping Strategies Predict EBV-antibody Titre Change Following a Stressor Disclosure Induction. *Journal of Psychosomatic Research* 38: 63-78.

Meichenbaum, D., and D. Fitzpatrick. 1993. A Constructivist Narrative Perspective on Stress and Coping: Stress Inoculation Applications. *Handbook of Stress: Theoretical and Clinical Aspects,* eds. L. Goldberger and S. Breznitz, 706-23. New York: The Free Press.

Miller, P. J. 1995. Personal Storytelling in Everyday Life: Social and Cultural Perspectives. *Advances in Social Cognition* 7: 177-84. Hillsdale, NJ: Lawrence Erlbaum Associates.

Olson, D. R., and D. J. Salter. 1993. Commentary. *Human Development* 36: 343-45.

Pennebaker, J. W., and S. K. Beall. 1986. Confronting a Traumatic Event: Toward an Understanding of Inhibition and Disease. *Journal of Abnormal Psychology* 95: 274-81.

Pennebaker, J. W., J. Kiecolt-Glaser, and R. Glaser. 1988. Disclosure of Traumas and Immune Function: Health Implications for Psychotherapy. *Journal of Consulting and Clinical Psychology* 56: 239-45.

Pennebaker, J. W. 1989. Confession, Inhibition, and Disease. *Advances in Experimental Social Psychology*, vol. 22, ed. L. Berkowitz, 211-44. San Diego, CA: Academic Press.

Pennebaker, J. W., M. Colder, and L. K. Sharp. 1990. Accelerating the Coping Process. *Journal of Personality and Social Psychology* 58: 528-37.

Pennebaker, J. W., and M. E. Francis. 1996. Cognitive, Emotional and Language Processes in Disclosure. *Cognition and Emotion* 10: 601-26.

Pennebaker, J. W., and M. E. Francis. 1999. *Linguistic Inquiry and Word Count: LIWC.* [Software Program for Text Analysis]. Hillsdale NJ: Lawrence Erlbaum Associates.

Pennebaker, J. W. 1997. Writing about Emotional Experiences as a Therapeutic Process. *Psychological Science* 8: 162-66.

Pennebaker, J. W., and J. D. Seagal. 1999. Forming a Story: The Health Benefits of Narrative. *Journal of Clinical Psychology* 55: 1243-54.

Petrie, K. J., R. Booth, J. W. Pennebaker, K. P. Davison, and M. Thomas. 1995. Disclosure of Trauma and Immune Response To Hepatitis B Vaccination Program. *Journal of Consulting and Clinical Psychology* 63: 787-92.

Pratt, M. W., C. Boyes, S. Robins and J. Manchester. 1989. Telling Tales: Aging, Working Memory, and the Narrative Cohesion of Story Retellings. *Developmental Psychology* 25.4: 628-35.

Range, L. M., S. H. Kovac, and M. S. Marion. 2000. Does Writing about Bereavement Lessen Grief Following Sudden, Unintentional Death? *Death Studies* 24: 115-34.

Reynolds, M., & C. R. Brewin. 1998. Intrusive Cognitions, Coping Strategies and Emotional Responses in Depression, Post-traumatic Stress Disorder and a Non-clinical Population. *Behaviour Research and Therapy* 36.2: 135-47.

Richards, J. M., W. E. Beal, J. D. Seagal, and J. W. Pennebaker. 2000. Effects of Disclosure of Traumatic Events on Illness Behavior Among Psychiatric Prison Inmates. *Journal of Abnormal Psychology* 109.1: 156-60.

Schank, R. C., and R. P. Abelson. 1995. Knowledge and Memory: The Real Story. *Advances in Social Cognition* 8: 1-85.

Segal, D. L., and E. J. Murray. 1994. Emotional Processing in Cognitive Therapy and Vocal Expression of Feeling. *Journal of Social and Clinical Psychology* 13: 189-206.

Segal, D. L., J. A. Bogaards, L. A. Becker, and C. Chatman. 1999. Effects of Emotional Expression on Adjustment to Spousal Loss Among Older Adults. *Journal of Mental Health and Aging* 5.4: 297-310.

Smyth, J. M. 1998. Written Emotional Expression: Effect Sizes, Outcome Types and Moderating Variables. *Journal of Consulting and Clinical Psychology* 66: 174-84.

Smyth, J., and J. W. Pennebaker. 1999. Sharing One's Story: Translating Emotional Experiences into Words as a Coping Tool. *Coping: The Psychology of What Works*, ed. C.R. Snyder, 70-89. New York: Oxford University Press.

Smyth, J. M., A. A. Stone, A. Hurewitz, and A. Kaell. 1999. Effects of Writing About Stressful Experiences on Symptom Reduction in Patients with Asthma or Rheumatoid arthritis. *Journal of the American Medical Association* 281: 1209-1304.

Spera, S. P., E. D. Buhrfeind, and J. W. Pennebaker. 1994. Expressive Writing and Coping with Job Loss. *Academy of Management Journal* 37: 722-33.

Stein, N. L. 1988. The Development of Storytelling Skill. *Child Language: A Book of Readings*, eds. M. B. Franklin and S. S. Barten, 282-97. New York: Cambridge University Press.

Stein, N. L., and E. R. Albro. 1999. Building Complexity and Coherence: Children's Use of Goal-structured Knowledge in Telling Stories. *Narrative Comprehension, Causality and Coherence: Essays in Honor of Tom Trabasso*, eds. S. R. Goldman, A. C. Graesser, and P. van den Broek, 5-44. Mahwah, NJ: Lawrence Erlbaum Associates.

Stein, N. L., M. D. Liwag, and E. Wade. 1996. A Goal-based Approach to Memory for Emotional Events: Implications for Theories of Understanding and Socialization. *Emotion: Interdisciplinary Perspectives,* eds. R. D. Kavanaugh and B. Zimmerberg, 91-118. Mahwah, NJ: Lawrence Erlbaum Associates.

Stein, N. L., and M. D. Liwag. 1997. Children's Understanding, Evaluation and Memory for Emotional Events. *Developmental Spans in Event Comprehension and Representation: Bridging Fictional and Actual Events,* eds. P. W. van den Broek, P. J. Bauer, and T. Bourg, 199-235. Mahwah NJ: Lawrence Erlbaum.

Stone, A. A., J. M. Smyth, A. Kaell, and A. Hurewitz. 2000. Structured Writing about Stressful Events: Exploring Potential Psychological Mediators of Positive Health Effects. *Health Psychology* 19: 619-24.

Stroebe, M., W. Stroebe, H. Schut, E. Zech, and J. van den Bout. 2002. Does Disclosure of Emotions Facilitate Recovery from Bereavement? Evidence from Two Prospective Studies. *Journal of Consulting and Clinical Psychology* 70: 169-78.

Suedfeld, P., and J. W. Pennebaker. 1997. Health Outcomes and Cognitive Aspects of Recalled Negative Life Events. *Psychosomatic Medicine* 59: 172-77.

Tait, R., and R. C. Silver. 1989. Coming to Terms with Major Negative Life Events. *Unintended Thought,* eds. J. S. Uleman and J. A. Bargh, 351-82. NY: Guilford Press.

Trabasso, T., and N. L. Stein. 1997. Narrating, Representing and Remembering Event Sequences. *Developmental Spans in Event Comprehension and Representation: Bridging Fictional and Actual Events,* eds. P. W. van den Broek, P. J. Bauer, and T. Bourg, 237-269. Mahwah, NJ: Lawrence Erlbaum Associates.

Van den Broek, P. 1989. Causal Reasoning and Inference Making in Judging the Importance of Story Statements. *Child Development* 60: 286-97.

Van den Broek, P., L. Rohleder, and D. Narváez. 1996. Causal Inference in the Comprehension of Literary Texts. *Empirical Approaches to Literature and Aesthetics*, eds. R. Kreuz and M. S. MacNealy, 179-200. Norwood, NJ: Ablex Publishing.

Van der Kolk, B. A., and R. Fisler. 1995. Dissociation and the Fragmentary Nature of Traumatic Memories: Review and Experimental Confirmation. *Journal of Traumatic Stress* 8: 505-25.

Van Minnen, A., I. Wessel, T. Dijkstra, and K. Roelofs. 2002. Changes in PTSD Patients' Narratives During Prolonged Exposure Therapy: A Replication and Extension. *Journal of Traumatic Stress* 15: 255-58.

Wegner, D. M., and L. Smart. 1997. Deep Cognitive Activation: A New Approach to the Unconscious. *Journal of Consulting and Clinical Psychology* 65: 984-95.

Wong, P. T. P., and L. M. Watt. 1991. What Types of Reminiscence Are Associated with Successful Aging? *Psychology and Aging* 6: 272-79.

Yehuda, R. B., K. Kahana, S. M. Binder-Byrnes, J. W Woutwcik, and E. L. Giller. 1995. Low Urinary Cortisol Excretion in Holocaust Survivors with Posttraumatic Stress Disorder. *American Journal of Psychiatry* 152: 982-86.

Zoellner, L. A., J. Alvarez-Conrad, and E. B. Foa. 2002. Peritraumatic Dissociative Experiences, Trauma Narratives and Trauma Pathology. *Journal of Traumatic Stress* 15: 49-57.

4

Semantics and Narrative in Therapeutic Discourse

WILLIAM FRAWLEY, JOHN T. MURRAY, AND RAOUL N. SMITH

1 Introduction

What do you get when you cross a scientific theory with experimental theater? '*Insignificance*', you might be tempted to say, referencing Terry Johnson's quirky and riveting play about a meeting of Marilyn Monroe, Albert
Einstein, Joe DiMaggio, and Joe McCarthy. We think we have a more recognizable, but probably no less surprising, answer: *therapy*.

Clients in therapeutic discourse develop empirical accounts of their
pasts that allow them to gather data and make testable predictions about
their futures; they perform these activities in a language that coheres with
the other sense-making stories they tell. Therapy thus sounds awfully like
scientific theory-building. Indeed, one might argue that therapy is, in essence, personal theory-construction. But the conditions of therapy require
that these sense-making stories be developed in a multivalent framework. In
therapy, as in experimental theater, discourse-specific events ('plot'), their
expression in text, and their management in a narrative line are not carried
out by any particular individual. Rather, they emerge in and by the interaction of the therapeutic moment. In this respect, therapy is very much like
performance art, where characters shift from role to metarole and back to
role throughout an enactment. What does it look like when science and
theater come together?

Narrative Theory and The Cognitive Sciences.
David Herman (ed.).
Copyright © 2003, CSLI Publications.

2 Toward a Semantic Analysis

The discourse parameters of conversational therapy have long been known—retellings, shifts in narrativity, truth-by-construction rather than depiction, stretching of pragmatic principles (e.g., via deliberate role playing), and so on (see Schafer 1976, 1980, 1992; Spence 1982, 1994). These properties make therapeutic conversation different from typical doctor-patient discourse, even though it would seem to be a subset thereof. For example, no matter how interactive it appears, doctor-patient conversation retains asymmetric power relations, with the physician ultimately giving advice that the patient accepts or rejects. Physicians may be storytellers—'chronicler(s) of bodily events' (Epstein 1995: 25)—but the stories they tell often yield to facts, as do the therapies they provide. It is difficult to see, e.g., cancer and its treatment constructed out of language.

Psychotherapy is arguably quite different. Interventions are co-constructed, and the therapy itself is made out of speech. Neimeyer's (2001: 266) observation in this respect is instructive: 'all of these [interventions] entail helping clients more adequately symbolize their experience as a precondition to its reflexive examination.' This does not reduce the therapeutic experience to the *therapy-is-conversation* solecism. Instead, therapeutic knowledge is constituted by insight in the moment of speaking, rather than uncovered in factual discovery. It is an insight through surprise. In the moment of uttering, it pulls the client out of the past. Borrowing Lee's (2000) observations about subjectivity in general, we might say that performativity—on-line sense-making and semiotic action—plays a significant role in therapy.

While science itself is likewise thought of as yielding to fact, the performativity of conversational therapy looks remarkably analogous to what constructivist views of science find to be constitutive of scientific inquiry and activity (Ceccarelli 2001). In such views, accounts of the patterns in the natural world function less as referential descriptions than semantic constructions that *determine* referential domains (i.e., the intensions determine the extensions).

How do we understand and analyze this performativity of therapy as personal science? A natural approach would be to use the tools of pragmatics and discourse, which have a long tradition in the analysis of therapeutic conversations (Litowitz and Epstein 1991). We propose instead to look more at the structural factors in such discourse, following the lead of such researchers as Litowitz (1991) for therapeutic discourse and Lee (2000) for narrative in general. This approach allows us to make the link between content and its deployment in performance. We can develop a kind of grounded pragmatics that explores the locutionary underpinnings of the illocutions and performatives that constitute the therapeutic speech act.

We also know that such a semantic analysis can contribute much to uncovering facts about theories. In many ways, a scientific theory is a semantic construct. Lexical choice and propositional structure are instrumental to scientific investigation and serve as a framework to drive inquiry of the natural world (Frawley 1988). No less holds for personal theory-construction, where the semantic inquiries—e.g., 'What do you mean by *depression*?'—are reliable barometers of the flow and progress of the therapy (Berg and de Shazer 1993).

Semantic analysis of therapeutic discourse allows us to reach back to three important features of therapeutic narrative: co-construction, plausibility, and reflexivity. We will see how semantic analysis of the discourse in therapeutic conversations helps unpack the ways these three contribute to the narrative of personal theory.

2.1 Three Features of Therapeutic Narrative

2.1.1 Co-construction

Consider the following excerpt from a therapy session of a woman talking about her powerlessness and inability to take control in a situation where her mother was dying (Neimeyer 2001: 274-5)[1]:

> ˢUm, the positive side I guess of all this has been that what I've been able to take with me with this experience is a 'Damn the consequences I'm gonna do what's right!' kind of attitude. ˢWhich is in contrast to... ˢWell *before*. I was in tremendous fear of authority... ˢI guess that if you've done battle with death, then the rest does kind of pale by comparison.

This discourse flows smoothly and seems to be the speech of a single person, the client. In fact, the excerpt involves *four speaker shifts*, each marked by a superscript ˢ. Such changes in narrative voicing are typical of therapeutic discourse, where the narrative as a whole emerges out of a blending of the rhetorical participants. As Schafer (1992: xv) observes: 'Psychoanalysis is conducted as a dialogue...In this dialogue, actions and happenings...are continuously being told by the analysand and sooner or later retold interpretively by both analyst and analysand. A life is re-authored as it is co-authored.'

---

[1] The article by Neimeyer (2001) includes the verbatim transcript of a therapy session conducted in front of a group of professional therapists in a theater setting. Its purpose was to demonstrate Neimeyer's approach to grief therapy.

The narrative reconfigurations that constitute therapy blur the line between the voice of the narrators and the voice of the focal participants. Indeed, in the excerpt above, who is telling the story, and who is the affected main character within? Who is *I*? Similarly, the turn-taking in the exchange is not one of structural systematics, with neat blocks assigned to contributors, but one more like what Bakhtin (1990) observed, where a turn is a place in speech where someone else has begun to talk, even if that speech involves saying nothing.

An obvious question that arises here is: if there is only one *I*, how does transference occur? Transference, in traditional Freudian psychotherapy, is, in a way, a form of cumulative projection. Over a long period of time the client projects an 'other' onto the psychoanalyst. The analyst then is *not* a co-constructor of the narrative. The narrative in that situation is closer to a monologue.

A more contemporary characterization of the therapist, as exemplified in Neimeyer, is that of someone whose role is to help the different foci of client and therapist converge on a co-construction. In our view traditional Freudian transference is actually diminished through co-authorization. And that is a good thing because of the long time span normally required for transference to occur. Gestalt therapy, on the other hand, relies on the currency of the therapeutic moment. In Gestalt therapy the client's so-called parataxic distortion (Sullivan 1954) is challenged in the session and the consequent awareness allows for healing to occur during the construction of the narrative in that moment.

All this makes the ecology of therapeutic narrative quite complex. It is difficult to chart voicing shifts, except by deictic markers, but even these are not so clear in the excerpt, which, in the last sentence, lacks an explicit marking of deictic shift even though the *I* has changed. But a semantic analysis of the narrative can help us follow the coherence of these exchanges and voicing shifts. As we will show, a significant framing parameter in the excerpt above is the tension between sources and results. How the source-result semantic relationships of lexical choices are played out in the exchange is a guide to the speech ecosystem.

2.1.2 Plausibility

The ultimate purpose of therapeutic conversation is not solely the referential depiction of past events nor the development of hypothetical solutions, but something between – something like functional plausibility. The self-narratives told and retold are designed to create the semblance of truth to gain insight. Schafer (1992: xiv) observes: 'narrative is not an alternative to truth or reality; rather, it is a mode in which, inevitably, truth and reality are presented. We have only versions of the true and the real...Each retelling amounts to an account of the prior telling.'

What, then, is a successful therapy session? And how can progress be understood and analyzed? As we all know, progress is not perfection. But progress is what therapy is all about. It is a matter of growing, which never ceases if the client is serious about changing. The *sine qua non* of successful therapy is when the client becomes aware of a misperceived reality. Before clients can truly work on their problems, they have to become aware of the root, historical causes of the problems, and with additional–usually linguistic—help from the therapist, they can learn tools to cope with the problem.[2] The 'Ah, hah!' effects that therapists seek to promote signal that clients have become aware of the cause of their affective reactions to troubling, contemporary events.[3] Schafer (1992: xv) addresses this issue by saying that the goal of narrative construction in therapy is 'progress toward insight. Insight itself refers to those retellings that make a beneficial difference in a person's construction and reconstruction of experience and adaptively active conduct of life.'

But if therapeutic narratives are continually retold, and if 'closure is always provisional to allow for further retellings' (Schafer 1992: xv), how do we chart the search for plausibility over truth? We need a mechanism to show how semantic structures can respond dynamically to the performative construction of meaning and model working semantic theories of critical lexical-conceptual choices as the therapeutic conversation unfolds. For example, we will show below how the choice of scalar questions in therapy–'On a scale of 1 to 10, how would you rate your happiness?'—may promote systematic misunderstandings that need to be resolved during the course of therapy. Resolution of these lexical misunderstandings can guide therapeutic conversations toward success and plausibility.

---

[2] Because reaction to an earlier traumatic event can continue throughout one's life, we refer to the client as *coping*. The client can learn tools to apply to ameliorate the continuing, long-term adverse effects necessitated by their experiences with a person, place, or situation. We agree with Neimeyer (2001: 267): 'The reconstruction of identity ... requires a *recursive* [emphasis ours] tacking between the self and social, between sensed and perhaps incompletely symbolized shifts in the client's self-narrative, and the responses of relevant others to these emerging features.'

[3] Other ways by which a client can signal that he or she has become aware can be textual, as in locutions such as 'I never thought of it that way' or 'I never said it that way before.' Awareness can also be felt and not uttered as a corrective emotional/affective experience. Or it can appear in a facial expression.

2.1.3 Reflexivity

All discourse 'has at least two dimensions. It is oriented toward its referential objects and toward another's discourse, toward someone else's speech' (Lee 2000: 281). Therapeutic discourse is no different in having both a non-reflexive, linguistic-referential function (expressing facts) and a reflexive, metalinguistic function (expressing the speech of others). Indeed, with respect to the latter, the co-construction of narrative in therapy partly achieves its purposes by the participants deliberately appropriating others' accounts as their own, for example in active role-playing and, as will be shown later, a therapist adopting a client's metaphors as an indication of subconscious focus. Hence this narrative is a potential goldmine for those interested in represented speech and thought.

But therapeutic narrative has further reflexivity that bears on our concerns here. The goal of the narrative in therapy *is the narrative*. That is, the purpose of co-constructing the narrative is to make the narrative–unlike, say, ordinary conversation, technical discourse, or even literary narrative. In therapy, the narrative is the reason for the narrative, and so therapy is intrinsically meta-narratological. Similarly, when one examines the content of therapeutic narrative, it is clear that the purpose of the content is to examine the content itself. As Berg and de Shazer (1993) note, therapeutic progress comes from the therapist and client co-exploring the semantics of critical terms. The goal of the semantics is semantic, and, thus, therapeutic narrative is intrinsically metasemantic.

The reflexivity of therapeutic narrative opens the discourse up to semantic analysis because the narrative is stocked with markers. In many ways, therapeutic narrative is easier to analyze than other kinds of discourse precisely because its world is so self-contained: facts can be very troublesome (see Spence 1994: 85-7)! Lexical choice, tenses, and deixis, however, can be very revealing of the way the therapeutic narrative is self-organizing. For example, many therapy sessions involve metaphor as a descriptive device and as an organizing principle (again, see Spence 1994: 77ff.). We will show, below, how metaphorical choices are framing devices and allow the participants in therapy different narrative positions in the co-construction of the discourse.

Therapeutic narrative is unique in that purpose and structure are uniquely connected. Therapy is designed for the co-construction of passing theories, personal theories, working alliances. The semantic strategies of the participants, we hope to show, reveal how they are seeking to re-narrate their past lives in order to narrate their futures.

3 Three Analyses

3.1 Semantic Networks

One way to uncover the semantic-conceptual information driving therapeutic exchanges is via the theory of lexical relations and semantic networks, which provides a nice model of the knowledge structures underlying statements in the narratives (Evens 1988; Saint-Dizier and Viegas 1995). In this theory, the meaning of a lexical item is a function of its embeddedness in a relational network (see Figure 1). Lexical items (words or fixed phrases) are nodes in a network, linked to each other by a finite, if large, set of abstract relations. The link is represented by an arc, which can be uni-directional (in either way) or bi-directional, depending on the relation represented.

Relation

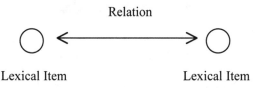

Lexical Item   Lexical Item

Figure 1. Nodes and Arcs in the Lexical Network

Because relations can be seen as conditions on the transition between two lexical items in a network, the node-arc representation has an equivalent linear form, shown in Figure 2:

Lexical ItemRELATIONLexical Item.

**Figure 2. A Linear Representation
of Relations in the Lexical Network**

One important relation is SYNONYMY (or lexical equivalence), represented formally by SYN: this is a bi-directional relation because all equivalence is reversible, by definition. SYN functions prominently in the narrative in Neimeyer's (2001) paper, where the client, Susan, and the therapist co-construct an equation of powerlessness and meaninglessness (271, ellipses ours):

> C5: Uh, It was reminiscent of the feeling of powerlessness, almost ludicracy…

T6:...as if there was no purpose for this in a way, that it was a...

C7: But still driven to do it, and still working very hard at it, and, um, I guess those types of feelings came flooding back ... A 'What's it all about, Alfie?' sort of thing, you know.

T8: At one level, it seems kind of meaningless...

Figure 3 represents the underlying semantic structure of the previous excerpt:

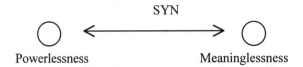

SYN

Powerlessness   Meaninglessness

(PowerlessnessSYNMeaninglessness)

Figure 3. The Semantic Structure of a Narrative Equating Powerlessness with Meaninglessness

We can use this formal apparatus of lexical networks to investigate further the therapeutic session in Neimeyer (2001), where he explores Susan's grief over the loss of her mother to cancer and her inability to take control over the situation. Part of what drives this narrative is the idea of powerlessness, and the therapy itself is very much an exploration of the local semantic neighborhood of this concept. But clear differences surface in the narrative between Susan and the therapist with regard to end-states and preconditions. Susan is focused on the end-states of powerlessness. Table 1 characterizes the notational system that we use to represent the *end-state* relations surrounding powerlessness and related concepts:

RESULT (RES) caused outcome of an of item ('fire makes heat': heatRESfire)

GOAL (GOAL): spatial or logical endpoint of item ('Sue went to the store': wentGOALstore)

PATIENT (PAT): changed recipient of item ('The window broke':

breakPATwindow)

EXPERIENCER: psychological undergoer of item ('Bob felt sad': feel-EXPBob)

PURPOSE (PURP): evidential consequence of an item ('I went to the doctor for a checkup': goPURPcheckup)

Table 1. A Notational System for End-state Relations

Note the following remarks, with our comments interspersed, and their conversion to lexical relational form (from Neimeyer 2001: 271ff.; T = therapist and C = client (Susan)):

T6:...as if there was no purpose for this in a way, that it was a...

C7: But still driven to do it, and still working very hard at it, and, um, I guess those types of feelings came flooding back...

Comment: Susan responds to the therapist observing that her situation lacks purpose (a negative end-state) by noting that her actions and feelings drive her, not that she controls them. The situation reveals no purpose for Susan:

Situation~PURPSusan
SusanPATfeelings

T8: What was pushing you in the direction of this kind of activity?

C9: ...The refusal to accept being powerless... in this situation. I guess that's what was the drive...[quoting herself in hypothetical discourse] C10: 'Even if it beats me, I'm going to do my best...'

Comment: Susan again focuses on her actions as results; even her own proactive effort is an experienced need.

SusanPATpowerlessness

T11: ...did you feel like your best was enough?...

C11: No... no. I um, that was very disappointing...[quoting herself in hypothetical discourse] 'Doesn't matter what you do, when it's gonna happen, it's gonna happen...'

Comment: Susan reaffirms that even her self-generated actions are the result of things out of her control.

SusanPATactions

Susan, in her focus on the consequences of powerlessness, uses the narrative to fill out the result-structure of these lexical items and related forms. Her hard work has no consequences, except for powerlessness: 'C5:...16 full... hours a day working very hard. And still at the back of our minds...to what end?' (Neimeyer 2001: 271): workRESpowerlessness. Powerlessness and these events drive her and overcome her: C12: 'It was terminal from the initial diagnosis' (273): SusanPATpowerlessness. Even her best efforts are experienced as results, not deliberate actions: C11: 'that was very disappointing': disappointEXPSusan. Likewise, her positive actions with respect to her mother—that she can still act against all odds—are a consequence of her being like her mother: C14: 'Well, that's the way she raised me!': SusanRESraise. When the therapist suggests that she acted in a new way toward her mother, of her own volition, Susan corrects and says: C16: 'But I knew it was always something she expected of me...' (274): SusanGOALexpect. Even her final assessment of her mother, after coming to terms with her death, is one of results: C48: 'she was a very demanding woman' (282): SusanEXPdemand.

These observations provide the following relational structure:

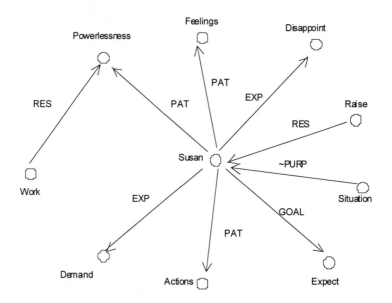

Figure 4. Susan's Result-oriented Semantic Network

In contrast to this semantic strategy of results, the therapist focuses on the preconditions of powerlessness and related concepts. The local semantic neighborhood for *preconditions* can be captured by the notational system given in Table 2:

PROVENANCE (PROV): material origin of item ('milk comes from cows': cowPROVmilk)

SOURCE (SOURCE): spatial origin of item ('Bill arrived from New York': arriveSOURCENewYork)

AGENT (AGT): deliberate doer of act ('beavers build dams': beaver-AGTbuild)

EFFECTOR (EFF): non-volitional instigator of act ('the rock broke the window': RockEFFbreak)

REASON (REAS): evidential source of item ('I ran from fear': fear-REASrun)

Table 2. A Notational System for the Semantics of Preconditions

With these relations in mind, note the following source-focused exchanges in the therapy session (Neimeyer 2001: 273ff.):

T12: That from the outset it was almost preordained...

C12: No, it had already metasta... I can never pronounce that right... It was terminal from the initial diagnosis.

Comment: The therapist tries to locate the reasons in the cause, but Susan rejects that and indicates that the situation was always a result.
ActionREASpreordained

C25: ... So I'd always taken a backseat to her stardom, you know,

T26: So somehow the limelight shifted... but you were more the leading character...

C26: ... I wouldn't say that I was the leading character...

Comment: Susan indicates that her role in the family has always been in the background, and the therapist tries to shift her perception of her role as the instigator of action. Susan rejects this and reaffirms her secondary role.
SusanEFFaction

C20: ...Um, the positive side I guess, of all this has been that what I've been able to take with me with this experience is a 'Damn the consequences I'm gonna do what's right!' ... kind of attitude.

T21: Which is in contrast to...

C21: Well *before*, I was in tremendous fear of authority... Now there doesn't seem to be any *reason* for that fear!

Comment: Susan regards even the positives of her condition as consequences. The therapist tries to refocus her attention to sources.
SusanSOURCEaction

The therapist suggests, early on, that Susan act on her desires and overcome the feeling of powerlessness: T10: '[quoting her hypothetical discourse] "I'm going to *do something*..."' (272): SusanAGTdo. In trying to reassert the agency and source vocabulary that Susan denies, the therapist remarks on the 'new Susan': T16: 'So something *new* came out in you' (274): SusanPROVnew. Susan denies this again, and asserts that it was not new but expected, which the therapist then counters with additional source-talk: T17: 'and then at the end you were able to, to give this to her' (274): SusanAGTgive. While Susan sees the positives as consequences (C20: 'Damn the consequences'), the therapist restates this as more source-talk: T23: 'Damn the torpedoes... I'm going to do what needs to be done...' (275): SusanAGTdo. Focusing again on the preconditions of Susan's actions, the therapist asks her to reconsider her role in the family, as a leading, rather than secondary, performer: T26: 'but you were more the leading character in the drama' (276): SusanEFFdrama. As with the structure for results, we can sketch out this local source-neighborhood:

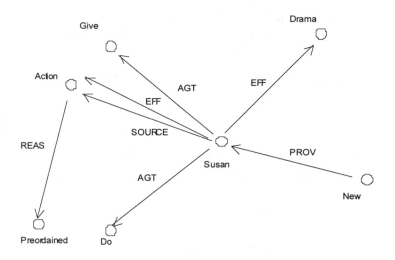

Figure 5. A Source-oriented Semantic Network

A much more detailed analysis of the lexical-semantic structure would reveal further details and focus, but our larger point is illustrated well enough. Semantic networks provide a way of capturing the knowledge structures underlying the narrative. What about the narratives themselves? How do semantic networks elucidate the three unique features of therapeutic discourse?

First, let us consider the co-construction of the narrative, the semantic ecology, as it were. Much of the therapy session revolves around the tension between—and failure to integrate—the source-focus of the therapist and the result-focus of Susan. As noted above, the therapist tries to locate the reasons for Susan's situation in pre-existing *causes*, but Susan converts these causes to consequences:

> T12: That from the outset it was almost preordained...
>
> C12: No, it had already metasta... I can never pronounce that right... It was terminal from the initial diagnosis.

The therapist locates a positive aspect of Susan as emanating from her, but Susan denies this and converts it to something she undergoes:

> T16: So something *new* came out in you...
>
> C16: But I knew it was something she always *expected* of me...

When Susan does indicate some agency of her actions—'I'm gonna do what's right!'—the therapist notes the shift to sources, and Susan finally picks up on this shift:

> T21: Which is in contrast to...
>
> C21: Well, *before*...

But this change of position, to where Susan engages in source-talk, is difficult to sustain and crashes:

> T26:... but *you* were more the leading character...
>
> C26: ... I wouldn't say I was the leading character...

The therapist tries to recover the source-talk by shifting to others' perceptions of her role, and Susan remarks that others have seen her new façade, a very telling lexical choice: she conceives of her new role as a kind of mask. The therapist tries to assert the agency behind the mask, but Susan again denies this and reverts to result-talk, where the façade is something she is the recipient of, not something she puts on:

> T30: ...I'm wondering if at that time it felt like it wasn't *fully* you...
>
> C30: ... It felt like a *new garment*.

Much of this narrative can thus be seen as the orchestration of two narrative positions: one where the voice is coming from the source and one where the voice is coming from the ends. The narrative is punctuated by the *disconnect* of these two positions. Susan even goes so far as to convert source-talk into ends-talk or deny the source-talk altogether. Indeed, when the therapist leads her to her acknowledged failures, Susan locates these in failed agency: C38: 'I couldn't quite deliver some of the times...' (279); C43: 'I wish I could have provided...' (282). And in the end, when she reconsiders her mother now after her death, Susan's final view of her is in result-terms: C48: 'she was a very demanding woman...' (282)

In many ways, this entire discourse is testimony to the semantic struggle of therapeutic conversation. This is *source vs. goal*, with little give on either side. One might wonder, at this point: is this progress? Given the nature of therapeutic narrative, progress can be measured here by the establishment of plausibility and the sustaining of the narrative itself. In that sense, there is progress. But one of the reasons that therapy may take a long time is that the client may not 'get it' the first time. Or, rather, practice at re-constructing one's thought structure is necessary. Re-cycling through an 'answer' is usually needed for it to become habit. A variant of the narrative has to be retold.

The networks do reveal the construction of local areas of truth—plausibility domains used to elucidate and justify source and goal. Susan's discourse purpose is to promote a theory of herself as a recipient and undergoer. But the therapist's purpose is to develop a theory of Susan's agency. How universal this is and whether these can be used as indicators of what stage a client is in his or her recovery is an interesting question. Importantly, these are both *passing theories*—ones developed on-line in the performative context of the therapy session. They are sustained by the therapy and endure as long as the therapy is sustained. We find overlaps and integration of these personal theories as Susan takes on the source-talk. But the question is whether she actually modifies her knowledge structure so as to change her ends into sources. At most, she appropriates the source talk into her own theory. In any case, transformation might not be the goal of the therapy or even a measure of its progress. Constructing these local areas of truth might be the best result.

Importantly for our analysis, the semantic networks can respond to the demands of performative theory-construction. They are simultaneously constant and dynamic. The formal structure of nodes and relations provides a framework of variables to be given values in any discourse, but the actual values assigned depend on the sense-making of the moment. If Susan were to decide that she is at the mercy of ghosts, then even this aspect of her recipient-oriented theory construction could be accommodated by the networks. As dynamic models, semantic networks are intrinsically amenable to the snapshots of plausibility and working, mini-truth sketches that constitute therapeutic exchange.

The semantic network presented here *is* a static representation. That is, it presents Susan's state of mind during a portion of that session. The network is a collapsing of a set of relations into one instant. In other words, we have taken a set of lexical relations being expressed diachronically and converted them into a synchronic statement. To represent the changes over time, we could number the relations sequentially as they are expressed. This would capture the diachrony and might be a way of capturing the moment of the occurrence of the 'Ah, hah!' effect, that is, when the client 'gets it' and what aspect of the therapy that he or she gets. In addition, a *lack* of presence of particular relations may be an indication of what concepts need further work.

We can clearly see the reflexivity in therapeutic discourse through these lexical semantic structures. Early on in the therapy, Susan traces many of her problems to lack of control (Neimeyer 2001: 271): C5: 'Uh, It was reminiscent of the feeling of powerlessness, almost ludicracy.' The therapist comments to the reader on the semantic nature of this issue and its role in the entire narrative (Neimeyer 2001: 271): C5: 'Susan makes clear that it is the feeling around the treatment that is most important now, and she offers two poignant terms to describe this: 'powerlessness' and 'ludicracy', to which she gives added emphasis. These then are the 'quality terms' whose meaning requires further interrogation. The therapeutic narrative takes on an entirely metasemantic function. A significant portion of the conversation involves the exploration of the term *powerlessness*, though not always explicitly so. Indeed, misunderstandings with respect to this term's semantics, and the client's and therapist's positions on this term, drive the discourse. In this therapy session, presumably as in all others, the data and the metalanguage converge. The purpose of this therapy is to explore the semantic structure of *powerlessness*, and the analysis of the data is the data. Use and mention converge.

Reflexivity also surfaces in another interesting way in this therapy session. At the one point where Susan and the therapist appear to be coming to a common viewpoint on Susan's need for agency (275), there is explicit meta-talk. The therapist achieves this acceptance in Susan by modeling her objectively against others and by talking about her role and theirs in social interactions. Freed from the *in situ* conditions of her life—and the therapy, for that matter—Susan responds by acknowledging her new role as an agent: C22: 'I guess it does...' (275). The therapist notes: T23: 'That's a dramatic shift...' (275), and follows up with: T24: 'Now, have others in your life noticed this shift?' (275). Note how the deictics *that*, *this*, and *now* are metadiscourse markers (Schiffrin 1987) and refer to properties of the discourse environment itself, not Susan's life: That [= 'The role that you have just acknowledged'] is a dramatic shift... Now [= 'At this point in the conversation that we are having'] have others in your life noticed this ['the aforementioned role'] shift? Much work remains to be done on how these framing devices further reflexivity in therapeutic narrative and how they might be marshaled as on-line tools by the therapist.

3.2 Metaphor

One of the first steps in therapy is for the client to become aware of the cause of his or her discomfort, rather than the discomfort itself. Awareness can then lead to cognitive control over the emotional discomfort so that when it re-surfaces, perhaps years later, the client can get control of it and attenuate the affective reaction.

What are some of the techniques that can be used to help a client become aware? In a truly professional setting, the client leads the narrative. Notorious cases of a therapist leading a client into thinking that he or she has been sexually abused have appropriately caused consternation in the profession. It is the client who must become aware of the cause/source of his or her discomfort and give the therapist clues, through language, about how he or she has constructed a worldview. The therapist's role is to notice the words that the client is using in order to understand how the client is construing his or her life.[4]

One technique is metaphor. As Soyland (1994: 91) has stated 'Emotion is perhaps inconceivable without metaphor[5]: a previous lexicon is needed, even to understand the most personal feelings.' Neimeyer (2001: 265) uses metaphor as a central tool in his practice of therapy:

> by exploring and elaborating those 'frozen metaphors' unreflectively used by a client to convey an experience (e.g., feeling 'burdened' or 'empty'), the therapist can prompt clients to articulate their meanings with greater precision and move the narrative of their engagement with the loss in new directions.

Metaphorical use of language, whether conscious or not, gives the therapist insight into how a client views the world and can assist the therapist in helping the client understand his or her worldview.

Indeed, metaphor is an area where scientific theory and therapy come together. Boyd (1979: 360) has defined theory-constitutive metaphors, the types of metaphors that we are discussing here, as figures of speech where 'metaphorical expressions constitute, at least for a time, an irreplaceable part of the linguistic machinery of a scientific theory.' That is exactly how metaphors are used in therapy—as the building blocks of theories in the client and therapist narrative.

---

[4] This, by the way, becomes very difficult when working with alexithymics, i.e., persons with an affective disorder characterized by a difficulty identifying and differentiating emotions (see Frawley and Smith 2001). It is clear that the therapist's job is made even more difficult in helping alexithymics express/construct their narratives.

[5] As is constructivism; see, for example, Spivey (1997).

How is metaphor used in the Neimeyer (2001) transcript? The first one is a very simple one, that of a flood[6]: C3: 'those feelings kinda, whoa, flooded back.' Significantly for the ultimate shift to metaphor, the deixis, *those feelings*, is literal and referential:

> C3: ...My mother, um, [1]died of lung cancer 3 years ago, and you know, [2]my parents were sepa- ... were divorced so [3]she had no one really to take care of her, um, when she was dying. My sister and I, [4]also divorced, [5]took her in and [6]took care of her. And [7]we brought her to the health center here twice a week, taking turns for chemotherapy and treatment. And [8]that went on it seemed like years, but it was from October 'til she died in July. And I haven't been back to the health center till today.

The eight superscripted phrases are all facts that had, at an earlier time, an affective quality; *those* refers to properties of the client's life outside the present session. In this situation, they could just as easily have been recited by a doctor in the 3rd person. However, the fact that the client refers to them as 'feelings' shows that there was, at the time of utterance, a reliving, or at least a re-feeling of some of those emotions.

The therapist then picks up on the metaphor: T4: 'And so those feelings that flooded in for you were feelings of re-evoking that sense of loss and the treatment.' This would be an obvious interpretation of 'those feelings' based on the client's report of these experiences, and the client's initial reaction is to agree with his interpretation: 'C: Right.' The client may have re-experienced the loss, but, in her current narrative, her interpretation of 'those feelings' (note the plural form in spite of the subsequent singular interpretation) is one that involves powerlessness. The client then corrects the therapist's interpretation of her feelings, not the facts per se: C5: 'Uh, it was reminiscent of the feeling of powerlessness ... She was terminal.' For the client the metaphor of a flood contributes to her position as the recipient of actions and events and supports the view that her experiences are something over which she is powerless and has no control. The advancing flood and her powerlessness to stop it are prominent for her.

The therapist seizes on this interpretation of the metaphor and, wanting the client to be truly consciously cognizant of its meaning, asks: T8: 'What was pushing you in the direction of this kind of activity?' The client begins by responding as follows:

---

[6] Actually, the very first metaphor is used by the therapist: T3: 'discuss some experience of loss of yours that ... has some unresolved pieces or growing edges to it.' These metaphors imply that loss is partitionable and can have edges. It is interesting that the client does not pick up on this. (It may be because of their obscurity!) But this is usually the case; it is the *therapist* who notices the metaphors used by the *client* and subsequently uses them, seldom the reverse.

C9: I, I kinda wish I knew, I just, I uh ... [4-second pause]. All right, I guess I *do* know. The need to *do something*, the need not to be powerless in this situation. The refusal to accept being powerless ... in this situation. I guess that's what was the drive.

This is one of those 'Ah, hah!' moments. Susan cognitively grasps what the feeling was that she had experienced. It was powerlessness over the situation.

To help her truly capture this interpretation the therapist then focuses on this feeling of powerlessness by verbalizing *for her*, as her persona, an interpretation of it: T10: 'I'm not going to let this leave me incapacitated, I'm going to do something ... for my mother.' This discourse strategy makes a double metaphor. Not only is there a metaphorical flood inducing powerlessness, but there is also an additional overlay of a new role of the interpreter of the flood. Susan then agrees with this and envisages herself saying: C10: 'Even if it beats me, I'm going to do my best.'

This portion of the narrative shows quite well the metaphorical method used by the therapist.

pick up on a metaphor used by a client,

give an initial, tentative interpretation of it,

pick up on any agreement or a clarifying insight on the part of the client,

then elaborate on the interpretation in a variety of ways so that the client can accept it and make it part of a conscious interpretation of his or her own actions and feelings.[7]

Because metaphor can suspend the pragmatic conditions on exchange, the double metaphor in the above excerpt is a particularly effective implementation of the metaphorical method because it creates a safe place to explain the facts and to allow the therapist and client to strategize.[8]

There are many other metaphors used throughout the narrative. If one were to treat the narrative as a single short text (which, of course, it is not) one would characterize them as mixed metaphors. But many times the metaphors are used just short-term (indicating that the therapy session is truly a *construction* of narrative). Others, more central to capturing/focusing on the client's condition, recur and are interwoven with one

---

[7] It should be noticed that in his transcript, it is always the therapist who initially picks up on the metaphor used by the client and never the reverse. Although work by Zoltan-Ford (1991) on covert language shaping in computer tutorials suggests that the reverse might also occur, it does not occur in this transcript. The differences in genres may account for this—on-line tutorials are monologues.

[8] The *sine qua non* of successful therapy is for the client to feel safe and to trust the therapist.

another throughout the co-construction of the narrative. One of these central metaphors, in this transcript, is that of the theater.[9] This is especially interesting in the context of our view that therapy is a cross between scientific theory construction and experimental theater. It begins with the client speaking of her sister: C25: 'So I'd always taken a back seat to *her* stardom.'[10]

This statement comes after a discussion of her realizing that, during her mother's illness, she had gone from a position of powerlessness, as a middle child, etc., to one of being in charge. She believed, until this session, that she was powerless. The interchange from T15 makes her cognizant of the fact that that is not the case. She had actually taken charge of many aspects of her mother's care. She had *not* been afraid of authority, etc.

The therapist picks up on the metaphor (almost overdoing it) and says:

T26: So somehow the <u>limelight</u> shifted, and she wasn't on <u>center stage</u>
so much in this <u>production</u>, but *you* were more the <u>leading character</u> in
the <u>drama.</u>

The client attempts to rein in this runaway image: C26: 'It was shared, yeah. I wouldn't say that I was the leading character, definitely <u>not</u>, but um, we shared.' The therapist elaborates: T27: 'So you were not just putting in a <u>cameo appearance</u> as you might have done before, but you were really <u>on stage</u> and had a <u>voice</u>.'[11] At which point the client interjects: 'C: Right, right, exactly.'

The metaphor adds to the previous narrative portion and helps further to overcome the client's belief that she is powerless. The therapist points out to her immediately that the very fact that she is participating in the session, especially in the context of the audience, shows that she is, in that moment, not fearful. Again, the functional consequence of metaphor is to suspend pragmatics and allow a safe zone for strategizing.

What does the extensive use of metaphor say about the narrative? First of all, it is an explicit tool in co-construction. The trained therapist picks up on a client's use of a lexical item that can have a metaphorical interpreta-

---

[9] We will not discuss the actual use of role-playing in therapy, however, even though it is a tool that is frequently used and *is* used in this very transcript.

[10] It should be noted that, contrary to all the other introductions of metaphors, the *therapist* introduced the metaphor much earlier: T15: 'So at the end of *her* [the mother's] life you found yourself being very much her daughter in this ... <u>enacting the role</u> in a way that was compatible with the way you had been as a child.' In this case the client uses the lexical item but does not extend the metaphor, using it in its frozen form: C15: 'I took on a *new* role during all this. I was the middle child, and um, was just kinda there growing up. And so taking charge was kind of a new role for me.'

[11] At this point the therapist puts the metaphor in a meta-context—the session actually occurred before an audience of therapists in a theater!

tion in its current context. The therapist repeats it and elaborates on it. The client then becomes aware of its metaphorical use, which gives her an interpretation of the events she has been discussing. This allows her to elaborate further and re-interpret them in a new, incisive light. Metaphor is a vehicle of overt, lexical cohesion and a method of co-construction.

Second, because the client acquiesces to or rejects a given figurative use, metaphor is one instrument by which plausibility is established and sustained in the narrative. It functions much the way metaphor functions in scientific theory-construction, as an organizing device and anchor to the sense-making (Boyd 1979). In the case of the theater metaphor above, it is used by the client to frame a possible interpretation of herself and then ask questions about it, such as, 'If I was an actress playing in a drama, what was my role? How was I projecting that role? Was I portraying that role correctly? Did I have the correct interpretation of that role?' And eventually, 'Is that the role I want to play now, and if not, how can I change it?'

Reflexivity is clearly present in metaphor as used in therapy. As a tool by which the client, with the help of the therapist, can frame the narrative, the reflexivity provided by metaphor can help the narrative flow in a positive direction, and lead to a realistic, and therefore healthy, self-concept.

3.3 Semantic Scales

Berg and de Shazer (1993) note that among the many tools that the therapist has at his disposal are scaling questions. These also are forms of metaphor and are means by which the therapist can ask the client to estimate the value of a behavior, feeling, outcome or any relevant phenomenon on some gradient: e.g., 'On a scale of 1 to 5, with 5 the highest, can you tell me how much progress you have been making in therapy?' Scaling questions are useful verbal instruments for therapists because they objectify knowledge. As Berg and de Shazer (1993: 10) observe, scaling questions can help '"measure" the clients own perception.' These questions can also stimulate the therapeutic narrative and push the discourse forward, especially at times of impasse: they 'motivate and encourage, and ... elucidate ...goals' (1993: 10).

Two important sets of semantic facts come with scaling questions. First, there are many different kinds of scales, each with their respective structural properties. Scales can be unidirectional, bi-directional, continuous, discontinuous, reflexive, multilayered, and so on (Cruse 1986). These varying structures have different truth conditions, semantic commitments, and, perhaps most importantly, inference and question patterns (Cruse 2000; Levinson 2000). Consider, for example, the difference between the two scales low to high and 0 to 5. The former is open-ended and internally continuous, but the latter is closed and composed of discrete intervals. Because of these different scalar structures, you can ask, 'On a scale of low to high, how high was X?' But you cannot ask, 'On a scale of 0 to 5, how 5 was X.' You can also estimate a position on these scales, but the scales' structures require different estimates. On a low-to-high scale, you can assert a more-or-less position: 'My feelings are somewhere in the low-to-middle range.' But this is not allowable on an interval scale. If you say, 'My feelings are somewhere in the 3 range,' you do not mean that the value 3 is fuzzy or slides into 4, as low is fuzzy and slides into middle. The phrase in the 3 range indicates something about your judgment of your relation to the scale, not the scale itself: i.e., 'I'm guessing I'm a 3,' not 'I'm definitely a sort of a 3.' In more technical semantics, these scales yield different conditions on the scope of the hedge. Continuous scales allow for the discrete assertion of hedged or fuzzy reference; discrete interval scales allow for hedged or fuzzy judgments of discrete references. Overall, then, the nature of the scale deployed in any question affects the way the statement containing that scale might contribute to the discourse.

The second set of semantic facts bears on the content of the scale. In principle, the content is independent of the scale itself, and so the conceptual basis of the scale is open to a variety of interpretations, even ones that can be constructed on-line. Still, the content must be consistently stated and must be compatible with the scale's formal structure in order to be appropriate. For example, asking someone to rate their confidence in their current mental health on a scale of 1 to 10, a seemingly benign scale, may offer the rater too many intervals for the confidence scale to be meaningful. Moreover, the intervals themselves may not be equal. Moving from 1 to 2 on a confidence scale may be easier or harder than moving from 9 to 10, in the same way that a moving from 300 to 350 on the GRE is easier than moving from 700 to 750. Careful thought must therefore be given to the conceptual content imposed on the scale when a scalar question is asked.

We can see the promises and problems of the uses of scales in therapeutic conversations in Berg and de Shazer's (1993) excellent article. We can also see how scales can underpin the narrative features of co-construction, plausibility, and reflexivity.

Note the following exchange, where a client is asked to rate her confidence in her diligence about her future actions with respect to her husband (Berg and de Shazer 1993: 10; T = Therapist; C = Client):

> T: How confident are you that you can stick with this? Let's say ten means you're confident that you're going to carry this out, that a year from now you'll look back and say, 'I did what I set out to do.' Okay? And one means you're going to back down from this. How confident are you, between ten and one?

C: Seven.

T: Seven?

C: Yeah.

T: Wow!

C: I don't have a choice.

A number of issues with regard to semantic scales arise immediately here and call into question the effectiveness of this rating method in this particular case. The conceptual content of the scale is not consistent. A rating of 10 means 'highly confident in actions'; however, a rating of 1 does not mean 'less confident' in actions, but 'failed action'. Confidence and action are conflated in this scale, and so any numerical value would not mean much as a choice in relation to another numerical value. Thus, we are not surprised that the client estimates her 'confidence' at 7, and then indicates that her choice is not a choice at all because the actions, and hence their likelihood, are entirely determined: 'I don't have a choice.' The therapist may be asking for confidence, but the client is talking about actions. It might have been better to phrase the question as consistent with a scale: e.g., 'On a scale of 1 to 10, estimate the success of your future actions.' In response to this kind of scalar question, a 10 means something with respect to a 1: 'more success'.

Because the scale is inconsistent, the client responds with stock answers, indicating a misfiring of the speech event as an invitation by the therapist to engage in on-line sense-making and to objectify behavior. The client is offered a scale of 1 to 10, and she places herself at 7, a nice conservative estimate toward the high end, thus saving face and preserving her positive identity in a discourse with a subtext of failed or ineffective action. The exchange that follows her estimate of 7 is extremely revealing (Berg and de Shazer 1993: 10-11; T is asking about C's mother-in-law's views of C's future actions):

T: What do you suppose Charlie's mother would say? About the same question, what do you think she would say?

C: She'd give me a lower one.

T: Probably...

C: She'd say we never stick to what we say we are going to do.

T: How low? What would she say between ten and one?

C: Four or five.

T: Four or five?

C: Yeah.

T: Ok. What if I asked Charlie about...

C: Me?

T: Yeah, about Joan. What would he say? What would he say you were at? How confident would he say he is that you're going to carry this out?

C: Three or four.

T: Three or four?

C: Yeah.

T: Lower than his mother. What about your mother? What would she say?

C: My mom would give me a one. She doesn't let me think anything...

What the client does here is offer averaging answers that cut up the scale in three-interval chunks. She rates herself at 7, Charlie and his mother at about 4, and her mother at 1. It is difficult to know what her estimates mean in these exchanges (a point Berg and de Shazer 1993 acknowledge). Arguably, she perceives this scale as completely deterministic because it is a scale of actions: 'I don't have a choice'; 'She doesn't let me think anything.' Additional evidence for this assessment of her view can be found in a later exchange, where the therapist asks for her friends' estimate of her actions:

T: What if I were to ask your friends, what would they say, on the same scale, about the same question?

C: They're not so worried that I'm going to be doing the things I want to be doing. They're just worried I'm going to take Charlie back again...

Here the client denies the applicability of the scale because to her, the scale concerns her actions, not confidence.

Clearly, the nature of a semantic scale and the applicability of conceptual content to that scale affect the way a therapeutic conversation might proceed. The discourse above, via its scales, promotes two aspects of therapeutic narrative, dynamic plausibility and reflexivity. As to the former, much of the exchange revolves, silently, around on-line sense-making—what a 7 or 4 means with respect to the scale. Reflexivity is also fostered. What a scalar question does is to invoke the framework of the discourse per se and ask for an assessment of that frame in the current speech event. Asking a client to estimate behavior on a scale of 1 to 10 makes the content of the conversation the object of the conversation. Consider the difference between the following two questions 'What did you do yesterday?' and 'On a scale of 1 to 5, with three as the present, how would you rate the time of your actions?' The former question uses tense as the content of the question. The latter mentions tense and raises it as the object of the question. Scaling questions are inherently metasemantic.

But narrative co-construction is tenuous here. This exchange is less a narrative than it is a conversation. The power of scaling questions to generate content and frame the discourse, coupled with the mixed signals sent by the inconsistent scale, push the exchange into what might be called a heterologue, an intrinsically varying and disjoint speech event. The client's scale estimates appear to reflect a discourse strategy by which she simply complies with the demands of the speech event to give answers. She divides a bounded and discrete scale by cutting it up regularly and safely. It is the scaling question that has positioned her to speak this way in order to play along.[12]

This observation about conversation vs. narrative is not meant as a criticism of the therapy. On the contrary, the exchange reveals how much on-line work there is in establishing a co-constructed narrative and it supports Berg and de Shazer's (1993) overall claim that therapy is driven by attempts to reconcile misunderstanding. Still, the whole therapeutic experience might have turned out differently if the therapist had asked the client to construct the scale with him and if they both assigned numbers in a more interactive fashion. Something like this eventually emerges in this therapy, as we can see below.

The therapist, still focusing on the client's actions with respect to Charlie, tries to convert confidence to probabilities and then to convert this bare odds estimate to a scale. This is a very challenging exercise in principle—switching conceptualizations—but especially difficult in practice:

> T: So if I were to ask your friends 'What are the chances that Joan is going to take Charlie back?' (client laughs) what would they say, on the same scale?
>
> C: Ten to one...
>
> T: Ten to one.
>
> C: Probably...
>
> T: What are the chances you give yourself?
>
> C: Probably about the same.

---

[12] A similar scenario is replayed later (Berg and de Shazer 1993: 16-18), where the client and therapist again miscommunicate about an inconsistent scale and the client offers averaged answers. The speech-event misfire has to do with the difference between scales of confidence and likelihood and the client's perception that a confidence scale does not have equal intervals: for her, it is very hard to go from a 2 to a 3.

T: Ten to one? So, you think not taking him back is good for you?

C: Yeah.

T: Really?

C: Right.

T: You're absolutely sure about that?

C: Positive.

T: Positive. So what do you need to do to increase the odds?

A number of interesting observations emerge from this excerpt. For one, it is not entirely clear that the switch from a confidence scale to probabilities has changed the client's perception. She responds to the therapist's question about odds by giving a 10 to 1 scale, arguably borrowed wholesale from the previous exchanges where the therapist established scaling as 10 to 1. Here, it looks as if the client is really saying: 'It is highly likely that others will say I'll take him back, and that's a 10 on our established scales. I see myself acting with the same likelihood.' (Indeed, when the therapist and client finally begin a co-constructed discourse, these meanings surface more transparently in their exchange: see below).

A second difficulty concerns the interpretation of the probabilities themselves. For pretty obvious therapeutic reasons, the therapist is talking about a scale of likelihood of refusal to take Charlie back. His goal is to get the client to stop what she has been doing. So the therapist's conceptualized scale is something like: PROBABILITY NOT X. Successful behavior with respect to this scale is an increase, which accounts for his statement 'So what do you need to do to increase the odds?' But when you look closely at the exchange, this suggestion of an increase does not really cohere with the way the conversation flows. The initial illustration of odds-making concerns the likelihood of the client accepting Charlie (PROBABILITY X), which the client judges as a 10 for both her friends' perception of her and her own action (i.e., highly likely). Successful behavior with respect to this scale is not an increase in the odds, but a decrease. When the therapist makes a subtle, yet significant semantic shift after the client's judgment—'Ten to one? So, you think not taking him back is good for you?'—this seems to be missed by the client. She then continues to explain her assessment of Charlie in response to the therapist's query about 'increasing her odds': C13: 'I always think he's going to change, he's going to be better... And then I sometimes think, well, okay... Who's going to take me with three kids?'

Her elucidation is not about increasing the odds of refusal, but about reasons why she continues to accept him. Increasing the odds of her refusal is not enhanced by Charlie changing, getting better, and so on. She's very worried about acceptance, which is why she asks, 'Who's going to take me...?' The client's perspective is a continuation of her initial odds-making about accepting him.

At this point in the exchange, two essential features of therapeutic narrative come to the rescue: reflexivity and dynamic plausibility. The therapist, sensing the conversation is going astray, explicitly introduces the content of the scale, from his perspective, and asserts a metasemantic statement: 'So, what do you have to do to increase the odds you're not going to take him back?' (13). The client's response is very revealing: 'I have no idea.' She is clearly telling the truth! She has no idea about a scale of the likelihood of refusal because she has been talking all along about a scale of likelihood of acceptance. The remainder of the session turns to performative sense-making, dynamic plausibility, and the therapist and client work jointly on what would constitute criteria for refusal.

The lesson here is fairly simple: scales are hard! And they contribute to the discourse in complicated ways. Scales position speakers and hearers and trigger inferences, so their use in therapeutic contexts might be more effective if they are the source of co-construction and worked out on-line, rather than something given by one participant to another. A question such as 'Where would you put yourself on a 1 to 10 scale of confidence?' presupposes both the structure of the scale and its content. But making these presuppositions the explicit content of questions in an exchange—'Could we put our behavior on a scale, and what would that look like?'; 'What would be the best basis of this scale, confidence, likelihood?'—would alter the flow of the exchange and promote co-construction. Indeed, this happens in the therapy under examination here. After the therapist works with the client on what constitutes the criteria for refusal, he says: 'What is the likelihood that he is going to come back to you...?' Both the scale and its content are worked out. The client responds: 'Pretty good', an intriguing answer because it is scalar but not numerical, and so very much like her answering '10'.

Thereafter, the therapy assumes a very different texture, with smoother flow and more cohesive utterances. Indeed, the therapist changes his scaling questions as a consequence: 'Let's say ten means you have every confidence that Charlie is going to change, to turn his life around, and one means, you know, the opposite' (16). This is a consistent scale, and the client responds in kind 'I'd give him a two.' Both the client and the therapist have changed by this point, which is exactly what should happen in good, co-constructed therapy.

4 Conclusion

In this paper, we have tried to show how a number of tools of semantic analysis might assist in the examination of narratives co-constructed in therapeutic discourse. Lexical inquiry, using semantic relations and semantic scales, reveals the conceptual structures that underlie informational organization and flow in therapeutic exchanges. Examination of the figurative language in therapeutic exchanges shows how therapists and clients frame their narratives and adopt a worldview in the exchanges. These semantic tools serve narrative analysis by uncovering structure in the narrative co-construction, performative sense-making, and reflexivity of therapeutic exchanges.

A number of possibilities for future work come out of the foregoing discussion. More detailed semantic analysis of the structures underlying the therapeutic exchange might reveal additional strategies of narrative co-construction. For instance, numerical scales trigger a range of implicatures (non-truth-conditional inferences)—so called *scalar implicatures* and *generalized conversational implicatures* (Levinson 2000). Some scaled items, like numbers, work in such a way that a higher value on the scale entails lower ones (if I have 5 dollars, I must also have 3); a lower value, however, does not entail a higher one, but is compatible with it (if I have 3 dollars, I may also have 5, but not necessarily). In discourse, asserting the lower member of a scale triggers the implicature that you are not in a position in this speech event to assert the higher, even though the higher is compatible and might, in fact, be true (if I have 3 dollars and may also have 5, I assert 3, because, for some reason, I just am not in a position to assert 5).

Now, consider these effects with respect to scales introduced in therapeutic conversations. Asking someone to position himself on a numerical scale is an invitation to scalar implicature. 'On a scale of 1 to 5, with 5 as most happy, where would you place yourself?' If you say 3, you are implicating that you may be 5, but for some reason are not in a position in this speech event to say so. This result would suggest that the therapy should focus not so much on the 3 but on why the speaker is not in a position to say 5, a very different pragmatic tack. Indeed, Berg and de Shazer (1993) have some success with this strategy, although they do not explain it in these semantico-pragmatic terms, when they focus their client on very particular reasons for her changing her estimate from a lower number to a higher one on a numerical scale. In general, a more detailed semantic analysis of the scalar context might yield both properties of the therapeutic narrative and practical suggestions for furthering such narratives as therapeutic strategies.

A second area that would benefit from the foregoing work is the development of intelligent computerized aids for psychiatric contexts (Smith and Frawley 1999). Networks and scales are inherently computationally tractable and have regularly been the formal basis of knowledge representation schemes for expert medical systems. But the significant role of figurative language in psychiatric narrative means that metaphor would also have to become computationally tractable to be brought into these projects. It turns out that metaphorical language can be captured formally by using the sorts of semantic networks we have described previously. Steinhart and Kittay (1994) and Steinhart (2001) describe a formal method of representing metaphors and a way of analyzing and generating them; Steinhart provides a computer program, NETMET, that supposedly does that. It incorporates semantic networks into an intensional version of the predicate calculus. It includes mechanisms for interpreting English sentences in terms of thematic roles. These, however, constitute just a small subset of a much larger set of relations that we use in analyzing narrative. More critically, Steinhart's description of NETMET is not sufficient to draw conclusions of its success. No complete descriptions of the algorithms that he uses are presented nor is there a printout of a complete analysis of a metaphor. Still, these theoretical findings and implementation with respect to metaphor are promising. We suspect that more focused work on the role of figurative expressions in the on-line sense-making of therapy will lead to important insights about therapeutic narrative itself.

References

Bakhtin, M. M. 1990. *Speech Genres and Other Late Essays*, trans. and ed. by C. Emerson and M. Holquist. Austin: University of Texas Press.

Berg, I. K., and S. de Shazer. 1993. Making Numbers Talk: Language in Therapy. *The New Language of Change: Constructive Collaboration in Psychotherapy*, ed. S. Friedman, 5-23. New York: The Guilford Press.

Boyd, R. 1979. Metaphor and Theory-Change: What Is 'Metaphor' For? *Metaphor and Thought*, ed. A. Ortony, 356-408. Cambridge: Cambridge University Press.

Ceccarelli, L. 2001. *Shaping Science with Rhetoric*. Chicago: University of Chicago Press.

Cruse, D. A. 1986. *Lexical Semantics*. Cambridge: Cambridge University Press.

Cruse, D. A. 2000. *Meaning in Language*. Oxford: Oxford University Press.

Epstein, J. 1995. *Altered Conditions*. London: Routledge.

Evens, M., ed. 1988. *Relational Models of the Lexicon*. Cambridge: Cambridge University Press.

Frawley, W. 1988. Relational Models and the Philosophy of Science. *Relational Models of the Lexicon*, ed. M. Evens, 335-72. Cambridge: Cambridge University Press.

Frawley, W., and R. N. Smith. 2001. A Processing Model of Alexithymia. *Cognitive Systems Research* 2:189-206.

Lee, B. 2000. *Talking Heads*. Durham: Duke University Press.

Levinson, S. 2000. *Presumptive Meanings*. Cambridge: MIT Press.

Litowitz, B., and P. Epstein, eds. 1991. *Semiotic Perspectives on Clinical Theory and Practice*. Berlin: Mouton de Gruyter.

Litowitz, B. 1991. Elements of Semiotic Theory Relevant to Psychoanalysis. *Semiotic Perspectives on Clinical Theory and Practice,* eds. B. Litowitz and P. Epstein, 81-109. Berlin: Mouton de Gruyter.

Neimeyer, R. A. 2001. The Language of Loss: Grief Therapy as a Process of Meaning Reconstruction. *Meaning Reconstruction and the Experience of Loss*, ed. R. A. Neimeyer, 261-92. Washington, DC: American Psychological Association.

Saint-Dizier, P., and E. Viegas, eds. 1995. *Computational Lexical Semantics*. Cambridge: Cambridge University Press.

Schafer, R. 1976. *A New Language for Psychoanalysis*. New Haven: Yale University Press.

Schafer, R. 1980. Narration in the Psychoanalytic Dialogue. *Critical Inquiry* 7:29-53.

Schafer, R. 1992. *Retelling a Life*. NY: Basic Books.

Schiffrin, D. 1987. *Discourse Markers*. Cambridge: Cambridge University Press.

Smith, R. N., and W. Frawley. 1999. ALEX: A Computer Aid for Treating Alexithymia. *Multiple Approaches to Intelligent Systems: Lecture Notes in Artificial Intelligence 1611*, eds. I. Imam, Y. Kodratoff, A. El-Dessoudi, and M. Ali, 362-71. Berlin: Springer.

Soyland, A. J. 1994. *Psychology as Metaphor*. London: Sage Publications.

Spence, D. 1982. *Narrative Truth and Historical Truth*. NY: Norton.

Spence, D. 1994. *The Rhetorical Voice of Psychoanalysis*. Cambridge: Harvard University Press.

Spivey, N. N. 1997. *The Constructivist Metaphor: Reading, Writing, and the Making of Meaning*. San Diego, CA: Academic Press.

Steinhart, E. C. 2001. *The Logic of Metaphor: Analogous Parts of Possible Worlds*. Dordrecht: Kluwer Academic Publishers.

Steinhart, E. C., and E. Kittay. 1994. Generating Metaphors from Networks: A Formal Interpretation of the Semantic Field Theory of Metaphor. *Aspects of Metaphor*, ed. J. Hintikka, 41-94. Dordrecht: Kluwer Academic Publishers.

Sullivan, H. S. 1954. *The Psychiatric Interview*. New York: W.W. Norton and Co.

Vaill, P. B. 1989. *Managing as a Performing Art: New Ideas for a World of Chaotic Change.* San Francisco: Jossey-Bass.

Zoltan-Ford, E. 1991. How to Get People to Say and Type What Computers Can Understand. *International Journal of Man-Machine Studies* 34: 527-47.

Part II

Narrative as Cognitive Endowment

5

Double-scope Stories

Mark Turner

The serpent, who was the subtlest beast in the garden, said to the woman, 'Did the Lord really tell you that you cannot eat whatever you like?' She answered, 'We may eat the fruit of the trees of the garden except for the tree in the middle. The Lord has commanded us not to eat its fruit, or even touch it, or we shall die.' The serpent countered, 'You won't die. The Lord knows that when you eat that fruit, your eyes will be opened, and you will be like gods.' When she understood that the tree was good for food, and pleasing, and to be desired for the knowledge it brings, the woman plucked the forbidden fruit, and ate it, and gave some to her husband, who ate it, too. And their eyes were opened.

Cognitively modern human beings have a remarkable, species-defining ability to pluck forbidden mental fruit—that is, to activate two conflicting mental structures (such as *snake* and *person*) and to blend them creatively into a new mental structure (such as *talking snake with evil designs*). In this study, I will present some principles of this 'forbidden-fruit' mental blending and explore some of the consequences for the science of narrative.

Consider the as yet unexplained human ability to conjure up mental stories *that run counter to the story we actually inhabit*. Suppose that you are buying a Rioja from a wine shop on University Avenue in Palo Alto. That is one mental story, with roles, actions, goals, agents, and objects. You must be paying attention to it, for otherwise, you would drop the bot-

Narrative Theory and the Cognitive Sciences.
David Herman (ed.).
Copyright © 2003, CSLI Publications.

tle and botch the transaction. But at the same moment, you are remembering a dinner you once had in San Sebastián. In that story, you are eating paella, drinking Rioja wine, and listening to a Spanish guitar.

Or suppose you are actually boarding the plane to fly from San Francisco to Washington, D. C. You must be paying attention to the way that travel story goes, or you would not find your seat, stow your bag, and turn off your personal electronic devices. But all the while, you are thinking of surfing Windansea beach, and in that story, there is no San Francisco, no plane, no seat, no bag, no personal electronic devices, no sitting down, and nobody anywhere near you. Just you, the board, and the waves.

We might have expected evolution to build our brains in such a way as to prevent us from activating stories that run counter to our present circumstances, since calling these stories to mind risks confusion, distraction, disaster. Yet we do so all the time. A human being trapped inescapably in an actual story of suffering or pain may willfully imagine some other, quite different story, as a mental escape from the present.

How can it be that quite incompatible stories do not suppress each other's activation in the human mind? How can we fire up incompatible mental patterns simultaneously? Psychologically, what are we doing when we attend to the present story—that is, our own present bodies, needs, impulses, and activities, and the many objects, events, and agents in our surroundings—but at the same time attend to some mental story that does not serve our understanding of the present? Neurobiologically, what is it in the functioning of our brains that makes it possible for us to resist the grip of the present? Evolutionarily, how did our species develop this ability? Remarkably, someone who is inhabiting the real story of the present and who is simultaneously remembering a different story can partition them, so as to monitor each without becoming confused about which items belong to which stories. Memory researchers offer as yet no explanation of this astounding mental feat of keeping simultaneous activations separate.

There is a tantalizingly similar, possibly related, rudimentary mental phenomenon, which we call 'dreaming', in which we ignore the present story while we activate an imaginary story. During sleep, our sensory attention to the real story is severely dampened. Before sleep, we place ourselves in the safest possible location, so that ignoring the present story is less dangerous.

It may be that dreaming—including the activation of stories other than the real one—is generally available to mammals (Frith, Perry, & Lurner 1999; Hobson 1988; Jouvet 1979; Jouvet and Michel 1959). Although a dog or cat cannot tell us whether it dreams, mammals do show the same stages of sleep as we do, including REM sleep, during which there are rapid eye movements, inhibition of skeletal and nucal muscular activity, and an electroencephalogram pattern much like the one associated with waking. In such a state of immobility, we, and presumably the mammal, can run alternative mental stories without incurring the risk that we will damage ourselves. As Michel Jouvet and his collaborators have shown, a cat with a certain kind of lesion in the pontine reticular formation retains muscle tone during REM sleep, and so apparently acts out, while sleeping, a variety of hunting behaviors: it raises its head, orients it, walks as if tracking prey, pursues, pounces, and bites. It is hard to resist the inference that the cat is inhabiting dreamed stories during REM sleep, stories that do not suit its actual present circumstances.

Consider a common situation. A man is participating in a wedding. He is consciously enacting a familiar mental story, with roles, participants, a plot, and a goal. But while he is fulfilling his role in the wedding story, he is remembering a different story, which took place a week before in Cabo San Lucas, in which he and his girlfriend, who is not present at the wedding, went diving in the hopes of retrieving sunken treasure. Why, cognitively, should he be able to inhabit, mentally, these two stories at the same time? There are rich possibilities for confusion, but in all the central ways, he remains unconfused. He does not mistake the bride for his girlfriend, for the treasure, for the shark, or for himself. He does not swim down the aisle, even as, in the other story, he is swimming. He speaks normally even as, in the other story, he is under water. We have all been in moments of potential harm or achievement—a fight, an accident, a negotiation, an interview—when it would seem to be in our interest to give our complete attention to the moment, and yet even then, some other story has flitted unbidden into consciousness, without confusing us about the story we inhabit.

Human beings go beyond merely imagining stories that run counter to the present story. We take a great mental leap that I liken to plucking forbidden mental fruit: we connect two stories that should be kept absolutely apart, and we then blend them to make a third story. The man at the wedding, for example, can make analogical connections between his girlfriend and the bride and between himself and the groom, and blend these counterparts into a daydream in which it is he and his girlfriend who are being married at this particular ceremony. This blended story is manifestly false, and he should not make the mistake, as he obediently discharges his duties at the real wedding, of thinking that he is in the process of marrying his girlfriend. But he plucks the forbidden mental fruit, with potentially serious consequences: he might come to realize that he likes the blended story, and so formulate a plan of action to make it real. Or, in the blended story, when the bride is invited to say 'I do,' she might say, 'I would never marry you!' Her fulguration might reveal to him a truth he had sensed intuitively but not recognized, and this revelation might bring him regret or relief.

Running two stories mentally, when we should be absorbed by only one, and blending them when they should be kept apart, is at the root of what makes us human. So far, I have stressed blends that combine a story we inhabit with a story we remember. But we can also blend two stories that are both attuned to our present circumstances. If we perceive someone dying under a tree as the autumn leaves fall, then the dying and the falling can be seen as different stories, which we can run and understand independently. The dying can happen without the leaves, and the leaves can fall without the dying. But we can also make a blend in which the present man is the present tree. As Shakespeare writes,

> That time of year thou mayst in me behold
> When yellow leaves or none or few do hang
> Upon these boughs which shake against the cold
> Bare, ruined choirs, where late the sweet birds sang.

On the one hand, it makes sense that memory would be designed so as to remain subordinate to our attempt to understand the present situation. Arthur Glenberg (1997) writes in 'What memory is for':

> To avoid hallucination, conceptualization would normally be driven by the environment, and patterns of action from memory would play a supporting, but automatic, role. (1)

But on the other hand, as Glenberg astutely observes, it is often the case that memory takes the upper hand in conceptualizing the story one is inhabiting:

> A significant human skill is learning to suppress the overriding contribution of the environment to conceptualization, thereby allowing memory to guide conceptualization. (Glenberg 1997: 1)

We confront a taxonomy of scientific puzzles related to the blending of stories:

> —We can make sense of a story in the immediate environment with the support of memory. This support can range from routine, invisible assistance to nuanced conscious remembrance of a particular memory that guides us in conceptualizing the present story.

> —We can bundle and compress two different but compatible stories that are both running in the immediate environment if we can assign them to places in a single conceptual 'frame', such as *chase*, or *race*, or *competition*, or *debate*.

> —We can dream an imaginary story during sleep, when our sensory attention to the present story is dampened. (One wonders about dol-

phins, who appear to sleep on one side of the brain at a time, keeping one eye open to attend to the immediate environment.)

—We can activate a memory while we are awake, even if it is not crucial to making sense of the present story.

—We can activate an imaginary story while we are awake, even if it is not crucial to making sense of the present story.

—We can blend a story tuned to the immediate environment with a remembered or an imagined story.

—We can even activate and blend two stories, both of which are supplied by memory or imagination, even if neither of them is tuned to the present story.

In *The Way We Think: Conceptual Blending and the Mind's Hidden Complexities*, Gilles Fauconnier and I focus on the remarkable human ability to blend different mental arrays (Fauconnier and Turner 2002). Blending is a basic human mental operation, with constitutive and governing principles. It played a crucial role, probably *the* crucial role, in the descent of our species over the last fifty or one hundred thousand years. Fauconnier and I offer the view that the mental operation of blending is a basic part of human nature, that human beings share its rudimentary forms with some other species, and that the advanced ability to blend incompatible conceptual arrays is a basic part of what makes us cognitively modern.

It is far from clear how this advanced human ability for blending evolved. It is tantalizing that it was preceded phylogenetically by both dreaming and memory, each of which requires that the brain differentiate between the immediate environment and a different story.

In *The Way We Think*, Fauconnier and I explore the ways in which blending is fundamental to a range of human singularities:

—Counterfactual thinking. (See chapter 11, 'The Construction of the Unreal', and its discussion of everyday examples such as 'Put the vegetables on the plate in front of the missing chair', 'I have a tooth missing', 'Nobody offered a proposal; *it* would have been shot down', See also chapter 12, 263-66, on the identity of missing people. See also Turner 2001 [chapter 2, 'Reason'].)

—The understanding of personal identity and character. (See chapter 12, 'Identity and Character'.)

—The understanding of cause and effect. (See chapter 5, 'Cause and Effect'.)

—Grammar and language. (See chapter 8, 'Compressions and Clashes', chapter 9, 'The Origin of Language', and chapter 17, 'Form and Meaning'. See also Coulson 2001; Coulson and Fauconnier 1999; Grush and Mandelblit 1997; Mandelblit 2000; Sweetser 1999.)

—The cognitive use of objects and material anchors. (See chapter 10, 'Things'. See also Hutchins In preparation)

—Mathematics. (See chapter 11, 233-38, and chapter 13, 270-74. See also Lakoff and Nuñez 2000.)

—Category extension and metamorphosis. (See chapter 13, 'Category Metamorphosis'.)

—Art (see also Turner 2002b), science, religion, dance, gesture (see also Liddell 1998), music (see also Zbikowski 2001), advanced tool use, fashions of dress, visual representation, literature (see also Turner 1996; Herman 1999; Hiraga 1999; Sinding 2001), rhetoric (see also Pascual 2002), and so on.

Here, I focus on how we blend two separate stories. I will begin with a small example from Racine brought to my attention by Gilles Fauconnier.[1] It is the celebrated avowal scene in Racine's *Phèdre* (Act II, scene v) involving Phaedra, the wife of Theseus, and Hippolytus, who is Theseus's son and Phaedra's step-son (Racine 1962 [1677]: 82-85). Phaedra, at the moment of speaking, is actually inhabiting a vibrant, emotional story involving Hippolytus. She has every reason to attend directly to Hippolytus and to the present moment. But she is cognitively modern, and does what we all do: she recalls a different story, namely, the legend of Theseus and the Minotaur.

PHEDRE

Oui, Prince, je languis, je brûle pour Thésée.

Je l'aime, non point tel que l'ont vu les enfers,

Volage adorateur de mille objets divers,

Qui va du Dieu des morts déshonorer la couche;

Mais fidèle, mais fier, et même un peu farouche,

Charmant, jeune, traînant tous les coeurs après soi,

Tel qu'on dépeint nos Dieux, ou tel que je vous voi.

Il avait votre port, vos yeux, votre langage,

Cette noble pudeur colorait son visage,

Lorsque de notre Crète il traversa les flots,

---

[1] Fauconnier and I have often discussed this example and presented it in talks. I presented an analysis of the passage at the Collège de France in 2000 (Turner, 2002a). Fauconnier (in preparation) also presents an analysis.

Digne sujet des voeux des filles de Minos.
Que faisiez-vous alors? Pourquoi sans Hyppolyte
Des héros de la Grèce assembla-t-il l'élite?
Pourquoi, trop jeune encor, ne pûtes-vous alors
Entrer dans le vaisseau qui le mit sur nos bords?
Par vous aurait péri le monstre de la Crète,
Malgré tous les détours de sa vaste retraite.
Pour en développer l'embarras incertain,
Ma soeur du fil fatal eût armé votre main.
Mais non, dans ce dessein je l'aurais devancée:
L'amour m'en eût d'abord inspiré la pensée.
C'est moi, Prince, c'est moi dont l'utile secours
Vous eût du Labyrinthe enseigné les détours.
Que de soins m'eût coûté cette tête charmante!
Un fil n'eût point assez rassuré votre amante.
Compagne du péril qu'il vous fallait chercher,
Moi-même devant vous j'aurais voulu marcher;
Et Phèdre, au Labyrinthe avec vous descendue,
Se serait avec vous retrouvée ou perdue.

HIPPOLYTE

Dieux! qu'est-ce que j'entends? Madame, oubliez-vous
Que Thésée est mon père et qu'il est votre époux?

PHEDRE

Et sur quoi jugez-vous que j'en perds la mémoire,
Prince? Aurais-je perdu tout le soin de ma gloire?

HIPPOLYTE

Madame, pardonnez. J'avoue, en rougissant,
Que j'accusais à tort un discours innocent.

Ma honte ne peut plus soutenir votre vue;
Et je vais...

PHEDRE

Ah! cruel, tu m'as trop entendue.

Richard Wilbur (Racine 1986 [1677]: 45-47) translates this scene as follows:

PHAEDRA

Yes, Prince, I burn for him with starved desire,
Though not as he was seen among the shades,
The fickle worshiper of a thousand maids,
Intent on cuckolding the King of Hell;
But constant, proud, a little shy as well,
Young, charming, irresistible, much as we
Depict our Gods, or as you look to me.
He had your eyes, your voice, your virile grace,
It was your noble blush that tinged his face
When, crossing on the waves, he came to Crete
And made the hearts of Minos' daughters beat.
Where were you then? Why no Hippolytus
Among the flower of Greece he chose for us?
Why were you yet too young to join that band
Of heroes whom he brought to Minos' land?
You would have slain the Cretan monster then,
Despite the endless windings of his den.
My sister would have armed you with a skein
Of thread, to lead you from that dark domain.
but no: I'd first have thought of that design,
Inspired by love; the plan would have been mine.
It's I who would have helped you solve the maze,
My Prince, and taught you all its twisting ways.
What I'd have done to save that charming head!
My love would not have trusted to a thread.

No, Phaedra would have wished to share with you

Your perils, would have wished to lead you through
The Labyrinth, and thence have side by side
Returned with you; or else, with you, have died.

HIPPOLYTUS

Gods! What are you saying, Madam? Is Theseus not
Your husband, and my sire? Have you forgot?

PHAEDRA

You think that I forget those things? For shame,
My lord. Have I no care for my good name?

HIPPOLYTUS

Forgive me, Madam. I blush to have misread
The innocent intent of what you said.
I'm too abashed to face you; I shall take
My leave . . .

PHAEDRA

      Ah, cruel Prince, 'twas no mistake.
You understood...

Phaedra escapes, partially, the present. She and Hippolytus call up the thought of Theseus, who is absent, and activate in imagination the story of Theseus and the Minotaur. Phaedra makes analogical connections between the present story, which involves Hippolytus, and the remembered story, which involved Theseus, Ariadne, and the Minotaur. In the cross-story analogy, Theseus and Hippolytus are counterparts. This analogy is natural, based on similarity, inheritance, and kinship: Hippolytus is the grown son of Theseus.

But then Phaedra does something that is at once highly imaginative and utterly routine for human beings: she blends the two analogical people, Hippolytus and Theseus, from the two separate stories. This launches a new, third, blended story. In the new blended story, Hippolytus does what Theseus did: Hippolytus, in Crete, enters the labyrinth and defeats the Minotaur. This imaginative story, launched by the analogy between Theseus and Hippolytus in the two original stories, quickly takes on emergent meaning. Phaedra blends herself with Ariadne, and so becomes in the blended story the assistant of the hero in the labyrinth. Having inserted herself into this new role, she comes to a new conclusion: the thread is not good enough; the hero's assistant, in this blended story, now dismisses the plan of giving the hero a mere thread as equipment for escaping, and concludes that the assistant must enter the labyrinth with the hero, to risk what he risks. The assistant is of course the hero's lover. In the blend, the hero is now Hippolytus, and the assistant is Phaedra, and so Phaedra is Hippolytus's lover. It is exceptionally revealing that Phaedra's love in the blend impels her to enter the labyrinth to help Hippolytus, because in the actual historical story, Phaedra did not feel this way about Theseus. She did not enter the labyrinth with Theseus. She did not give him the thread. (In some versions of the story, she was not even there.) The essential difference between the historical story with Theseus in the labyrinth and the blended story with Hippolytus in the labyrinth is that now Hippolytus replaces Theseus and Phaedra replaces Ariadne. All the new feelings, all the new meanings are caused by these changes, which are developed only in the blended story.

How could Phaedra know that in the counterfactual blend she would be so passionately attached to Hippolytus? One available implication is that she loves Hippolytus in the blend because he is blended there with Theseus, her husband. But another available implication is that she knows how she would feel in the blend because that is how she feels now in front of Hippolytus, in the present story. In that case, she is telling him, through this fantastic blended story, that she loves him not just as a woman loves a man, but with the most extreme passion and dedication. Hippolytus cannot fail to recognize this implication.

To summarize, Phaedra's words prompt us, and prompt Hippolytus, to run two stories at the same time—the present story and the historical story—and also to form a highly imaginative blended story in which Hippolytus is integrated with Theseus. In that blended story, that false story, new meaning develops. That new meaning turns out to deliver to us the deep truth for the actual human situation. Plucking the forbidden fruit brings insight and knowledge.

The blended story of Phaedra and Hippolytus manifests standard features of blending:

Mapping between elements of the two stories. Blending two stories always involves at least a provisional mapping between them. The mapping typically involves connections of identity, analogy, similarity, causality, change, time, intentionality, space, role, part-whole, or representation. In *Phèdre*, the mapping involves analogy and time. There is a causal link as well, because Phaedra's existence in Theseus's household is a result of his earlier trip to Crete and his vanquishing of the Minotaur.

Selective projection. Different elements of the stories are projected to the blended story. In *Phèdre*, we take from the historical story of the myth the scene of the labyrinth, the Minotaur, and the roles of both the hero and the daughter of Minos who helps him, but now we bring Hippolytus and Phaedra in from the other story as the values of those roles. In the story of the Minotaur, the daughter of Minos who helps Theseus is Ariadne, not Phaedra.

Emergent structure. In the blended story of Phaedra and Hippolytus as lovers, we have astonishing emergent structure. Now it is Hippolytus who conquers the Minotaur, and it is Phaedra who helps him. Moreover, Phaedra goes into the labyrinth because of her great love. Emergent structure in integrating stories comes from three sources: composition, completion, and elaboration. Composition is putting together elements from different conceptual arrays. Completion is the filling in of partial patterns in the blend. Elaborating the blended story occurs when we develop it according to its principles. In the case of *Phèdre*, elaboration of the blend leads to a great range of new meaning.

Phèdre is a story of sexual passion involving psychological subterfuge. Now consider a radically different story, one that connects divinity to humanity.

Human beings are able to invent concepts like *punishment, revenge,* and *retribution.* These concepts are the result of blending. In each case, there is an earlier scenario in which a character does something that is regarded as an offense, and a later scenario in which something is done to that person. If we took the two scenarios as separate, we would have two actions, and the second one (killing, inflicting physical pain, locking someone up, taking money from someone, depriving someone of a right or a privilege, even yelling at someone) could be regarded as a gratuitous offense, no different from the first. But when we integrate these two scenarios into one, we compress the two actions into one balanced unit. This compression does not change the facts of the first scenario, but it does change their status. The emergent meaning for the integration network is very rich. While the two scenarios, each on its own, are offensive, the blend is just, and this has consequences for the two scenarios themselves: because they sit in this blending network, the second action is permissible, and the first offense is *removed* or *neutralized* or *paid for*.

The human concept of *punishment* goes far beyond any evolutionary psychological motivation to dominate, intimidate, or discipline another person, as we see from the fact that a human being can be disturbed when an offender dies *unpunished*. Obviously, we cannot modify the future behavior of a corpse by dominating, intimidating, or disciplining it, and the corpse offers no threat or competition, so there is no possible evolutionary benefit to us of expending energy trying to do so. But human beings have double-scope imaginations. They can conceive of a hypothetical punishment, revenge, or retribution, and feel aggrieved that this blend is permanently counterfactual because the offender has died. Here is a revealing story on this subject: Spanish conquistador Don Juan de Oñate was accused, perhaps apocryphally, of having handed down extreme punishments to rebellious Acoma Pueblo Indians in 1599, including amputation of the right foot of all young Acoma men. Nearly four centuries later, an anonymous group claiming to be 'Native Americans and Native New Mexicans' took credit for cutting off the right foot of the monumental, heroic statue of Oñate at the Visitor Center at Alcalde north of Española, New Mexico (Lee 2001).

If we imagine a *just punishment* blending network in which the first story has reference to reality but both the second story and the blend are only hypothetical, then the offending party in the first story counts as *worthy of punishment*. The punishment is furthermore *unrealized*. This is a general template for a blending network. Applying this network not to a single person but instead to all of us in the aggregate, we have the familiar grand story of *guilty or sinful humanity, worthy of punishment*. That is one blending network. Now let us activate alongside that network an altogether different story in which a blameless man is crucified. Now we blend *guilty or sinful humanity* with the blameless man. In the new hyper-blend, we have the blameless man from one story but the sins of the human beings from the other. His crucifixion, according to the logic of the *just punishment* blending network, becomes recompense for the sins of humanity. His suffering excuses humanity from bearing the punishment.

This is a spectacular blended story, of the sort Fauconnier and I have called 'double-scope'. In a double-scope story network, there are input stories with different (and often clashing) organizing frames that are blended into a third story whose organizing frame includes parts of each of the input organizing frames. The blended story has emergent structure of its own. In the double-scope story of the crucifixion, one element in the blend, Jesus Christ, has, from the story of Jesus the Carpenter, the identity, biography, and character of Jesus, but also has, from the story of human beings who sin, the sins of the human beings. In the blend, Jesus is an individual who bears away the sins of the world, the *agnus dei qui tollis peccata mundi*. As Paul says in Romans 4:25, 'he was delivered over to death for our sins.' The punishment in the blend has a profound consequence for the input story with the human beings: they no longer must bear the punishment! The punishment has spent itself. Some of the human beings concerned may even feel, in virtue of this double-scope story, that their sins have been *removed*.

In the story of Jesus, he is *unsinning*. His counterpart in the story of humanity is the human beings, who are *sinful*. This is an absolute clash. In the blend, we integrate features of Jesus with features of the human beings, producing emergent structure according to which the human beings no longer must bear the consequences of their sins.

Perhaps not surprisingly, it is common for other inputs to be used to strengthen this double-scope story. We all know the abstract story in which someone bears a heavy burden for us, and the abstract story in which a force that results in displacement is balanced out by applying a countervailing force, and the story in which some specific animal, often a lamb, is sacrificed to allay a god or gods and thereby to dissuade them from bringing harm. All of these inputs are themselves complicated, and the story of the sacrificial lamb is itself already a complicated blend. In the final hyperblend that arises from integrating these many different input stories, Jesus Christ is at once the sacrificial lamb, the bearer of the burden, and the individual who is punished for the sins.

This blended story, like many double-scope blended stories, achieves the invaluable mental feat of compressing great and diffuse ranges of conceptual structure down to human scale. Although we are gripped by our sense of inadequacy and transgression, our minds cannot grasp at a shot all its origins and nuances. If we multiply that sense over all humankind, we obtain a result that is beyond human understanding, or would be, absent the conceptual power of double-scope blending. The Christ The Redeemer blending network provides one way to compress the human condition down to a comprehensible human-scale story, thereby to give us global insight. The blend contains one main man, Jesus, and one human-scale story of His suffering. The story happens in one place and lasts one day. He is crucified and mocked. He dies. He is deposed and buried. In the blend, our existential and ethical relation to the cosmos takes on the compressed intelligibility and memorability of a blow for a blow. Many, very many human beings, indeed *all* human beings are compressed into one. All their sins are compressed, and one man's pain pays for all. One death atones for all.

As we have already seen, a blended story can itself be an input to another blend. Cascading networks, of blend upon blend, can compress, in stepwise fashion, great reaches of thought and meaning to human scale. For example, *The Dream of the Rood*, passages of which, carved on the Ruthwell Cross, date from at least the early eighth century A.D., is a spectacular example of a cascade of blends. It uses the story of Christ the Redeemer, which we have seen is already a double-scope hyper-blend, as an input story to a further, more elaborate blend. *The Dream of the Rood* has many contributing scenarios. In it, a sinner relates a dream in which the Rood—the Holy Cross—appears to him and speaks to him about its experiences. This pyrotechnic blend is based on an everyday blending pattern according to which our perception of a physical object makes us feel as if the object is communicating to us something of its history. A souvenir, for example, communicates to us about the time, place, or event of which it is a souvenir. This is a minimal personification blend: one input has a person, another has a physical object in the presence of which we have memories or make inferences, and the blend has an object that is communicative about these memories and inferences and perhaps even intentional without actually being able to talk.

In *The Dream of the Rood*, this conventional blending network is developed so that the personified object receives even more projection from the concept of a person: the Cross can actually speak like a person, and in fact does.

Typically in everyday blends for 'communicative' objects, the content of the communication comes from memories we possess that are associated with the object, or from inferences we derive from seeing the object. In such typical cases, the communication cannot extend beyond memory and inference. But in *The Dream of the Rood*, the content of the Cross's speech goes beyond anything the auditor might remember or infer. The talking Cross has therefore received even more elaborate projection from the input containing the person than is usual: the Cross, like the person, can tell us things we would never have guessed or remembered. The reader becomes the audience for the talking sinner who relates his story, and so indirectly the audience for the Cross, which relates its story.

Remarkably, the Cross is also blended with Christ, for not only is the Cross stained with blood on the right side, it also bleeds on the right side. This is a blend of an instrument (the Cross) with a patient (the person crucified on the Cross). The story of the manufacture of the Cross out of a tree and its use as an instrument of crucifixion is blended with the story of Christ and his crucifixion: Christ is blended with Cross, and being crucified is blended with being used as the instrument of crucifixion. The Cross reports the history in which it was taken by foes from the forest and forced into shape for an evil design. It suffered like Christ and was wounded with the same nails; Cross and Christ were both mocked. The Christ-like suffering of the Cross confers upon it both immortality and the ability to heal sinners: the Cross informs the sinner that those who wear the Cross need not be afraid, that the kingdom of heaven can be sought through the Cross.

The Cross is also blended with the sinner who relates the dream, creating a blend of identification. The sinner is stained with sins, wounded with wrongdoings, downcast. The Cross, too, felt sinful: it had been the slayer of Christ. But it was redeemed, and in just the same way, the sinner can be redeemed. This is the crucial moral of the blended tale.

Perhaps most interestingly, the Cross is also blended with a thane, and Christ with the lord served by that thane. In the story remembered and related by the Cross, Christ is a strong, young hero, who hastens to the Cross, stouthearted, in order to climb it, who strips and climbs the cross, bold in the sight of the crowd. The Cross describes itself as having done its duty to serve the Lord's will, even though it was afraid and was tempted to fail the Lord. As Peter Richardson has shown, the purpose of this blend is to give a model of what a good thane is and does (Richardson 1999).

The author of *The Dream of the Rood* blends Cross and thane so the Cross can count as a thane. The Cross represents its actions as perfect and praiseworthy service to a lord, and this evaluation, combined with the holy status of the Cross and its evident prestige (all that gold, all those adoring angels) makes it, in the blend, not just a thane but a paragon among thanes. As a result, it provides a model for those who would be thanes. The poem therefore has a particular rhetorical purpose which Richardson calls 'making thanes'. It offers a complicated blend, in which the history of the Cross as a physical object is blended with the frame of a thane's life, making the Cross the counterpart of the thane and Christ the counterpart of the thane's lord, and resulting in a particular emergent biography in the blend, of an exceptionally honored and successful thane-Cross, all with the purpose of projecting back to the contributing story of *thane* a divinely approved model of how a thane should act. To the extent that this poem is meant to persuade a reader to be a good thane through aspirational identification with the ideal, it prompts yet a further blend in which the reader is blended with the ideal thane.

Very many individual human beings, along with their complicated, aggregate, overarching story, can be compressed to human scale if we blend that diffuse array with a story that is already compressed, such as the story of a single agent involved in a clear, human-scale set of events. The diffuse story thereby acquires the compression of the compressed story. This is exactly what we see in the case of Christ the Redeemer. But here is another example of the same phenomenon , which on its surface looks completely different. In *Seabiscuit: An American Legend,* Laura Hillenbrand tells the story of a racehorse as if it were an allegory of the American people during the Depression (Hillenbrand 2001). *USA Today* borrowed this portrayal in its announcement of *Seabiscuit* as its 'book club pick':

> *Seabiscuit* tells how an unimpressive older horse with crooked legs and a short tail stole the hearts and minds of the American people during the Depression. In 1938, the No. 1 newsmaker was not FDR or Hitler; it was a horse that defined the word 'underdog'.

> It was the indefinable quality of 'being game' that captured Americans. As one observer put it, Seabiscuit would rather die than be beaten in a race. Yet, unlike many champion thoroughbreds, his off-track personality was low-key, appealing and, frankly, lazy. He was a glutton for food and enjoyed the friendship of a horse named Pumpkin.

> In short, he seemed the American Everyhorse, the equine version of how we see ourselves. Yet his race against the favored War Admiral is considered the greatest horse race in history. (Donahue 2002)

In this Seabiscuit-Americans network, one story has the American populace with its sufferings, poverty, and challenges, facing Hitler, who, in 1938, took control of Austria and the Sudetenland and showed signs of annexing Poland. The other story has a horse, supported by a ramshackle team, who competes against the intimidating War Admiral and wins. In the double-scope blend, we have an element that is both Seabiscuit and the American people. This compresses 'the American people', something diffuse and vague, to human scale. Nationalism, like religion, depends on such compressed, double-scope stories for its existence, which is why robust nationalism, like religion, did not come into existence until after human beings evolved the capacity for double-scope blending.

The story of Phèdre belongs to elite literature, both Greek and French, and the story of Christ the Redeemer belongs to successful religion. The story of *The Dream of the* Rood belongs to both. The story of Seabiscuit belongs to adult nationalism. But double-scope stories are not restricted to a particular human rank, a class of conceptual domains, or a kind of cultural practice. On the contrary, they are everywhere, the inescapable hallmark of all cognitively modern human beings. Children pluck forbidden fruit routinely, as part of what it means to be a human child and to learn human culture. My nine-year-old son, Jack, whose younger brothers are Peyton and William, and whose twenty-year-old sitter is Elizabeth, said at the dinner table ten minutes ago, entirely out of the blue, 'If we were all chickens, you, William, would be about Elizabeth's age, you, Peyton, would be about dad's age, and me, dad, and mom would all be dead of old age. We are all five alive. We are lucky we are not chickens.' However ridiculous it may seem at first blush, I assert that the ability to pluck such forbidden fruit—blending chickens and human beings, for example, which we should never confuse—is the defining mental ability of cognitively modern human beings, and the source of our creativity and knowledge. These mental operations—disobeying the command of the present to activate alongside it the story of chickens as they progress through life, and then plucking forbidden mental fruit by blending the chickens with specific members of a human family—these are instances of the basic mental operations that make us cognitively modern.

Activating incompatible stories and blending them results in dramatic emergent meaning. In the We-Are-Chickens blend, the six-year-old Peyton is in advanced middle age and the parents and the eldest child are dead. This emergent meaning has inferential consequences for the real story, where human beings are now *lucky*, a feature that, like *hapless, safe,* and *mistaken*, is inconceivable without forbidden-fruit blending.

Such blends depend upon backstage precision and care in the mapping and the blending. For example, in the We-Are-Chickens blend, dad is dead because of his chronological age, but Peyton, who is 'dad's age' in the blend, is not dead. How can this be? The answer is that 'dad's age' for Peyton in the blend is advanced middle age *for a chicken*, a life-stage which a chicken (we infer from the assertion) reaches after about six years, Peyton being six years old; while dad's state for dad in the blend is the state of a chicken born 48 years ago, that is, dead. In interpreting the assertion, we all immediately and unconsciously make complicated calculations to arrive at this emergent structure, even as we project elements and relations selectively to the blend. My nine-year-old son is not Racine, but they belong to the same species. Any normal member of our species is equipped with these mental operations, and no member of any other species has them.

Double-scope blending is also manifestly evident in children from an early age. *The Runaway Bunny*, published in 1942, is one of the two most popular and successful picture books for two-year-olds (Brown 1942). In *The Runaway Bunny*, a little bunny talks with his mother (already a blend, if one of the most routine). He says that he is going to run away, and his mother quite predictably says she is going to come after him. Already we have a blended story. We activate the story of a human mother and her child and a story of a little bunny who is being chased by its bunny mother. The opening illustration shows a depiction that could be a representation of the bunny story. But then the blending takes off. The little bunny says, 'If you run after me, I will become a fish in a trout stream and I will swim away from you.' The illustration now shows a bunny in a stream. His mother responds, 'If you become a fish in a trout stream, I will become a fisherman and I will fish for you.' So the already-blended story of the talking bunnies is now blended with the story of a fisherman fishing. The accompanying illustration refers undeniably to this new blend with the fish, and not just to normal bunnies, as we see from the fact that, in it, the mother is walking on two legs and reaching up toward fishing equipment. In the next illustration, the mother, wearing waders and holding a net, stands in the trout stream, casting a line with a carrot at the end. The little bunny is swimming toward the carrot.

Two-year-olds have not the slightest difficulty constructing the blended story and drawing the appropriate inferences. If a two-year-old who knows that fishermen use hooks and bait to fool fish, to snag them, to hurt them, to haul them in, and to eat them is looking at the illustration of the mother-bunny-fisherman fishing for the baby-bunny-fish with a carrot-hook on the end of the line, and you begin to ask questions, the dialogue goes like this: 'What is this?' 'A carrot.' 'What is it for?' 'To catch the baby bunny.' 'What will the baby bunny do?' 'Bite the carrot.' 'Will he swim away down the river.' 'No. He bites the carrot.' 'What is the mommy bunny doing?' 'Fishing for the baby bunny.' 'What is she?' 'She's a fisherman.' 'Does the baby bunny know his mommy is fishing for him.' 'No. He wants the carrot.' 'Can the baby bunny swim?' 'Yes. He's a fishie.' 'Does he have a fishie tail.' 'No. He's a bunny.' 'Will the carrot hurt the baby bunny?' 'No! The mommy doesn't hurt the bunny!' 'What will happen when the baby bunny bites the carrot?' 'The mommy bunny will pull him in and hug him and kiss him.' 'Will he smell like a fish?' 'No! He's a baby bunny!'

When the little bunny says he will become a fish, he is asserting a new blended story as a vehicle for escape from the first blended story in which bunnies talk and the little bunny runs away from home. In the little bunny's new blended story, the bunny is a fish, but its mother, in the little bunny's view, is projected to the new story as merely a talking-mommy-bunny, and is, as planned, incapacitated. But the mother asserts a corre-spondence between herself and a fisherman. She insists that she projects in to the new story as a talking-mommy-bunny-fisherman. The mechanism of this projection is *change*: she will 'become a fisherman.' Here, she simply follows the pattern originally laid down by the little bunny, who asserted that he could escape the first blended story and land in a new blended story through an act of willful change on his part, transforming himself into a fish (or more accurately, a talking-baby-bunny-fish).

This sets the pattern for the rest of the book. Every time the little bunny insists that he will escape the blended story by creating a new blend, the mother projects herself into that new blend by assuming a role there that gives her more power and ability than the baby bunny foresaw. The little bunny cannot seriously deny her power to project herself in this fashion, because it was he who provided the pattern of projection in the first in-stance, and, more forcefully, because she has an absolute motivation that nothing can withstand: 'For you are my little bunny.'

Thus, when the little bunny says 'If you become a fisherman, I will become a rock on the mountain, high above you,' the mother responds 'if you become a rock on the mountain high above me, I will be a mountain climber, and I will climb to where you are.' And so the little bunny becomes a crocus in a hidden garden, and so the mother becomes a gardener and finds him, and so the little bunny becomes a bird and flies away, and so the mother becomes the tree that the bird comes home to (the tree looks like topiary, in the shape of a mother bunny, to which the winged bunny flies), and so the bunny becomes a sailboat and sails away, and so the mother becomes the wind and blows the little bunny where she wants, and so the little bunny joins a circus and flies away on a flying trapeze, and so the mother becomes a tightrope walker and walks across the air to the little bunny, and so the little bunny becomes a little boy and runs into a house, and so the mother becomes the little boy's mother and catches him and hugs him (the illustration shows the mother bunny rocking the little boy-bunny in a rocking chair).

The little bunny at last realizes it is hopeless: the mother has the general trick of coming into any story, no matter how ingeniously blended, and catching him. Therefore, none of the blended stories removes him from his mother. 'Shucks,' says the little bunny. 'I might just as well stay where I am and be your little bunny.' And so he does. 'Have a carrot,' says the mother bunny. The last illustration returns us to the original blended story, in which mother and little bunny are in a comfortable room, which is a rabbit hole in the bottom of a tree. The mother gives the little bunny a carrot.

I expect that for many children, there is another story that is being blended with each of these blended little bunny stories, namely, the story of their own lives. In that case, the children who are hearing the story blend themselves with the little bunny as it goes through each of the blended stories in the cascade. This feat of multiple double-scope blending provides the inference that no matter what the human two-year-old does to explore its freedom and assert its independence from its mother, in the end, mother will always be there, to find, retrieve, catch, cuddle, and rock the human child. Perhaps this accounts in part for the popularity of the book among two-year-olds.

It is worth taking a moment to marvel at the fact that a complicated string of fantastic blended double-scope stories ends up being profoundly persuasive and reassuring for the real story which the real child actually inhabits. The child cannot actually test its independence so thoroughly in reality without running unacceptable risks, but it can do so through mental simulation, and the simulations change the child's view of its own reality. The adult reading the story might also be persuaded by these simulations to conceive of the relationship in a certain way. Mother and child have the opportunity to conceive of their real roles by activating stories they in fact could not possibly inhabit. This is amazing.

There is another familiar situation that calls for persuasion: a suitor courting a young woman. In the Provençal song 'O, Magali,' embedded in Frederic Mistral's 1858 *Mireille*, a suitor calls from the street below to his beloved, Magali, who is in her room above (Mistral 1996 [1858]).[2] The song uses the identical abstract pattern deployed in *The Runaway Bunny*: Magali launches a blended story as a means of escape from the present story, but it doesn't work, and so, repeatedly, a new blend must be launched from the old. Each time, the resourceful suitor finds a way to enter the new blend as something linked to his beloved. These links emphasize physical pursuit, touch, and possession. Magali says she will not respond to the serenade but instead turn into a fish and escape into the sea. In this way, the beloved, like the child, issues a challenge. Here is the ensuing cascade of metamorphoses:

—If you become a fish, I will become a fisherman.

—Well then, I will become a bird and fly away.

—Then I will become a hunter and hunt you.

—Then I will become a flowering herb in the wild.

—Then I will become water and sprinkle you.

—Then I will become cloud and float away to America.

—Then I will become the sea breeze and carry you.

—Then I will become the heat of the sun.

—Then I will become the green lizard who drinks you in.

—Then I will become the full moon.

—Then I will become the mist that embraces you.

—But you will still never have me, because I will become the virginal rose blossoming on the bush.

—Then I will become the butterfly who kisses you and becomes drunk on you.

—Go ahead, pursue me, run, run. You will never have me. I will become the bark of the great oak hidden in the dark forest.

—Then I will become the tuft of ivy and will embrace you.

---

[2] I am grateful to Manuela Carneiro da Cunha for bringing this poem to my attention.

—If you do that, you will cling only to an old oak, for I will have turned into a novice in the monastery of Saint Blaise.

—If you do that, I will become a priest and be your confessor and hear you.

Now, in *Mireille,* this song is being recounted by Noro to a group of young women, who at this point tremble and beg Noro to tell them what happens to this novice, this 'moungeto', who was an oak, and a flower, moon, sun, cloud, herb, bird, and fish. Noro says, 'If I recall, we were at the place where she said she would take refuge in a cloister, and her ardent admirer responded that he would enter as her confessor, but we see again that she sets up a great obstacle':

—If you pass through the portal of the convent, you will find all the nuns walking in a circle around me, because you will see me laid out under a shroud.

This is an absolute obstacle indeed. But the suitor is undeterred:

—If you become the poor dead girl, I will therefore become the earth. And then I shall have you.

This suite of blends has a profound persuasive effect on Magali, and it leads her to think about changing her judgment of the suitor's character, or at least her visible response to his courtship. She says, 'Now I begin to believe that you are not merely engaging in pleasantries with me. Here is my little glass ring for remembrance, handsome young man.'

The Runaway Bunny and 'O, Magali' rely on another kind of double-scope blending that is both common and effective. The pattern of the story-telling has a form that is blended with the event structure of the narrated human interactions. The lives of the mother and child, or lover and beloved, are vast, uncertain, and diffuse, stretching over time and place, conditioned by every kind of environment, emotion, and intentionality common to human lives. The question is, what will happen in these lives? Will these lives have any reliable structure? By contrast, the form of the expression has a very crisp structure: two people speak in a short, witty conversation. The conversation consists of a challenge begun by one of them, and each time, the challenge is answered. Whenever the child or beloved escapes into a new blend, the mother or lover follows ingeniously and to the same effect, until the child or beloved becomes convinced by the pattern. The pattern of the brief *conversation* is blended with the pattern of the extended *life.* The dedication of the mother or lover in staying with the witty *conversation*, always rising to the *rhetorical* challenge during the ten or fifteen minutes it takes to conduct the conversation, is blended with the dedication of the mother or lover in *life*, always rising to the *biographical* challenge of staying with the child or beloved through changes over years.

Quite interestingly, the quality of the rhetorical performance of the mother or lover is indicative of the biographical performance toward the child or the beloved. Why should the beloved give the lover her little glass ring just because he can conduct the exchange? Why should a brief, human-scale conversation between two people have any influence on her judgment of his character and his future performance as a lover? The answer is that she, like all cognitively modern human beings, can do double-scope blending, and in this case, blends two radically different things, namely a brief rhetorical form and the rhythm of an extended life. Fiction, poems, and plays are brief and cannot contain patterns that are diffuse in life. But they can prompt us to blend such diffuse patterns with human-scale stories and human-scale forms to produce blends that count as human-scale representations of the otherwise diffuse stories. The result is compressed blends that give us insight into what is otherwise beyond our grasp.

Here is an example which depends explicitly on blending two radically incompatible scenarios, one of them centrally concerned with form. In *Harold and the Purple Crayon* (Johnson 1981), written for three-year-olds, Harold uses his purple crayon to draw, and whatever he draws is real. His world is a blend, of spatial reality and its representation. In the blend, the representation is fused with what it represents. When Harold needs light to go for a walk, he draws the moon, and so he has moonlight. The moon stays with him as he moves. In the real story of walking in the moonlight, the moon cannot be created by drawing or come into existence at someone's will. Alternatively, in the little story of a child drawing a moon, the drawn moon cannot emit moonlight or float along in the sky as the artist's companion. But in the blend, there is a special blended moon with special emergent properties: it comes into existence by being drawn, and it hangs in the sky and gives light.

The mechanisms of blending that give us this special blended moon work generally throughout *Harold and the Purple Crayon*. When Harold wants to return home, he draws a window around the moon, thereby positioning the moon where it would appear in his window if he were in his bedroom, and so he is, ipso facto, presto-chango, in his bedroom, and can go to sleep. Child Harold's blended world has new kinds of causality and event shape that are unavailable from either the domain of drawing or the domain of spatial living.

The projection to this blend, and the completion and elaboration of the blend, are not algorithmic, not predictable from the contributing spaces, but instead have considerable room for alternatives. For example, when one draws, one often makes practice sketches, erasures, and mistakes that do not count as the finished drawing. Which kinds of marks made with the purple crayon shall count as reality in the blend? The answer chosen by the author of the book is all of them. When Harold's hand, holding the purple crayon, shakes as he backs away in a line from the terribly frightening dragon, the resulting mark is a purple line of wavy scallops: 'Suddenly he realized what was happening. But by then Harold was over his head in an ocean.'

The principle for connecting the purple sketches to elements of reality is, predictably, image-schematic matching: if the sketch matches the iconic form of something, it is that thing. But it appears that this matching is constrained: a given purple sketch can be matched to exactly one reality. For example, once the wavy line is an ocean, Harold cannot transform the ocean into a cake by perceiving the wavy line as icing on a cake. Yet in a differently conceived blend, in a different book, the character who does the drawing might possess the power to recast reality by perceiving the sketch first one way and then another.

In Harold's blend, all of physical space is a piece of paper on which to draw. What are the possibilities in the blend of blank paper/empty space? Can Harold move as he wishes through it? The answer chosen by the author is that once something is drawn that gives Harold relative location, he is constrained by some of the physics of the real world and his relative location. For example, once he draws the hull of a boat and part of the mast, he must climb the mast to draw the parts of the boat he could not reach from the ground. When he wants to find his house, he begins to draw a mountain which he can climb for a better view. He climbs the part he has drawn so he can draw more to climb. But as he looks down over the other side of the mountain, he slips, and since he has been positioned with respect to the mountain, the blank space is now thin air, so he must be falling. He is obliged to draw a balloon to save himself from crashing.

There is another blend at work in *Harold and the Purple Crayon*: the parent who reads this story to a child is prompting the child to make a blend of himself and Harold so the child will be more tractable at bedtime. This is a conventional blend in children's literature, at least children's literature of the sort that weary parents prefer to read to children at what the parents regard as the child's bedtime. In this template for a blending network, the story in the present environment is blended with whatever story is being read, in the hope of leading the child to make the present story conform to a favored event in the blend, namely, the child's pleasant willingness to go to bed.

The human ability to conceive of a small story—with objects, agents, and actions—that counts as an understanding of the present environment is by now well-recognized for its central role in cognition. This ability to parse the world as consisting of stories is leveraged by two additional mental abilities. The first is the ability to activate simultaneously, without confusion, two or more different stories that conflict resolutely. The second is our amazing creative ability to pluck forbidden mental fruit by blending two conflicting stories into a third story with emergent structure and meaning.

We are at the beginning of a period of research into the principles of double-scope blending, the neurobiological mechanisms that make it possible, the pattern of its unfolding in the human infant, and the path of its descent in our species. This is a challenging research program, one that will require the combined efforts of cognitive neuroscientists, developmental psychologists, evolutionary biologists, and scholars of story. Any child can pluck forbidden fruit, but we adults are only now starting to explain it.

References

Brown, M. W. 1942. *The Runaway Bunny*. With Pictures by Clement Hurd. New York: Harper and Row.

Coulson, S. 2001. *Semantic Leaps: Frame-shifting and Conceptual Blending in Meaning Construction*. New York and Cambridge: Cambridge University Press.

Coulson, S., and G. Fauconnier. 1999. Fake Guns and Stone Lions: Conceptual Blending and Privative Adjectives. *Cognition and Function in Language*, eds. B. Fox, D. Jurafsky, & L. Michaelis, 143-58. Palo Alto, CA: CSLI Publications.

Donahue, Deirdre. 2002. Book Club Is Spurred to Choose 'Seabiscuit'. *USA Today*, Thursday, 23 May 2002, page 1D.

Fauconnier, G. In preparation. Compressions de Relations Vitales dans les Réseaux d'Intégration Conceptuelle.

Fauconnier, G. and M. Turner. 2002. *The Way We Think: Conceptual Blending and the Mind's Hidden Complexities*. NY: Basic Books.

Frith, C., R. Perry, and E. Lumer, 1999. The Neural Correlates of Conscious Experience: An Experimental Framework. *Trends in Cognitive Sciences* 3.3: 105-14.

Glenberg, A. M. 1997. What Memory Is For. *Behavioral and Brain Sciences* 20: 1-55.

Grush, R., and N. Mandelblit. 1997. Blending in Language, Conceptual Structure, and the Cerebral Cortex. *The Roman Jakobson Centennial Symposium: Acta Linguistica Hafniensia* 29, eds. P. A. Brandt, F. Gregersen, F. Stjernfelt, and M. Skov, 221-37. Copenhagen: C.A. Reitzel.

Herman, V. 1999. Deictic Projection and Conceptual Blending in Epistolarity. *Poetics Today* 20.3: 523-42.

Hillenbrand, L. 2001. *Seabiscuit: An American Legend*. New York: Random House.

Hiraga, M. 1999. Blending and an Interpretation of *Haiku*. *Poetics Today* 20.3: 461-82.

Hobson. J. A. 1988. *The Dreaming Brain*. New York: Basic Books.

Hutchins, E. In preparation. Material Anchors for Conceptual Blends.

Johnson, C. 1981. *Harold and the Purple Crayon*. New York: Harpercollins.

Jouvet, M. 1979. What Does a Cat Dream About? *Trends in the Neurosciences*, 2: 280-85.

Jouvet, M. and F. Michel. 1959. Correlations électromyographiques du sommeil chez le chat décortiqué et méséncephalique chronique. *Comptes rendus des séances de l'Académie des Sciences*. 153.3: 422-25. <http://ural195-6.univ-lyon1.fr/articles/jouvet/cras_59-2/sommaire.html>.

Lakoff, G., and R. Núñez. 2000. *Where Mathematics Comes From: How the Embodied Mind Brings Mathematics into Being*. Basic Books.

Lee, M. 2001. 'Oñate's Foot: A Legend Grows.' *ABQjournal*, Friday, March 23, 2001.<http://www.abqjournal.com/paperboy/text/news/284240news03-23-01.htm.>

Liddell, S. 1998. Grounded Blends, Gestures, and Conceptual Shifts. *Cognitive Linguistics* 9.3: 283-314.

Mandelblit, N. 2000. The Grammatical Marking of Conceptual Integration: From Syntax to Morphology. *Cognitive Linguistics* 11.3-4: 197-252.

Mistral, F. 1996 [1858]. *Mireille. Œuvres Poétiques Complètes*, vol. 1, ed. Pierre Rollet, 14-456. Barcelona: R. Berenguié. 'O, Magali' is printed on pages 112-123.

Pascual, E. 2002. *Imaginary Trialogues: Conceptual Blending and Fictive Interaction in Criminal Courts*. Utrecht, The Netherlands: Landelijke Onderzoekschool Taalwetenschap.

Racine, J. 1962 [1677]. *Phèdre*, trans. M. Rawlings. New York: E. P. Dutton & Co., Inc.

Racine, J. 1986 [1677]. *Phaedra*, trans. R. Wilbur. San Diego: Harcourt Brace Jovanovich.

Richardson, P. 1999. Making Thanes: Literature, Rhetoric and State-Formation in Anglo-Saxon England. *Philological Quarterly* 78 (Winter/Spring): 215-32.

Sinding, M. 2002. Assembling Spaces: The Conceptual Structure of Allegory. *Style* 36.3: 503-23.

Sweetser, E. 1999. Compositionality and Blending: Semantic Composition in a Cognitively Realistic Vramework. *Cognitive Linguistics: Foundations, Scope, and Methodology*, eds. T. Janssen and G. Redeker, 129-62. Berlin and New York: Mouton de Gruyter.

Turner, M. 1996. *The Literary Mind: The Origins of Thought and Language*. New York: Oxford University Press.

Turner, M. 2001. *Cognitive Dimensions of Social Science: The Way We Think About Politics, Law, Economics, and Society.* New York: Oxford University Press.

Turner, M. 2002a. *L'Imagination et La Créativité: Conférences au Collège de France.* Berkeley: The Berkeley Electronic Press. <http://www.bepress.com/casbs/monographs-imagination.>

Turner, M. 2002b. The Cognitive Study of Art, Language, and Literature. *Poetics Today* 23.1: 9-20.

Zbikowski, L. 2001. *Conceptualizing Music: Cognitive Structure, Theory, and Analysis.* New York: Oxford University Press.

6

Unnarratable Knowledge: The Difficulty of Understanding Evolution by Natural Selection

H. PORTER ABBOTT

1 Introduction

It is a commonplace that broad acceptance of evolution by natural selection has been impeded by factors built into the concept itself. Three are invoked almost everywhere in the literature. It is incompatible with religious accounts of creation. It is indifferent to vice or virtue in its system of rewards. And it requires us to think in terms of 'deep time', a capability which has gone unselected because we have had no species need for it. My argument is that there is an additional factor: the immense difficulty of narrativizing natural selection. This argument assumes that, as a general rule, human beings have a cognitive bias toward the clarity of linear narrative in the construction of knowledge.[1] At the same time, of course,

---

Narrative Theory and the Cognitive Sciences.
David Herman (ed.).
Copyright © 2003, CSLI Publications.

the argument has to assume that we can exceed this bias. In the final section of this chapter, I suggest that the kind of narrative challenge Darwin required of his readers can be found in areas of knowledge quite distant from the evolution of species (including economics and mob behavior). The special problem Darwin faced, and that Darwinians still face, is the combination of his idea's immense, wide-ranging importance and the fact that there is no unencumbered way of packaging it in narrative form without serious distortion. This inherent narrative difficulty may help explain why this theory in particular, more than all other major scientific theories, is rejected by the nonscientific public (Scott 1997: 263). It may also help explain why many scientists who otherwise supported Darwin were resistant to the key principle of natural selection (Mayr 2001: 86-7). And it may finally explain why Darwinian evolution has been subjected to so many narrative re-workings that invariably distort to the degree that they seek a clear narrative rendering.

Put briefly, the difficulty with evolution by natural selection arises because neither *natural selection* nor *species*, as they were conceptualized by Darwin, are entities with agency. Worse, they do not seem to be narrative entities at all (neither Propp's 'characters' [Propp 1968 (1928)] nor Greimas's 'actors' and 'actants' [Greimas 1983 (1966)], nor Chatman's 'existents' [Chatman 1978]). One faces, then, the difficulty of constructing an explanatory narrative that shows agency but that has to make do with an apparent lack of entities and even an apparent lack of events, without which, of course, there can be no narrative. Yet because natural selection is a way of understanding change over time, which in turn would appear to be a kind of action, it is difficult to find other terms with which to describe it.

This is a difficulty that has persisted to the present day. In *The Selfish Gene*, for example, Richard Dawkins, one of Darwin's hardest nosed exegetes, exacerbated the difficulty by training attention on an entity that could be isolated—the gene—and then endowing it, not only with agency, but purpose: 'what is a single selfish gene trying to do? It is trying to get more numerous in the gene pool. Basically it does this by helping to program the bodies in which it finds itself to survive and reproduce'. Dawkins acknowledged that he was allowing himself 'the license of talking about genes as if they had conscious aims', but claimed that we can always reassure 'ourselves that we could translate our sloppy language back into respectable terms if we wanted to' (Dawkins 1976: 88). As Katherine Hayles points out, Dawkins' 'sloppy language' is 'much more than attractive giftwrap. On the contrary, it is central to the construction of a narrative in which the gene is cast as protagonist' (Hayles 2001: 148). The

---

evolutionary, cited later in this essay would seem also to lend strong support to the hypothesis that humans are indeed equipped with this sort of bias.

result is an unresolved contradiction that goes to the heart of the problem of narrativizing natural selection. One finds this everywhere in evolutionary discourse. Dawkins's coinage for the basic unit of cultural replication, the 'meme', for example, was taken over by Susan Blackmore along with Dawkins's 'sloppy language': 'memes compete among themselves and evolve rapidly in some direction, and genes must respond by improving selective imitation—increasing brain size and power along the way. Successful memes thus begin dictating which genes will be most successful. The memes take hold of the leash' (Blackmore 2000: 69).

But already in 1859 such language and the narrative paradigm it invokes can be found almost everywhere in *The Origin of Species*: 'Natural selection will modify the structure of the young in relation to the parent, and of the parent in relation to the young. In social animals it will adapt the structure of each individual for the benefit of the whole community; if the community profits by the selected change' (Darwin 1915a: 105-6). Here we have an action in which agency and intention are attributed to non-purposive insentience—'will modify', 'will adapt', 'for the benefit of'—and we have an entity without physical or empirical embodiment that is said to drive a process that is necessarily and inescapably physical. There is, in fact, neither an entity or actor driving something, nor an entity or actant being driven. There is simply, in Daniel Dennett's words, 'a cascade of algorithmic processes feeding on chance', a cascade that is 'itself the product of a blind algorithmic process' (Dennett 1995: 59).[2]

Darwin shows the same guarded awareness that Dawkins does regarding his 'characterization' of genes, but he deals with it more aggressively, as in this passage added to the third edition of *The Origin of Species*: 'It has been said that I speak of natural selection as an active power or Deity; but who objects to an author speaking of the attraction of gravity as ruling the movement of the planets? Everyone knows what is meant and is implied by such metaphorical expressions; and they are almost necessary for brevity. So again it is difficult to avoid personifying the word Nature; but I mean by Nature, only the aggregate action and product of many natural laws, and by laws the sequence of events as ascertained by us. With a little familiarity such superficial objections will be forgotten' (Darwin 1915a: 99). Darwin's focus here is on the problem of 'personifying' or anthropomorphizing 'Nature'—a problem in the discourse on natural selection that has been taken up by others.[3] But personification is only a

---

[2] But notice how, even in Dennett's careful language, conventional narrative can lurk in a metaphor: 'feeding on chance'.

[3] Gillian Beer (2000) placed a substantial part of the blame for Darwin's expressive difficulty on language itself, which, in her words, is 'anthropocentric' and 'always includes agency'. For an extended treatment of Darwin's anthropomorphizing of natural selection, including the implications of the phrase itself, see Robert M. Young (1985: 92-125). Young proposes three

trace element of the more serious problem of narrativization. From this perspective, the analogy Darwin invokes doesn't work to show that the problem is a 'superficial' one. Those who invoked 'the attraction of gravity', at least prior to 1859, were assuming gravity to be an actual physical force that could be said with some empirical justification (yet to be discovered) to 'rule' the planets. Even today, there are those physicists who invoke the currency of as yet undiscovered 'gravitons' through which this force can be said to propagate. Whether the concept is right or wrong, it can be clearly narrativized since it involves events that are explicable in terms of an agential force, that is, a narrative entity. But natural selection not only is not human, it is not a 'force'. Nor does it propagate. Nor, for that matter, does it 'select'. It is instead a pattern: the continually changing aggregate result of survivals and deaths, of propagation and the absence of progeny.

It is possible that Darwin sought a rhetorical advantage by casting natural selection as a narrative actor capable of agency. It allowed him to slide his discourse into functions occupied by the common narrative of divinely guided history. But it is more likely that he, like Dawkins and Blackmore and numerous others, found it difficult to speak of his subject in any other way. The result was a conceptual conflict that undermined the rhetorical advantage he sought and that made the theory vulnerable to popular incredulity or misinterpretation.[4]

2 Complex Causation: Narrative by Inference and Indirection

The central cognitive problem can be approached by attempting to define evolution by natural selection while remaining true to the conception of species that it entails. Here is one attempt at a definition: *the continually changing aggregate of ranges of trait variation throughout the complete palette of species traits as driven by the continually changing tally of the*

---

reasons for Darwin's language: it was an inevitable 'accident' of the available language; it reflected a persistence of theological rhetoric that was a pervasive aspect of Darwin's education; and it was a necessity of the level of abstraction at which Darwin had to operate if his exposition was to be persuasive (Young 1985: 97-98). Again, in my own argument, I am claiming a more universal cause of the problem—one that makes natural selection difficult to describe in any historical context or at any level of sophistication.

[4] Even among novelists who read Darwin favorably, his impact often meant not an abandonment but an alteration of narrative. As both Gillian Beer (2000) and George Levine (1988) have shown exceptionally well, the incompatibility of Darwin's idea with conventional narrative form had an immense impact on how novels were shaped in the latter part of the nineteenth century. In my view, however, Darwin's idea is yet more deeply resistant to narrative than scholars such as Beer and Levine have indicated.

procreative outcome of a multitude of little stories of love and death. Clearly this encompasses much narrative business (little stories of love and death). But, to grasp this process requires negotiating two levels of understanding, as represented in (1) below: the species level of evolutionary change and the level of events in the quotidian world. The former is usually (though as I hope to show quite imperfectly) narrativized in a single arc while the latter is jammed with narratable incidents. If the entire process can at all be described as narrative, it is narrative by inference or indirection.

(1)   Level 1: Species → Species → Species → Species
       Level 2: Individuals dying without issue or surviving and
                procreating

Separating the process into two levels helps expose the challenge to narrative imagining that Darwin forced upon his readers. There are at least three principal parts to this challenge.

1) *Narrative disjunction.* To understand the concept requires dissociating the lively narrative business in level two from the progression of species in level one. In other words, though all the little stories of love and death in level two are themselves quite absorbing, involving as they do creatures powered by fierce needs, and including even ourselves, there is no concern anywhere in this rich narrative tapestry for what is going on in level one. In fact, there is no entity anywhere in this entire process that has for an object the survival of the species. There is neither an intervening Force at work nor is there any imminent part of the process itself that is struggling, or even designed, to do something about species. There is not, for sure, any gene 'trying to get more numerous in the gene pool....by helping to program the bodies in which it finds itself to survive and reproduce.' Level two operates in complete indifference to level one. It is important to stress that this is not an absolute impediment to imagining the relationship of the two levels. Scientists engage in this kind of move all the time. But such imagining requires releasing oneself from the kind of narrative engagement that is represented in level two in order to see the relationship of that activity to what is going on in level one. The kind of narrative disengagement this requires is especially difficult when the stories involved are stories of beings like ourselves. I return to this feature of my argument when I take up evolution by acquired characteristics in section 3 below.

2) *The stochastic repetition of initiating conditions.* This difficulty concerns natural selection's dependency on random variation, perhaps the most frequently cited (and misunderstood) feature of natural selection. From the start, Darwin was excoriated for the depressing sovereignty of what George Bernard Shaw called 'mere dead luck and accident' (Shaw

1974: 278). But looked at as narrative, the constancy of the role of chance makes for a very bad story. Chance, of course, has always been a vital part of narrative and in both tragedy and comedy it has time and again played a key role: Oedipus happening to run into his father on the road to Thebes, Claudius happening to be at his prayers when Hamlet is ready to kill him. But in the great narratives chance draws its power from its infrequency. It occurs within a larger narrative shaped by human agency, and the feelings of both tragic helplessness and tragic dignity are magnified by the feeling that chance intervenes only at rare, if decisive, moments. Increase the frequency of chance events and you weaken the force of the story. Thomas Hardy, whose sense of tragedy was deeply inflected by his reading of Darwin, ran this risk often. But spread chance everywhere and you have something that transcends the limits of tolerable narrative, something strangely postmodern, like John Cage's *Concerto Grosso for 4 TV Sets and 12 Radios*. In Darwin's scheme of gradual change by infinite variations, chance is not simply decisive but a matter of starting anew always and everywhere, throwing the dice over and over. In this regard, Darwin's was a dull masterplot, an incursion of postmodern discord into one of the great ages of narrative orthodoxy. Again, as with the first difficulty discussed above, it is possible to adjust to, to understand, to tell this bad story, but such adjustment requires an active resistance to the narrative frames of common experience.

3) *The re-conception of species.* The third narrative difficulty is the most serious. It has to do with the fact that, where the second level involves the activity of entities in the real, empirical world (hamsters, humans), the first is a succession of averages with no real existence at all. One of the ironies of Darwin's title, *The Origin of Species*, is that the book it belongs to made the concept of species terminally indeterminate. Making the case for natural selection as the prime agent of species change required what Ernst Mayr called an 'entirely new way of thinking' by substituting variable populations for classes or types. During epochs of change, that is, species have no empirical reality but are rather floating averages of organic and behavioral traits. In Mayr's words: 'The ultimate conclusions of the population thinker and of the typologist are precisely the opposite. For the typologist, the type (*eidos*) is real and variation an illusion, while for the populationist the type (average) is an abstraction and only the variation is real. No two ways of looking at nature could be more different' (Mayr 2001: 75, 84). Species exist nowhere; what we have instead are individuals. Species are not selected; individuals are. But—and here's the rub—in the process, species change.[5]

---

[5] Some advocates of the theory of 'punctuated equilibrium'—that is, evolution by comparatively rapid change in smaller, isolated (allopatric) communities, succeeded by long

Figure 1 represents the two levels in another way.

Level 1: A running average of ranges of trait variation in combination

Length of tail
□□□□→ □□□□
Thickness of tail
□□□□→ □□□□
Flexibility of tail
□□□□→ □□□□
Rapidity of tail movement
□□□□→ □□□□
Depth perception
□□□□→ □□□□
Color perception
□□□□→ □□□□
Movement perception
□□□□→ □□□□
Acuity of night vision
□□□□→ □□□□
Peripheral vision
□□□□→ □□□□
etc. . . .

Range of procreative viability
□□□□→ □□□□

Level 2: Individual stories

Max & Mindy Mole mate & multiply.
Mort Mole mates not. Dies.
etc.

Legend: □□□□ = measurement numbers at the low end of the range of trait variation
□□□□ = measurement numbers at the high end of the range of trait variation

Figure 1. Expanded Bi-Level Narrative Model

---

periods of species stasis—have included in their arguments against 'Darwinian' gradualism the concept of 'species selection' (Eldredge 1985, 1995). I do not completely understand this latter concept, but whether one opts for the greater constancy of species change in gradualist schemes or the shorter epochs of change in 'punctuationist' schemes, I am convinced that the model I am suggesting must hold. In the punctuationist scheme, the evolutionary process still takes many generations covering periods of tens of thousands of years, and it is during such periods that species must necessarily be moving targets of aggregate average traits.

Here the first level is pictured as running averages of an enormous number of traits belonging to creatures, all of whom successfully inter-procreate; the second is pictured as an enormous number of stories involving these same creatures.

Granted, the entries under level one are much too crudely stated. 'Color perception' alone covers a myriad of variable features of color perception which lie well beyond my knowledge. But if you can imagine this list extending for perhaps a quarter of a mile, then imagine after each entry in level one a constantly changing digital read-out that is in some way recording the average range of that trait based upon the changing aggregate result of all the stories involving 'moles' in level two. Note especially that each digital read-out expresses at any one time not a single figure but a *range* of figures, since the idea of species encompasses not just traits but trait variations.

But with this third condition, have we finally passed the limits of the narratable? Can one not object, for example, that an aggregate of average traits is a kind of *entity*, and, if so, is there not a narrative of sorts in the combined action of all these little micro-narratives involving individual creatures as it *changes* this aggregate? Isn't this a narratable *event*? And why does it matter that this aggregate of traits is always and forever changing? Can the same not be said of the aggregate traits of a human being, surely the most common kind of entity to be found in narrative? Are not human beings constantly changing, both physically and mentally, with every passing minute of the day and night? And, finally, isn't it especially the case that there is an *event* (the *sine qua non* of narrative) at that moment when all the extant creatures of the allopatric community have lost the capability of successfully producing fertile offspring with any of the existing members of the original host community? This is the moment when the trait-range following the last entry in level one—'range of procreative viability'—excludes the possibility of producing fertile offspring with the original host community. What is the difference between this and any moment in the summer of 1941 when Ted Williams swung his bat and hit 400? Wasn't that an act in the physical world that changed an average in the virtual world? And didn't the fans go wild?

Well, yes and no. There are really two issues here, and for both of them the example of Ted Williams is somewhat misleading. The first has to do with treating abstractions as entities, narratable entities moreover that are affected by events in the empirical world. The example does indeed indicate one of many valid narratable instances when an act in the physical world is seen to have an effect in a world of abstraction. However, in this instance we have a single act (a hit) by a single entity (Ted) that directly causes a change in another entity (Ted's batting average) that then stays the same until his next at-bat. As an entity, the product of Ted's at-bats divided by his hits is at any time fixed and only changes when Ted does or does not get a hit when he is at bat. The narrative structure is lean, and the sequence of cause and effect is clear. By contrast, species ooze. They ooze, moreover, in no particular direction. In fact, they ooze in many directions at once. As for the moment when the range of procreative viability excludes the possibility of producing fertile offspring with the original host community, yes, this is an event, a silent, hidden event that takes place unheralded within the still ongoing ooze of species.

The second issue has to do with the 'real' bio-psychological complexity of Ted Williams and the way it seems to be quite irrelevant to the story as narrated. What we do in this case, and quite validly, I think, is essentialize Ted Williams. To grasp this narrative we do not have to have any awareness at all that Ted Williams is not only a mass of fluctuating bodily functions and shedding brain cells, but also a congeries of shifting self-reflexive subjective schemata that may actually screen the fact that there is no essential Ted there at all. Sanity in fact dictates that we do not. What we do when we narrate such short stories about Ted Williams is something we do with equal validity all the time. 'The judge sentenced Larry to thirty years in the pen; he got out in twelve and immediately robbed another bank. Alas, this was Larry's third strike, and the judge put him away for life.' This is a narrative that can be not only true but sufficient. We do not have to worry about the complexity of Larry or the judge. But what if we tried to tell this same 'story' without essentializing its main characters? What if, instead of featuring two characters of which it is sufficient to know that they had agency—that is, that they could act of their own will—we tried to see them instead as two continually changing semi-porous fields of bio-psychological processes interacting within a larger field? This is more like what we are up against.

So, is this the knock-out blow? Is evolution by natural selection, finally, unnarratable? The answer would appear to be No. But in order to understand this extraordinary narrative, you have to keep somewhere in your mind the enormous complexity not only of the running tally of aggregate average trait ranges (that is, species de-essentialized), but also the immense narrative complexity of what goes on in level two of the model. As narrative, it is narrative by inference and indirection, and it tells a story that is more grand and convoluted by some exponential factor than *War and Peace* or *A la recherche du temps perdu*. Somehow, in grasping the concept of evolution by natural selection, we register this complexity.

3 Narrative Sufficiency and Rhetorical Power

One implication of my argument is that, if acceptance of natural selection is impeded by its challenge to narrative thinking, causal theories that involve narrative clarity have a greater chance of broad acceptance among the general public. This is the case with creationism.[6] In its 'young earth' version, the creationist argument is not only free of the encumbrance of the evolution of species but also anchored in a cosmic masterplot that purports to account for all entities and all events. Unlike the theory of evolution by natural selection, it features an absolute entity ('I am that I am') with absolute agency. All earthly history, including the geological and paleontological record, is comprehended by 'young earth' creationists in three events—the creation, the fall, and the flood—with a fourth yet to come. 'The main key . . . to the true interpretation of the physical data relating to earth history, must lie in full recognition of the effects of creation, the Curse and the Flood' (Morris 1974: 215). What we have here is not simply narrative but a particular *story* compounded of what Barthes called 'nuclei' and Chatman called 'kernels': that is, constituent events, without which it would not be the story that it is. (2) illustrates:

(2)   Creation → Disobedience → Fall → Further disobedience →
         Flood…

There is room for much narrative business in the interstices, and it can be found amply in the Bible, but the constituent events stand out clearly at the level of a history featuring only one significant species and one near-extinction event.[7]

What works for creationists and against Darwinians is the principle of narrative salience. Creationists maintain narrative salience not simply by stressing the linearity of the masterplot and the singularity of its causal agent, but also by regularly avoiding any detailed accounting of how that causal agent is motivated in particular instances of His creation. One might assume, for example, that creationism's sheer lack of parsimony as a theory of universal history would necessarily generate extensive elaboration to accommodate objections that arise on every hand. For example, if the

---

[6] I hope it is clear to readers that, in what follows, I am in no way taking creationism seriously as a scientific theory. What interests me is its persistence as a popular theory, despite its extraordinary weakness as science.

[7] Because so much of the subject of evolution turns on a modern understanding of the history of the earth, much creationist discourse focuses on the Flood as a key event. Arguably the most influential text in 'young earth' creationism, Whitcomb and Norris's *The Genesis Flood* (1961), is entirely absorbed in accounting for the geological record as the effects of the flood recorded in Genesis.

Creator is not simply a primary and sustaining cause, but also endowed with absolute goodness, at once just and merciful and lacking in cruelty, then why must some babies be born without brains? Why must cats play with mice? Can the production of brainless babies and the torture of mice be redeemed? But in most 'young earth' discourse very little effort is made to respond to objections of this kind.

Focus is maintained instead on Norris's three constituent events of Biblical history. Where difficulties emerge, quite often a line is drawn and a mystery declared, since God's ways are beyond our mortal understanding.[8] Most obviously, this strategy can be seen as a way of cutting losses, that is, of avoiding the effort of defending the indefensible and, seen as such, it has driven critics to distraction. But my point is that whatever this strategy lacks in argumentative fair play it makes up for in preserving the narrative salience of the masterplot. As such, it actually confers rhetorical force, since the very lack of elaboration that mystery guarantees maintains focus on the single narrative. In other words, what the theory loses in scientific parsimony it gains in narrative portability. This would appear to be a distinct cognitive advantage: it can be stored in the mind, is readily accessible, and features an agent with wide-ranging permission to be mysterious. It is this combination that makes the theory portable, that is, that allows it at once to be easily carried about and to be freely applied and re-applied across the whole spectrum of creation. The cost of the strategy comes due when the sense of mystery is threatened by some other sense, like that of whimsy. Why, for example, should a rational god have carefully distributed the fossil record in such a way as to suggest that complex organisms evolved from simpler ones? Is this a joke? A test? A temptation to go astray?

A more sophisticated creationism was developed over 175 years ago by Georges Cuvier, who adapted the paleontological record to the Bible by multiplying Noah's flood into a series of deluges. This move toward a 'catastrophist' view of deep time accommodated both the uncomfortable fact of species extinction, which Cuvier was the first to demonstrate, as well as the gaps in the fossil record, which have always plagued evolutionists.

---

[8] It is, of course, also true that creationist arguments are in large part polemical. The object has been to attack Darwinian and neo-Darwinian evolution, not to develop a comprehensive defense of creationism. But when they appear, attempts to account for the vulnerable details of creationist natural history are almost inevitably sectarian. The narrative accounting of cat and mice, implicit in young earth creationism, runs something like the following. When Adam and Eve fell, all Creation including cats fell with them. The cruelty of cats, reborn from generation to generation, is a mark of their fallen nature. Mice, though seemingly innocent, are fallen as well. Therefore, the torture they endure, unjust as it may seem, is simply a working out of the higher justice. But rarely is there this degree of narrative elaboration, and the move of drawing the veil of mystery, though with greater sophistication, continues into some (though not all) present-day proponents of 'intelligent design'.

154 / H. PORTER ABBOTT

At the same time, Cuvier's catastrophism preserved creationism's narrative force *at the level of species* since each deluge was a case of divine intervention that included the creation of a new set of species. As (3) suggests, each of these events is a direct intervention at the level of species with no requirement of a second level:

(3)   Species → Intervention → Species → Intervention → Species

At the other end of the spectrum, some present-day advocates of 'intelligent design' have sought to avoid the embarrassments of 'young earth' creationists by taking no stand, at least as evolutionary theorists, on the nature of the supernatural entity who/which has intervened from time to time in the course of natural history. Michael Behe (1996), for example, without *specifically* implicating either God, gods, or extraterrestrials, refers to the 'irreducible complexity' of phenomena like the coagulation of the blood as sufficient evidence for the necessary intervention of some super-terrestrial entity. But here again, in a faint paradox, molecular complexity is invoked to support an overarching simplicity. In other words, irreducible complexity at the level of being supports causal simplicity at the level of narrative.

Creationism in all its forms is an excellent example of an accounting of human life and history that requires no 'reduction'. If it is accepted, in other words, there is no explanatory need to move downward to a more molecular level of explanation. The masterplot of divine causation sustains explanation at the level of narration, because that is the only level that counts. The entities that perform and the agency that they have are absolute.

At the center of my argument, however, has been the point that it is not evolution *per se* that resists narrative understanding but evolution by natural selection. What Darwin proposed was an idea that was not simply shocking to received ideas and dependent on a conception of time that was immense, but a version of evolution that was, quite literally, impossible to narrativize *at the level of species*. But evolution was in fact frequently narrativized at the species level. And there were any number of alternative versions of evolution that enjoyed both an historical reassurance and a narrative advantage similar to that of creationism. There were so many of these that the term 'evolutionism' was commonly taken to imply a positive, melioristic, teleology (Morton 1984: 58). Some were frankly Christian, like those of Charles Kingsley and Henry Drummond. Some were not, but depended all the same on the periodic interventions of supernatural agency. Advocates included the popular and influential St. George Jackson Mivant and, of all people, Alfred Russel Wallace. Wallace, with Darwin, was a co-discoverer of natural selection, and it was their joint presentation before the

Linnaean Society in 1858 that first gave the idea to the world. But Wallace came to restrict the operation of natural selection to the non-human natural world. Human evolution for Wallace had to be a separate process that required repeated intervention from a higher force. Here again, whatever complexity may exist in life itself, human evolution as a process guided by a mysterious hand was seen to have narrative sufficiency. Needless to say, these theories had other attractions, but doubtless an important advantage of narrative sufficiency was to make the theory portable, that is, easy to carry in the mind and easy to apply.

There were also versions of 'evolutionism' that did not necessarily invoke a process of intervention. Quite common was the 'saltationist' view that species change is sudden, represented in (4):

(4)   Species → Saltation → Species → Saltation → Species

In this view, species change occurs abruptly—members of the old species simply start giving birth to the new. This was the view relied upon by Robert Chambers in his 1844 volume, *Vestiges of Natural Creation*, and I believe it was also what Tennyson (1951) had in mind when he described Arthur Hallam, the subject of his 1850 elegy, *In Memoriam*, as 'a noble type / Appearing ere the times were ripe' (Epilogue, lines 138-9). Evolution by saltation, of course, can as equally accommodate a 'devolutionary' or even non-teleological view, but whatever the teleology, or lack of it, it is an easier concept to narrativize than that of evolution by natural selection because cause operates at the level of species:

Some other theories (but not all) involving the operation of a creative principle or life force are also more amenable to a clear narrative model working at the level of species. Far and away the commonest non-supernatural mechanism for evolution was that of acquired characteristics, and it creates an interesting complement to my argument. Originating with Lamarck, the theory argues that habitual use leads to augmentation of a capability, while habitual disuse leads to its diminution and eventual elimination. The habitual efforts of generations account for why hawks have sharp eyes, just as habitual neglect accounts for the mockery of eyes in moles. Part of the appeal of acquired characteristics lies in the way it mitigates the first and second narrative difficulties discussed in the two-part model above. With acquired characteristics, the narrative disjunction between levels one and two is less pronounced because the willed agency of the entities in the stories of level two is featured as a direct agent of species evolution in level one. At the same time, the agency of chance variation is replaced by the agency of the will. The narrative engagement aroused by this theory is especially gripping when the species is our own, for it credits the power of the will as an agent shaping the larger history that contains us. What we strive for as individuals we contribute to the species.

Since behavior in this sense is directly connected to species shaping, the two levels of change harmonize. Much melioristic evolutionary theorizing emphasized the theory of acquired characteristics specifically in accounting for the finer capabilities of civilized humans. No one pushed this theory further than the enormously influential and revered philosopher, Herbert Spencer. But even Darwin felt the appeal of Lamarck's idea, since it allowed us to build on the basic moral sense that we derived through natural selection, our 'sympathies having been rendered more tender and widely diffused through the effects of habit, example, instruction and reflection. It is not improbable that after long practice virtuous tendencies may be inherited' (Darwin 1915b: 626).

Darwin's hope, and to some degree Spencer's, was in effect to reduce the narrative disharmony between levels one and two by conceiving of the entire process as a team effort, with all of us pulling together in the same direction, acting as joint agents of the species to which we belong, and thus continually increasing the distance between us and the 'savage' Fuegians who so appalled Darwin (1915b: 633-34). The refinement of Europeans is a testimony of how, through combined effort, we remake ourselves. To this extent, the whole process can be narrativized without distortion at the level of species. (5) illustrates:

(5)   Species → Combined Effort → Species → Combined Effort →
        Species

But the possibility of such a final step in decomplicating the two-part narrative model through a theory of Lamarckian adaptation falls of its own weight. Without some supernatural coordinating power, evolution by acquired characteristics is no more a team endeavor than evolution by natural selection. If we may at times pull together, we also more commonly pull in different directions. It follows that a fully developed accounting of evolution by acquired characteristics would require something of the same two-level complexity that is needed to encompass evolution by natural selection.

4 Further Implications

The example above involving Larry and the judge suggests that the problem of narrativizing natural selection may be seen as an instance of a more general problem concerning levels of narrative knowing. Just as Darwin may have demystified species as clearly definable categories, so at the same time he may have, by example and without necessarily intending it, exposed the distortion that in comparable instances is created by narrative at the molar (species) level of representation. It is in fact possible that the narrative problem of grasping natural selection may be the rule rather than the exception. That is, when it is necessary to understand complex causalities by 'reduction' (to use the term in the sense commonly intended in scientific methodology[9]), overarching narratives (or, in more precise narratological terms, 'stories' or 'fabulas') must give way to a vision that includes a vast subsidiary field made up of swarms of interacting micro-narratives.

For example, the common descriptive currency regarding economic markets is highly narrativized. It speaks of the 'behavior' of putative 'entities' like the *stock market* or even individual *stocks*. On a daily basis we are told encouraging stories ('the market rallied after hearing the good news from leading indicators') and sad ones ('Cisco dove 40 points and failed to recover in late action'). What is happening descriptively here flows from the same kind of necessity that Dawkins spoke of when he invoked the 'license' to use 'sloppy language'. But, whatever the necessity, what is being freely narrativized is in fact something much more like Dennett's 'cascade of algorithmic processes feeding on chance.' And many are the investors who know from bitter personal experience that serious liabilities can flow from trying to understand the market, or the course of an individual stock, as a story. The same general problem can undermine the narrativization of other complex phenomena from the behavior of mobs to the evolution of electronic communication. In such instances, the problem of conceptual understanding seems to arise when one is required to move by reduction 'downward' from any overarching, or molar, representation of phenomena to a more discrete, or molecular, understanding of what goes on.

Recently, proponents of 'complexity theory' (and, even more recently, 'emergence theory') have subjected these and other instances of change in complex phenomena to a form of analysis that is fundamentally non-narrative. Referring to the 'interactive revolution', Steven Johnson writes that we should abandon narrative models altogether in trying to grasp its

---

[9] See Dawkins (1985: 13) and Wilson (1988: 83-5). There are actually two ways in which the term 'reduction' has commonly been used, the one usually affirmed in scientific discourse, the other usually condemned in humanistic discourse. The model of indirect narrative that I am proposing in this argument helps bring out the difference between these two senses of the term, a difference that I think Dawkins fails to recognize. In scientific discourse, reduction is the complexity-revealing process by which we move from level one to level two. In humanistic discourse, reduction is a fallacy that arises from simplistic explanations, one example of which would be taking level one for the whole truth about evolution.

trajectory through time, since the 'revolution' proceeds without any internal or external agency of control. What structure there is simply emerges out of a complexity that is more than the sum of its moving parts: 'There isn't a story. It's more like tending a garden, only you're growing it with 10,000 other gardeners' (Johnson 2001: 28). On this view, evolution and the stock market are systems in which the patterns of change are not the direct product of the combined cause-and-effect actions of the myriad parts, but rather an emergence that exceeds all real or imagined narratable models. Whether or not these arguments prevail, my focus in this essay has been restricted to the part played by our cognitive predisposition toward narrative models of understanding in the general resistance to evolution by natural selection. My operating assumption has been that any *necessary* move toward a more granular level of understanding increases the level of cognitive resistance to the degree that it reduces narrative salience. In the ordinary course of our lives, we generally do not have to make this move in order to get by—to make judgments, solve problems, earn a living. Indeed, the move can be enormously disruptive. In the area of ethics and the law, for example, the consequences of a more granular understanding of human behavior can be immense, since so much of the moral and legal fabric of a culture is predicated on a narrative understanding of persons as individual entities capable of agency, that is, as *characters*. It is only on this presumption that the jury can find Larry guilty. Perhaps nothing shows this so vividly as the threat of narrative disaggregation that is introduced by the insanity defense.

The special problem that evolution by natural selection raised, and continues to raise, is the degree to which it requires either non-narrative thinking or some kind of abbreviated awareness of extraordinary narrative complexity *simply to be grasped*. Because of this special need, as I have argued above, evolution by natural selection is different from the broader concept of evolution, which in its general contours can be narrativized with a certain degree of success. The story of an evolutionary descent from a species of carnivorous quadrupeds in the Eocene to present-day whales can be rendered, as in Figure 2, by treating transitional species as the narrative entities and indicating the action or events by the repeated use of the verb-construction 'evolved into'.

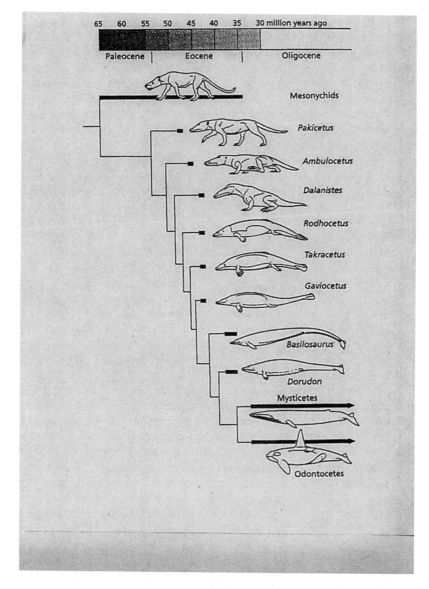

Figure 2: Evolution of Whales, from Mayr (2001: 17)

Thus Mesonychids evolved into Pakicetus, which evolved into Ambulocetus, and so on until you get to present-day whales. This is a story that sets aside questions regarding both the nature of species and the way an event like 'evolved into' works. It is worth noting in passing how much cleaner the graphic representation of this sequence is, lacking as it does the connotative noise that must afflict almost any other verb that one might try to use in this context. But the key problem is that the story represented in this chart works equally well for evolution by acquired characteristics, by saltation, by the Life Force, or by periodic intervention of a supernatural power. When Darwin redirected attention to the evolutionary mechanism of natural selection, he forced us to abandon this workable narrative structure simply to understand his concept.

In making the argument I have, I am both supporting and qualifying the theory, mainly associated with the psychologists Roger Schank and Robert Abelson, that 'all knowledge is encoded as stories' (Schank & Abelson 1995a: 2). In what they have called their 'strong' position, Schank and Abelson (1995a) argue that 'Stories...are the basis of understanding. Understanding means retrieving stories and applying them to new experiences' (33).[10] If my argument has merit, then it suggests, at the least, that human cognition inclines toward narrative. Our thinking is not only most comfortable in this mode of understanding, but seems to require it, especially in grasping the order of events. In Schank and Abelson's (1995a) words, 'Stories are a way of preserving the connectivity of events that would otherwise be dissociated over time' (40). But my argument also suggests that there is some other cognitive operation that allows us to transit between levels one and two of the explanatory model at issue in order to see their intimate connection.

Given our weakness for narrative clarity, it is a credit to human cognitive ability that so many have grasped Darwin's concept, despite his and his many supporters' misleading narrativizations. Of course, as I have noted frequently, our understanding of natural selection was built by Darwin on a vast assortment of valid narratives involving the survival and procreation, or the failure to procreate and death, of individual creatures. Narrative understanding, in other words, is still highly operational over the course of his long argument. But it is only by some process of cognitive triangulation that we grasp without distortion the larger concept of

---

[10] In the *Advances in Social Cognition* volume that features their long essay, 'Knowledge and Memory: The Real Story', Schank and Abelson are consistently criticized by their respondents for their insistence on the exclusivity of narrative as a mode of cognition. In their concluding response, 'So All Knowledge Isn't Stories?' (Schank and Abelson 1995b), they seem to relent a bit from their 'strong' position: 'Perhaps we *have* overstated our case. In the last analysis, however, the debate about *all* vs. *most* vs. *some* is beside the point. The heart of our proposal is concerned with the consequences for memory and knowledge of the preparation and telling of stories' (1995b: 228)

evolution by natural selection. Moreover, though narrative may be the only efficient language we have for representing the general course of evolution, to understand that course specifically as evolution by natural selection, we must let go of the overarching narrative model, even as we preserve narrative understanding for the host of events that make evolution possible.

References

Beer, G. 2000. *Darwin's Plots: Evolutionary Narrative in Darwin, George Eliot, and Nineteenth-Century Fiction*, revised ed. Cambridge: Cambridge UP.

Behe, M. J. 1996. *Darwin's Black Box: The Biochemical Challenge to Evolution.* New York: Free Press.

Blackmore, S. 2000. The Power of Memes. *Scientific American.* 283.4: 64-73.

Chatman, S. 1978. *Story and Discourse: Narrative Structure in Fiction and Film.* Ithaca: Cornell University Press.

Darwin, C. 1915a. *The Origin of Species by Means of Natural Selection*, 6th ed. New York: Appleton.

Darwin, C. 1915b. *The Descent of Man and Selection in Relation to Sex.* New York: Appleton.

Dawkins, R. 1985. *The Blind Watchmaker: Why the Evidence of Evolution Reveals a Universe Without Design.* New York: Norton.

Dawkins, R. 1989. *The Selfish Gene.* New York: Oxford University Press.

Dennett, D. C. 1995. *Darwin's Dangerous Idea: Evolution and the Meanings of Life.* New York: Simon & Schuster.

Eldredge, N. 1985. *Time Frames: The Rethinking of Darwinian Evolution and the Theory of Punctuated Equilibria.* New York: Simon & Schuster.

Eldredge, N. 1995. *Reinventing Darwin: The Great Debate at the High Table of Evolutionary Theory.* New York: John Wiley.

Greimas, A. J. 1983 [1966]. *Structural Semantics: An Attempt at a Method*, trans. D. McDowell, R. Schleifer, and A. Velie. Lincoln: University of Nebraska Press.

Hayles, K. 2001. Desiring Agency: Limiting Metaphors and Enabling Constraints in Dawkins and Deleuze/Guattari. *SubStance*, 30.1-2: 144-59.

Johnson, S. 2001. *Emergence: The Connected Lives of Ants, Brains, Cities, and Software.* New York: Scribner.

Langer, E. J. 1975. The Illusion of Control. *Journal of Personality & Social Psychology* 32: 311-328.

Levine, G. 1988. *Darwin and the Novelists: Patterns of Science in Victorian Fiction.* Chicago: University of Chicago Press.

Mancuso, J. C. 1986. The Acquisition and Use of Narrative Grammar Structure. *Narrative Psychology: the Storied Nature of Human Conduct*, ed. T R. Sarbin, 91-110. New York: Praeger.

Mayr, E. 2001. *What Evolution Is.* New York: Basic Books.

Morris, H. M. 1974. *Scientific Creationism.* San Diego: Creation-Life Publishers.

Morton, P. 1984. *The Vital Science: Biology and the Literary Imagination, 1860-1900.* London: Allen & Unwin.

Propp, V. 1968 [1928]. *Morphology of the Folktale*, 2nd ed., trans. L. Scott, revised by L. A. Wagner. Austin: University of Texas Press.

Scott, E. C. 1997. Antievolution and Creationism in the United States. *Annual Review of Anthropology* 26: 263.

Schank, R. C., and R. P. Abelson. 1977. *Scripts, Plans, Goals, and Understanding*. Hillsdale, NJ: Lawrence Erlbaum Associates.

Schank, R. C., and R. P. Abelson. 1995a. Knowledge and Memory: The Real Story. *Advances in Social Cognition* 8: 1-85.

Schank, R. C., and R. P. Abelson. 1995b. So All Knowledge Isn't Stories? *Advances in Social Cognition* 8: 227-33.

Shaw, B. 1974. *The Bodley Head Bernard Shaw*, vol. 7, ed. D. Laurence. London: Max Reinhardt.

Tennyson, A. 1951. *The Selected Poetry of Tennyson*, ed. Douglas Bush. New York: Random House.

Whitcomb, J. C., and H. M. Morris. 1961. *The Genesis Flood*. Philadelphia: Presbyterian and Reformed Publishing Company.

Wilson, E. O. 1998. *Consilience: the Unity of Knowledge*. New York: Knopf.

Young, R. M. 1985. *Darwin's Metaphor: Nature's Place in Victorian Culture*. Cambridge: Cambridge University Press.

7

Stories as a Tool for Thinking

DAVID HERMAN

1 Introduction

People incorporate stories into a wide array of practices, using narrative as a problem-solving strategy in many contexts. In this sense, narrative functions as a powerful and basic tool for thinking, enabling users of stories to produce and interpret literary texts, carry out spontaneous conversations, make sense of news reports in a variety of media, create and assess medical case histories, and provide testimony in court. The interdisciplinary research tradition that has grown up around the study of 'cognitive artifacts' (Herman forthcoming; Herman and Childs 2003; Hutchins 1995a, 1995b, 1999; Norman 1993; Shore 1996)—that is, material as well as mental objects that enable or enhance cognition—can help account for the problem-solving abilities supported by narrative. My essay draws on this work to address the following question: what is it about narrative (viewed as a cognitive artifact) that explains its multi-situational serviceability, the richness and longlastingness of its processes and products, its power to organize thought and conduct across so many different domains of human activity?

A decade ago, Jerome Bruner (1991) developed a synoptic account of how narrative 'operates as an instrument of mind in the construction of reality' (6).[1] Beginning from the premise that knowledge is domain-specific

---

[1] Writing even earlier, Louis O. Mink (1978) also characterized narrative as an instrument of mind—indeed, as 'a primary and irreducible form of human comprehension, an article in

Narrative Theory and the Cognitive Sciences.
David Herman (ed.).
Copyright © 2003, CSLI Publications.

(see Hirschfeld and Gelman 1994), Bruner focused on 'how we go about constructing and representing the rich and messy domain of human interaction' (1991: 4). In particular, Bruner argued that like the domains of logical-scientific reality construction, the domain of social cognition, i.e., the mode of thinking that both enables and is shaped by social experience (Fiske and Taylor 1991),

> is well buttressed by principles and procedures. It has an available cultural tool kit or tradition on which its procedures are modelled, and its distributional reach is as wide and as active as gossip itself. Its form is so familiar and ubiquitous that it is likely to be overlooked...we organize our experience and memory of human happenings mainly in the form of narrative—stories, excuses, myths, reasons for doing and not doing, and so on. (Bruner 1991: 4)

Bruner went on to itemize ten features of stories viewed as a 'symbolic system' supporting a particular domain of knowledge, i.e., the domain of social beliefs and procedures (21). The ten features include, inter alia, particularity, hermeneutic composability (story parts take shape in the context of narrative wholes and vice versa), canonicity and breach (narrativity emerges from the nonfulfilment rather than from the fulfilment of expectations about behaviors or occurrences), context sensitivity and negotiability, and narrative accrual (stories can be cobbled together to form a 'culture', 'history', or 'tradition').

More than just identifying key properties of narrative, Bruner's account sought to map those properties onto forms of cognition enabled by stories. For instance, the hermeneutic composability of narrative supports humans' ability to situate the behavior of social actors in wider contexts of interpretation and evaluation. When an interlocutor tells me a story incriminating a mutual acquaintance, I am likely to construe specific details in light of what I know about the storyteller's past history with the person who is the focus of the story. Conversely, the storyteller is likely to tailor his or her narrative in accordance with the amount of background knowledge he or she assumes me to have. In addition to being basic requirements for narrative understanding, though, attributing intentions and drawing on background knowledge are also crucial features of the process by which people make sense of the words and deeds of others. Narrative thus affords an optimal environment for social cognition.

In the remainder of this essay, I extend Bruner's model in an effort to throw additional light on how stories constitute tools for thinking. The essay grows out of an ongoing attempt to blend insights from several

---

the constitution of common sense' (132). Mink argues that narrative alone can identify and describe aspects of the world in a way that makes constant and necessary reference to their location in some process of development (146).

fields, including narrative theory, discourse analysis, cognitive science, anthropology, and literary studies. Synthesizing ideas developed in these disciplines, I argue that stories provide crucial representational tools facilitating humans' efforts to organize multiple knowledge domains, each with its attendant sets of beliefs and procedures. Relevant domains include not only those standardly subsumed under social cognition (in a narrow sense), but also a variety of other problem-solving activities.[2] My hypothesis is that stories provide, to a degree that needs to be determined by future research, *domain-general* tools for thinking.[3] The approach outlined here is thus broader in scope than Bruner's, shifting from an account of how narrative helps construct (social) reality to a taxonomy of the core problem-solving abilities supported by stories. Although the forms of problem-solving in question bear importantly on matters of social cognition, they can be construed as extending into other knowledge domains as well, suggesting the domain-generality of narrative as a resource for thought.

Sketching out how stories enable or support cognition, section 3 of my essay concentrates on a sample narrative elicited during a sociolinguistic interview and taken from the corpus of North Carolina ghost stories that I have discussed in recent work (e.g., Herman 1999, 2000, 2001b).[4] In this story, the informant (TS) recounts her grandfather's encounter with a 'shapeshifter' who transforms himself from a human into a squirrel and then, when he is fatally wounded by the grandfather and a friend during a hunting expedition, back into a human again. (See the Appendix for a

---

[2] I add the proviso 'in a narrow sense' because, in recent research influenced by the work of Lev Vygotsky (e.g., Frawley 1997; Lee 1997; John-Steiner 1997; Nunes 1997; Resnick, Pontecorvo, and Säljö 1997; Wertsch 1985, 1991, 1998), a number of theorists have argued that the individual's participation in social life causes, conditions, and enables her cognitive activity as such (see especially Rogoff 1990: 3-61). Indeed, Vygotsky's concept of 'psychological tools' anticipates the later research on cognitive artifacts on which I draw in the present essay. For Vygotsky, such tools include, among other semiotic systems, "'language, various systems for counting; mnemonic techniques; algebraic symbol systems; works of art; writing; schemes, diagrams, maps, and mechanical drawings; all sorts of conventional signs; and so on'" (quoted in Wertsch 1985: 79; cf. Resnick, Pontecorvo, and Säljö 1997: 3-4; Rogoff 1990: 51-55).

The Vygotskian perspective informs my remarks about cognitive artifacts and users of them as parts of a larger functional system (section 2.1); about narrative as a resource for coordinating communicative behavior (section 3.4.1); and about stories as a means for the social distribution of intelligence (section 3.5).

[3] My claim for the domain-generality of narrative squares, I believe, with Ellen Spolsky's (2001) argument that 'narratives are themselves the processes that human beings have evolved to understand, express, and meet the need for revised and revisable behavior in an unstable world' (181).

[4] Research informing my discussion of TS's ghost story was supported by NSF Grant SBR-9616331.

complete transcription of the story.) A basic assumption guiding my analysis is that, like narrative in general, TS's story about her grandfather's run-in with the shapeshifter can be studied both as an achieved representation of experience and as an instrument enabling a class of comparable representational achievements—a class whose members are linked by shared strategies for problem-solving in the broadest sense. The problems at the heart of TS's narrative are among the most basic issues facing human beings—for example, how to divide the manifold of experience into knowable and workable increments, as well as how to reconcile constancy and change, stability and flux. The question to be addressed in section 3 of my essay is how TS comes to grips with these and other problems by recruiting powerful representational tools associated with narrative.

2 Narrative as Cognitive Artifact

2.1 Some Background on Cognitive Artifacts

As specified by theorists working in a range of fields, from cognitive anthropology to human-computer interaction, cognitive artifacts encompass material as well mental objects—calendars and spreadsheets as well as proverbs and rules of thumb. All such artifacts can be used for the purposes for which they were initially designed or else for novel, unanticipated purposes (Hutchins 1995a, 1995b, 1999; Norman 1993), there being a continuum from cases of targeted use of cognitive artifacts, to cases in which artifacts with a targeted purpose are used for some other purpose, to wholly opportunistic uses of structures existing independently in nature (Hutchins 1999: 127).

For example, I can write down appointment times on a calendar, in the manner for which it was designed; but I can also place the calendar itself in a particular location within my office, thereby reminding myself that I need to check my appointments at a specific stage in the sequence of actions with which I start my work day. By the same token, in order to describe to coworkers how the furniture in our office could be moved around, I might pick up some pens and pencils (themselves cognitive artifacts that can be used to support humans' ability to represent, calculate, and remember), arranging the writing implements on my desk in a way that iconically captures my proposed scheme for the furniture (Norman 1993: 47-9). Edwin Hutchins (1999: 126-7) reviews research on other opportunistic uses of cultural artifacts. For instance, shoppers develop routine trajectories through the grocery store to remind themselves about what they need to buy. For their part, bartenders use the shapes of drink glasses and their placement on the bar to help themselves remember what drinks to make when they are faced with multiple drink orders. Similarly, airline pilots can detect fluctuations in speed simply by looking at their instrument displays in a particular way, rather than expending the additional processing effort required to use the displays to *calculate* speeds (see Hutchins 1995b). Structures not made by humans, i.e., natural artifacts, can also be exploited in cognitively beneficial ways, as when Micronesian sailors use the night sky to navigate a course between islands (Hutchins 1995a), or farmers use the cycle of the seasons to regulate activities such as tillage, planting, and harvesting. David Kirsh (1995) articulates as follows the general principle underlying all these examples: 'Preprocessing the world saves processing the representation of the world. Put another way, the greater our understanding of the organization we maintain outside, the less we have to memorize' (66).

Perhaps because of the sheer pervasiveness of humans' preprocessing efforts, it has proven difficult to draw clear boundaries around the idea of cognitive artifacts. As Hutchins indicates (1999: 127), the notion encompasses not only prototypical cases (e.g., pocket calculators, heart monitors) but also 'fuzzier' instances such as social routines and patterns of phenomena (rather than objects proper) existing in the natural world.[5] Across these variable artifactual forms or instantiations, however, a constant feature is the provision of representational tools for understanding and managing the complexities of experience. Thus, defining cognitive artifacts as 'tools of thought . . . that complement abilities and strengthen mental powers' (43), Don Norman (1993) goes on to write:

> The powers of cognition come from abstraction and representation:
> the ability to represent perceptions, experiences, and thoughts in some
> medium other than that in which they have occurred, abstracted away
> from irrelevant details . . . . we can make marks or symbols that repre-
> sent something else and then do our reasoning by using those marks.
> (47)

Similarly, commenting that complex cognitive performances require the application of component cognitive abilities, Hutchins suggests that tools facilitating these component abilities 'provide...representational media in which the computation is achieved by the propagation of the representational state' (1995a: 154). The tools in question also organize problem-solving activities into functional systems. For Hutchins—and to underscore a point that will resurface in my discussion of narrative representa-

---

[5] Such considerations prompt Hutchins himself to argue that '[t]he cognitive artifact concept points not so much to a category of objects, as to a category of processes that produce cognitive effects by bringing functional skills into coordination with various kinds of structure' (Hutchins 1999: 127).

tions in particular—such systems are not representational technologies that stand between 'users' and 'tasks'. Rather, users and tasks can be construed as nodes of more basic—yet supraindividual—functional systems in which cognitive activities take root (1995a: 154-55 and 1995b).[6]

The shift of perspective just mentioned necessitates an adjustment of methods and ideas from cognitive science, some strands of which traditionally focus on the representation-processing properties of individuals (Frawley 1997: 13-34). At issue here are rather functional gestalts in which intelligence is distributed between two or more agents (whether human, computational, or other) making a coordinated effort to come to grips with a problem in their environment—via a complex interweaving of individual and shared representations. The study of cognitive artifacts thus requires abandoning the axiom of 'methodological individualism', the postulate that "'no purported explanations of social (or individual) phenomena are to count as explanations, or . . . as rock-bottom explanations, unless they are couched wholly in terms of facts about individuals'" (Lukes 1977, quoted by Wertsch 1998: 19). To avoid such 'individualistic reductionism' (Wertsch 1998: 21), researchers 'need to go beyond the isolated individual when trying to understand human action, including communicative and mental action' (Wertsch 1998: 19). The focus shifts from the mental contents of individuals to cognition viewed as 'mediated action'. Thinking, that is, can be redescribed as a particular use of cultural tools (semiotic systems, computational devices, etc.) by agents engaged in mental, communicative, and other forms of behavior that display a basic synergism with the larger environment in which their behavior unfolds (Wertsch 1998: 23-72; cf. Wertsch 1991: 28-43; 119-47).[7] It follows that 'the notion of mental function can properly be applied to social as well as individual forms of activity' (Wertsch 1991: 27).

The problem-solving abilities of a surgical team, for example, cannot be explained by reference to the representational states or activities of individual team members. Instead, the ability to detect and manage problems encountered during a surgical procedure is a function of representations arising from (mediated by) multiple sources and modes, including perceptions of changes in the patient's appearance, more or less strictly task-oriented verbal interchanges, visual or auditory signals provided by assorted monitors, inferences based on training and previous operations, and so on. Below, in characterizing stories as an instrument for distributing intelligence across

---

[6] Analogously, see Jon Barwise and Jerry Seligman's (1997) account of how structural regularities make possible the flow of information within distributed systems.

[7] Note that James Wertsch (1998: 73-108) analyzes narrative in particular as a 'cultural tool' for representing the past.

groups (section 3.5), I argue for an analogous shift from the individual mind to the larger, encompassing narrative situation as the primary unit of analysis.

2.2 From Targeted to Opportunistic Uses of Story Artifacts

Along the cline or continuum identified by Hutchins—the continuum linking targeted and opportunistic uses of cultural artifacts as well as natural phenomena—narrative can be assigned multiple locations. At one end of the continuum, a particular instantiation of the narrative text type matches up with the communicative profile of the discourse context in which it occurs.[8] In this case, which parallels the use of a calculator to balance one's checkbook or the use of an outdoor thermometer to measure the temperature, humans exploit elements of narrative structure with the predominant purpose of cuing interlocutors, viewers, or readers to reconstruct a sequence of *states*, unplanned *events*, and deliberately initiated *actions* (Herman 2002: 27-51). In such canonical usages, to be sure, narratively organized representations provide significant cognitive benefits. They enable tellers and interpreters to establish spatiotemporal links between regions of experience and between objects contained in those regions. Narratives also allow people to adopt relatively distant or intimate (and relatively fixed or variable) perspectives on the storyworlds they evoke.[9] Storyworlds, in turn, are inhabited by participants about whose physical as well as mental behavior tellers and interpreters are licensed to make a vast number of inferences. Indeed, narrative comprehension *requires* situating participants within networks of beliefs, desires, and intentions.

But narrative structure can also be exploited opportunistically, i.e., put in the service of discourse contexts whose communicative profile is not predominantly narratively organized. In such cases, different cognitive benefits accrue. Thus—to mention instances ranging over a fairly wide stretch of the form-function continuum—stories can be used to give support for positions presented in arguments (Virtanen 1992), but also as a resource for comparing and contrasting features of past and present situations (Turner 1996). Further, narrative can function to expand the participation frame-

---

[8] Here I anticipate a point to be developed in greater detail in section 2.3 below, where I draw on Tuija Virtanen's (1992) argument that narrative can be construed as a basic type of *text* because of the relative ease with which it lends itself to use in a variety of *discourse* types (i.e., overarching communicative contexts).

[9] Here, as in Herman (2002), I use the term *storyworld* to denote a global mental representation of who did what to and with whom, when, where, why, and in what fashion in the world to which recipients relocate—or make a deictic shift (Zubin and Hewitt 1995)—as they work to comprehend a narrative.

work of disputes: a story about a disputant's past behavior can be used to undercut his or her present position by eliciting negative evaluations from other ratified participants in a current discourse (Goodwin 1990). Narrative, as well, helps generate and assess counterfactual, what-if scenarios—hypothetical scenarios by means of which the consequences of current circumstances and behaviors can be traced through and evaluated (Doležel 1999).

2.3 Narrative as a Basic and General Resource for Thought

Further complicating matters, the notion 'story' itself spans both an abstract cognitive structure and the material trace of that structure left in writing, speech, sign-language, three-dimensional visual images, or some other representational medium. As Bradd Shore (1996) puts it, on the one hand the term *narrative* 'refers to the activity of adjusting and creating reality through talking it out', i.e., the activity whereby people use stories to 'make sense of their worlds "on the fly"' (58). On the other hand, *narrative* 'also refers to the instituted result of this structuring process' (58). Hence, narrative is at once a class of (cultural) artifacts and a cognitive-communicative process for creating, identifying, and interpreting candidate members of that artifactual class.

The artifact-producing power of narrative is what induces Leonard Talmy (2000) to claim for narrative the status of a basic pattern-forming cognitive system bearing on sequences experienced through time. Functioning 'to connect and integrate certain components of conscious content over time into a coherent ideational structure' (419), this system is in Talmy's account domain-general: 'its characteristics share the properties that are common across cognitive systems generally, so that it can, in turn, be used to better understand the nature of those properties' (420; cf. 446-81). In this model, narrative can be construed as a system for structuring *any* time-based pattern into a resource for consciousness, making it possible for cultural as well as natural objects and phenomena to assume the role of cognitive artifacts to begin with. Indeed, in the case of objects fashioned to accomplish particular tasks, the very notion of 'artifact' implies sequence (Kirsh 1995: 51-54), which narrative helps make cognizable. A tool presupposes a sequentially organized activity in which things are more or less constrained with respect to an order of operations, a form of practice. And narrative is a primary means of mapping processes not directed toward any particular goal—that is, mere temporal *flux*—onto patterns of temporal *progression*.

Stories, then, afford structure that can be used in both a targeted and an opportunistic fashion. Moreover, there are grounds for characterizing narrative as a pattern-forming cognitive system that organizes all sequentially experienced structure, which can then be operationalized to create tools for thinking. Narrative thus provides cognitively beneficial structure in a wide range of ways; that range furnishes independent support for Tuija Virtanen's (1992) hypothesis that narrative is a *basic* type of text, i.e., a type that is in some sense more fundamental than descriptive, instructive, expository, or argumentative types of text.

Virtanen proposes a two-tiered classificatory scheme of *discourse types* and *text types*. For example, a text of the narrative type, more or less readily identifiable as such, may be slotted into a discourse whose overarching purpose is argumentational, with the narrative used to provide backing for a position being argued for (cf. Schiffrin 1987: 132-3). As Virtanen puts it, '[t]he superordinate discourse type need not always be realized through the corresponding text type. An apparent mismatch of a discourse type and the corresponding text type may be accounted for in terms of notions such as the "direct" and "indirect", or "primary" and "secondary" uses of various text types' (298). In all Virtanen discusses five types of texts—narrative, descriptive, instructive, expository, and argumentative—and their direct and indirect usage in discourse environments. But whereas 'the narrative type of text seems to be able to realize any type of discourse, i.e., argumentation, exposition, description, instruction in addition to the narrative discourse type', by contrast 'the argumentative type of text . . . seems to be more or less restricted to direct use, i.e., to the realization of the argumentative discourse type' (303). For her part, Virtanen outlines several structural as well as functional reasons for the ease with which stories can be slotted into discourse contexts that are not narratively organized overall.[10] The foregoing discussion supplements Virtanen's account by suggesting that stories' polyfunctional communicative profile, their actual or potential manifestation in multiple discourse environments, is a reflex of their extraordinary serviceability as a tool for thinking. Indeed, a more specific research hypothesis suggests itself in this connection: namely, that the narrative *text type* can surface in virtually every *discourse type* because of the domain-generality of stories as a resource for thought, i.e., the pertinence of stories for multiple problem domains.

---

[10] The following are among the factors that Virtanen (1992) lists as contributing to narrative's being amenable to 'indirect' uses in multiple discourse types: 'very little material is in fact needed for a text to qualify as a narrative' (304); narrative is a text type acquired early in life; and the structure of the prototypical narrative is highly iconic, 'and the more iconic text types may be assumed to be more universal than text organized according to various culture-specific designs, such as . . . patterns of argumentation or exposition' (305).

3 How Narrative Supports Core Problem-Solving Abilities

Of course, it will require more than a single chapter to begin testing out the hypothesis just stated; but in what follows I present strategies for exploratory investigation along these lines. Specifically, I focus on five (overlapping) problem-solving activities—'chunking' experience into workable segments, imputing causal relations between events, managing problems with the 'typification' of phenomena, sequencing behaviors, and distributing intelligence across groups—for which the representational tools bound up with narrative can be argued to furnish crucial support. Described in more detail in subsequent sections, these activities encompass but are not limited to problems entailed by social cognition. Further, the five activities are pertinent to narrative viewed both as product and as process; they reveal ways in which particular narratives can be exploited as a tool for thinking about specific situations, as well as ways in which narrative in general constitutes a primary resource for building, recognizing, and using cognitive artifacts across variable circumstances.

Working under the assumption that theorists can gain insight into narrative as process by studying instituted narrative products—in the same way that linguists arrive at hypotheses concerning the human language faculty by studying attested linguistic behavior—I use the sample narrative mentioned earlier as a point of reference in the ensuing discussion. To reiterate, however, my aim is indeed twofold: to characterize TS's account of the shapeshifter as a cognitive artifact in its own right, but also to characterize the more general representational processes that subtend and make possible all such narrative accountings.

3.1 Chunking Experience

From early on, the notion of 'chunking'—i.e., the process by which the stream of experience is segmented into units that are bounded, classifiable, and thus more readily recognized and remembered—has played an important role in cognitive-scientific research. For instance, what Marvin Minsky (1975) called *frames*, or structures for representing and remembering stereotypical situations (e.g., being in a classroom or an art gallery), were for Minsky a means of organizing knowledge of the world into discrete, manageable chunks (cf. Nebel 1999). It is easier to organize knowledge and behavior if the vast realms of experience are subdivided; indeed, the world would quickly become unmanageable if I had to sort through every possible concept and potential course of action at every given moment. Minsky's idea of frames was designed to explain how knowing what one does when in a classroom can be separated from knowing what one does in an art gallery, so that one can avoid staring at the blackboard as though it were great abstract art and, inversely, refrain from writing in chalk on a framed portrait from fourteenth-century Italy.

Meanwhile, Herbert A. Simon and William G. Chase (1973) used the notion of chunking to account for what constitutes expertise at chess (see also Gobet 1999). Simon and Chase argued that skill at chess depends on segmenting the chessboard into small chunks or sets of pieces that encapsulate typical patterns of pieces and suggest possible moves, with expertise increasingly proportionally with the number of chunks that a player can access. Kirsh (1995: 66) discusses an analogous phenomenon. Strings of letters can be stored in working memory more easily if they are preprocessed by being clustered or chunked into well-known units. To store the string ANAECURCTSGNIEAM, much more processing effort is required than if I chunk this string into two bounded segments (in this case, lexemes), i.e., CRUSTACEAN ENIGMA.

Likewise—and arguably in a global or domain-general way—narrative affords representational tools for addressing the problem of how to chunk the ongoing stream of experience into bounded, cognizable, and thus usable structures. Stories organize experience by enabling people to select from among the total set of sequentially and concurrently available inputs; preprocess those inputs into internally differentiated chunks with (as Aristotle 1971 put it) a beginning, middle, and end; and then use those temporally structured segments as a basis for further cognitive operations on new experiential inputs. Life stories, as interpreted by Charlotte Linde (1993), can be characterized in just these terms. They are the output of segmenting operations ('First I studied X, but then, after a period of reflection, I realized that I was bored so I began a career doing Y') that in turn provide structure for additional or alternative segmentations. Indeed, by marking off a point on the temporal continuum and assigning it the role of origin or beginning, decisions about where to begin a story not only constrain the design and interpretation of the narrative itself, but also index competing ways of understanding the world—i.e., alternative strategies for tracing current states of affairs back to a point of origin. Competing accounts of the Troubles in Northern Ireland, for instance, might trace its root-cause back to (among other candidate causes) the events of 1867 (the Fenian Rebellion), 1916 (the Easter Uprising), 1972 ('Bloody Sunday'), or 1695 (the advent of more than a century of anti-Catholic 'Penal Laws').

By the same token, narrative is a resource for closure. Any particular telling of a narrative has to end, even if the narrative being told is presented as unfinished or unfinishable. In coming to a conclusion, tellings mark even the most painful or disturbing experiences as endurable because finite. In such contexts, narrative is a tool for representing events not as over and done with, but as reaching a terminus that imposes a limit on the trauma-inducing (and cognition-disrupting) power of the events at issue.[11]

TS's account of the shapeshifter, by segmenting experience into a bounded sequence of states, events, and actions—i.e., by structuring what happened into *a* shapeshifting incident with an identifiable inception and terminus—reveals the power of narrative to chunk phenomenal reality into classifiable, knowable, and operable units. Indeed, the first, shorter narrative included in the transcription rehearses, in miniature, the same narrative-enabled strategy for chunking that structures the subsequent, longer narrative about TS's grandfather and the squirrel/man. In the first story, TS's cousin shot the owl; the shot ricocheted off the owl, who was in fact a shapeshifter and who could not be shot with impunity; the cousin died from the resulting wound. This narrative situates the cousin and the owl/man in an action structure that involves conflicting goals and plans—and hence causal relations of the sort described in my next section.[12] It thereby extracts from the stream of experience a delimited set of participants, states, actions, and events and structures into a coherent whole what might otherwise be reabsorbed back into the atelic and unbounded process of time's passing. In effect, the telling of this abbreviated story provides a cognitive template, a paradigm for segmentation that guides both the production and the interpretation of the more extensive span of talk required to complete the telling of the story about TS's grandfather and the squirrel/man. The prior narrative enables TS's interlocutors to monitor subsequent discourse for markers indexing the inception and the terminus of an analogously structured (i.e., bounded) unit of experience.

Thus, although it is told much less elliptically than the first story, at a pace approximating what Gérard Genette (1980 [1972]: 93-95) specifies as 'scene' in contrast to 'summary', TS's second narrative uses as a cognitive and communicative resource the strategies for chunking encoded in the prior story. After evoking the concept of 'shape shifts' in line (i), TS uses the discourse marker *and* clause-initially in lines (k-m), triggering the inference that there is a global tie linking the current topic of talk with the topic (shapeshifting) that was previously in focus (Schiffrin 1987: 128-52). In this way, TS sets up an expectation for structure—an expectation that the

---

[11] Compare, in this connection, H. Porter Abbott's (2000) remarks concerning the evolution of narrative as a coping strategy for grief, a way of accommodating death by 'memorializing...death-dealing events' (251).

[12] Here I draw on Rachel Giora and Yeshayahu Shen's (1994) definition of *action structure* as 'a higher-order organization which hierarchically connects not only adjacent events...but also events which are remote from one another on the temporal axis of a given discourse. Thus a story...is more than pairwise relationships among events, but rather, a string of events combined into a psychological whole' (450).

second narrative, too, will center on a shapeshifting incident resulting in conflict between a human protagonist and an antagonist blending animal with human traits. What William Labov (1972) would call the abstract of the second story, i.e., the pre-announcement in lines (k-l) that the grandfather 'killed somebody', reinforces the expectation that the segment of experience encapsulated in the second narrative will be structured in parallel with that presented in the first story.[13]

Lines (m-n) mark the opening boundary of the narratively packaged experiential unit: the grandfather was a little boy, at that time living in Cherokee, NC, at the inception of the incident. The 'middle' of this internally differentiated unit consists of stages of the unfolding conflict, as told by the grandfather and re-narrated by TS: shooting the big squirrel that yells when it falls from a tree and then cannot be found (r-gg); being stared at meanly by the man into whom the squirrel has re-morphed (jj-nn); finding the old man dead from a wound mirroring, point-for-point, the injury suffered by the squirrel (qq-xx). The closing boundary or terminus of the shapeshifting incident is afforded by the grandfather's own comments on the encounter (zz-fff), comments quoted as well as summarized by TS. Line (ggg) operates metacommunicatively, so to speak, signalling that the narratively bounded unit has reached its completion point. Functioning as what Labov (1972) calls a 'coda', this utterance bridges the world of the past and and the world of the present, preparing the way for further discourse and—potentially—different strategies for segmenting experience.

3.2 Imputing Causal Relations between Events

In a very basic way, TS's story centers on the problem of identity, and more specifically on the problem of how something can be identified as 'the same' entity despite changes over time. To establish identity over time, producers and interpreters of narrative must use a cause-and-effect algorithm to map storyworld occurrences onto more or less radical changes in the nature, appearance, or behavior of participants in the situations and events being recounted. Indeed, given that narrative prototypically roots itself in causal-chronological relations—in sequences of happenings in which earlier happenings are at least causally necessary for, though not fully determina-

---

[13] In this connection, compare Elinor Ochs's and Lisa Capps's (2001) suggestion that the 'use of second stories in everyday conversational interaction is similar to the use of precedent in legal decision-making' (209). Although Ochs's and Capps's argument builds on Harvey Sacks's (1992) account of second stories told by interlocutors in response to a different narrator's first story, their claim also bears on second stories told by the same narrator, as in the present case: 'Second stories highlight criteria of a first story that lay foundations for categorizing experience' (209).

tive of, later ones (Carroll 2001)—the problem of identity over time would seem to be one for which stories are ideally suited. One of the hallmarks of narrative is its linking of phenomena into causal-chronological wholes; stories provide structure for connecting otherwise isolated data into elements of episodes or 'scenes' (Fillmore 1977), whose components can then be represented as systematically interrelated via causal networks. To put the same point another way, stories function as a kind of judgment heuristic or 'meta-heuristic' (Tversky and Kahneman 1971, 1974; see also Kahneman, Slovic, and Tversky 1982), i.e., an assemblage of rules of thumb for interpreting experience, with attendant *biases* whose effects warrant closer scrutiny.[14] In this respect, stories like TS's can be construed as the reflex of a narrative-supported—and domain-general—predisposition to find causal links between states, actions, and events in a sequentially presented array.

Roland Barthes (1977 [1966]: 94) once made a similar claim, describing narrative as a culturally sanctioned application of the fallacy *post hoc, propter hoc* ('after this, therefore because of this'). To paraphrase: narrative understanding depends fundamentally on a generalized heuristic according to which interpreters assume that if Y is mentioned after X in a story, then X not only precedes but also causes Y. Indeed, one can detect the operation of this same heuristic in a variety of discourse contexts, as when language users are able to 'read in' temporal and causal relations in the case of conjunctions that do not contain explicit time-indices or markers of causality (cf. Grice 1989 [1975]; Kehler 2002). Most speakers of English would agree that the string (S) *Tom bought a security system and had his house burgled* differs from the string (S$_1$) *Tom had his house burgled and bought a security system.* Yet there is nothing 'in' the connective *and* to mark a particular temporal ordering of (or causal relation between) the two conjuncts—(a) Bob's buying a security system and (b) Bob's having his house burgled—contained in both strings. An argument could be made for the view that narrative is the source of this 'post-hoc-propter-hoc' judgment heuristic. From this perspective, language users' default, automatic tendency to superimpose causal and temporal relationships onto the logico-semantic structure of sentences like (S) and (S$_1$) is an extension or derivation of narratively organized thinking.[15]

---

[14] Heuristics of this sort, influentially explored by Amos Tversky and Daniel Kahneman (1971, 1974; see also Fischhoff 1999), enable people to determine the probability of rain, the size of a crowd on the street, or the time needed to write an academic essay—though they also lead to systematic errors that researchers have technically defined as the *biases* attendant upon distinct kinds of judgment heuristics.

[15] To put the same point another way, narrative may be the ultimate source of the more localized judgment heuristics that Grice (1989 [1975]) identified as the 'maxims' adherence to which yields 'results in accordance with the Cooperative Principle' (26). For example, the

In any case, in narrative itself the heuristic at issue is indispensable to tellers as well as interpreters. By using the heuristic, tellers can safely leave things unstated that it would otherwise take far too much time and effort to spell out, and interpreters can make sense of those abbreviated reports, which would otherwise remain hopelessly elliptical and opaque. If in telling a story I recount that someone got into bed and then report that the person in question fell asleep, I need not elaborate the causal link between these two events. Instead, I can assume that you will use your general world-knowledge about beds as places for sleeping to sketch in the link yourself.

In her story about the shapeshifter, TS relies on (and relies on her interlocutors' reliance on) this same heuristic to impute causal links between storyworld occurrences and what might otherwise be construed as a random sequence of change-of-state predicates attaching to the shapeshifter.[16] (Or rather, in the absence of the post-hoc-propter-hoc heuristic, the predicates might be assumed to attach to a pair of distinct entities—squirrel and man—in contrast to entities that are transforms of one another.) Indeed, the sequence of occurrences organized by the narrative involves not just the alteration of a few accidental predicates but rather a being's wholesale transformation from animal to human. Further, a transformation from human to animal must be assumed to have occurred prior to the grandfather's shooting of the squirrel. Narrative provides representational tools enabling TS to dovetail this metamorphosis with the emergent conflict between the grandfather (along with his hunting companion), the squirrel, and the man in the house.

In this case, TS draws on resources available to conversational storytellers, using emphatically lengthened speech productions to cue a series of causal inferences. Collectively these inferences define a causal network in

---

post-hoc-propter-hoc heuristic associated with narrative may be the foundation for, rather than derive from, what Grice characterized as the maxim of Manner ('Be orderly'). Adherence to the maxim of Manner prompts my interlocutor to assume that if I produce an utterance in which two or more events are mentioned, I will not mention those events out of order unless I have some special reason for (or wish to achieve some special effect by) doing so. If the maxim of Manner indeed has narrative origins, that may help explain why such temporal ordering standardly generates additional implicatures concerning causal relations—even in the absence of explicit cues pertaining to causality. Stories are, as already suggested, a primary resource for transforming sets of events into causally as well as chronologically structured wholes.

[16] For discussion of the way interpreters of discourse (e.g., recipes and stories) must continuously update their mental representations of entities undergoing more or less radical changes of state, see Gillian Brown and George Yule (1983: 190-222) and Catherine Emmott (1997: 103-235). For an attempt to use narratological theories of actants to describe the causal networks associated with story interpretation, see Herman (2000).

which the storyworld occurrences can be mapped onto changes in the participants, including the shape shift.   TS's emphatic utterances, which constitute the skeleton of the entire story, include SQUIRRELS (q), BIGGER (t), YELLED (x), YELLED (ee), FIND (gg), WENT (ii), MAN (kk), THEM SO ^MEAN (kk), MEAN (nn), SEE (rr), KNOWED (aaa), SQUIRREL (eee).   *SQUIRRELS* identifies the type of entity being hunted, while the inclusion of information about its size serves to mark one particular squirrel as unusual; i.e., *BIGGER* flags this entity as noteworthy—reportable—in the current and upcoming discourse context.   As the narrative proceeds this size-related predicate can be interpreted retrospectively as the first prompt to build a causal connector between the entities 'squirrel' and 'man'.   The next two emphatic utterances, both of them productions of *YELLED*, ascribe a key human property to the squirrel, namely, the capacity for speech.   In yelling, the squirrel is at its most human, just as later on, given the kind of wound sustained by the squirrel (z-cc), the dead man in the house with 'blood down his back' (uu) is at his most animal.

But further, *YELLED* (along with the nonemphatic *screamed* at line (y)) cues construction of a causal network subtending a pattern of conflict between hunters and hunted.   This pattern organizes understanding of TS's utterances as a narrative, involving pursuit of a goal (the hunt), conflict (the hunters shoot the squirrel), and subsequent reprisal (the man's mean stare that convinces the grandfather forever that he is a murderer).   On the basis of this narratively structured pattern of conflict, the yelling squirrel can be inferred to be fundamentally continuous with the man who stares so meanly at TS's grandfather and then dies.   TS's emphatic productions of *FIND* (gg) and *WENT* (jj) reinforce the causal inferences linking the squirrel, TS's grandfather, and the angrily staring man in a pattern of offense-and-reprisal. Insofar as the grandfather is unable to find the squirrel he shot, interpreters of the story infer that another shape shift has occurred and that the man who stares him down is a transform of the mortally wounded squirrel, exacting a form of revenge.   Indeed, because of the causal inferences it triggers, the narrative enables two, ostensibly incompatible referents ('squirrel' and 'man') to be assigned to the definite description *that MAN* (kk), overriding semantic constraints imposed by the explicit lexical content of the phrase itself.   With TS's account, then, identifying discourse referents, computing causal inferences, and making sense of the story are mutually conditioning processes.   To be able to track discourse entities across shifts of shape, one must grasp the narrative structure that encodes those entities as participants in an emergent pattern of conflict.

3.3 Managing Typification Problems

Under this heading, I include ways in which stories provide tools for solving the problem of how to balance expectations against outcomes, general patterns against particular instances—in short, the typical against the actual. Bruner (1991) discusses related issues under the rubric of 'canonicity and breach', noting that 'to be worth telling, a tale must be about how an implicit canonical script has been breached, violated, or deviated from in a manner to do violence to . . . the "legitimacy" of the canonical script' (11). Shore (1996) makes a similar point, but he also suggests how the narrative representation of anomalous or atypical events can in turn reshape a culture's or community's sense of what is normal or typical, and thereby help build new models for understanding the world:

> The role of narrative in meaning construction becomes especially clear following anomalous or otherwise disturbing events . . . . Any such unexpected event is, for normal people, relatively indigestible until it is processed by talk into palatable form. Following such disturbing events, people . . . tell and retell the story until the events are gradually domesticated into one or more coherent and shared narratives that circulate among the community of sufferers . . . . Through narrative, the strange and the familiar achieve a working relationship. (Shore 1996: 58)

In this connection, Alfred Schutz's (1962) concept of typification—his notion that '[a]ll our knowledge of the world, in common-sense as well as in scientific thinking, involves constructs, i.e., a set of abstractions, generalizations, formalizations, idealizations specific to the respective level of thought organization' (5)—can be brought productively into play.

For Schutz, typifications are a means of preprocessing the world, and they thus link up with what I discussed previously as strategies for chunking experiencing. As Schutz puts it, human beings

> have preselected and preinterpreted this world by a series of common-sense constructs of the reality of daily life, and it is these thought objects which determine their behavior, define the goal of their action, the means available for attaining them—in brief, which help them find their bearings within their natural and socio-cultural environment and to come to terms with it. (1962: 6; cf. Husserl 1973: 321-38)

Schutz thus assigns the process of typification domain-general status, with that process facilitating a broad variety of cognitive tasks—from the organization of objects into classes and members-of-classes, to the learning of the lexical and syntactic patterns of a language, to the ascription of motives to others during social interaction (Schutz 1962: 7-23). The constant feature across all these tasks is the expectation-creating modes of preprocessing that typification affords. If assimilated to pre-existent types, any encountered object, situation, or event can be placed within a 'horizon of familiarity and pre-acquaintanceship which is, as such, just taken for granted until further notice as the unquestioned, though at any time questionable stock of knowledge at hand. The unquestioned pre-experiences are...at hand as *typical*, that is, as carrying open horizons of anticipated similar experiences' (Schutz 1962: 7).

Stories fill the breach when typification fails; in line with Bruner's (1991) remarks about transgressions of canonicity, narrative is a means of redressing problems that arise when anticipated similar experiences do not materialize. Thus, TS's account is designed to redress a number of abrogated expectations: the larger-than-expected size of the squirrel; the squirrel's ability to yell; the hunters' failure to find the squirrel despite their expertise (one assumes) in computing the probable location of quarry that has been shot; the surprising meanness of the man's stare; and the unanticipated parallelism between the squirrel's and the man's wounds, along with the man's unforeseen death. More than this, however, stories can be told prior to or in the absence of any real failure of expectation, in order to question the explanatory limits of expectation-inducing and –sustaining typifications. In such contexts, narratives can be used to question 'the stock of knowledge at hand' that is, as Schutz emphasizes, 'at any time questionable'.

TS's story serves precisely this retypifying or rather meta-typifying function, questioning the coherence of standard membership criteria for the classes 'human' and 'animal'. In other words, by representing a sequence of actions and events in which a key participant blends canonically human and canonically animal traits, TS's narrative demands that interpreters reorient themselves within a new horizon of familiarity—one in which the distinction between humans and non-humans (specifically, rodents) must be viewed as gradient and fuzzy instead of binary and clear-cut. The new horizon opened by TS's tale is therefore literally super-natural. It compels a rethinking of what have been taken to be natural categories or kinds, and *ipso facto* a retypification of experience.

3.4 Sequencing Behaviors

What exactly should one do, where, when, and in what order? As intractable as it sometimes seems, this too is a problem for whose solution narrative provides important representational tools. When it comes to stories, the problem manifests itself at two different levels: at the level of narrative communication, and also at the level of the storyworlds that get constructed and reconstructed during narrative communication.

3.4.1 Narrative and Communicative Behavior

On the one hand, narrative helps manage the sequencing of behaviors during face-to-face communicative interaction. Specifically, stories organize the coordination of turns at talk by enabling participants in conversation to collaborate on the accomplishment of extensive, multi-unit turns (Schegloff 1981). Allowing interlocutors to overcome conversation's interactionally motivated bias towards smallest possible turn-size (Sacks, Schegloff, and Jefferson 1974), stories facilitate the creation of carefully structured, pre-planned discourse segments. The production and interpretation of these stretches of talk require participants to reflect on and evaluate previous, on-going, or possible experiences. Hence—to anticipate claims developed in section 3.5 below—narrative contributes primordially, it would seem, to the sustained exercise of thought jointly accomplished by social interactants.

The narrative profile of TS's contribution structures communicative behavior in the context in which it is embedded. Displacing a dyadic interview format marked by pairs of questions and answers, the narrative organizes a relatively monologic type of speech event, one accommodating the extensive turns at talk required for storytelling. Thus, once TS's story is underway, the interviewer (BA) passes on opportunities for interrogative or other utterances in favor of minimal forms of 'backchanneling' (lines h, j, u, bb, dd, mm, vv, yy, and ccc). In addition, in a portion of the interview not transcribed in the appendix, TS and BA co-construct a story preface in which BA demonstrates her willingness to adopt the role of listener by way of explicit requests that TS 'tell some stories'. The preface also contains emphatic speech productions in which BA underscores her interest in and appreciation of stories in general, tales of the supernatural in particular:

```
TA:   'Cause of the ^stories..I just..all the stories
      and my house is the world's worst
      to tell you things /inaudible word/ (laughs)
      [
BA:   ^Tell some stories
      I ^love stories like that.
      ^Tell us some (claps hands)..^yes.
```

TS's account therefore organizes the turn-taking behavior of the parties engaged in narrative communication. Specifically, in narratively organized discourse, there is an overall preference for a current speaker's turn at talk to continue, and a dispreference for potential next speakers to truncate that turn by self-selecting. Yet this mode of communication is not tantamount to activity on the part of the teller and passivity on the part of an interlocutor (or group of interlocutors). Rather, stories require a dovetailing of sequencing strategies by interpreters as well as producers of narrative. All parties must actively enable the production of the narrative via an intercalated sequence of behaviors performed and behaviors withheld.

3.4.2 Narrative Representations of Behavior

On the other hand, narratives also support the sequencing of behaviors by modeling, in the storyworlds they encode, what, how, where, and when a particular course of action can or should be pursued. This representational function can accrue to storyworlds no matter what their modality status, whether fictional, actual, or indeterminate. Commentators as diverse as Horace, Sir Philip Sidney, and Tipper Gore have assumed the power of fictional worlds to impinge on actual human conduct. Likewise, censorship debates and recent protests against violence in Hollywood movies have turned on questions about the capacity of narrative to model ways of behaving—to represent what might or should be done after someone else does X but before a third party can react by doing Y.

But this aspect of stories viewed as a tool for thinking can be studied more microanalytically, suggesting ways narrative provides templates for behavior in physical as well as moral-cultural worlds. For example, stories typically feature a protagonist orienting herself in space as well as time. In this respect, narratives of all sorts can function to support human navigational abilities, representing how agents might pursue a particular trajectory through a complex, dynamically emergent spatial environment—whether that environment is physical and actual or computer-mediated and virtual (Herman and Young 2000). Putting the same point another way, narrative supports 'cognitive mapping' (Downs and Stea 1977; Gould and White 1986; Herman 2001b; Ostroff 1995), i.e., the process by which things and events are mentally modeled as being located somewhere in the world.

In fact, narrative affords a range of structures for encoding emergent spatial relationships among agents, places, and objects—for representing potential paths of motion, or possible routes through space. Motion verbs, for instance, are instrumental for the construction and updating of cognitive maps for storyworlds. In English, these verbs are located on a semantic continuum whose poles are *come* and *go* (Brown 1995: 108-24; 188-91; Landau and Jackendoff 1993; Zubin and Hewitt 1995). By encoding the directionality of movement, motion verbs express viewer-relative locations of entities being perceived by narrators, as well as paths taken by entities as they move or are moved from place to place. In the natural-language narratives Gillian Brown (1995) studied, verbs such as '*come, arrive, walk in* are used of entry into the space...which is nearest the observer..., whereas *go, walked off/out* and *leave* are used as characters leave that space' (190).

Similarly, TS uses motion verbs to encode the direction of the two hunters' movements along the paths that lead to and away from the shapeshifter's house. Relevant forms include *were headed to* (hh), *went* (jj), *left* (oo), *went on* (pp), and *come back* and *went around* in (qq). These forms encode the shapeshifter's house as located at the distal end of an axis whose proximal end is the vantage-point of the storyteller. Except for the single construction describing the grandfather's movement *around* the shapeshifter's house, these verb forms encode linear paths cutting bidirectionally through space.

In representing the hunters' comings and goings as (for the most part) linear paths of motion through space, TS's account suggests how narrative is anchored in—and perhaps provides structure for—what Barbara Landau and Ray Jackendoff (1993) have characterized as a distinction between the 'what' and 'where' systems of human cognition. According to this hypothesis, spatial thinking involves a rich what-system concerned with objects (object shapes, names, and kinds), and relatively impoverished where-system concerned with places. Humans use thousands and thousands of count nouns to name objects and draw on a rich combinatorial system to describe object geometries; by contrast, and as TS's story demonstrates, the relatively small number of spatial prepositions used to represent locations preserve only very basic geometric object properties—chiefly their main axes. More than this, however, in TS's account the man's house serves as a kind of landmark, a figure standing out against a ground. The directions in which the grandfather and his friend travel on the paths leading to and away from this landmark correlate with stages of the conflict between them and the shapeshifting squirrel/man. In particular, the grandfather's final change of direction back towards the house can be mapped onto the mental reorientation needed to cognize the wounded squirrel and glaring man as one and the same being. Narrative thus provides a resource for coordinating behavioral sequences with the progress of thought; stories are a tool for interweaving doing and thinking, navigating and knowing.

3.5 Distributing Intelligence

Two heads are better than one. But too many cooks spoil the pot. Stories provide a means of balancing the two countervailing truths captured in these maxims.

In the first instance, narrative at once reflects and reinforces the supra-individual nature of intelligence—i.e., the inextricable interconnection between *trying to make sense of* and *being within* an environment that extends beyond the self (Gibson 1979; Rosch 2001). Grasping this self-environment nexus means thinking against the grain of explanatory schemes that posit a central, controlling intelligence that stands out like a foreground against a backgrounded context for mental and other forms of activity. What is required instead is some concept of agents-within-an-environment—a 'molar' notion greater than the sum of its 'molecular' components—to explain how individual as well as collective cognitive processes are organized (cf. Wertsch 1998: 20-21). Narrative, arguably, is at once a vehicle for and target of such distributed cognition, which is *enabled* by the shared construction and revision of stories, but which also *eventuates* in the fashioning and refashioning of accounts of how the world is, might be, or should be. By the same token, the methods and stakes of narrative theory change when the object of analysis is neither tellers, nor tales, nor interpreters of tales, but rather the combined product of all of these factors bearing on stories viewed as a tool for thinking.

Narrative helps distribute intelligence by facilitating more or less sustained and far-reaching blends between the individual and his or her environment. Described by Erving Goffman (1974, 1981) as a fundamental resource for 'laminating' experience—that is, a tool for embedding imagined or noncurrent scenarios within a current context of talk—stories also afford a basis for various forms of imaginative projection, including those required for empathetic identification with others. It is not just that by narrating the experiences of others, storytellers like TS (and for that matter epic poets, rhapsodes, historians, and science fiction writers) can extend the focus of concern to places, times, events, and participants beyond those that lie within their own or their interpreters' personal acquaintance. What is more, by building on their understanding of the 'social mind in action' (Palmer 2002), i.e., by drawing on the same sociocognitive processes of attribution they use to make inferences about their cohorts' unstated feelings, motives, and dispositions, readers of literary narrative have no trouble accepting the fiction writer's premise that other minds can be dipped into, reported on, even quoted verbatim by a heterodiegetic or 'third-person' narrator (cf. Herman and Childs 2003; Zunshine forthcoming). Conversational storytellers work from the same premise, as when TS relates what her grandfather wanted when he went back to look at the old man (rr) and also what he never forgot (fff). Narrative bridges self and other, creating a network of relations between storytellers, the participants whose experiences they recount, and the larger environment embedding those experiences, including the setting afforded by the activity of storytelling itself.

More generally, narrative is both an instrument for multiplying and detailing the perspectives that can be adopted on a given set of events, and also for enriching the total store of past, present, and (possible) future events that constitutes humans' knowledge base. Narrative therefore serves a dual function: correcting for biases and limitations that can result from a particular cognizer's efforts to know; and integrating such individual efforts into a larger human project that takes its character from the way it is ongoingly distributed in social and historical space. In short, the process of telling and interpreting stories inserts me into the environment I strive to know, teaching me that I do not know my world if I consider myself somehow outside of or beyond that world.[17]

Neither, though, do I know my world if I merge with it haphazardly, as one structureless, indistinguishable mass absorbed into another. If cognition is, as Hutchins (1995a, 1995b) suggests, a functional gestalt, stories afford ways of differentiating between elements within that gestalt and assigning them complementary functional roles. TS's account is made possible by a participation framework specifying roles for the storyteller and her interlocutors (Goodwin 1990: 239-57); this framework enables the social elaboration of knowledge by warding off the scenario in which everyone makes every effort to know everything all at once. Insofar as it is distributed, intelligence requires, instead, an ongoing coordination of cognitive activities—an orchestration of precisely the sort that the telling and interpreting of stories entails. Most basically, then, stories furnish a way of structuring the individual-environment nexus, constituting a principled basis for sharing the work of thought.

4 Conclusion

Far from implementing an approach to narrative analysis, this essay merely outlines a program for future research. In essence, I have been arguing for the advantages of viewing narrative theory as a subdomain of cognitive science, broadly conceived (cf. Herman 2001a, 2002). From that perspective, stories can be studied as a primary resource for building and updating models for understanding the world—and also for creating and sustaining the supra- or transindividual 'society of mind' (Minsky 1986) in which such intelligence consists. Much more interdisciplinary exchange, of the sort represented by the current volume, will be required before a cognitively grounded theory of narrative can come to full fruition. As I have argued in

---

[17] In a deep sense, this is the subject of TS's account, and not just the dynamic it exemplifies. The story involving her grandfather is in this interpretation a cautionary tale, warning against attempts to impose a rigid boundary between the human and animal worlds. Indeed, the narrative reveals the impossibility of radically separating self and other, human individual and surrounding environment.

this chapter, however, it is now possible to identify at least some of the relevant parameters for an inquiry into stories taken as a tool for thinking.[18]

Appendix

This story was elicited during a sociolinguistic interview that occurred in the trailer home of PS, one of the participants in the interview and a 22-year-old Anglo American female. The other participants included BA, the fieldworker, and TS, a 24-year-old Cherokee female. The interview occurred on 21 March 1997, in Robbinsville, North Carolina. Robbinsville is located in Graham County, which lies in the mountainous extreme western portion of the State. For ease of reference, the story has been divided into alphabetically labeled clauses. (As noted in section 3.1 above, the transcription actually features a *pair* of stories; the first focuses on the experiences of the narrator's cousin and provides an introduction or bridge to the analogous—but more meticulously recounted—experiences of TS's grandfather in the second narrative.)

TS: (a) And I've had a COUSIN~..
     (b) he was a GEORGE~..
     (c) um..that shot an OWL~..
     (d) and it ricocheted straight off that owl
     (e) and it hit him and it killed him.
     (f) That meant that that was somebody...
     (g) that was in the owl.
               [
BA: (h) Are you SERIOUS?
TS: (i) They call them shape shifts~
BA: (j) Uh huh.. uh huh.
TS: (k) And uh..Grandpa told me this years ago
     (l) and he.. swears up and down he..he's killed somebody.
     (m) And uh..he uh..when he was littler
     (n) he used to live in Cherokee
     (o) and there was two of them
     (p) and they went out...
     (q) and uh..they was hunting for SQUIRRELS and stuff~
     (r) And he saw one..it was a pretty good-sized squirrel.
     (s) He said it wasn't..a little squirrel or nothing
     (t) he noticed it was BIGGER.
BA: (u) Um hm.
TS: (v) They SHOT that squirrel.

---

[18] I am grateful to H. Porter Abbott and William Frawley for their invaluable comments on earlier drafts of this chapter.

(w) And..they could..when it fell

(x) he said it..YELLED..

(y) it screamed.

(z) And he said it from..like from its head back on its back

(aa) it just had this..you know the bullet just went.. right through=

                  [

BA: (bb)   Um hm.

TS: (cc) =and..kind of scraped it open and stuff=

             [

BA: (dd)   Um hm.

TS: (ee) =and he said that..it YELLED going down

(ff) and they tried to find it

(gg) and they couldn't FIND that squirrel.

(hh) He said he was..they were headed to some man's HOUSE

(ii) and he knows..he knowed the names and everything

(jj) and he WENT to that house

(kk) and he said that MAN looked at THEM SO ^MEAN.

(ll) And he said that normally he doesn't do that=

               [

BA: (mm)   Um hm.

TS: (nn) but he said he just looked at them..so MEAN.

(oo) And he said that..they left and everything

(pp) the other BOY had just went on

(qq) he said he come back and went around the house

(rr) and he sa..he wanted to SEE...

(ss) what was going on

(tt) he said he looked and the man had rolled over

(uu) and he had..blood down his back..=

       [

BA: (vv)   Ohhhh.

TS: (ww) =and he said he was bleeding.

(xx) And he said that man died.

BA: (yy) I'll be ^darned.

   [

TS: (zz) And he said "I ^didn't mean to do that"

(aaa) he says "but I KNOWED that..he said that..was me."

(bbb) He said "We shot him."

BA: (ccc) /I'll be darned/

   [

TS: (ddd) And he said that was him..

(eee) and that's..he was a SQUIRREL (laughs)

(fff) And he said he'll never forget that.. you know

(ggg) and he told us over and over about that story.

Transcription Conventions
(adapted from Tannen 1993 and Ochs et al. 1992):
... represents a measurable pause, more than 0.1 seconds
.. represents a slight break in timing
. indicates sentence-final intonation
, indicates clause-final intonation ("more to come")
Syllables with ~ were spoken with heightened pitch
Syllables with ^ were spoken with heightened loudness
Words and syllables transcribed with ALL CAPITALS were emphatically lengthened speech productions
[indicates overlap between different speakers' utterances
= indicates an utterance continued across another speaker's overlapping utterance
/ / enclose transcriptions that are not certain
( ) enclose nonverbal forms of expression, e.g. laughter
(( )) enclose interpolated commentary

References

Abbott, H. P. 2000. The Evolutionary Origins of Storied Mind: Modeling the Prehistory of Narrative Consciousness and Its Discontents. *Narrative* 8: 247-56.

Aristotle. 1971. *Poetics. Critical Theory Since Plato*, ed. H. Adams, 48-66. San Diego: Harcourt Brace Jovanovich.

Barthes, R. 1977 [1966]. Introduction to the Structural Analysis of Narratives. *Image Music Text*, trans. S. Heath, 79-124. New York: Hill and Wang.

Barwise, J., and J. Seligman. 1997. *Information Flow: The Logic of Distributed Systems*. Cambridge: Cambridge University Press.

Brown, G. 1995. *Speakers, Listeners and Communication: Explorations in Discourse Analysis*. Cambridge: Cambridge University Press.

Brown, G., and G. Yule. 1983. *Discourse Analysis*. Cambridge: Cambridge University Press.

Bruner, J. 1991. The Narrative Construction of Reality. *Critical Inquiry* 18: 1-21.

Carroll, N. 2001. On the Narrative Connection. *New Perspectives on Narrative Perspective*, eds. W. van Peer and S. Chatman, 21-41. Albany: State University of New York Press.

Doležel, L. 1999. · Fictional and Historical Narrative: Meeting the Postmodern Challenge. *Narratologies: New Perspectives on Narrative Analysis*, ed. D. Herman, 247-73. Columbus: Ohio State University Press.

Downs, R. M., and D. Stea. 1977. *Maps in Minds: Reflections on Cognitive Mapping*. New York: Harper and Row.

Emmott, C. 1997. *Narrative Comprehension: A Discourse Perspective*. Oxford: Oxford University Press.

Fillmore, C. 1977. The Case for Case Reopened. *Syntax and Semantics*, vol. 8, eds. P. Cole and J. Sadock, 59-81. New York: Academic Press.

Fischhoff, B. 1999. Judgment Heuristics. *The MIT Encyclopedia of the Cognitive Sciences*, eds. R. A. Wilson and F. C. Keil, 423-25. Cambridge, MA: MIT Press.

Fiske, S. T., and S. E. Taylor. 1991. *Social Cognition*, 2nd ed. New York: McGraw-Hill.

Frawley, W. 1997. *Vygotsky and Cognitive Science: Language and the Unification of the Social and Computational Mind*. Cambridge, MA: Harvard University Press.

Genette, G. 1980 [1972]. *Narrative Discourse: An Essay in Method*, trans. J. E. Lewin. Ithaca: Cornell University Press.

Gibson, J. J. 1979. *The Ecological Approach to Visual Perception*. Boston: Houghton-Mifflin.

Giora, R., and Y. Shen. 1994. Degrees of Narrativity and Strategies of Semantic Reduction. *Poetics* 22: 447-58.

Gobet, F. 1999. Chess, Psychology of. *The MIT Encyclopedia of the Cognitive Sciences*, eds. R. A. Wilson and F. C. Keil, 113-15. Cambridge, MA: MIT Press.

Goffman, E. 1974. *Frame Analysis: An Essay on the Organization of Experience*. New York: Harper and Row.

Goffman, E. 1981. *Forms of Talk*. Philadelphia: University of Pennsylvania Press.

Goodwin, M. H. 1990. *He-Said-She-Said: Talk as Social Organization Among Black Children*. Bloomington: Indiana University Press.

Gould, P., and R. White. 1986. *Mental Maps*, 2nd ed. Boston: Allen and Unwin.

Grice, P. 1989 [1975]. Logic and Conversation. *Studies in the Way of Words*, 22-40. Cambridge, MA: Harvard University Press.

Herman, D. 1999. Towards a Socionarratology: New Ways of Analyzing Natural-language Narratives. *Narratologies: New Perspectives on Narrative Analysis*, ed. D. Herman, 218-46. Columbus: Ohio State University Press.

Herman, D. 2000. Pragmatic Constraints on Narrative Processing: Actants and Anaphora Resolution in a Corpus of North Carolina Ghost Stories. *Journal of Pragmatics* 32: 959-1001.

Herman, D. 2001a. Narrative Theory and the Cognitive Sciences. *Narrative Inquiry* 11: 1-34.

Herman, D. 2001b. Spatial Reference in Narrative Domains. *TEXT* 21: 515-41.

Herman, D. 2002. *Story Logic: Problems and Possibilities of Narrative*. Lincoln: University of Nebraska Press.

Herman, D. Forthcoming. Regrounding Narratology: The Study of Narratively Organized Systems for Thinking. *What is Narratology?*, eds. Jan-Christoph Meister, Tom Kindt, and Hans-Harald Müller. Berlin: de Gruyter.

Herman, D., and B. Childs. 2003. Narrative and Cognition in *Beowulf*. *Style* 37.2: 177-202.

Herman, D., and R. M. Young. 2000. Narrative Structure in Intelligent Tutoring Systems. Paper presented at the annual meeting of the Society for the Study of Narrative Literature. Atlanta, Georgia.

Hirschfeld, L. A., and S. A. Gelman, eds. 1994. *Mapping the Mind: Domain Specificity in Cognition and Culture*. New York: Cambridge University Press.

Husserl, E. 1973. *Experience and Judgment*, ed. L. Landgrebe, trans. J. S. Churchill and K. Ameriks. Evanston: Northwestern University Press.

Hutchins, E. 1995a. *Cognition in the Wild*. Cambridge, MA: MIT Press.

Hutchins, E. 1995b. How a Cockpit Remembers Its Speeds. *Cognitive Science* 19: 265-88.

Hutchins, E. 1999. Cognitive Artifacts. *The MIT Encyclopedia of the Cognitive Sciences*, eds. R. A. Wilson and F. C. Keil, 126-28. Cambridge, MA: MIT Press.

John-Steiner, V. 1997. *Notebooks of the Mind: Explorations of Thinking*, revised ed. New York: Oxford University Press.

Kahneman, D., P. Slovic, and A. Tversky, eds. 1982. *Judgment under Uncertainty: Heuristics and Biases*. Cambridge: Cambridge University Press.

Kehler, Andrew. 2002. *Coherence, Reference, and the Theory of Grammar*. Stanford, CA: CSLI Publications.

Kirsh, D. 1995. The Intelligent Use of Space. *Artificial Intelligence* 73: 31-68.

Labov, W. 1972. The Transformation of Experience in Narrative Syntax. *Language in the Inner City*, 354-96. Philadelphia: University of Pennsylvania Press.

Landau, B., and R. Jackendoff. 1993. 'What' and 'Where' in Spatial Language and Cognition. *Behavioral and Brain Sciences* 16: 217-65.

Lee, B. 1997. *Talking Heads: Language, Metalanguage, and the Semiotics of Subjectivity*. Durham: Duke University Press.

Linde, C. 1993. *Life Stories: The Creation of Coherence*. Oxford: Oxford University Press.

Lukes, S. 1977. Methodological Individualism Reconsidered. *Essays in Social Theory*, ed. S. Lukes, 177-86. New York: Columbia University Press.

Mink, L. O. 1978. Narrative Form as a Cognitive Instrument. *The Writing of History: Literary Form and Historical Understanding*, eds. R. H. Canary and H. Kozicki, 129-49. Madison: University of Wisconsin Press.

Minsky, M. 1975. A Framework for Representing Knowledge. *The Psychology of Computer Vision*, ed. P. Winston, 211-77. New York: McGraw-Hill.

Minsky, M. 1986. *The Society of Mind*. New York: Touchstone.

Nebel, B. Frame-Based Systems. 1999. *The MIT Encyclopedia of the Cognitive Sciences*, eds. R. A. Wilson and F. C. Keil, 324-26. Cambridge, MA: MIT Press.

Norman, D. 1993. *Things That Make Us Smart*. Reading, MA: Addison-Wesley.

Nunes, T. 1997. What Organizes Our Problem-Solving Activities. *Discourse, Tools, and Reasoning: Essays on Situated Cognition*, eds. L. B. Resnick, R. Säljö, C. Pontecorvo, and B. Burge, 288-311. Berlin: Springer.

Ochs, E., and L. Capps. 2001. *Living Narrative: Creating Lives in Everyday Storytelling*. Cambridge, MA: Harvard University Press.

Ochs, E., C. Taylor, D. Rudolph, and R. Smith. 1992. Storytelling as Theory-Building Activity. *Discourse Processes* 15: 37-72.

Ostroff, S. 1995. Maps on My Past: Race, Space, and Place in the Life Stories of Washington D.C. Area Teenagers. *Oral History Review* 22: 33-53.

Palmer, A. 2002. The Construction of Fictional Minds. *Narrative* 10: 28-46.

Resnick, L.B., C. Pontecorvo, and R. Säljö. 1997. Discourse, Tools, and Reasoning. *Discourse, Tools, and Reasoning: Essays on Situated Cognition*, eds. L. B. Resnick, R. Säljö, C. Pontecorvo, and B. Burge, 2-20. Berlin: Springer.

Rogoff, B. 1990. *Apprenticeship in Thinking: Cognitive Development in Social Context*. New York: Oxford University Press.

Rosch, E. 2001. 'If You Depict a Bird, Give It Space to Fly': Eastern Psychologies, the Arts, and Self-Knowledge. *SubStance* 94/95: 236-53.

Sacks, H. 1992. *Lectures on Conversation*. Cambridge: Basil Blackwell.

Sacks, H., E. A. Schegloff, and G. Jefferson. 1974. A Simplest Systematics for the Organization of Turn-Taking for Conversation. *Language* 50: 696-735.

Schegloff, E. A. 1981. Discourse as an Interactional Achievement. *Analyzing Discourse: Text and Talk*, ed. D. Tannen, 71-93. Georgetown: Georgetown University Press.

Schiffrin, D. 1987. *Discourse Markers*. Cambridge: Cambridge University Press.

Schutz, A. 1962. Common-Sense and the Scientific Interpretation of Human Action. *Collected Papers*, vol. 1, ed. M. Natanson, 3-47. The Hague: Martinus Nijhoff.

Shore, B. 1996. *Culture in Mind: Cognition, Culture, and the Problem of Meaning*. New York: Oxford University Press.

Simon, H. A., and W. G. Chase. 1973. Skill in Chess. *American Scientist* 61: 393-403.

Spolsky, E. 2001. Why and How to Take the Fruit and Leave the Chaff. *SubStance* 94/95: 177-98.

Talmy, L. 2000. A Cognitive Framework for Narrative Structure. *Toward a Cognitive Semantics*, vol. 2, 417-82. Cambridge, MA: MIT Press.

Tannen, D. 1993. What's in a Frame? Surface Evidence for Underlying Expectations. *Framing in Discourse*, ed. D. Tannen, 14-56. Oxford: Oxford University Press.

Turner, M. 1996. *The Literary Mind.* New York: Oxford University Press.

Tversky, A., and D. Kahneman. 1971. Belief in the 'Law of Small Numbers'. *Psychological Bulletin* 76: 105-10.

Tversky, A., and D. Kahneman. 1974. Judgment under Uncertainty: Heuristics and Biases. *Science* 185: 1124-31.

Virtanen, T. 1992. Issues of Text Typology: Narrative—a 'Basic' Type of Text? *TEXT* 12: 293-310.

Wertsch, J. 1985. *Vygotsky and the Social Formation of Mind.* Cambridge, MA: Harvard University Press.

-----. 1991. *Voices of the Mind: A Sociocultural Approach to Mediated Action.* Cambridge, MA: Harvard University Press.

-----. 1998. *Mind as Action.* New York: Oxford University Press.

Zubin, D. A., and L. E. Hewitt. 1995. The Deictic Center: A Theory of Deixis in Narrative. *Deixis in Narrative: A Cognitive Science Perspective*, eds. J. F. Duchan, G. A. Bruder, and L. E. Hewitt, 129-55. Hillsdale, NJ: Lawrence Erlbaum.

Zunshine, L. Forthcoming. Theory of Mind and Fiction. *Narrative.*

Part III

New Directions
for Cognitive Narratology

8

'Awake! Open your eyes!' The Cognitive Logic of External and Internal Stories

MANFRED JAHN

1 Introduction

Narratology's standard objects of analysis are stories which exist in some physically tangible form—'external' stories such as one encounters in novels, anecdotes, movies, and plays. This chapter argues that postclassical narratology must wake up to the existence of 'internal stories', too—the stories which are stored in memory and performed in the mental theater of recollection, imagination, and dream.[1] While theorists from various disciplines—philosophy, anthropology, and cognitive science—have emphasized the psychological and cultural importance of internal stories, their narratological relevance has generally escaped notice. Accepting internal stories as crucial counterparts of external stories, the chapter presents a model of the 'cycle of narrative' which connects external and internal stories. Three test cases are used to point up the model's implications—conversational storytelling in Billy Wilder's *The Apartment*, Coleridge's account of the genesis of 'Kubla Khan', and operatic storytelling in Richard Wagner's *Ring*.

---

[1] On the notion of postclassical 'narratologies', see Herman (1999) and Fludernik (2000).

Narrative Theory and the Cognitive Sciences.
David Herman (ed.).
Copyright © 2003, CSLI Publications.

2 The Object(s) of Narratology

When narratologists talk of the beginnings of their discipline, they typically hark back to the year 1966 and issue number 8 of the French periodical *Communications*. Although the term narratology has yet to be coined (by Todorov, in 1969), the title of the special issue succinctly anticipates what narratology is going to be all about—*L'analyse structurale du récit*, the structural analysis of narrative. As a matter of fact, mustering authors like Roland Barthes, Gérard Genette, Tzvetan Todorov, Algirdas-Julien Greimas, Umberto Eco, and Christian Metz, the list of contributors reads like a Who's Who of contemporary structuralists. Introducing the subject in the lead essay ('Introduction à l'analyse structurale des récits'), Barthes begins by presenting his famous list of story forms (I am bolding the terms which denote possible medial realizations):

> There are **countless forms of narrative** in the world. First of all, there is a prodigious variety of genres, each of which branches out into **a variety of media**, as if all **substances** could be relied upon to accommodate man's stories. Among the **vehicles of narrative** are articulated language, whether oral or written, pictures, still or moving, gestures, and an ordered mixture of all those **substances**: narrative is present in myth, legend, fables, tales, short stories, epic history, tragedy, *drame* [suspense drama], comedy, pantomime, paintings (in Santa Ursula by Carpaccio, for instance), stained-glass windows, movies, local news, conversation. Moreover, in **this infinite variety of forms**, it is present at all times, in all places, in all societies; indeed narrative starts with the very history of mankind; there is not, there has never been anywhere, any people without narrative; all classes, all human groups, have their stories, and very often those stories are enjoyed by men of different and even opposite cultural backgrounds: narrative remains largely unconcerned with good or bad literature. **Like life itself**, it is there, international, transhistorical, transcultural. (Barthes 1975 [1966]: 237)

Stressing the ubiquity of stories and storytelling, Barthes details a long list of genres as instances of narrative 'media', 'substances', 'vehicles', and 'forms'. As narratology grows into a full-fledged discipline in the nineteen-seventies, this broad conception of narrative forms quickly becomes a disputed issue, and to this day, the narratological community is largely divided on what constitutes the objects and the scope of the discipline. Commentators usually either claim that the list buries crucial differences or that it inundates the structuralist project in a sea of heterogeneous data. Embracing the latter view, Barthes presents a case for a 'deductive' approach which begins by hypostatizing a general 'model of description' and proceeds 'from that model down, towards the species, which at the same time partake in and deviate from the model' (1975 [1966]: 239). In Genette's version of the deductive model, however, the objects of narratology are already restricted to verbally narrated texts so that novel and drama not only appear as different species but as incompatible categories. It is on this ground that he considers drama an 'extranarrative' medium—'extranarrative if one defines narrative *stricto sensu*, as I do, as a *verbal* transmission' (Genette 1988 [1983]: 16).[2]

On reflection, however, there are notable pitfalls to restricting the field of analysis and pursuing a straight top-down approach. Restrictions can be arbitrary, and a general model of description may fail to generalize appropriately. Nothing goes if everything must always remain *stricto sensu*. A narrative enacted in a performance is anything but a contradiction in terms. Indeed, from a postclassical narratological vantage, Barthes's argument for a set of initial terms and principles appears less important today than his equally sustained emphasis on the 'plurality of narrative acts' and 'their historical, geographical, and cultural diversity' (1975 [1966]: 239). Heeding Barthes's twofold orientation, Seymour Chatman has passionately argued for the commonality of all narrative forms, a commonality which, according to Chatman, manifests itself in cross-generic modes of telling and showing, a large inventory of common plots and techniques, and the 'double chrono-logic' (Chatman 1990: 9) of action and performance/reception. Proposing a taxonomy of 'text types' (1990: 115), Chatman manages to impose a top-down order on Barthes's list and to treat novel, drama, and film as related narrative forms (Jahn 2001). Although quite rigid in a superficial sense, Chatman's taxonomy is in fact open to Barthes's notion of the 'infinite variety' of narrative forms and easily accommodates deviant and marginal types. Needless to say, it is just these latter cases that are the preferred objects of analysis in much of today's critical discourse. Against this background, the perceived danger of broad definitions—of not seeing the wood for the trees—recedes behind the evil of the exclusionary generalizations that so often float in the wake of *stricto sensu* definitions.

---

[2] Quite a few narratologists have followed this line of reasoning, though some are less certain, and others shift position from time to time. Gerald Prince, for instance, adopts Barthes's broad definition in *Narratology* (1982), whereas in his *Dictionary of Narratology* he argues, along with Genette, that a play is 'not a narrative because it is performed by actors on stage' (1987: 58).

3 External vs. Internal Stories

Adopting Barthes's and Chatman's broadly conceived narrative objects, I find myself wondering whether the screw could not be given another turn, or rather, be loosened further. Saying this, I do not mean to complain that this or that genre or text-type is missing either in Barthes's list or in Chatman's tree—programme symphony, say, or soap opera, or hypertext fiction, or some other new-fangled form. Chatman's taxonomy includes a number of empty 'Other' slots so that extras and newcomers are easily accommodated. But what about internal stories? These are such significant Others that there is no provision for them in Chatman's taxonomy, open and flexible as it is. If dreams, memories, or fantasies find any acknowledgment in narratological accounts at all (which is a rare enough occurrence) they are usually treated as 'embedded narratives' (Ryan 1991: 156), i.e. located within and framed by an external narrative. As a matter of fact, it is Barthes who makes a move towards internal stories when, toward the end of the passage quoted earlier, he associates narrative with 'life itself', that is, something which transcends substance, media, and form.

If one looks beyond the confines of narratology, even broadly defined, independent consideration of internal, 'mental', or 'untold' stories is not as extravagant as may appear at first glance. There are a number of observers who view stories and storytelling as psychological and cognitive *forces* rather than as *forms* of communication or entertainment. Thus Eric Berne, a psychoanalyst, argues that a person's life plans are 'scripted' on fairy-tales. Daniel C. Dennett, a philosopher, claims that 'everyone is a novelist' (1988: 1016) writing his or her life story. Paul Ricoeur, a literary theorist, argues that life and identity are 'in quest of narrative' (1991: 20). Roger C. Schank (1995), an Artificial Intelligence pioneer (and co-inventor of the 'script' concept), suggests that human memory is a database of stories. Finally, Mark Turner, a cognitive critic, holds that 'most of our experience, our knowledge, and our thinking is organized as stories' (1996: i). Many more testimonials of this kind could be added. Although one of the observers, Paul Ricoeur, strictly denies that any analytical move toward 'narrative understanding stemming from the creative imagination' (1991: 24) could fall within the province of narratological inquiry, the testimonials quoted above raise two questions directly related to basic narratological issues. One of these questions is whether 'the study of narratives can help us understand the workings of the mind' (Chafe 1990: 96); the other is how internal stories impact on narratological theory.

Let us tentatively assume, at this point, that the general concept of *story* subdivides into external and internal stories, and that this is a primary distinction before any additional distinctions come into play. This decision allows us to think in terms of 'contrastive features' and perhaps a table of oppositions such as presented in Table 1. To include a level of exemplification, I have, somewhat arbitrarily, associated external stories with a fairy-tale, and internal stories with a dream.

1	external story (e.g., a fairy-tale)	internal story (e.g., a dream)
2	physical	virtual
3	recordable	reportable
4	public	private
5	addressee orientation	no addressee orientation
6	permanent	fleeting

Table 1. External and Internal Stories in a Table of Oppositions

Generally speaking, contrastive tables are highly efficient because they offer two definitions for the price of one. To make them work, one needs crisp and polar features, preferably features that can be rewritten as plus/minus pairs (for instance, one could use *+public* and *-public* rather than *public* vs. *private*). Unfortunately, however, most of the terms used in Table 1 are fuzzy rather than crisp, and this may be a reflection of the fact that the objects involved are too heterogeneous to allow a well-defined set of distinctive features. For instance, *recordable* vs. *reportable* in line 3 is an awkward opposition, and *reportable* in particular is not distinctive to internal stories. Nor are all external stories necessarily public, as is asserted in line 4, considering the evidence of the diary form. Hence *public* is only a *typicality* feature, at best, as is *addressee orientation* (line 5). The degree of permanence claimed for external stories (line 6) is not absolute either, considering that stories can be erased from public record—in which case their continued existence may paradoxically depend on somebody's 'internal record' of them.

In the final analysis, all the seemingly clean divisions suggested by the table are deceptive and the two types of stories are just as difficult to categorize as mundane objects like marrows and pumpkins (fruit or vegetable?). As happens so often, the range of properties of an object is neither immediately manifest nor can it be absolutely delimited by a set of clear-cut conditions. External and internal stories, in particular, are highly indeterminate when viewed in isolation and prone to shift status erratically as soon as contextual factors come into play. Suppose you had a dream and you recount what you remember of it. The person who hears your report gets an external story of an internal story. Again, suppose your mother tells you the (external) story of Little Red Riding Hood. Subsequently, you may *internalize* it, script your life on it, and rely on it as one of your personalized internal stories (a similar scenario will be discussed in more detail, below). The contrastive features of Table 1 cannot tell us anything about such associations, transitions, and adaptations, not to mention the chicken-and-egg question of which comes first—the internal story which turns into an external one, or the external story which people adopt as an internal one.

At this point narratologists are likely to throw up their hands in frustration. If Barthes's inventory of story types was too heterogeneous already, gratuitous addition of internal stories appears to compromise systematic investigation beyond hope. No wonder that there is so little communication between narratologists, focusing on external narratives, and psychologists, anthropologists, and cognitivists, focusing on internal narratives.

4 A Cyclical Model

Nevertheless, giving up at this point amounts to a classic case of throwing out the baby with the bath water. As a matter of fact, the table's weaknesses are a strong clue as to where to look for a way out of the structuralist prison-house. We are not, after all, entirely unfamiliar with chicken-and-egg scenarios. The expression 'internalization', which insinuated itself into the discussion above, strongly suggests that what one needs is a model of *transitional states* rather than one of contrastive categories. Indeed, the theoretical precedent that immediately springs to mind is Bremond's model of the French folktale, whose plot line cycles through two main states—a 'satisfactory state' and a 'state of deficiency'. Each state change is the product of a 'procedure' in Bremond's model—logically enough, it is a procedure of 'improvement' which leads to the satisfactory state, and a procedure of 'degradation' which leads to the state of deficiency (Bremond 1970: 251). For convenience, the following graphic shows a version of Bremond's model as part (a), while part (b) presents the obvious extrapolation.

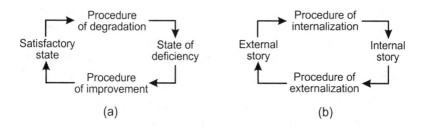

(a)   (b)

Figure 1. Appropriating Bremond's Model of the French Folktale (a) for a Cycle of Narrative (b)

As one can see, adaptation of Bremond's model simply consists of making some substitutions and introducing a procedure of *externalization* as the logical counterpart of the procedure of *internalization*. Let us see what happens when we add some detail. Consider Figure 2.

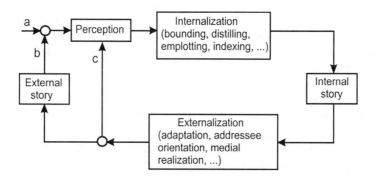

Figure 2. Flow-Charting the Cycle of Stories

The flowchart features of the refined design emphasize that we have shifted gears, so to speak, and begun to conceptualize external and internal stories as data structures connected by flows of information. (One of the practical advantages of a computational model is that it allows us to employ 'structured' strategies such as top-down design, modularity, and virtual testing.) Note that, in order to use the computational concepts, internal stories are here treated as if they were 'realized' (and thus transmittable) as 'mental representations'.[3]

---

[3]Interestingly, Ryan's treatment of 'embedded' internal stories rests on a similar assumption (1991: 274n2). Needless to say, the notion of mental representations is open to serious

On the whole, the revised model pursues a more dedicated orientation towards how a human mind—treated as a 'computational mind' as suggested by Jackendoff (1987)—handles stories, particularly how it gets them, how it adapts and adopts them, and how it makes them. As is common in flowcharts, the model presents its procedures as 'black boxes' of which, at the present level of refinement, we know no more than their input and output. The major addition introduced at this point is the box labeled Perception. This actually means that the narrative cycle is no longer considered to be a hermetically closed one. Rather, the perception device provides an interface for three channels of information (marked a, b, and c). If input routes through channel a, the mind emplots a story from an ongoing stream of real-life events (typical cases: on-the-spot reporting and teichoscopy ['viewing from a wall'] in classical drama). If perceptional input comes via route b, the mind is in the recipient mode of reading or watching a story cast in one of the forms and media listed by Barthes. Finally, channel c represents an internal feedback route which supplies story data for imaginary perception and offline thinking.

As I have argued on a prior occasion, imaginary perception is a crucial concept in cognitive narratology (Jahn 1996). According to the flowchart logic of the present model, imaginary perception is closely bound up with the procedure of Externalization and associates with three major types of events: (i) drafting a story for possible actual production, (ii) remembering, daydreaming, and similar mental activities, (iii) dreaming. In the first two cases, imaginary perception is a functional part of wakefulness, while during the act of dreaming the perception device mistakes channel-c (internal) input for channel-a (external) input. Actual composition of a story is understood to cycle through channels c (imagining, remembering) and b (external reception, reading) in close or near-simultaneous succession—a scenario which provides an interesting theoretical ground to Henry James's statement that 'the teller of a story is primarily, none the less, the listener to it, the reader of it, too' (1984 [1908]: 1089).

The next level of refinement of the model will have to address further specifics of the Procedures of Internalization and Externalization, and on an informal level Figure 2 already anticipates some likely subprocedures. Thus Internalization is likely to factor out into 'bounding' (i.e., setting the beginning and closure boundaries of a story), 'distilling' (selection of relevant detail), 'emplotting' (selection of a plot schema), and 'indexing'

---

challenge. No precise formalization of mental representations is available at present, nor does anybody know whether it ever will be in the future. The closest narratologists have come to mental representations of stories are the linguistics-inspired 'story grammars' drawn up in the structuralist period of the discipline.

(more on this below). Similarly, the Externalization box will presumably submodularize into an 'adaptation' procedure (for creating a specific media type), an 'addressee orientation' procedure (tailoring the story to the needs of actual or hypothetical recipients, including oneself), and a 'translation' procedure (mapping visual matter into lingual representations, and vice versa).

I will break off discussion of technicalities here, and will also deliberately evade the question whether a model synthesizing human story processing can ever be made to 'work', and if so, for what purpose. Rather, at this point, I would like to assess the explanatory gains established already. To begin with, the model's attention to dynamic processes and transitions resolves most of the problems besetting the contrastive features of Table 1. Second, the cycle of Internalization and Externalization creates a causal chain linking reception and production and suggesting that both processes are perhaps mutually dependent (a point to be further explored below). While this explicit linkage closes the door to a 'mentalist' model in which 'the thinker' appears to be the solitary manipulator of self-contained mental representations, it opens the door to a system which accepts cognizers as participants in an essentially social process. Third, on a level of disciplines, the model generates a number of postulates and hypotheses which directly feed into investigative frameworks such as 'narrative psychology' (Sarbin 1986) and 'psychonarratology' (Bortolussi and Dixon 2003). (As far as I can see, it transcends these approaches by presenting a more holistic picture of the relatedness of reception and production.) And, fourth, the model situates real and imaginary perception in a framework of story-based memory processes.

Since memory processes are inherent in the model's design, a brief excursion into the role of stories in cognitive theories of memory may be in order. In the cognitive literature, 'semantic' memory is often opposed to 'episodic' memory (Schacter 1996), or 'MOP memory' and 'story memory' in Schank's terms (1995: 118). MOPs (memory organization packages) store information by disconnecting it from its original context and by filtering out irrelevant and distractive elements. Cognitive taxonomies, for instance, are potentially useful substructures of MOPs. For instance, one usually has an answer to the question of whether a flounder has gills even if one has never encountered the question before. The likely reason for this is that one has access to a highly organized knowledge database which first tells one that a flounder is a fish and then supplies the information that fish have gills. Hence, most people will claim that they 'know' that a flounder has gills even though they really deduce this on the fly (Schank 1995: 118). By contrast, story memory stores and recalls a sequence of events retaining the connectivity of episodes. Moreover, often stories are memorized (internalized) so as to maximize future tellability. According to Schank, the ability to recall and produce a perspicacious external story is a major indicator of human intelligence. Another ingredient, as we shall see in more detail below, is the teller's ability to adapt the story to the pragmatic requirements of the narrative situation, that is, to activate a suitable process of Externalization.

5 Three Test Cases

While it is one thing for a model to have a certain face validity, the true test of it lies in the question of whether it adds to our understanding of actual cases. In the remainder of this essay, I will discuss three test cases which crucially revolve around memory retrieval, adaptive storytelling, feedback loops, and forgetting. Illustrating the applicability of the model, I will focus on a hyponarrative (or embedded story) from a film, an author's anecdotal account of the genesis of a poem, and the climax scene of a romantic opera. The recalcitrant data contained in some of these cases will put the model under considerable strain. Ideally, this will show us how far it (and we) can go.

5.1 Conversational Storytelling in *The Apartment*

In *Tell Me a Story*, Schank presents a fine example of intelligent storytelling. Schank is mainly interested in how an external story told by speaker A reminds hearer B of an internal story of his own, and how speaker B's subsequent narrative response pursues certain pragmatic goals. In the scene from Wilder's film, 'Bud' Baxter (Jack Lemmon) has barely managed to save Fran Kubelik (Shirley McLaine) from committing suicide. Earlier, she had told him the story of her 'talent for falling in love with the wrong guy in the wrong place at the wrong time' [Wilder and Diamond 1998: 118]). This reminds Bud of a story in which *he* is the protagonist (the following passage has been directly quoted from Schank):[4]

> I know how you feel, Miss Kubelik. You think it's the end of the world
> - but it's not, really. I went through exactly the same thing myself.
> Well maybe not exactly - I tried to do it with a gun. She was the wife of
> my best friend, and I was mad for her. But I knew it was hopeless - so I
> decided to end it all. I went to a pawnshop and bought a .45 automatic,

---

[4]I quote from Schank rather than from the original because he conveniently filters out both the playscript format and all conversational interruptions and turntakings that encumber the original text. (This, too, is an example of appropriating an external story for one's own goals.)

and drove up to Eden Park - do you know Cincinnati? Anyway, I parked the car and loaded the gun - well, you read in the papers all the time that people shoot themselves, but believe me, it's not that easy - I mean, how do you do it? Here or here or here [with cocked finger, he points to his temple, mouth, and chest]. You know where I finally shot myself? [Indicates knee.] Here. While I was sitting there, trying to make my mind up, a cop stuck his head in the car, because I was illegally parked - so I started to hide the gun under the seat and it went off - pow! Took me a year before I could bend my knee - but I got over the girl in three weeks. She still lives in Cincinnati, has four kids, gained twenty pounds - she - Here's the fruitcake. [Shows it to her under Christmas tree.] And you want to see my knee? (Schank 1995: 42-43)

Being reminded of something, Schank argues, is like searching a database of indexes to stories in memory. Whether something reminds one of a story partly depends on the quality of the index which was generated when the story was originally prepared for possible recall. (Note that our model makes 'indexing' part of its procedure of Internalization.) However, as Schank points out, being able to access an efficient relational database is only one aspect of intelligent storytelling. Equally important is how a speaker manages to adapt a story to the pragmatic needs of the situation. Bud Baxter excels in this area. One of his main 'YOU-goals' is to get across a piece of sensible advice—namely, that drastic action isn't always the proper cure. In addition to this, Bud also pursues a number of less obvious 'ME-goals'—from the simple goal of 'getting attention', which usually attends story-telling (Schank 1995: 43), to the more specific goals of establishing himself as a humorous person, an ideal confidant, and a better candidate than the married men in Ms. Kubelik's life.

Ms. Kubelik's own story, which precedes Bud's story and in which she confesses to her fatal attraction to married men, is just as significant an example of conversational storytelling because it lets her hearer get a glimpse of the psychological dilemma she is caught up in. While Schank mainly focuses on the cathartic intention of her confession, the story also presents a 'life script' (this is Eric Berne's term, not to be confused with Schank's own script concept). This script contains a sequence of roles and action patterns which Fran Kubelik feels compelled to enact and repeat until it either works out in a happy ending or climaxes in a catastrophe (the latter is the more likely outcome). The existential plight created by malign scripts is well understood in Bernean transactional psychology, and it is no coincidence, perhaps, that it frequently recurs as a trait of character in Wilder's films. To bring out the scripted nature of obsessive behavior it is standard procedure for the transactional therapist to inquire after the patient's favorite fairy tale (Berne 1973: 435). To which Ms. Kubelik might well reply, Beauty and the Beast (cp. Berne's note on the tale, 1973: 47). A script abstracted from this tale might well instruct Ms. Kubelik to look out for and have an affair with a disguised Prince. Sooner or later, the Prince is likely to transform into a married beast and abandon her, happy endings being less frequent in real life than in fairy tales. Eventually, not having the strength to repeat the familiar moves of the script, she will try to commit suicide, as she does in the film. Potent as Ms. Kubelik's script is, it is the perfect cue for Bud Baxter's intelligent narrative response, which highlights the flaws inherent in the script and at the same time suggests a more sensible alternative.

5.2 Coleridge on 'Kubla Khan'

Although 'Kubla Khan' was written in 1798, Coleridge did not initially feel that it merited publication. When he finally did allow publication, in 1816, he added a one-page prefatory note written in the third person. 'The poem is here published', he states, 'at the request of a poet of great and deserved celebrity' (this is usually taken to be a reference to Byron). Otherwise Coleridge strongly deprecates the poem, calling it 'a fragment' and adding that 'as far as the Author's own opinions are concerned', the poem is published 'rather as a psychological curiosity, than on the ground of any supposed *poetic* merit'. I will come back to these judgments, but my main interest lies in the author's subsequent story of the genesis of the text:

> In the summer of the year 1797, the Author, then in ill health, had retired to a lonely farm-house between Porlock and Linton, on the Exmoor confines of Somerset and Devonshire. In consequence of a slight indisposition, an anodyne had been prescribed, from the effects of which he fell asleep in his chair at the moment that **he was reading the following sentence, or words of the same substance in 'Purchas's Pilgrimage'**: 'Here the Khan Kubla commanded a palace to be built, and a stately garden thereunto. And thus ten miles of fertile ground were inclosed with a wall'. The Author continued for about three hours in a **profound sleep**, at least of the **external senses**, during which time he has the most vivid confidence, that he could not have **composed** less than from two to three hundred lines; if that indeed can be called composition in which all the **images rose up before him as *things*, with a parallel production of the correspondent expressions, without any sensation or consciousness of effort**. On awaking he appeared to himself to have a distinct **recollection** of the whole, and taking his pen, ink and paper, instantly and **eagerly wrote down the lines** that are here preserved. At this moment he was unfortunately called out by a person on business from Porlock, and detained by him above an hour, and on his return to his room, found, to his no small surprise and mortification, that [...] all the rest had **passed away** like the images on the surface of a stream into which a stone has been cast, but, alas!

without the after restoration of the latter! (Coleridge 1966: 295-296; all bolded emphases mine)

Today it is generally acknowledged that this account suffers from an abundance of factual mistakes, to say nothing of the blatant aesthetic misjudgment that provides the frame in which it is presented. Many critics are also fascinated by what Coleridge censors out in this particular account, namely that the medication he took for his 'slight indisposition' consisted of three grains of opium. Less attention is usually given to the cognitive oddity or even absurdity of the case, even though this is what makes the story anecdotally tellable in the first place. What is quite pertinent, in the present context, is the poet's description of the 'effortless' translation of vision into words, a process that supposedly begins even before he sets pen to paper. None of this sounds very credible at face value, but on the strength of the model presented here, and on the strength of assumptions common in cognitive studies today, the account is in fact far more plausible than critics are generally inclined to accept.

As a matter of fact, Coleridge's story presents a striking example of what Jackendoff (1997: 192) calls the 'dumb, and obsessive conversion of mental representations', in this case, the conversion of vision into concept, and of concept into vision, speech, and action. Inaccurate as Coleridge's story may be on historical facts, it is also a vivid confirmation of the cognitive commonplace that one has to rehearse what one wants to remember, especially in cases of fleeting data such as dreams. Once awake, Coleridge proceeds to create and produce the external narrative he has all the while been composing, claiming that he only needed to write down what had already been finished. Then the fateful interruption by the messenger from Porlock apparently causes the rest of the dream vision, including its internal pre-composition, to pass away into oblivion. Again, while it is difficult to accept this on a level of historical accuracy, the story illustrates what our model presents as an entirely natural psychological process.

As Coleridge points out, the dream vision at the heart of the poem revives *and continues* the imaginary perception triggered by reading *Purchas His Travels*, an external story. Coleridge even quotes the pre-text's sentence that in the poem's subsequent intertextual adaptation translates into the initial lines of the poem. The author's paratext itself is not an original account either but an account of something recollected in tranquillity and rephrased to fit a particular narrative situation. In this light, the text's explicit addressee orientation and its transposition into the third person (a 'transvocalization' in narratological terms) are significant stylistic moves. Treating this as an instance of 'faulty' memory, drug-induced hallucination, and after-the-fact authorial spin-doctoring is only half of the truth. If one disregards the supernatural paraphernalia what remains is a sensible account of the processes of modification, adaptation, and incremental interpretation which our model suggests is the perfectly ordinary course of events. Moreover, nothing is ultimately settled; the cycle is only temporarily interrupted when Coleridge reaches his 'final' verdict. Even as he utters his disparaging disclaimer, the rhetoric of the gesture is obvious. Admitting the celebrity testimonial, the author, too, has embarked on a process of re-evaluation. 'Memory', as Schank puts it most succinctly (1995: 138), 'tends to lose the original and keep the copy. The original events recede, and the new story takes its place'.

5.3 Siegfried's Story

All of Richard Wagner's operas run on elaborate plots, and the *Ring* tetralogy, which weaves and binds the fates of generations, races, and worlds, has the most tightly knitted plot of all. Anything worth mentioning is directly or indirectly related to everything else. Tightly knitted plots encourage storytelling, and story-telling takes up much of the opera's time and action. Often, the second-degree stories told by the characters merely serve the standard function of exposition and reminder, sometimes they trigger major courses of action, and occasionally they stand as central moments of action itself. Act III, Scene 2, of *Götterdämmerung* is one the latter cases, but it begins harmlessly enough with a story told for the manifest purpose of entertaining and distracting King Gunther, who is under a cloud. Naturally, there is a twist: in a moment, the story will get out of hand, and its teller will be killed for telling it. These are clearly storytelling circumstances of a special nature, and in this case they are compounded by the fact, of particular interest to narratologists, that the teller will never return to the narrative level from which he sets out.

Though not a born storyteller, Siegfried's heroic status assures access to a rich store of tellable stories of personal experience, and it needs only a little priming to set him off. *People say you understand the language of birds*, Hagen, his unsuspected antagonist, prompts him, and, like many storytellers, Siegfried begins not *in medias res* but by going back a bit, knowing well enough that while one thing leads to another it is caused by something that happened earlier. He therefore begins by relating how he made himself a sword; how he used the sword to kill a dragon; how he found and appropriated the dragon's hoard; how, bathing in the dragon's blood he became invulnerable to external weapons. Then, tasting the dragon's blood, he began to understand the language of birds, and understanding their language helped him dispose of the foes who were after his life. Yet there is a complication to Siegfried's storytelling, a complication of which the audience knows all and the character knows nothing. Despite the fact that everything is tied up with everything else, Siegfried's recall is not total because he has earlier been tricked into consuming a magic drink which made him forget one particular episode—how he first met and fell in love with a woman, Brünnhilde. Siegfried is now offered the counterpotion—*to refresh your memory*, as Hagen duplicitously puts it. The potion takes effect while the music pauses dramatically.[5] Then Siegfried finds himself narrating a sequel which he, only a moment ago, had not known to have taken place: how the bird whose language he understood led him to a mountainous rock encircled by a wall of fire. How, negotiating the wall of fire he found a sleeping girl. How he kissed her, as the rules of folklore demand that he do, and how she woke and smiled at him.

What makes the story gripping at this point is the fact that the sudden re-experience of the forgotten incident entirely floods the narrator's consciousness, blocking out all real-world circumstances—particularly the fact that he is at present engaged to be married to another woman, and has indeed sworn that there never was another woman in his life. In a word, telling this story perjures the teller and gives Hagen the political legitimacy to run a spear through him. (Suitably enough, the hero has a proverbial chink in his armor.) Beyond reaction or defense, Siegfried escapes into a wish-fulfillment fantasy replaying the boy-meets-sleeping-beauty scene. However, looked at closely, the story presents a considerably modified copy:

Brünnhilde,	Brünnhilde,
heilige Braut!	holy bride!
Wach auf! Öffne dein Auge!	Awake! Open your eyes!
Wer verschloß dich	Who sank you
wieder in Schlaf?	**again** in sleep?
Wer band dich in Schlummer so bang?	Who shackled you in uneasy slumber?
Der Wecker kam;	Your wakener came
er **küßt** dich wach,	and **kissed** you awake,
und **aber** der Braut	and **again broke**
bricht er die Bande	the bride's bondage:
da **lacht** ihm Brünnhildes Lust!	Brünnhilde **laughed** in delight at him!
Ach, dieses Auge,	Ah, her eyes,

---

[5] According to Schank, the main cause for failing to remember is a faulty or missing index rather than any wholesale erasure. Corrupting a story index, the drink of forgetfulness causes Siegfried's local loss of memory; the counterpotion repairs the faulty index and makes the story retrievable again. Cognitive theory in the service of practical criticism...

ewig nun offen!	forever open!
Ach, dieses Atems	Ah, the blissful stirring
wonniges Wehen!	of her breath!
Süßes Vergehen,	Sweet passing,
seliges Grauen -	blessed terror -
Brünnhild' **bietet** mir - Gruß!	Brünnhilde **bids** me welcome!

(Wagner 1983: 187-91)

Climaxing in lustful oxymorons, Siegfried meets his fate. It is a strange end to a none-too-bright character, a hero who was never more than a pawn in the power games played by people of superior knowledge, and a figure absurdly defenseless against the invisible malice of magic potions. Still, one must grant there are worse things than to die remembering the best moment of your life, *and* believing it to have come round a second time, *and* telling the story of it, too. Clinging to the detail of the situation, the speaker's discourse reverberates with the wave of emotion thus released. Although manifestly engaged in the mode of retrospective first-person narration, Siegfried makes the striking mistake of counting the re-lived experience as a second occurrence of the event. 'Who sank you *again* in sleep', he asks (both himself and his imaginatively present bride), and then continues to tell himself and his audience that he must 'again' break '*the bride's* bondage'. The discourse's conflicting impulses here not only affect the deictics of pronouns and referring expressions but also of tenses. The shift from the past tense to present (line 8 of the original text; line 18 in the translation) can be understood as a perfectly regular shift into the historical present, used in the standard function of foregrounding a significant past moment. On the other hand, the present tense is clearly also the natural mode of directly reported experience. Aware as he is of continuing his tale, the speaker's discourse attempts to negotiate a twofold orientation: of *addressing* Brünnhilde in the second person and *telling about* her in the third. The speaker himself is past being able to tell the difference between what is real and what is imaginary (nor, indeed, does he care), whereas the audience, supposing it gets the deictic signals right, knows that Brünnhilde's second awakening is an experience directly *created* by the teller's report. In a word, Siegfried's story and Siegfried's discourse connect in a feedback loop that makes the one dependent on the other.

6 Conclusion

The exceptional test cases paraded in the preceding section were used to test the validity and resilience of the model and to obtain a glimpse at aspects of storytelling which are so habitual as to be invisible under ordinary circumstances. Siegfried, the benighted storyteller who confuses story and discourse, seems to commit every fault in the book:

> The narrator can only report events: he does not literally 'see' them at the moment of speaking them. The heterodiegetic narrator never saw the events because he/she/it never occupied the story world. The homodiegetic or first-person narrator *did* see the events and objects at an earlier moment in the story, but his recountal is after the fact and thus a matter of memory, not of perception. He tells or shows what he remembers *having seen*. In other words, narrative discourse recognizes two different narrative beings moving under the same name: one, the heterodiegetic narrator, inhabits only discourse time and space, another, the homodiegetic or character narrator, also speaks from discourse time and space but previously inhabited story time and space. ... If we are to preserve the vital distinction between discourse and story, we cannot lump together the separate behavior of narrators and characters under a single term, whether 'point of view', 'focalization', or any other. (Chatman 1990: 145)

Coming to terms, Chatman is mainly concerned with the ecology and common sense of narratological concepts. Against the background of the law as set down, Siegfried seems to be doing the impossible—he is narrator and experiencer at the same time, he tells *and* he sees, he sees what he tells, and he tells what he sees. A case such as this will not necessarily faze Chatman, however. As was pointed out above, Chatman freely welcomes exceptions and even allots them a comfortable niche in the greater narratological scheme of things. This is the niche of 'games', 'alterations', 'infractions', 'metalepses', or 'scandals', whose exceptional status becomes discernable precisely against the pattern of the cardinal rule which they violate. Hence, controverting the 'logic of narrative', the exceptional cases really uphold and reinforce it.

Unless one questions Chatman's fundamental tenets, the logic of this argument is impeccable. What gives one pause is that neither Siegfried nor Wagner are playing any pre- or postmodernist game of alteration. As our discussion of the table of oppositions showed, a rigid take-it-apart-and-keep-distinct approach can easily pose the wrong questions and in its prefigured answers lead to error and confusion. Conducting a spirited debate with Chatman, Harry Shaw has recently stressed the necessity of addressing the emotional involvement of narrators—an orientation practically precluded by the rule that narrators 'can only report' (Chatman 1995; Shaw 1995). Equally suspect are Chatman's conclusions on the sense and scope of focalization. As James Phelan points out in an essay entitled 'Why Narrators Can Be Focalizers', Chatman's 'discussion of narrators inadequately captures the dynamics of narration as it is experienced by readers. If narrators are, in effect, blind to the story world, then audiences must be too' (Phelan 2001: 57; see Jahn 1996: 258-260 for a similar argument). Indeed, on the cognitive logic of the model presented here, the feedback loop which sustains Siegfried's storytelling is not exceptional at all but indicative of the internal-external dynamic of all storytelling. Like Brünnhilde, postclassical narratology must wake up—wake up *again*, too—to the strange loops by which we perceive, remember, imagine, and tell stories which are like life itself.

References

Barthes, R. 1975 [1966]. An Introduction to the Structural Analysis of Narrative. *New Literary History* 6: 237-72.

Berne, E. 1973. *What Do You Say After You Say Hello*. New York: Bantam.

Bortolussi, M., and P. Dixon. 2003. *Psychonarratology: Foundations for the Empirical Study of Literary Response*. Cambridge: Cambridge University Press.

Bremond, C. 1970. Morphology of the French Folktale. *Semiotica* 2: 247-276.

Chatman, S. 1990. *Coming to Terms: The Rhetoric of Narrative in Fiction and Film*. Ithaca: Cornell UP.

Chatman, S. 1995. How Loose Can Narrators Get? (And How Vulnerable Can Narratees Be?). *Narrative* 3.3: 303-306.

Chafe, W. 1990. Some Things that Narratives Tell Us About the Mind. *Narrative Thought and Narrative Language*, eds. B. K. Britton and A. D. Pellegrini, 79-98. Hillsdale: Erlbaum.

Coleridge, S. T. *The Complete Poetical Works*. Oxford: Clarendon, 1966.

Dennett, D. C. 1988. Why Everyone Is a Novelist. *Times Literary Supplement* September 16-22: 1016-28.

Fludernik, M. 2000. Beyond Structuralism in Narratology: Recent Developments and New Horizons in Narrative Theory. *Anglistik* 11.1: 83-96.

Genette, G. 1988 [1983]. *Narrative Discourse Revisited*, trans. Jane E. Lewin. Ithaca: Cornell University Press.

Herman, D. 1999. Introduction: Narratologies. *Narratologies: New Perspectives on Narrative Analysis*, ed. D. Herman, 1-30. Columbus, OH: Ohio State University PRess.

Jackendoff, R. 1987. *Consciousness and the Computational Mind*. Cambridge, Mass.: MIT Press.

Jackendoff, R. 1997. *The Architecture of the Language Faculty*. Cambridge, Mass.: MIT Press.

Jahn, M. 1996. Windows of Focalization: Deconstructing and Reconstructing a Narratological Concept. *Style* 30.2: 241-67.

Jahn, M. 2001. Narrative Voice and Agency in Drama: Aspects of a Narratology of Drama. *New Literary History* 32: 659-679.

James, H. 1984 [1908]. Preface to *The Princess Camissamira*. *Literary Criticism*. New York: Penguin.

Phelan, J. 2001. Why Narrators Can Be Focalizers—And Why It Matters. *New Perspectives on Narrative Perspective*, eds. W. van Peer and S. Chatman, 51-64. Albany: State University of New York Press.

Prince, G. 1982. *Narratology: The Form and Functioning of Narrative*. New York: Mouton.

Prince, G. 1987. *A Dictionary of Narratology*. London: University of Nebraska Press.

Ricoeur, P. 1991. Life in Quest of Narrative. *On Paul Ricoeur: Narrative and Interpretation*, ed. D. Wood, 20-33. London: Routledge.

Ryan, M.-L. 1991. *Possible Worlds, Artificial Intelligence, and Narrative Theory*. Bloomington: Indiana University Press.

Sarbin, T. R., ed. 1986. *Narrative Psychology: The Storied Nature of Human Conduct*. New York: Praeger.

Schacter, D. 1996. *Searching for Memory: The Brain, the Mind, and the Past*. New York: Basic Books.

Schank, R. C. 1995. *Tell Me a Story: Narrative and Intelligence*. Evanston: Northwestern University Press.

Shaw, H. S. 1995. Thin Description: A Reply to Seymour Chatman. *Narrative* 3.3: 307-314.

Turner, M. 1996. *The Literary Mind*. Oxford: Oxford University Press.

Wagner, R. 1983 [1874] *Götterdämmerung*, ed. K. Pahlen. Mainz: Atlantis. [Trans. L. Salter, 1968, DGG 1991, conductor J. Levine]

Wilder, B., and I. A. L. Diamond. *The Apartment*. London: Faber, 1998.

9

Cognitive Maps and the Construction of Narrative Space

MARIE-LAURE RYAN

1 Introduction

The concept of cognitive map means different things to different people. It was introduced in 1948 by the psychologist Edward Tolman to describe the navigational skills that enable rats in a maze to reach a food box, when the familiar path has been blocked. In more recent years, the term has been applied to people's memorizations of graphic maps (as I will call what we commonly regard as 'geographic' maps: road maps, topographical maps, world maps); to mental images of complex spatial environments, such as a city (Lynch); to the knowledge that enables people to draw free-hand images of city streets, countries, or continents (Tuan 1975); to private representations of geographical entities that ascribe personal values to different areas: dangerous, safe, desirable, vacation spot, good place to live, and so on (Gould and White 1974). Tuan (1975: 210-11) further proposes five functions for mental maps: (1) They make it possible to give directions to strangers; (2) They enable people to 'rehearse spatial behavior' (as does a rider who goes mentally over an obstacle course before a jumping competition); (3) They are used as mnemonic devices ('memory palaces'); (4) They are means to structure and store knowledge; (5) They serve as 'fields of dreams' to the imagination (for instance dreaming of California).

In a 1981 article Richard Bjornson proposed to extend the term to the cognitive processing of literature. Relying principally on Lynch's idea that

Narrative Theory and the Cognitive Sciences.
David Herman (ed.).
Copyright © 2003, CSLI Publications.

'the observer [of an environment] selects, organizes, and endows with meaning what he sees' (quoted p. 53), Bjornson uses the term of cognitive map to denote a global mental representation of the literary text that involves not just spatial relations, but any type of meaning and formal organization. Drawing a broad analogy between graphic maps and mental representations of texts, Bjornson writes that cognitive maps 'are necessarily incomplete and schematized; they can never achieve exact correspondence with the territory they represent, and any claim that they embody absolute truth deserves to be regarded with skepticism' (55). But it took the adoption of the term by a critic as prominent as Fredric Jameson to put 'cognitive mapping' on the literary-critical map. Also claiming inspiration from Lynch's *Image of the City*, Jameson proposed to extend the concept from the purely spatial to the social domain. To draw a 'cognitive map' of social phenomena, in Jameson's sense, is to study these phenomena not in isolation but as part of a world-spanning network of relations. The 'phenomenological experience' of somebody living in London may for instance be bound up to 'the whole colonial system of the British Empire', as this system 'determines the very quality of the individual's subjective life' (349). Jameson's concept of cognitive mapping paved the way for cultural and globalization studies, and it opened the floodgates to the mapping of anything that passes through the mind of the postmodern subject.

Here I will work from a much narrower and literal definition: a cognitive map is a mental model of *spatial* relations. But this definition presents sufficient versatility to reach into narrative territory. The space represented by the map can indeed be real or imaginary. The representation can be based on embodied experience (moving through space, seeing, hearing, smelling the world), or on the reading of texts. The text can be a graphic map, or a verbal evocation. The verbal evocation can be narrowly focused on space (directions, descriptions, travel guides) or treat space as a stage for narrative events. My focus will be on the second term of each alternative.

Stories tell about the actions of intelligent agents. These agents are situated within a world, and so are the objects they act upon. One may infer from this description that telling a story necessitates, in the words of David Herman, 'modeling, and enabling others to model, an emergent constellation of spatially related entities' (534). Narrative thus entails 'a process of cognitive mapping that assigns referents not merely a temporal but a *spatio*-temporal position in the storyworld' (535). But cognitive maps, like graphic ones, can represent worlds in various degrees of detail and precision. While it seems evident that narrative comprehension requires *some kind* of mental model of space—how else could readers imagine character movements?—the issue of the form and content of this model remains to be explored. What are the relations between cognitive maps and graphic maps? To what extent and in what detail do mental maps of textual worlds need to represent spatial relations between objects? Through what strategies do texts facilitate the conceptualization of these relations? Is a totalizing, bird's-eye-view mental image of narrative space necessary to a proper understanding of plot, or do readers work from cartographic fragments? Such are the questions that I would like to address in the present essay. I will do so by comparing my own 'master-map' of a narrative text, a map reconstructed through close attention to spatial cues, with maps drawn by readers with a much broader focus—readers who do not construct narrative space for its own sake, but as a background for the understanding of plot, character motivations, and the moral issues articulated in the text.

For my investigation of readers' construction of narrative space I have chosen *Chronicle of a Death Foretold* by Gabriel García Márquez (García Márquez 1982). This text recommends itself for the study of mental maps through its meticulous attention to spatial configuration. It tells about the death of Santiago Nasar, a twenty-year-old member of an Arab minority in a Caribbean town. Presented as the investigation of a crime by a narrator-witness, *Chronicle of a Death Foretold* is a murder story without suspense. The reader knows from page one that Nasar will be murdered, and he or she learns the identity of the killers on p. 16. If there is any mystery in this pseudo-detective novel, it concerns the identity of the man for whom Nasar vicariously dies: for Nasar is killed by the brothers of a bride (Angela Vicario) who was returned to her mother on her wedding night because she was no longer a virgin. When Angela denounces Nasar as the perpetrator, her twin brothers Pedro and Pablo restore the family's honor by slaughtering the alleged culprit. But the unconcerned attitude of Nasar, as he walks to his death, make it amply clear that Angela was covering up for somebody else. We never learn the identity of her secret lover, though Gonzalo Díaz-Migoyo (1988) has ingeniously argued that he must have been the narrator himself. But Nasar does not die for Angela's lover only: he becomes the scapegoat whose expulsion reaffirms the unwritten law that defines the institution of marriage in this society, a law that preserves the proprietary rights of husbands over wives by limiting male sexual activity to wives, servants and prostitutes, and by forbidding expressions of female desire. (There is indeed no suggestion that Angela acted against her will.) The ritual dimension of his death explains the ambivalence of the towns-people vis-à-vis the murder. Everybody is aware of the killers' intent, and many people make discreet attempts to warn the future victim, but nobody is willing or able to stand up and stop the unfolding of a sacrifice that both repulses the soul and upholds the values of the community.

As in most detective stories the topographical layout of the setting fulfills a strategic function of utmost importance. It is common for investigators to draw a map of the scene of the crime and to plot on this map the movements of victim and suspects. In García Márquez' novel this map is implicitly drawn by the narrator's minute-by-minute reconstruction of the events that lead up to the murder of Nasar. The first section relates Santiago Nasar's actions on the morning of his death up to half an hour before the murder (which takes place at 7:05 am). Nasar gets up at 5:45 in the morning after one hour's sleep, hung-over from the wedding celebration of the previous day and a visit to the local madam, to greet the bishop who is visiting the town on a river boat. The whole town is there to honor the bishop, but he merely gives a blessing from his boat and sails on. After the departure of the bishop, Nasar is invited by the narrator's sister to have breakfast at their house further down on the river, but he decides to change clothes first, and he heads back toward his house with a friend, Cristo Bedoya. The second section narrates in a flash-back the courtship and wedding of Bajardo San Román and Angela Vicario. The third retraces the events following the end of the wedding celebration: the bride being returned to her mother; her brothers learning about her shame; the preparations for the murder; the brothers' waiting for Nasar at the milk shop (which doubles as bar) across the square from Nasar's house; and Nasar getting home safely through the back door. The fourth section narrates the aftermath of the crime: the autopsy, the trial, and Bajardo San Román returning to Angela twenty years later. The last section picks up the chronicle of the last hour of Nasar's life where it had been left: Nasar gets separated from Bedoya when an Arab shopkeeper tries to warn Bedoya of Nasar's impending fate; he visits his fiancée's house; and finally returns home, to be butchered like a pig by the front door of his house, which had been inadvertently closed by his mother a few minutes earlier. The last scene shows Nasar staggering through the neighbor's house to get to the back of his own house. He sees the narrator's aunt, Wenefrida Márquez, on the other side of the river, answers her question 'what has happened to you' with a laconic 'they've killed me, Wene child' (García Márquez 1982: 143), enters his house through the open back door, and falls dead in the kitchen.

2 Reconstructing the Map of the Fictional World

It takes a specific agenda—such as the present project—to attempt the systematic reconstruction of the 'textually correct' map of a fictional world. It was only on my third reading of *Chronicle of a Death Foretold* that I reached what I hope is a reasonably complete and accurate representation of the topography of the novel. My first reading was a reading for pure pleasure. I had no intent to write about the text, and it left me with a vivid, though spotty visualization of the setting: something like those reconstructed Cretan frescoes made of pictorial fragments separated by blank areas. The purpose of my second reading was to decide whether the novella was suitable for the experiment described in this essay: I wanted to ask a group of high school students to draw their representation of the textual world. During this second pass I did sketch a map as I went along, but I had forgotten so much of the text that I had to concentrate on other dimensions of the plot, such as the psychological underpinning and the patterns of foretelling. This led me to overlook some important pieces of spatial information, and as I drew my map in the course of my reading I had to perform several corrections. Even when I was through, I was not sure about the location of many items. It was only on my third reading, after I had collected the students drawings and learned a few things from them, that I could concentrate entirely on the mapping project. From a practical cartographer—one who makes maps in order to use them—I had reverted to a pure surveyor: somebody who regards the exact representation of space as a goal in itself. I present the results of that third pass not as the mental image that any 'good' reader should reach, but as the representation of a mythical 'model reader' or 'super-reader' with whom no real reader will identify, because this model reader has near perfect recall, and reads purely for the map. The purpose of this exercise is to build a standard of comparison for the drawings and reading acts of my flesh-and-blood informants.

The major difficulty that faces the cartographic efforts of the reader of a narrative texts is the discrepancy between the temporal dimension of language and the spatial nature of maps. Researchers in cognitive psychology and discourse analysis (Linde and Labov 1975; Tversky 1996) have identified two discourse strategies that assist the transposition of sequentially given information into synchronous spatial representations: the *map* and the *tour*, also called the survey and the route. In the map strategy, space is represented panoramically from a perspective ranging from the disembodied god's-eye point of view of pure vertical projection to the oblique view of an observer situated on an elevated point. Space is divided into segments, and the text covers the segments according to a systematic algorithm: east to west and north to south; left to right; or front to back. In contrast to the more or less disembodied and static perspective of the map, the *tour* strategy represents space dynamically from a perspective internal to the territory to be surveyed, namely the perspective of a moving object. The tour thus simulates the embodied experience of a traveler.

Another variable parameter in the topographic presentation of textual worlds is the timing of the disclosure of spatial information. The text can either sketch the map all at once to set the stage for the action, or distribute information relevant to its construction throughout the narrative. With its neat gathering of information, the all-at-once approach facilitates the task of the investigator who reads for the map, but it taxes the memory and attention span of those who read for the plot: How many of us can honestly say that we never skip descriptions? Some narratives bypass this difficulty by presenting a graphic map of the setting. But the most widely practiced alternative is to unfold the map gradually, by linking the disclosure of spatial information to the actions of characters or by interleaving short descriptions with the report of narrative events. This is indeed the mapping strategy of *Chronicle of a Death Foretold*. Whereas the information tied to the moving bodies of characters creates mini-tours, the short descriptions outline mini-maps. To gain a panoramic view of narrative space the reader must be able to synthesize this information through a bottom-up process of construction.

Here is a sample of the variety of statements from which I derived cartographic data (all page references to García Márquez 1982):

Direct description:

> [Santiago Nasar's] house was a former warehouse, with two stories, walls of rough planks, and a peaked tin roof...(10)

Mapping action: Give two storeys to the house.

Implication from report of events:

> By the time Ibrahim Nasar arrived with the last Arabs at the end of the civil wars, seagoing ships no longer came here because of shifts in the river, and the warehouse was in disuse. (10)

Mapping action: Put Nasar's house reasonably close to an arm of the river; put the town at some distance from the ocean (on a delta or estuary).

Narrativized description:

> Ibrahim Nasar bought [the warehouse] at a cheap price in order to set up an import store that he never did establish, and only when he was going to be married did he convert it into a house to live in. On the ground floor he opened up a parlor that served for everything, and in back he built a stable for our animals, the servant's quarters, and a country kitchen with windows opening onto the dock. (10)

Mapping action: The entire floor plan of the house can be drawn from the narration of Ibrahim Nasar's remodeling.

Object movement:

> one morning when a servant girl had shaken the case to get the pillow out...the pistol went off as it hit the floor and the bullet wrecked the cupboard in the room, went through the living room wall, passed through the dining room of the house next door with the thunder of war, and turned a life-size saint on the main altar of the church on the opposite side of the square to plaster dust. (4)

Mapping action: Put Nasar's house on the town square. Next to it put another house. On the opposite side of the square put a church.

Character movement:

> It was through [the front door] that [Santiago Nasar] went out to receive the bishop, despite the fact that he would have to walk completely around the house in order to reach the docks. (11)

Mapping action: Place the front door on the square side, away from the docks. This passage also reinforces the location of the back side of Nasar's house near the docks and the river.

Explicit specification of character position:

> The only place open on the square was a milk shop on one side of the church, where the two men were who were waiting for Santiago Nasar in order to kill him. (16)

Mapping action: Place the milk shop next to the church and at a short distance from Nasar's house. Since these two buildings are on the side opposite to Nasar's house, and since Nasar's house can be observed from the milk shop, make the square fairly small.

Character act of perception:

> The landlady of the bachelor's boarding house where Bayardo San Román lived told of how he'd been napping in a rocking chair in the parlor toward the end of September, when Angela Vicario and her mother crossed the square carrying two baskets of artificial flowers. Bayardo San Román half awoke, saw the two women...and asked who the young one was. (30-31)

Mapping action: Put a bachelor's boarding house on the square.

Disembodied act of perception:

[About the house of the widower Xius, which Bayardo San Román has bought to live there with his future wife Angela Vicario]

clear summer day you could make out the neat horizon of the Caribbean and the tourist ships from Cartagena de Indias. (39)
Mapping action: Place the house on a hill at a distance from the town
square; place the town in the vicinity of the ocean; situate the town in a
simulacrum of real-world geography.

Omniscient representation of what characters do and do not perceive:
From the place where [Plácida Linero, Nasar's mother] was standing
she could see [the killers] but she could not see her son, who was running toward the door from a different angle. [138]
Mapping action: Since at this point we know that the killers are
coming from the milk shop, and Nasar from his fiancée's house,
place the milk shop and fiancée's house on different sides of the
square.

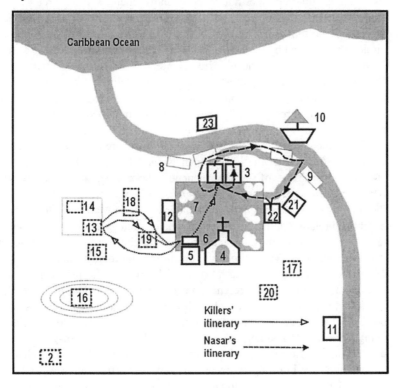

Figure 1. Master Map of *Chronicle of a Death Foretold*

My mapping of the textual world is shown in Figure 1. (Table 1 in the Appendix provides a legend for this map.) I present the diagram not as *the* map but as one of the possible maps of the textual world. Just as texts project many possible worlds—one for every imaginative concretization—they project many topographies. The famed incompleteness of texts and the need to fill in informational gaps to reach a coherent interpretation is particularly acute when one tries to translate textual information into mental models of space, and these mental models into visual representations. A graphic map after all is not a cognitive map, but only the more or less faithful image of a cognitive map. Whereas texts and the reader's mental image of textual worlds can leave the location of objects unspecified, graphic maps must situate every feature somewhere on the page. Figure 1 is therefore much more explicit than my original mental image.

What the diagram does not properly show, then, is the degree of precision of the textual mapping. The world of *Chronicle of a Death Foretold* is organized into four zones of decreasing sharpness and resolution. The inner circle is constituted by the house of Nasar, the beginning and ending of the journey of both his day and his life. The text facilitates the drawing of the floor plan by chronicling Ibrahim Nasar's remodeling of the former warehouse. This strategy, which builds the house before the reader's inner eyes, follows Lessing's recommendation that the temporal medium of poetry turn static descriptions into narrative action.

The middle circle, which encompasses the square and the docks by the river, is the theatre of the last hour in Nasar's life. The location of landmarks in this area is of great hermeneutic importance, since it enables the reader-investigator to trace the movements of the victim and the killers, but the strategy of space presentation adopted by García Márquez allows only a partial and relative situation of objects. This strategy falls into a no-man's land between the various systems of representing space distinguished by discourse analysis: viewer-relative, absolute, and object-relative (Tversky 1996). A viewer-relative description (which can take the perspective of either character or narrator) presents objects as being left, right, in front of, or in back of the observer. An absolute description uses the coordinates south, north, east and west. An object-relative description will locate an object as being 'in front' of another, from this other object's 'point-of-view'; thus a bench can be described as being in front of the church, because a church is an asymmetrical building, with an implicit front (the entrance) and back. García Márquez's text occasionally uses the object-relative system (i.e. the front and back door of Nasar's house), but the vast majority of spatial notations do not belong to a particular system: for instance, the information that the milk shop is 'next' to the church can be used in all three approaches.

The absence in the text of what Ferguson and Hegarty (1994) call anchors does not facilitate the reconstruction of a spatial relations within the second circle. An anchor is a landmark that serves as point of reference for the location of other items: for instance 'square' in this made-up description: 'In the middle of the square is a fountain; on its south side; a church and a bar. The other three sides are lined with houses and shops. A narrow street takes off from the north-west corner of the square and leads past the jail and brothel to the river docks'. Though the square forms the strategic center of the plot, it is not used in García Márquez's text as an orienteering tool; it is only through relatively complex deductions that the reader can place some landmarks around it (cf. the description of the bullet flight quoted above).

The third strategic zone in the novel encompasses the outskirts of the town. This is the scene of the events that lead up to the murder: the courtship, the wedding, and the activities of characters between the end of the wedding and the visit of the bishop on the next morning. Here buildings are mentioned, but we only know that they lie at some distance from the square. The arbitrary location of a building on the map is indicated by broken lines.

The last zone, not sketched on the map, is the liminal area from which characters emerge (for instance, Bajardo San Román arriving one day on the weekly boat) or into which they disappear: the killers sent to jail in Riohacha, or Angela Vicario exiling herself to a village in the interior. In this broadest circle the fictional world blends with real geography (Riohacha, Cartagena), but real-world locations lay far away on the horizon, leaving the town and its surroundings a free-floating area on the map of Colombia.

3 The Experiment

To investigate the formation of mental models of space I asked a group of high school students to draw a map of the world of *Chronicle of a Death Foretold*. The students, all college-bound seniors participating in an advanced literature course, had read the novel in the summer of 2001. They discussed it with their teacher for about three weeks in December 2001 and January 2002. The test took place before the classes moved on to the next text. Some of the students may have re-read the book and some others may not. There were about five copies of the text available for each class of twenty students, and some of them used the book to remember character names; but there was no time to check the text for spatial cues.

I am not presenting this undertaking as a scientific experiment, but as an informal attempt to probe into readers' memory and imagination—a term taken here in its most literal sense: the faculty to form mental images. Whereas the scientific approach to narrative cognition decontextualizes the act of reading, presents readers with texts specially designed for the occasion (texts usually so bland that nobody would have reason to read them in real life), and evaluates mental processes in strictly quantitative terms (usually the time taken to perform specific tasks), the informal approach, whose representatives include Victor Nell and Richard Gerrig, attempts to penetrate into the mind of readers by inviting them to talk freely about their experience of 'real' narrative texts—texts worth reading on their own merit. It is as a visual form of self-expression that I asked the students to draw pictures of the topographical layout of *Chronicle of a Death Foretold.* I encouraged the students to use their imagination when their memory failed, and I made it clear that I was not conducting a test of how well they had read the text.

Sixty students participated in the experiment, but five of them limited their pictures to the floor plan of Nasar's house, and one returned a blank map. (See below for the reason.) The floor plans were in general much more accurate than the larger maps, but the task was easier because the configuration of the house is described very clearly in the passage narrating Ibrahim Nasar's remodeling, and also because it is reinforced by several episodes that take place indoors. In my discussion I will ignore the floor plans and concentrate on the far more complex task of drawing a map of the whole town. The blank map, however, is taken into consideration in the statistical tallies, since it can be regarded as an empty representation of the town.

As an expression of readers' representation of the textual world, the maps can be evaluated in terms of three criteria: inventory, spatial relations, and mapping style.

3.1 Inventory

Examining maps in terms of inventory means paying attention to what kind of objects readers include on their drawing, to where these objects come from—the text, or other sources—and to what the selection tells us about the map maker's conceptualization of the plot. Table 2 in the Appendix lists the most frequently mentioned features in decreasing order. Not surprisingly, the most prominent landmark is the house of Nasar. This suggests that the drawings are plot-centered, which means that the map makers retrieve from memory the salient features of the fictional world by mentally replaying the fate of the hero. The plot can be replayed in terms of two parameters: the spatial movements of Nasar on the morning of his death, and the network of interpersonal relations that cause his murder. The spatial system explains the importance of the river, square, docks, bishop's boat, front door of Nasar's house, and narrator's house, while the interpersonal system produces the buildings associated with the wedding (Angela Vicario's house, the widower Xius's house, Bajardo San Román's hotel), as well as those directly involved with the killers' actions (milk shop, knife shop, butcher's shop[1]). Of the items at the top of the list the least connected to the characters and to the logic of the plot are the church and the fountain. The church is the object of several textual references, but it is most strongly called to mind by the cover of the book, which shows a plaza with an imposing Baroque cathedral. The fountain is harder to explain, since it is not mentioned in the text nor depicted in an illustration. My only explanation is that the students used standard cultural images of what a South American plaza looks like; they may also have been influenced by the cityscape of their home town, Fort Collins, Colorado. The social center of Fort Collins is indeed a pedestrian plaza with a fountain in the middle.

The bottom of the list (i.e. the features mentioned only once or twice) was divided between landscape elements of purely atmosphere-creating importance (fields, mango grove, flower pots, dogs, chicken coops, hills), houses of minor characters (Divina Flor, Pablo Vicario's fiancée, Yamil Shaiun) and non-textual items brought into the picture by cultural schemata, personal experience, or (I suspect) by the pure pleasure of letting the imagination loose: cemetery, cactus, school, cow pen near the milk shop, restaurant, drugstore, coffee shop, ghetto, trailer park, beach, and even a road sign pointing to the U.S. The maps were just as revealing of their authors' conceptualizations of the plot for what they omitted as for what they included or added. In general, the landmarks mentioned in the early episodes were much better represented than the features of the later ones. The scene of the bishop's visit on a river boat, told in the first section, had a strong impact on the readers' imagination (78% drew the river, 40% drew the bishop), while the dramatic last scene, in which the mortally wounded Nasar staggers through the neighbor's house and sees the narrator's aunt

---

[1] Literally speaking there is no butcher shop in the text. The brothers raise and slaughter pigs, and keep knives in their workshop. They sell the meat at the meat market. Applying the cultural schema of the town square as shopping center, the readers who mentioned these locations turned the workshop into a knife store, and the meat market into a butcher shop. They also added a coffee shop, though it is at Pablo Vicario's fiancée's house that the killers drink coffee.

across the river, left minimal cartographic traces: only 4 maps (7%) mentioned the neighbor's house, and none included the house of Wene García. This suggests that in reading matters as in other domains of experience, the first impression is the strongest: The representation of textual worlds gels early on, providing to the imagination a playfield for the moves of characters, and it expands from a dense core which remains vividly inscribed in memory.

3.2 Spatial Relations

The evaluation of spatial relations is much more difficult than the analysis of the inventory because it deals with scalar rather than binary categories: While an item is or isn't on the map (the only doubt here is what the reader meant with the label), it can be located at variable distances from another item. How close, for instance, does a house have to be from the river to be scored as 'on the river'? (In my evaluation I used the criterion that an item is next to another if there is no other item in between.) Once we decide on criteria, though, the diagramming of spatial relations can be scored in a more rigorous way than the mapping of what is there. Inventories are more or less complete, but never totally wrong, since the presence of non-textual items can be attributed to the imaginative need to flesh out the textual world. But in their representation of spatial relations, the sketches can be shown to be accurate or inaccurate on the basis of solid textual evidence.

Table 3 summarizes findings for a group of textually verifiable spatial relations. Most of these relations select the square as anchor point, a decision justified by its thematic and strategic prominence, even though, as we have seen, the text does not systematically use it as spatial point of reference. The lowest percentage of error concerns the placement of the church and of the widower Xius's house. The location of the church on the square is multiply enforced by textual description, cultural schemata, and the cover's illustration. As for the widower Xius's house, it is the subject matter of a memorable episode, during which the text makes it very clear that it is situated on a hill at a distance from the town center. The items that fall in the middle range of errors (60-80%) display a tendency to bring strategically important characters or locations from the periphery toward the center: Angela is a main character; she must therefore be located at the heart of the action. The knife 'shop' (see note 1) is moved to the square not only because of its connection to the killers, themselves important characters, but also as part of the commercial zone that surrounds the plaza. The misplacing of the brothel further suggests a tendency to allocate a central location to all the buildings that belong to the cultural image of a town, even though such buildings are usually hidden in the outskirts.

If we discount the placement of some items too rarely mentioned to be statistically significant, the largest proportion of errors concerns the most important landmarks: the house of Nasar and the milk shop. How in particular can we explain the fact that only 17% of informants located Nasar's house correctly between the square and the river? I believe that misplacements are due to an ambiguous distribution of textual information. The text scatters hints that Nasar's house is close to the river as well as hints that it is on the square, but it never presents these hints in the same passage, nor does it explicitly mention that the square is close to the river—a mandatory inference, if Nasar's house borders on both.

But the factors that determine the placement of buildings are not necessarily textual. In their mapping of the textual world, many students seem to have started with the two most important landscape features, the river and the square. Other objects could have been added according to one or the other of two drawing strategies: either cluster objects around the two anchors; or try to fill the empty space between the square and the river, so as to produce a well-balanced picture. Students may also have been reluctant to erase a false start that left no room for proper location. Purely graphic considerations may thus explain why a large percentage (41%) of those students who had both a river and a square on their map placed Nasar's house at a distance from both of these landmarks.

3.3 Mapping Style

A map, technically, is a model of a reference world drawn from a vertical perspective. Its symbols are conventional rather than iconic. This is also known as a plan view. A picture, by contrast, is a representation drawn from a horizontal point of view. It attempts to reproduce the visual perception of an observer, and its elements are iconic. This is known as an elevation or perspective view. Most maps, however, contain iconic elements and elevation symbols: for instance the church in the master map. Conversely, many pictures tend toward the plan-mode by capturing a wide-angle and by selecting an elevated point of view. Table 4 represents the various mapping styles chosen by the students. 'Pure plan' tolerates elevation-style elements only for the sake of differentiation; for instance, the church icon on the master map allows the viewer to distinguish two types of buildings, churches and houses. 'Iconic plans' are consistently represented from a vertical perspective, but there is an attempt at reproducing visual perception. These plans show for instance the pitch of roofs, the waves on the river, the peb-

river, the pebbles on roads. 'Mixed plan-picture' adopts a vertical point of view but represents many elements in elevation, usually houses. 'Predominantly pictorial representation' selects an oblique point of view, and while it shows spatial relations, it attempts to convey a sense of what the landscape looks like. Pure image renounces the elevated point of view altogether. The four maps discussed here were categorized as follows: Figures 1 and 2, 'pure plan'; Figures 3 and 4, 'mixed plan-picture'.

The maps do not merely represent the world of *Chronicle of a Death Foretold*, they also tell their own story—the story of the reader's reading. Here I will discuss briefly the mapping strategies and narrative emphasis of three of the sketches. The examples were selected for their diversity, as well as for their (obviously relative) accuracy in terms of either richness of inventory or representation of spatial relations.

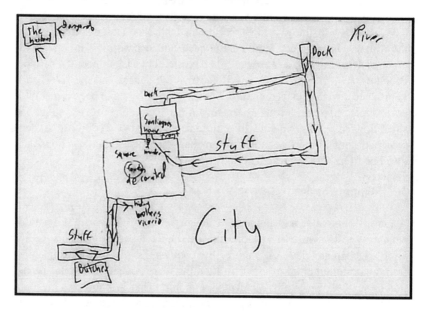

Figure 2. Map of Character Movement

3.3.1 Map of Character Movement

The map represented in Figure 2 could have been produced by a detective investigating the case. Consistently drawn from the vertical perspective of a city plan, it combines time and space by representing the respective itineraries of Nasar and the killers. It is one of the few sketches that places Nasar's house both on the square and close to the docks. The line of the river mean-anders away from Nasar's back door, but this is consistent with the text, since the river is said to have changed its course since Ibrahim Nasar acquired the warehouse. The two-directional arrow for the murderers' itinerary from their slaughtering shop to the milk store indicates their back-and forth movement, itself a symptom of their hesitations: They take knives from their shop, go to the milk store, return home, get new knives, and go back to the milk store. The map, drawn by a male student, conceptualizes the plot as the interaction of three parties, all represented by male characters: the husband, Nasar, and the killers. Visual details are generally omitted, which makes it all the more surprising to find a fountain on the square. Though the fountain is not a textual element, it helps differentiate the town square from the other square shapes on the map.

Figure 3.   Symbolic Map

3.3.2 Symbolic Map

With its drawing of the town square as the intersections of the two arms of a gigantic cross, the map represented in Figure 3 privileges graphic design and symbolic meaning over the logic of the plot. Was the map maker (female) influenced, perhaps subconsciously, by the religious theme of the novel and by the crossings of the square performed by Nasar and Angela? (Nasar, the innocent who dies for another, is a Christ figure who ends up literally crucified on the front door of his house.) The dominant episode here is the wedding of Angela and Bajardo; no explicit mention is made of the murder. But the map alludes to the killers' ambush of Nasar by situating the milk shop catercorner from Nasar's house, with nothing in between to block the view of the brothers. Another diagonal runs from the brothel to the wedding house, suggesting the contrast of marriage and prostitution, while a symbolic triangle links the Vicario house to the church and to the wedding house, bypassing the brothel: the triangle of socially approved marital love. One of the apexes of the triangle is a building either misplaced or invented by the map maker: In the text the wedding takes place at the Vicarios and at the house of their next-door neighbor.

Figure 4. Storyspace Map

3.3.4 Storyspace Map

Many of the maps tell me that the assignment was a chore for the cartographer. The reader (his or her gender was left unspecified) who produced the map represented in Figure 4 took it as an opportunity to let the imagination embroider new tales on the canvas of the narrative world. On the borderline between map (vertical perspective of the spatial layout) and illustration (frontal perspective of the individual objects), this drawing may not meet the highest standards of accuracy in the area of textual topography, but it captures beautifully the verve, tall-tale exaggerations, and gossipy quality of García Márquez' narrative style—a style deeply influenced by oral storytelling. With the Halloween motif in the foreground, the beach and sea monsters in the background, and the shopping mall lining Main Street, the map turns the South American town into a hybrid of amusement park and American city. But the thematics of the novel are not entirely forgotten. By making the church, on the left, and the brothel, on the right, the two salient features of the landscape, the drawing suggests the ambiguous opposition that dominates the life of the townspeople: Should we read it as good versus evil (as would the official ideology), or as the repression versus the liberation of sexual energies? Sacrificing textual accuracy to symbolic meaning, the drawing underscores the public nature of the murder and the complicity of the whole town by moving the death of Nasar from the doorsteps of his house to the center of the plaza.

4 Discussion

4.1 From Cognitive Maps to Graphic Maps

What can we learn from this experiment about the importance of cognitive mapping, or mental models of space, for narrative comprehension? It is important to avoid confusing the students' sketches with their purely mental models of narrative space. The drawings are in a sense the exact opposite of a cognitive map: Whereas cognitive maps internalize an experience of space which is usually based on visual cues (studying a graphic map; walking through a city; scanning a text[2]), the sketches drawn by the students are graphic transpositions of mental images. Even though the experiment was conducted informally rather than staged in the controlled environment thought to be necessary to scientific rigor, it cannot avoid the fundamental

---

[2] As the case of blind people forming a representation of the arrangement of their houses suggests, mental maps can also be built on the basis of non-visual experience.

ambiguity of scientific observation, an ambiguity known in theoretical physics as the uncertainty principle and in the social sciences as the Hawthorne principle.[3] This principle states that scientifically observed facts are at least partly created by the presence of the observer and the technique of measurement. A graphic map is a heuristic tool that feeds back into the reader's mental image, shaping it through the very process of representing it. In my original inner vision of the world of *Chronicle of a Death Foretold*, for instance, I placed the river at the bottom, but when I drew the master map I changed its position to remain consistent with the cartographic convention of placing the north at the top and the south at the bottom. I used to visualize the movements of Santiago Nasar as going down to the river, but after drawing the map I reversed my mental scenario. Similarly, the buildings that I arbitrarily located on the diagram no longer float in space, but occupy specific coordinates in my inner vision.

By asking the students to draw a map rather than a picture, I implicitly imposed a visual form on the graphic transposition of their mental images. (As Table 4 shows, however, many of the students resisted this suggestion by choosing a compromise between the map and the picture.) Most students regarded the experiment as an opportunity to develop rather than mirror a vision of the textual world, but at least one of them took the assignment as a literal invitation to reproduce a pre-existing image. This student declined to draw a map, justifying his or her decision with the comment 'I never gave any thought at all to trying to place locations in relationship to one another or map them while reading the text'. But a mental model of narrative space developed through the drawing of a map is no less legitimate as a response to the text than an interpretation formed after discussing a book with friends or revisiting the text mentally after other input. Reading and interpreting a text, especially a literary one, are not mental activities that stop when the eye moves away from its visual inscription. There are indeed readers who spontaneously draw sketches of fictional worlds to clarify their cognitive maps.[4]

The fact that the students represented their view of the textual world in map or semi-map form does not necessarily mean that mental models of space constructed on the basis of narrative texts resemble graphic maps—as does, for instance, our internal representation of the map of the world. The

---

[3]For a definition of the principle and a sketch of its background, see http://users.netlinc.net/tlc/dee3.htm.

[4] See for instance the sketches of Vladimir Nabokov in the notes for his lectures on literature.

issue of the resemblance between graphic and mental maps and of the importance of visualization for the construction of spatial models has received considerable attention in cognitive science. In work dating back to the sixties, the cognitive psychologist Allan Paivio (1986) suggested that information can be stored in either pictorial or propositional, quasi-verbal form, depending on the mindstyle of the subject (some people are 'visualizers' while others are not) and on the nature of the data. Some types of information—for instance the meaning of a sentence like 'the cat chased the dog'—can be stored in both forms while other types ('I think therefore I am') can only be stored verbally. This is known in cognitive psychology as the 'dual-coding' theory (Esrock 1994: 96-104). A mental model of a narrative world is clearly a type of information that can be represented both ways.

Experimental research on the nature and functioning of mental models of space associated with texts has taken two directions. The first (Bower and Morrow 1990; Morrow, Bower, and Greenspan 1989) consists of asking subjects to memorize a graphic map before reading a story that takes place in the represented setting. Bower and Morrow have argued that readers perform on such models the same types of operations they would on a graphic map. The travel of characters is simulated by locating them on the mental map, moving them from spot to spot, and visualizing the objects that surround them at every stop. It takes a longer time for subjects to imagine travel that covers a long distance on the cognitive map than to mentally move characters between close locations, and objects located near the character's current coordinates are more easily retrieved from memory than objects located far away from the character. While this research demonstrates the possibility of map-like mental models of space, its relevance to the processing of narrative texts is at best limited to the case of novels that include a graphic map (Jonathan Swift's *Gulliver's Travels*, Robert Louis Stevenson's *Treasure Island*, Michel Butor's *L'Emploi du temps*, Jean Auel's *The Shelters of Stone*, etc.).

The second type of research (Tversky 1991, 1996; Ferguson and Hegarty 1994) addresses the issue of the construction of mental maps from a purely textual input. But it tends to deal with short descriptive texts that foreground the representation of space. For instance, Ferguson and Hegarty (1994) asked informants to draw a sketch map on the basis of this passage:

> The little town of Crestview is an old mining town. To reach Crestview by car, drive north along the highway. Crestview begins when you cross the Green River. The river flows out of some low hills that lie on your left. Just after you drive across, you can see Crestview High School, which lies on the back to your left at the base of the hills. The small curvy Frontier Road begins on your left and provides the connection to

the high school from the highway. On your right, directly across from the entrance to Frontier Road, you pass a gas station. The gas station is on the river bank, and fishing bait and tackle can be purchased there. (Ferguson and Hegarty 1994: 472)

This type of data is not particularly useful for the investigation of the importance of cognitive maps for the processing of semantically complex literary texts that treat space as a stage for narrative action. It should come as no surprise that the sketch maps obtained by Ferguson and Hegarty (1994) were infinitely more faithful to the text than the drawings of my informants.

The maps I collected seem far too incomplete, the salient features too randomly distributed on the page, and the representation of spatial relations too inaccurate to suggest that their authors followed the narrative by moving the image of Nasar on the mental equivalent of a comprehensive plan of the town, as a pawn is moved on a gameboard. This does not mean that readers do not form vivid mental pictures of the hero at various points in his itinerary. Even the authors of the sloppiest drawings may have been able to visualize Nasar leaving his house, waiting for the bishop by the docks, heading home through the streets, turning the corner to the square, being attacked by his front door, or entering the kitchen to die. But these individual visualizations are too ephemeral to be assembled into a global representation comparable to the master map of Figure 1.

4.2 Cognitive Maps and Memory Processes

To understand the disparity and relative inaccuracy of the students' sketches we must take into consideration the full complexity of the reading process. As the cognitive scientists Marschark and Cornoldi observe, '[T]ext processing simultaneously "occurs" at several different levels, corresponding to words, sentences, paragraphs, passages' (1991: 165). To this list one may add the level of the global meaning, or narrative macro-structure. Reading also involves two levels of memory: Whereas the global representation is stored in long-term memory, smaller textual units affect primarily what has been called the sketch-pad of short-term, or episodic, memory. It is on this sketch-pad that readers form their most detailed visualizations. My personal experience tells me that these visualizations are picture-like representations that encompass both the character and the character's field of vision. We see the characters, but we also see with them, and we share their horizontal point of view. If we are able to contemplate textual space from a bird's-eye perspective, it seems safe to assume that these images will be constructed on the basis of information stored in long-term memory.[5]

The divergence of the students' sketches from the master map can be attributed in part to the fact that the master map is only one possible way to represent the textual world. But I would like to suggest that it mainly derives from the transient nature of short-term memory. The master map of Figure 1 represents an attempt to retain the images of short-term memory, to turn them into cartographic symbols, and to situate them on the global map of long-term memory. But on the sketchpad of short-term memory, the visualizations generated by the individual scenes merely replace each other. The reader may thus be perfectly able to imagine the story's main episodes without precisely situating each event on a global map. Or if the reader does indeed situate events, the coordinates may be forgotten when the next event fills the screen of the mind. If spatial imagination proceeds piecemeal, we will situate site a with respect to site b; then site b with respect to site c when a character is shown moving between these points, but we will not necessarily situate c with respect to a in our mental model. In other words, we may be able to imagine very vividly Nasar turning the corner from his fiancée's house into the town square. Then we may visualize, again very vividly, Nasar walking toward the front door of his house. But we will not visualize his path it its entirety, and we will not create a global map that encompasses the square, the fiancée's house and Nasar's house. As Stephen Kosslyn found, 'suitably instructed subjects could either move the focus of a mental image by continuous scanning of a path from start to finish, or by discrete jumps in the mental image' (Bower and Morrow 1990: 47). We make use of this faculty to jump when one of the partial maps of short-term memory has been replaced by another.

The act of reading has often been compared to 'cinema in the mind'. If the metaphor is accurate, we construct the story scene by scene, as a series of camera shots or 'fields of vision', as Gabriel Zoran (311) has called these discrete mental units. When we watch a movie, we see individual images of the strategic locations of the narrative world—for instance, the hero's house,

---

[5] The cognitive psychologist Barbara Tversky (1996) has argued that mental models of space constructed on the basis of texts are neither map-like nor tour-like in nature, but manipulable images which do not come with a fixed perspective. Adopting different points of view on their mental models, readers can answer 'map-like' questions ('is a north or south of b') on the basis of tour-like descriptions, and tour-like question ('what does a traveler see on the left after passing the lake') on the basis of map-like descriptions. Tversky's findings, however, were obtained on the basis of short texts exclusively focused on spatial relations, similar to the Ferguson and Hegarty (1994) passage quoted above.

the neighbor's house, the high school, the hero's work place, some streets of the town in the movie *American Beauty*—but we are usually unable to locate these sites with respect to each other.[6] Our mental model of the narrative world of *American Beauty* is not a city plan taken from a bird's-eye perspective but rather a stereotyped image (American small town), and a collection of snapshots of the fields of action. Novels are more conducive to the construction of plan-like models of space than movies because the reader sets his own pace through the story, and also because their abstract signs leave more room to the imagination. But the example of movies tells us that most plots can be followed with the help of very rudimentary sketches of global space. The role of mental maps is to provide a common background to the individual images (or 'little movies') of short-term memory, allowing these individual images to cohere into a world and a story. But the background is not constructed by fitting together the images of short-term memory like the pieces of a puzzle, for this would mean that long-term memory collects everything that affects short-term memory, and also that comprehensive images of textual space cannot be fully formed before the end of the text. If mental maps help readers follow the plot, they are needed throughout the reading process. I believe therefore that readers work from the very beginning with a global, but very schematic, vision of the spatial configuration of the textual world.

The items most frequently included on the students' sketches give us a good idea of what permanent landmarks readers find indispensable to make themselves at home in the world of *Chronicle of a Death Foretold*: a town, a river, a public square, a church, and a house for the main character. These landmarks surround a drama that involves Nasar and the characters associated with the next few items on the frequency list: Angela, San Roman (widower Xius's/newlywed's house) and the killers (milk shop/bar). The students' sketches may not be transparent images of cognitive maps, but they provide a useful document of the selective work of long-term memory. In their emphasis on characters' houses they corroborate the observation of Ralf Schneider: 'readers focus their interest in the fictional world on the characters rather than, for instance, fictional time or space or narrative situations' (2001: 628). Mental models of narrative space are centered on the characters, and they grow out of them, in contrast to the stage setting of a play, which normally starts out as a fully furnished but unpopulated space, and gradually fills up with characters.

---

[6] The bird's-eye view of the town that begins *American Beauty* gives us a good idea of what kind of town this is, but it is not very useful in helping the spectator conceptualize spatial relations.

4.3 The Construction of Cognitive Maps

We can only speculate about the dynamic formation of mental models of narrative, but it seems evident that it differs from the production of the master map and of graphic maps in general. To draw the master map I started with a blank page, added spatial features one by one as I went through the text, and I relocated these features when my placement on the map turned out to conflict with later information. It took a lot of erasing, throwing away versions and starting over from scratch to create a map consistent with the text. The novel offered far more spatial information than my memory could hold, and the mapping activity would not have been possible without a piece of paper. The production of the master map further resembled that of a graphic map in the sense that the drawing phase was distinct from the using phase: It is only at the end of the surveying work that my map allowed me to retrace the movements of characters across narrative space.

In contrast to graphic maps, mental maps are drawn and used by the same individual, and the processes of surveying and consulting are conducted almost simultaneously. Readers need mental maps to follow the plot, but they construe these maps on the basis of the plot. Out of the movements of characters (what Zoran [313] calls chronotopic space) we construct a global vision (Zoran's topographic space) that enables us to situate events. While this global vision is constructed through a bottom-up activity, it provides top-down guidance to the explorer of the textual world. This interplay of bottom-up and top-down processes is the cognitive implementation of the hermeneutic circle.

Since the reader's imagination needs a mental model of space to simulate the narrative action, it is important to achieve a holistic representation of the narrative world as quickly as possible. In Table 3, the most frequently occuring elements are indeed all landscape features that appear in the first few pages of the novel. I would like to speculate that once the map has been mentally sketched, it will be relatively resistant to new input or modifications. When new information conflicts with the reader's mental model of space, it is easier to concentrate on the visualization of the current scene, and ignore the discrepancy, than to reorganize the whole map. This would explain the inaccuracies of the students' maps with respect to the letter of the text. If this hypothesis is accurate, the relative stability of mental models of space contrasts with the dynamic character of character models (Schneider 2001: 628). Whereas space functions as a background, characters stand in the foreground of narrative interest; and whereas space mainly consists of permanent features, characters are evolving bodies and minds who continuously add events to their personal history. It seems reasonable to expect that the changing foreground will be the object of a more intense updating activity than the stable background.

While the reader's exploration of the textual world is complicated by the necessity of constructing the map as she goes along, the map-making activity is somewhat simplified by the fact that the map does not have to meet the needs of any other user. Published maps contain information for a wide variety of users, both travelers and dreamers; they must consequently include an equally wide variety of possible landmarks, destinations, and routes. But the mental map of a textual world is exclusively geared toward the mind that constructs it. Though one cannot speak of a specific destination in the case of narrative texts—here the goal to be reached is a rich imaginative experience of the entire action and a reasonable understanding of narrative logic—the mental map of a textual world can fulfill its cognitive function of getting the reader into the narrative without being complete, or narrowly faithful to the text. As I observed above, people read for the plot and not for the map, unless they are literary cartographers. We construct mental models of narrative space only as far as we find a cognitive advantage in this activity—only as far as is needed to achieve immersion in the textual world.[7]

Appendix

Table 1:
Legend to Figure 1

Features numbered in the approximate order of their mention in the text.
Number in parentheses = number of mentions (out of 55) in student maps.

1 Santiago Nasar's house. (Murder by front door, death in kitchen by back door) (54)
2 The Divine Face, Santiago Nasar's ranch (2)
3 Neighbor's house, through which Nasar goes through after being mortally wounded (4)
4 Church (30)

---

[7] This article is part of a larger project, *Literary Cartography*, supported by a grant from the Guggenheim Foundation. I would like to thank Darren Marshall and his 12th grade students in the International Baccalaureate program at Poudre High School, Fort Collins, Colorado, for their participation.

5 Clotilde Armenta's milk shop / bar, where killers wait (26)
6 Bench, where killers fall asleep (6)
7 Square and almond trees (square, 37)
8 Old docks
9 New docks, where people wait for bishop (docks or boardwalk: 34)
10 Bishop's boat (22)
11 House of narrator's family (7)
12 Bajardo San Román's hotel (7)
13 Angela Vicario's house (31) (+ 3 mentions of 'Vicario brothers' house)
14 Pigsty in Vicario yard (2)
15 Vicario neighbor's house, borrowed for wedding (4)
16 House of widower Xius, bought by Bajardo San Román to live there with Angela (27)
17 Brothel of Alejandrina Cervantes (12)
18 Meat market (butcher, 22; market, 2)
19 House of Prudencia Cotes, Pablo Vicario's fiancée (1)
20 Jail (8)
21 Yamil Shaium's house (1)
22 House of Flora Miguel, Santiago Nasar's fiancée (7)
23 House of Wenefrida Márquez, the narrator's aunt (0)

Table 2:
The Most Often Mentioned Items on the Maps

Feature (*=Not Mentioned in Text)	Mentions (out of 55)	Percentage (truncated)
Santiago Nasar's house	54	98
River	43	78
Square	37	67
Docks	32	58
Angela Vicario's house	31	56
Church (cathedral)	30	54
Widower Xius's/ newlyweds' house	27	49
*Fountain on square	25	45
Milk store/bar/saloon	23	41
Bishop on boat	22	40
Butcher (*butcher shop)	22	40
Front door of Nasar's house	18	32
Brothel	12	21

Table 3:
Representation of Spatial Relations

*Relevant field = number of maps that include all the locations named in the relation: for instance, number of maps that have both Nasar's house and a square for the relation "Nasar house on square"

Name of Relation (*Textually Inaccurate)	Number of maps showing relation	Relevant Field*	Percen- tage of relevant field
Nasar house on square	19	37	51
Nasar house near river	15	43	34
N house on square and near river	6	34	17
*N house not on square nor river	14	34	41
Church on square	19	20	95
Milk shop on square	11	17	64
Milk shop next to church	4	9	44
Milk shop on square opposite Nasar house	3	12	25
Church opposite Nasar house	12	20	60
Angela house away from square	16	21	76
Xius / San Roman house away from square	27	27	100
Butcher away from square	6	15	40
Brothel away from square	2	7	29

Table 4:
Map Styles

* = Subset of 'Pure Plan'

Map style	Number (out of 55)	Percentage (truncated)
Pure plans	20	36
*Iconic plans	2	3
Mixed plan-picture	26	47
Predominantly pictorial representations	6	10
Pure pictures	3	5

References

Barthes, R. 1982. The Reality Effect. *French Literary Theory Today*, ed. T. Todorov, 11-17. Cambridge: Cambridge.

Bower, G., and D. Morrow. 1990. Mental Models in Narrative Comprehension. *Science* 247: 44-8.

Bjornson, R. 1981. Cognitive Mapping and the Understanding of Literature. *SubStance* 30: 51-62.

Denis, M. 1996. Imagery and the Description of Spatial Configurations. *Models of Visuospatial Cognition*. eds. M. de Vega et al., 128-97. New York: Oxford University Press.

Díaz-Migoyo, G. 1988. Truth Disguised: Chronicle of a Death (Ambiguously) Foretold. *Gabriel García Márquez and the Powers of Fiction*, eds. J. Ortega and C. Eliot, 74-85. Austin: University of Texas Press.

Esrock, E. 1994. *The Reader's Eye: Visual Imaging as Reader Response*. Baltimore: Johns Hopkins University Press.

Ferguson, E., and M. Hegarty. 1994. Properties of Cognitive Maps Constructed from Texts. *Memory and Cognition* 22.4: 455-73.

García Márquez, G. 1982. *Chronicle of a Death Foretold*. New York: Ballantine Books.

Gerrig, R. 1993. *Experiencing Narrative Worlds: On the Psychological Activities of Reading*. New Haven: Yale University Press.

Gould, P., and R. White. 1974. *Mental Maps*. London: Penguin.

Herman, D. 2001. Spatial Reference in Narrative Domains. *Text* 21.4: 515-41.

Jameson, F. 1988. Cognitive Mapping. *Marxism and the Intrepretation of Culture*, eds. N. Cory and L. Grossberg, 347-60. Urbana: University of Illinois Press.

Kosslyn, S. 1980. *Image and Mind*. Cambridge: Harvard University Press.

Lessing, G. E. 1984. *Laocoön: An Essay on the Limits of Painting and Poetry*, trans. E. A. McCormick. Baltimore: Johns Hopkins University Press.

Linde, C., and W. Labov. 1975. Spatial Networks as a Site for the Study of Language and Thought. *Language* 51.4: 924-39.

Lynch, K. 1960. *The Image of the City*. Cambridge: MIT Press.

Marschark, M., and C. Cornoldi. 1991. Imagery and Verbal Memory. *Imagery and Cognition*, eds. C. Cornoldi and M. A. McDaniel, 133-82. New York: Springer.

Morrow, D., G. Bower, and S. Greenspan. 1989. Updating Situation Models during Narrative Comprehension. *Journal of Memory and Language* 28: 292-312.

Nabokov, V. 1980. *Lectures on Literature*, ed. F. Bowers. New York: Harcourt Brace Jovanovich.

Nell, V. 1988. *Lost in a Book: The Psychology of Reading for Pleasure*. New Haven: Yale University Press.

Paivio, A. 1986. *Mental Representations: A Dual Coding Approach*. New York: Oxford University Press.

Schneider, R. 2001. Toward Cognitive Theory of Literary Character: The Dynamics of Mental-Model Construction. *Style* 35.4: 607-40.

Tolman, E. 1948. Cognitive Maps in Rats and Men. *The Psychological Review* 55.4: 189-208.

Tversky, B. 1991. Spatial Mental Models. *The Psychology of Learning and Motivation* 27: 109-46.

Tversky, B. 1996. Spatial Perspective in Descriptions. *Language and Space*, eds. P. Bloom, M.. Peterson, L. Nadel, and M. Garrett, 463-92. Cambridge, Mass: MIT.

Tuan, Yi-Fu. 1975. Images and Mental Maps. *Annals of the Association of American Geographers* 65.2: 205-13.

Zoran, G. 1984. Towards a Theory of Space in Narrative. *Poetics Today* 5.2: 309-36.

10

Natural Narratology and Cognitive Parameters

MONIKA FLUDERNIK

1 Introduction

Towards a 'Natural' Narratology (Fludernik 1996) formulated a narratological paradigm based on conversational narrative ('natural narrative' in the Labovian terminology) and predicated on cognitivist parameters. Since 1996 several reviews and other discussions of the theory have appeared.[1] The main criticisms levelled against the theory have focussed on two areas of interest. For one, reviewers were concerned about the universality of the cognitivist setup proposed, querying whether the cognitive parameters outlined in *Towards a 'Natural' Narratology* were really applicable beyond a restricted period of English literature. Secondly, reviewers focussed on the diachronic aspect of narrativization, arguing—no doubt correctly—that the book provided too little discussion and illustration of the interplay of universal cognitive schemata and the development of new forms of (literary) fiction. The two issues are related since diachronic considerations impinge on both concerns. Thus, some of the disaffection with the universality of cognitive parameters stems from the suspicion that readers' real-world schemata may have changed over time.

---

[1] See Alber (2002), Gibson (1997), Lieske (1998), Minami (1998), Ronen (1997), Surkamp (1998), Witt (1998), Zerweck (2000). I have myself written a number of papers that have extended my previous proposals, especially Fludernik (2000, 2001, 2003). I would like to use this opportunity to thank Lisbeth Brouwer and Els Jongeneel, who organized a workshop on my work in Groningen (Netherlands) in June 2000, for having provided invaluable feedback which led to my current reappraisal of *Towards a 'Natural' Narratology*.

Narrative Theory and the Cognitive Sciences.
David Herman (ed.).
Copyright © 2003, CSLI Publications.

Since 1996 I have given some consideration to these issues and have also continued analyses of late medieval and early modern texts. The present paper is a response to the questions raised by the original formulation of the theory, and it attempts an extended presentation of the cognitive framework which supports it. The essay starts with a summary of my model (section 2), then proceeds to a consideration of cognitive issues (section 3), and closes with a discussion of universalist and diachronic issues (section 4) and some general conclusions (section 5).

2 Natural Narratology in Nuce

The theory of Natural Narratology is based on insights from cognitive linguistics and was inspired by the analysis of conversational narratives. One of the key tenets of Natural Narratology is the assumption that the cognitive framework of natural narrative can be applied to *all* narrative, even though later, especially fictional, texts extend the original oral design in significant ways. Secondly, and more importantly, the reading process was argued to be fundamental to the constitution of narrativity—that which makes a narrative narrative. Narrativity, according to my model, is not a quality adhering to a text, but rather an attribute imposed on the text by the reader who interprets the text *as narrative*, thus *narrativizing* the text.

Between the deep-structural level of cognitive parameters attaching to narrative (including the notions of experientiality, reportability, and point) and the reception level of the narrativization process are located four levels of narrative transmission which, in their turn, rely on cognitive parameters. These transmission levels refer to (a) basic-level schemata such as readers' real-world understanding of what an action, a trajectory, a goal, etc., consist in; (b) schemata that define the narrative material within a perspectival paradigm: the ACTION, TELLING, EXPERIENCING, VIEWING, and REFLECTING frames;[2] (c) generic and historical frames such as the 'satire' or 'dramatic monologue' schemata; and (d) the level of narrativization that utilizes elements from the first three levels in order to constitute narrativity (1996: 43-45).

These four levels of narrative transmission interface with the mediation of narrative through consciousness, which is as much as to say: through cognitive frames. Thus, not only is the subject of narrative defined as experientiality—a cognitive category; the ways and means of rendering this subject in narrative discourse also rely on cognitive parameters.

---

[2] I am using the terms *schema* and *frame* more or less interchangeably.

For readers unfamiliar with *Towards a 'Natural' Narratology* I here provide a more extensive summary of this basic groundwork.

Towards a 'Natural' Narratology constitutes narrativity not—as is traditionally the case—in reference to *plot* or *story*, but in reference to what I have called *experientiality*. This term refers to the dynamics between *tellability* and *point* noted by Labov and other discourse analysts and describes the typical quality of natural narratives in which surprising events impinge on the protagonist (usually coterminous with the narrator) and are resolved by his (or her) reaction(s)—a sequence that provides an illustrative 'point' to the story and links the telling to its immediate discourse context.

By introducing the concept of experientiality, I was concerned to characterize the purpose and function of the storytelling as a process that captures the narrator's past experience, reproduces it in vivid manner, and then evaluates and resolves it in terms of the protagonist's reactions and of the narrator's often explicit linking of the meaning of this experience with the current discourse context. To cite an example: In Norrick (2000: 96-99), Norrick quotes a story about a barn burning in which the narrator's father breaks down crying since he is unable to save the animals from dying in the flames. The story is a memorable childhood event for the narrator in which the horrible moment of arrival at the farm features prominently, when the lurid glow seen on the horizon while driving home turns out to be the fire on their own property. This moment constitutes the traumatic core of the experience. Its horror is cathartically purged by the father's reaction.

The memorableness of these events for the narrator lies in the *conjunction* of the tragedy ('we had to sit there all night [...] and listen to those animals die' [97]) with his father's breakdown, or, in other words, in the narrator's first-hand experience of human frailty in view of higher forces impinging on human affairs. The father's breakdown ('The only time I have seen my father weep') signifies an appropriate reaction to the events (not a weakness), since the frustration of being unable to rescue the animals warrants an emotional overreaction. This is a situation in which even men are allowed to give free rein to their emotions. For the narrator the experientiality of the story resides not merely in the events themselves but in their emotional significance and exemplary nature. The events become tellable precisely because they have started to mean something to the narrator on an emotional level. It is this conjunction of experience reviewed, reorganized, and evaluated ('point') that constitutes narrativity. Narrativity therefore depends on events (story) only to the extent that the large majority of our memorable experiences occur in the context of events or series of actions and reactions by human subjects. The crucial ingredient, as I have argued, is not the series of narrative actions in themselves but their experiential (emotional and evaluative) overload. It is for this reason that I have defined the object of narrative as partaking of human consciousness.

Having characterized the *what* of narrative, let me now clarify more precisely in what way the *how* is to be defined in terms of cognitive frames. I have distinguished five cognitive frames in *Towards a 'Natural' Narratology*: ACTION, TELLING, EXPERIENCING, VIEWING, REFLECTING. These frames relate to basic perspectives on human experience and its narrative mediation. The experiential core can be presented as a series of events and reactions to them. Secondly, the core of experientiality can be focussed on the TELLING frame in which our familiarity with storytelling is being foregrounded. Medieval narrative typically institutionalizes the figure of the bard as a key element of romance and other narrative genres. The frequent presence of a personalized narrator in fiction can be interpreted as a reflection of this basic cognitive parameter. Third, the VIEWING frame goes back to witness narratives and rests on a cognitive mode that conceptualizes an on-the-scene spectator watching the narrative events. Fourth, the EXPERIENCING directly touches on the experiential core of the narrative, focussing on the protagonist's immersion in the experience. This focus provides the cognitive prototype for reflector-mode (Stanzel) narrative. Finally, the REFLECTING frame, which relates to the mental evaluation of the experience, can in turn give rise to a mode of narrative transmission. Examples are mostly postmodernist texts but also the traditional essay literature (Montaigne) or the moralizing discourse of Fielding, Sterne, or other eighteenth-century authors.

These five cognitive frames are used in *Towards a 'Natural' Narratology* to define modes of narrative transmission through schema-generated types of perspectives on experientiality. (See Figure 1.) They are designed to complement F.K. Stanzel's bipartite model of mediacy in which the story is transmitted either by means of a teller character (i.e. narrator) or by means of a reflector character (in which case the illusion of an unmediated rendering of the story world is foregrounded). What my proposal attempts to do is to reveal Stanzel's two basic modes as cognitively based on the TELLING and EXPERIENCING frames and to add to these three more frames that will help to explain narratives of report (e.g., historical narratives)—based on the ACTION frame; neutral narrative of the camera-eye type and 'empty deictic center' texts (Banfield 1987; Fludernik 1996: ch. 5), here treated within the VIEWING frame; and the essayistic and postmodernist type of narrative which no longer correlates with TELLING as a storytelling activity and invokes instead a cognitive frame of REFLECTION.

Besides these macrostructural functions, the five frames also relate to basic constituents of natural narrative, i.e. conversational storytelling, which provides the cognitive source for these parameters. Thus, when one analyses natural narrative, one can clearly distinguish between non-experiential narratives (ACTION schema); experiential narratives of personal experience and experiential narratives of vicarious experience (TELLING and EXPERIENCING schemata); witness narratives (VIEWING schema); and narrative comment (REFLECTING schema). Both experiential types of narrative combine the TELLING and EXPERIENCING schemata since they have an on-the-stage narrator. Narratives of vicarious experience that are non-experiential combine the ACTION with the TELLING schema.

Human experientiality = topic of narrative

↓

Mediation (narrativization) by means of consciousness
(a complex natural category with several available frames to choose from)

↓

Narrativity = mediated experientiality

Different forms of constituting consciousness:
(a) protagonist's consciousness	(EXPERIENCING)	reflector-mode narrative
(b) teller's consciousness	(TELLING)	teller-mode narrative
	(REFLECTING)	much experimental, self-reflexive fiction
(c) viewer's consciousness	(VIEWING)	neutral narrative; Banfield's empty center; reflectorization

(from Fludernik 1996: 50)

Figure 1. Narrative Mediation

The theory therefore utilizes insights from the analysis of conversational narrative (providing basic *types* of natural narrative) and extrapolates from these to construct cognitive macro-frames to which, it is argued, readers resort when cognizing and analyzing latter-day written narratives. In a third, more specifically narratological move, these five basic types are then also argued to correspond to typical historical forms of narrative, with the ACTION and TELLING frames responsible for most narratives until the eighteenth century and the EXPERIENCING and REFLECTING frames emerging belatedly to come into their own in the twentieth century. The VIEWING frame, the most marginal of basic-level frames, makes a brief appearance in the late nineteenth and early twentieth centuries, but never acquires the same prominence as the other schemata.

It is no doubt the triple utilization of the five frames in *Towards a 'Natural' Narratology* that has given rise to critics' uneasiness with my proposals. The five frames are related to the basic types of natural narrative; they are employed macro-structurally as modes of narrative transmission (with the ACTION frame relating to non-experiential or zero-degree narrative); and they are in addition aligned with historically specific types of narration that only emerge over time. In fact, they trace a programme of possible narrativizations (in the sense of cognitive explanations) for new types of narrative which—at first blush—seem to be entirely non-natural since they do not have a correlative in the corpus of natural narratives. However, and this is part of my diachronic argument, these frames are accessed over time in the development of increasingly NEW forms of narrative. In section three I will discuss this more fully.

To conclude section two, I want to highlight the two major purposes of my model of Natural Narratology. These were, for one, to provide a definition of narrativity that is as far as possible applicable to all types of narrative and does not merely serve to describe the realist novel; secondly, to provide a model that allows one to integrate the two least researched areas of narrative texts—pre-eighteenth-century narrative (medieval and early modern) and postmodernist narrative. Since the model is an extension of Stanzel's narrative theory, my aim was to integrate a larger corpus of texts and to modify the theory in such a way that it could both accommodate the older and newer texts and still deal with the realistic eighteenth-century novel to its early twentieth-century successor. In addition, the model takes its inspiration from natural narrative, arguing that natural narrative is the prototype of all narrative. It therefore significantly goes beyond the exclusively literary framework of all previous narratology.

3 Cognitive Groundwork

In this section, I want to explicate more fully where the cognitive groundwork of *Towards a 'Natural' Narratology* lies. I will discuss the three sources of the term 'natural', turn to an analysis of the relevant parameters, and address the issue of how new prototypes arise.

3.1 Sources

The three sources for the term *natural* in *Towards a 'Natural' Narratology* (1996: 13-19; 31-35) were *natural narrative* (i.e., conversational narrative), the area of linguistics variously called *natural linguistics* or *cognitive linguistics*, and Jonathan Culler's term *naturalization* (Culler 1975). All three sources connect with cognitive parameters and processes, though to a varying extent.

3.1.1   Spontaneous Conversational Narrative

Natural narrative, as already indicated above, is used as a cognitive resource by the model. It does so, on the one hand, by taking natural narrative to be prototypical of narrative in general, and, on the other, by linking story schemata with basic cognitive parameters. Thus, by locating narrativity in what I have dubbed experientiality, i.e., the dynamics between tellability and point, I am providing a cognitively anchored common denominator for all types of narratives, since experientiality equally determines narrativity in novels. Rather than focussing on the presence or absence of plot, therefore, the model of *Towards a 'Natural' Narratology* relies on the human reworking of experience in terms of its emotional and evaluative significance. That complex is linked to the schema of incidence and reaction, i.e., the schema of an encounter with the surprising and unexpected and one's reaction to it, and to the retrospective evaluation given to the narrative core in the elaboration of 'point'. This basic storytelling schema from natural narrative is then deployed as a prototype to explain the operation of narrativity in more complicated written narratives. Thus, the prototypical correlation of experientiality with narratives of personal experience is backgrounded in favor of creating third-person texts in which the focus of experientiality relates to the major protagonist, thereby creating that typically fictional situation outlined by Käte Hamburger: 'Epic fiction is the sole epistemological instance where the I-originarity (or subjectivity) of a third person qua third person can be portrayed' (Hamburger 1993: 83). Novels that, like Virginia Woolf's, feature extensive portrayals of characters' consciousness are therefore paradigmatic of experientiality, extending fiction's inherent potential for the representation of third-person consciousness. Section four below explores these issues further.

Secondly, the prototype nature of natural narrative in *Towards a 'Natural' Narratology* is also instanced by the more immediate structure of natural narrative (or conversational narrative), particularly by the various slots of the Labovian narrative structure—abstract, orientation, delayed orientation, comment, coda, etc. These slots *functionally* survive into written narrative where they may be present on the textual surface structure in quite different form. Thus, the typical brief oral orientation section already in medieval romance has been extended to a more lengthy passage presenting the ancestry of the hero, and by the time of Balzac may come to span one or several lengthy initial chapter(s). The basic structure of (oral) episodic narrative can in fact be treated not only as a secondary schema that is later applied to written texts; it can also be argued to be a cognitive frame in and by itself. The constituents, or slots, at issue correspond to necessary cognitive elements within a narrative structure: the framing for contextual alignment, the experiential core, and the superadded levels devoted to explanation and commentary. For readers unfamiliar with the structure of episodic narrative outlined in *Towards a 'Natural' Narratology*, Figure 2 presents the basic model:

Abstract — Orientation — {[episode 1][episode 2][...][episode n]} — evaluation — Coda
$\qquad\qquad\qquad$ ↑ $\qquad\qquad\qquad\qquad\qquad\qquad\qquad$ ↑
$\qquad\qquad\qquad$ initial incipit $\qquad\qquad\qquad\qquad\qquad$ final resolution

Episode pattern:
$\qquad$ incipit — (narrative clauses) — setting — incidence(s) — situative — result(s)

(from Fludernik 1996: 65)

Figure 2. Episodic Narrative Structure

The pattern is a recursive one. Within the framing structure of abstract and coda a series of episodes is inserted, which in turn are structured on the basis of an initial incipit point and a final result/resolution point, with the core of the episode consisting in a central incidence impinging on the setting. This model is a further development of Labov's schema (Labov and Waletzky 1967). Figure 2 does not take the off-plot level into account. At any point within the recursive schema explanatory or evaluative comments can interrupt the plotline level of the story. To mark such digression, a much more complex, multi-level diagram would need to be developed.

3.1.2 Prototype Theory

The second source for the term *natural* was natural linguistics, a branch of cognitive linguistics linked with the name of Wolfgang Dressler at the University of Vienna. Dressler and Mayerthaler (Klagenfurt) have produced numerous studies that propose an analysis of linguistic form and function from the perspective of 'naturalness'.[3] These theoretic proposals invoke cognitive parameters, and in their results overlap with prototype theory.

In particular, the notion of a cognitive frame of naturally occurring storytelling situations and its prototypical use in latter-day fictional

---

[3] See Dressler (1989, 1990), Dressler et al. (1987) and the Dressler *Festschrift* (Schaner-Wolles et al., 2001).

narratives played a central role in the development of my model. Thus, the communication model of narrative (Petrey 1990; Sell 2000) can be explained as a transfer of the prototypical storytelling frame, just as first-person narrative corresponds to narrative of personal experience, and third-person narrative to narrative of vicarious experience. Even more importantly, the notion of prototypicality explains preferred interpretative options and the existence of more marginal types of narration which require a boost to become active options for writers and readers. Again, this will be clarified in greater detail in section four, where the movement from non-natural storytelling situations to accepted and productive new narrative paradigms will be sketched.

3.1.3 Synthesizing Inconsistencies

Jonathan Culler's concept of *naturalization*, finally, is also based on a cognitive grounding. According to Culler, readers try to erase or synthesize textual inconsistencies by establishing overarching interpretative patterns that neutralize the inconsistency and provide an explanation for it. The (in)famous unreliable narrator[4] is a typical instance of such a reading strategy. Since the discourse of such a first-person narrator displays evidence of contradictory features, the reading strategy aimed at resolving these incompatibilities posits that the narrator is 'unreliable', that he is hiding something. Thus, in Kazuo Ishiguro's *The Remains of the Day* (1990 [1989]), memorably filmed by Merchant Ivory, the butler Stevens, the novel's first-person narrator, keeps talking about the necessity of control and restraint, while he is impulsively seeking a reunion with Ms. Kenton, the former housekeeper. One increasingly comes to feel that he was in love with her but could not tell her and is now extremely sorry about how things turned out. That story is never told by him; it is reconstructed by the reader in a bid for explaining the various inconsistencies in Stevens's argumentation.[5]

This process of naturalization is related to interpretative frames: rather than seeing textual inconsistencies or contradictions as a frame clash (Stevens as the perfect butler vs. Stevens as emotional wreck), the process of naturalization manages to link both areas within one common frame: repression of one's sexuality; fear of emotional involvement, etc. In this

---

[4] For the latest proposals about unreliability see Nünning (1998a). See also Yacobi (1987) and Zerweck (2001).

[5] Cp. Wall (1994) and Phelan and Martin (1999) for excellent discussions of *The Remains of the Day* as unreliable narration.

manner, the contradictions become necessary functional elements within the superadded pathological frame.

3.2 History of Narrative Frames

I have briefly summarized the cognitive bases of *Towards a 'Natural' Narratology* on the level of its three source areas. Let me now turn to the question of (historical) development. How do new prototypes arise?

Basically, when one starts out from natural storytelling situations one can distinguish between narratives of personal experience, narratives of vicarious experience (telling about another person's experiences), and witness narratives (observing what happens to others, usually with both personal involvement and a vicarious empathy for the observed protagonist. Conversational discourse also contains reporting without experiential parameters, a frame that underlies much later historical writing.

The first major move that occurred was the merging of historical discourse with the vicarious experiential narrative paradigm. Alternatively, one can say that, in the context of *written* narrative, where third-person reference predominated,[6] the oral pattern of narratives of personal experience (constituting the bulk of oral narrative) was transferred to the most common type of written narrative; or, in other words, when first composing narrative in the vernacular, the best-known oral schemata were resorted to in contexts where Latin did not provide the primary reference point. This development can be observed in Old French as well as Middle English and Old High German, with these vernacular traditions influencing one another, especially the French tradition providing useful models for Middle English writing in the vernacular. Wittchow (2001) also discovers an oral substrate in Medieval Latin, which could therefore have served as an additional model.

The best-documented transfer and extension occurs in the eighteenth century when what is realistically impossible, the presentation of a fictional protagonist's consciousness from his/her own perspective, begins to constitute an ever larger portion of fictional narratives. What in real life is only possible, if at all, in first-person accounts of previous experience, is here inserted into the third-person novel and extended drastically to allow for internal presentation of characters' thoughts much in excess of real-world first-person accounts. Since the experiential pattern had already been

---

[6] Historically, first-person narratives only occurred in dream poems in the fourteenth century and, in prose, did not emerge before the sixteenth century—not including religious tracts of personal conversion or spiritual development which are, in fact, anticipations of the typical Renaissance spiritual autobiography. As a scholar of English literature, I here refer to the situation in England exclusively.

transposed into third-person texts, this introduction of the EXPERIENCING schema only constituted an extension of a pattern already familiar to readers, and hence did not require any additional efforts at comprehension.

The later twentieth-century types of non-natural narrative, on the other hand, are much more difficult to naturalize; it takes some time to become accustomed to them. Thus, although peripheral first-person narration (Thady in Maria Edgeworth's *Castle Rackrent* or Lockwood and Nelly Dean in *Wuthering Heights*) is the equivalent of natural narrative's witness schema, the extension of this pattern to 'empty deictic center' (Banfield 1987) contexts or to passages of figuralization (Fludernik 1996: 192-213; 217-21) requires much more effort on the reader's part. Although the extension of the VIEWING pattern to an anonymous or abstract viewing point/subject (as in Hemingway or Chandler) does not seem such a radical move, the de-anthropomorphization which it involves comes as a major shock. Camera-eye narration extends this mode of VIEWING to the context of film and by its refusal to allow experientiality to surface as a protagonist's consciousness deliberately aligns the narrative with non-experiential report patterns. (However, as I have also shown, the narrativization processes at work immediately result in the attribution of consciousness to the viewing point—as in Robbe-Grillet's *La jalousie*, where the discourse, despite a lack of experiential markers, is often attributed to the jealous husband's watching through the shutters.) In impressionistic ('empty center') contexts, on the contrary, one does not miss the persona of the experiencer.

Consider the following passage from Katherine Mansfield's 'At the Bay', in which a large number of expressive markers are used which should by rights be referable either to a speaker or to a reflector character on stage:

There ahead was stretched the sandy road with shallow puddles, the same soaking bushes *showed* on either side and the same shadowy palings. Then *something* immense *came into view*; an enormous shock-haired *giant* with his arms stretched out. It was the big gum-tree outside Mrs. Stubb's shop, and as they [shepherd and flock] passed by there was a strong whiff of eucalyptus. And *now* big spots of light *gleamed* in the mist. The shepherd stopped whistling; he rubbed his red nose and wet beard on his wet sleeve and, screwing up his eyes, glanced in the direction of the sea. The sun *was rising*. It was *marvellous* how quickly the mist thinned, sped away, dissolved from the shallow plain, rolled up from the bush and was gone as if in a hurry to escape; big twists and curls jostled and shouldered each other as the silvery beams broadened. The far-away sky — a bright, pure blue — was reflected in the puddles, and the drops, swimming along the telegraph wires, flashed into points of light. *Now* the leaping, glittering sea was so bright it *made one's eyes ache to look at it*. The shepherd drew a pipe, the bowl as small as an acorn, out of his breast pocket, fumbled for a chunk of speckled tobacco, pared off a few shavings and stuffed the bowl. *He was a grave, fine-looking old man.* As he lit up and the blue smoke wreathed his head, the dog, watching, *looked* proud of him.

(Mansfield 1984 [1912]: 442; bold italics my emphasis)

The highlighted deictic and expressive features in this passage seem to relate to a person 'on stage', a witness of the shepherd coming into view, but there is no such character. The reader nevertheless feels immersed within the fictional world as if he or she were that missing consciousness situated on the scene.

Second-person narrative is another new development which came into its own in the twentieth century. Here non-fictional models included trial discourse, instruction manuals, and imperatives, but the resulting narratives clearly establish experiential deixis and align this with the you-protagonist who may or may not additionally have a clear addressee function. The two most prominent types of second-person narrative, as I have tried to show (Fludernik 1994a, 1994b, 1996), either merge the EXPERIENCING schema with the use of *you* in interior monologues to achieve an even more realistic illusion of direct access to a character's mind; or, by means of its foregrounded address function, seem to take hold of the reader and transport him/her into the fiction where he/she finds him/herself in the role of a fictional character. In this second version a combination of TELLING and EXPERIENCING is at work whose audacity relies on the link between the protagonist and the reader figure with its metaleptic implications.

Finally, in *Towards a 'Natural' Narratology* and Fludernik (2001) I also noted a strategy called reflectorization, in which a prominent authorial discourse starts to align itself with the experiencing self of a fictional protagonist, either empathetically (*What Maisie Knew*) or ironically (George Eliot) (cp. *Towards a 'Natural' Narratology*, chapter 5). By erasing the neat distinction between teller and character, this narrative technique implicitly undermines the natural TELLER schema where teller and told are neatly separated. Whereas Hardy or Gaskell had alternatively presented information about the fictional world in the narratorial discourse and provided insights into their characters' psyche, the technique of extended reflectorization makes possible what is the acme of fictional écriture—experientiality rendered in the prism of an external perspective yet with full access to the protagonist's subjectivity. The technique shares some of the non-naturalness of film where the quasi-objective external image is suffused with subjectivity to such an extent that the medium loses its objective 'feel' and likewise seems to render experientiality from the inside but in images on the screen.

4 Universalist and Diachronic Issues

Having outlined what I see as the major extensions of non-natural storytelling situations and their incorporation within the narrational field of natural narratology, I would now like to address the two issues that have bothered most reviewers of the study.

4.1 Generating New Frames

Let me start with the question of narrative development since it can be treated in sequence with my preceding remarks on non-natural storytelling situations and their successful narrativization. Rather than privileging naturally occurring storytelling situations, Natural Narratology, by contrast, attempts to show how in the historical development of narrational forms natural base frames are again and again being extended. In this manner, the originally quite realistic storytelling frames of ACTION, TELLING and VIEWING are transferred to new contexts in which, realistically, they can no longer apply. Indeed, already with the advent of literacy, the replacement of a real-life teller of the story by a surrogate, the narrator *qua* bard, marks a first important extension of the naturally occurring storytelling scenarios. With the transposition of the experiential parameters from narratives of personal experience to historical and romance third-person contexts, another logical impossibility is allowed to become constitutive of the narrative genre.

Two lessons can be drawn from this repeated naturalization of non-natural narrational frames. On the one hand, these early developments have become so 'natural', in the sense of generally accepted and non-salient, that the momentousness of the transfer can no longer be appreciated. After all, third-person narrative, in its authorial mode, seems the most natural thing to us. This implies, secondly, that once an originally non-natural storytelling situation has become widely disseminated in fictional texts, it acquires a second-level 'naturalness' from habituality, creating a cognitive frame (on level III in my model) which readers subconsciously deploy in their textual processing. Even more paradoxically, fiction as a genre comes to represent precisely those impossible naturalized frames and to create readerly expectations along those lines.

Having come to expect full access to protagonists' consciousness, readers start to take this for granted, and experience frustration when that access is suddenly denied, as in Hemingway. Moreover, this initiates a clearly modernist preoccupation with newness or unexpectedness in and for itself which helps to train readers to naturalize even stranger new narrative set-ups later on (for instance, second-person narratives). The development of narrational frames therefore relies on prior natural storytelling frames; if these no longer apply, readers—for the benefit of narrativity—are willing to suspend disbelief (or, in this instance, criticism). Such new forms in turn can become so naturalized that they are no longer perceived as actually quite 'impossible' storytelling scenarios. A good example of this is second-person fiction. Initially, the use of an address pronoun to refer to the major fictional protagonist in narrative clauses of a novel or short story constituted a major stumbling block and required very sophisticated techniques of easing readers into such texts by means of interrogational or instruction manual-related frames. Since the 'epidemic' spread of the form, and due to its popularity, the initial surprise factor has become much muted, to the extent that readers now quickly move into an EXPERIENCING frame without undue worry about the impossibility of such narration in the real world. Similarly, in the wake of the interior monologue—itself a major violation of verisimilitude if seen from a commonsense point of view—it has become quite fashionable to present the moment of a protagonist's death through his/her mind. F.K. Stanzel has discussed this technique in his section 'Dying in the first person' in *A Theory of Narrative* (1984: 229-32). Not only do readers fail to balk at such impossibilities; they are in fact delighted at the author's ingenuity since—in an extension of the by now customary mind-reading—we are allowed a glimpse into logically inaccessible experience.

Fiction, we can therefore say, provides readers with experiences that they cannot have on their own—and this constitutes the fascination of all narratives. Whether we are transported into strange countries or into the mythic past, into the minds of figures that people these narratives, or into situations that cannot occur in real life—in all of these cases we are indulging in the thrill provided by poetic licence.

To summarize. There are at least three levels on which the naturalization of non-natural storytelling situations occurs. Most basically, *habit* and frequency of encounter determine the acceptance, subsequent loss of saliency, and eventual naturalization of non-natural story forms. As in the previous paragraphs, I am here using the term *naturalization* in the sense of 'converting' the non-natural into a basic cognitive category, not in Culler's sense of the term. Secondly, this process of acceptance is significantly enhanced *thematically* by fiction's subject of the strange, the extraordinary or the exotic—since readers expect something new, they are more willing to accommodate themselves to the impossible, the fantastic, the supernatural even. Finally, however strange the actual set-up, narrativization takes care of focusing the *reading experience* on a protagonist. Only if the text resists narrativization—i.e. resists our efforts to elicit some kind of experientiality—do we stop short and start to take the non-natural make-up seriously.

The model is arranged in a way that allows newer developments to occur in any direction, and it is also open as to what kind of newer developments there might be. Thus, the invention of film provided an entirely new viewing experience that soon came to have an influence on what readers were willing to accept by way of montage or other 'filmic' techniques used in fiction; moreover, the filmic experience also created readerly expectations and desires which fiction either needed to fulfill or to set aside entirely in order to demarcate the potential of the written from the visual medium. (Conversely, film has of course been significantly influenced by fictional technique—for example, in the use of voice-over or interior monologue, to name just two prominent devices.)

Rather than proposing a natural bias, the model, on the contrary, tries to provide a framework that allows for easy transitions between the basic natural storytelling scenarios, new scenarios offered by new real-life experience (including the movie, the theater, video games, the computer, etc.), and the logically impossible but fictionally useful and exciting frames found in modernist and postmodernist novels. It also takes account of external changes in aesthetics (modernism's flair for the new), in the advent of new media, and in the status of written narrative. These changes in attitudes and expectations do not, however, affect the basic cognitive categories of the model, but merely add to the parameters on levels II and III, perhaps also on level IV, as I will argue below. Moreover, it is in principle possible to imagine that real-life frames from level I that, so far, have not been productive of narrativization might be resorted to at some point in the future.

4.2 Universality Reconsidered

This takes me to the second query that has frequently been raised in relation to *Towards a 'Natural' Narratology*: how universal is the model? In particular, it has been argued that my cognitive categories are either too realistic (and do not fit postmodernist texts)[7]; that they rely too much on a modernist aesthetics and lose sight of readers' commonsensical realist reading strategies[8]; or that they do not take account of major changes in perception introduced in the wake of the media revolution.[9] The first of these points of criticism focuses on cognitive categories on levels IV and/or II, and argues that postmodernist narratives no longer take experientiality to

---

[7] This is the criticism of Gibson (1997), Feldmann (1998) and Alber (2002).

[8] Implied in Nünning (1998b) and explicit in Nünning (2001).

[9] See Alber (2002). Some of these arguments were also raised at the seminar discussing *Towards a 'Natural' Narratology* at the University of Groningen (see footnote 1).

be the ground of narrativization. The third critique, by contrast, focuses on level I and argues that level I cognitive schemata like GOAL or ACTION constituents have perhaps changed in the wake of the media revolution and that these basic-level cognitive parameters must not be treated as universals. Since I consider the model's anti-realistic groundings as one of its major assets, I will not address point 2.

Now it is perfectly reasonable to assume that the media have significantly changed our perception. As we can see from our students, they are not only inured to louder and less harmonic types of music, they additionally have acquired an uncanny facility with visual orientation in window menus which people like myself find rather disorienting. However, these different perception strategies (scrolling, click-hopping, etc.) do not, I would argue, affect level I-related cognitive parameters such as the knowledge of what constitutes an event, intentional action, goal-directedness, etc. However, even if certain types of human behavior did indeed change drastically in the past few decades and have resulted in lasting cognitive reconfigurations that are starting to influence our basic-level cognitive inventory, I still would not regard that as really threatening to the theory, either. Since the purpose of level I is merely to create an inventory of subconscious cognitive parameters by which authors and readers cognize the world in terms of fundamental processes of human being in the world, the changes are likely to be minimal, and they would in any case be accommodated during narrativization.[10] Influences from the technological revolution are much more likely to result in new cognitive frames on level II and on level III, where video-clips alongside the dramatic monologue or filmic montage may be added to a growing inventory of generic frames.

In response to the criticism that my concept of experientiality is too 'realistic' and that *Towards a 'Natural' Narratology* is unable to deal with maximally anti-realistic or experimental texts, my answer is as follows. For one thing, the model of Natural Narratology is, basically, built on the prototypicality of conversational narrative. To this extent, it admittedly sees the prototype as a fairly conventional case of narration. Having said that, however, what I have demonstrated above regarding the easy narrativization of non-natural story frames seems to suggest that the model is very well able

---

[10] Gibson (1997: 237) and Feldmann (1999: 451) imply that the cognitive bases of *Towards a 'Natural' Narratology* may be essentialist. I agree with Gibson's estimation that I am, after all, a pragmatist. In parallel to the cognitivists, my interests are ultimately empirical, though they are informed by anti-realist insights loaned from poststructuralism. Feldmann's more precise query can be answered by saying that cognitivism, like all natural sciences, is in the business of projecting theoretical constructs (e.g., cognitive frames) that are provisionally treated as real, even if, theoretically, we know they are not.

to deal with more experimental types of fiction. For this reason, the accusation of being too 'modernist' is a point well-taken — I am certainly guilty in this respect, and proud to be so.

Nevertheless, I can comprehend why some doubt would remain about highly experimental texts which resist the strategies for narrativization outlined in my model. This specifically concerns texts that do not allow the reader to establish a human source of subjectivity in the text and do not align their self-reflexive, formal experiments with a persona to whose mind (or consciousness) such self-reflexivity can be related. In particular, texts that fragment the attribution of subjectivity by alternating between a number of diffuse referents that never become full-fledged protagonists, or texts that deconstruct language itself put up great resistance to being narrativized. My view in *Towards a 'Natural' Narratology* had been that such texts are closer to poetry than to narrative and that their most effective aesthetic appreciation consists in an analysis of word play, or of a series of disconnected images—both decidedly aesthetic readings but not necessarily narrative ones. In other words, there *are limits to* narrativization, and these limits have tended to lie in texts that move either towards the lyric use of language[11] or the deconstruction of language (or both). This is the argument presented in Chapter 7 of *Towards a 'Natural' Narratology*, which uses the work of Gertrude Stein as one example. However, this recognition of the limits of narrativization does not disqualify my model from dealing with postmodernist texts. Rather than describing postmodernist novels and short stories negatively as having too little plot, no proper characters, etc., *Towards a 'Natural' Narratology*, on the contrary, offers the critic an explanation for how many readers who are not particularly poststructurally oriented nevertheless manage to interpret these texts as narratives. Only some highly experimental works resist such recuperation.[12]

---

[11] In view of Alber (2002), a word on narrativity in relation to the lyric may be in order. It has long been recognized that some modernist and some postmodernist texts, by reducing the importance of plot, seem to move towards a greater affinity with the lyric mode—an argument underlying Frank's 'spatial novel' and literary impressionism with its imagistic associations. Taking these insights seriously, I have argued in *Towards a 'Natural' Narratology* and Fludernik (2000) that there exists a significant overlap between the lyric and some types of narrative. Not only is a large amount of traditional poetry *narrative* poetry, many lyric texts—though they do not tell a story—purvey hints of experientiality in the intermittent evocation of a specific human consciousness embodied in a specific time and place. That still leaves a large number of properly lyric texts which are neither narrativizable nor interpretable in terms of aesthetic illusionism (Wolf 1998). If radically non-narrative texts like Beckett's "Lessness" can be narrativized (even though this may not be a desirable or useful reading strategy), then I fail to see why one should not also narrativize some poems.

[12] In fact, Alber's example of 'Lessness'—a serialist text—in my view is easily recuperable as narrative as long as one is unaware of its serialist generation.

What my critics argue by way of contrast is that extreme experimental texts are based on typically postmodern perceptual strategies, for instance on serial composition (arranged according to numbers and mechanical patterns of ordering) or on impressionistic sequences of word material. From this perspective, postmodernist prose seems to resuscitate Walter Pater's dictum that all art aspires towards the condition of music, only that in this post-classical age the music is not harmonious but a deliberate clashing of sounds, a planned cacophony, an arrangement of sounds in geometric images. This type of cognitive structure (serialization, fragmentation), the argument then continues, corresponds to new cognitive perceptions of the world, and my model fails to take that cognitive revolution into account.

My response relates to the level on which these serial and other arrangements obtain. In my view they refer to the surface structure level of the text and to its aesthetic qualities. Neither have been the *points de repère* of *Towards a 'Natural' Narratology*, which has been built on a deep-structural account of narrativity. Having said that, I would, however, agree that a cognitive analysis of the *reading process* is an eminently useful approach, and that this is the level on which observable changes can be described and shown to relate to the media revolution. Next to the thematic and ideological planes of narrative, this is certainly the level on which most developments take place. It needs to be pointed out also that the syntactic surface structure of narrative texts (which I have analyzed in detail in *Towards a 'Natural' Narratology*) has likewise changed considerably over time, and relates precisely to those issues of linearity which are important for the most recent media revolution as well.

If one wanted to integrate these insights into *Towards a 'Natural' Narratology*, one would have to accommodate them on the level of narrativization and perhaps distinguish between deep-structure-related narrativization and surface-structure-related narrativization. My contention that narrativity is not generated by plot but by experientiality was obviously directed at the deep structure of narrative texts, though that deep structure was partly signalled by the linguistic markers associated with episodic surface structure.

Alternatively, one could try to contrast three types of narrativization: narrativization as related to cognitive frames; narrativization as related to the fictional world; and narrativization as related to the reading process. In *Towards a 'Natural' Narratology* I had concentrated on the first two aspects and taken it for granted that conventional reading strategies ('naturalization') were in operation on the third level of the reading process. Although my model already posits the existence of fairly flexible narrativization strategies and opens itself to possible future developments, a more poststructuralist conception of narrativization would have to both redefine the *what* of narrativity *and* to elaborate the cognitive load of the narrativization process in relation to postmodernist aesthetics.

Such a project, although not formally linked to cognitive narratology, has in fact been attempted by Andrew Gibson (1996). However, that model—though it perfectly explains postmodernist texts—is much less suited to classical narrative and even less applicable to medieval or conversational narratives. Alber's criticism in fact repeats Gibson's charges that *Towards a 'Natural' Narratology* is not able to adequately deal with postmodernist texts. As I see it, this viewpoint confuses the theoretical positions of poststructuralism with the explication of postmodernist literature in its variety. There are numerous playful and self-reflexive postmodernist texts that profit from a strategy of narrativization, although they can also be read as resisting commonsense notions of narrative coherence. As Gibson himself notes (1997: 238), the train has been moving in the direction of 'pragmatism' (cultural studies, the ethics of narrative, and postcolonial issues), and recent fiction has warmed to good old storytelling traditions. For critics mainly interested in experimental texts, *Towards a 'Natural' Narratology* obviously is not useful enough since the book tries to embrace narrative forms both diachronically and synchronically and is therefore constrained to find common denominators and continuities between postmodernist and earlier fiction. On the other hand, a theory of postmodernist narrative based on poststructuralist theoretical groundings is just that—it merely deals with *one type* of narrative, however well.

Since my model relies on a deep-structural definition of narrativity and tries to span a long diachronic stretch of narrative, I do not see the necessity to redefine narrativity in order to incorporate the few extremely experimental texts of the late twentieth century which have already gone out of fashion again. However, if one were more concerned with the *aesthetics* of narrative than I have been so far, then the cognitive sources of aesthetic pleasure, and the reliance of the narrativization process on different (and historically changing) cognitive processing modes, would require immediate attention. Towards the end of an already longish chapter, I can merely articulate the desirability of such an extension. Perhaps others more versed in the newer media have a better chance of coming up with interesting solutions.

5 From Reading to Theory

I should like to raise two further issues before closing this chapter. The first issue concerns the transfer of reading strategies to the theoretical conceptions of narratology. The second also touches on the notion of objectivity and historical situatedness, and on the vexed relationship between constructivism and empiricism in my work.

In *The Fictions of Language and the Languages of Fiction* (Fludernik 1993) and *Towards a 'Natural' Narratology* I repeatedly criticized the communicational models of narrative theory, especially with regard to the essentialization of a narrator figure in texts which had no clear deictic or expressive textual markers to warrant the existence (linguistically) of such a persona. I argued that what we were observing in narratologists needing a narrator for *A Portrait of the Artist as a Young Man* was an illicit transfer of real-life frames of storytelling onto the communicational process of narrative and into the theoretical structures of the discipline of narratology.

Since beginning work on this chapter, I have increasingly wondered whether in my own model I am guilty of a similar transfer, this time from my analysis of the reading process (narrativization) to the theoretical level of natural narratology. One could argue that it is this adoption of narrativization as a *theoretical* constituent of natural narratology that is responsible for the criticisms regarding my book's treatment of postmodernist texts. As long as it is merely readers who narrativize Beckett's late prose, one can legitimately ignore these benighted individuals. When it is the theory that establishes narrativization as the central sense-making reading strategy within the theoretical model, the term becomes much more threatening.

I have indicated above that a special aesthetic dimension of the reading process may well be worth pursuing theoretically. Perhaps a subjective level should also be added. Narrativization certainly operates in readers' creative perceptions of texts that they know are supposed to be narratives, just as poetic reading strategies motivated the students of Stanley Fish to interpret a list of names as a poem. What was problematic for readers of *Towards a 'Natural' Narratology* was the *kind* of narrativization and the underlying definition of narrativity that I had proposed. Although I am far from modifying my definition of experientiality (which, since it is *not* synonymous with 'experience', can be neither male nor female, eighteenth-century or contemporary), I do believe that the aesthetics of the narrative text changes drastically over time and that these developments will tend to influence narrativization. Moreover, individual readers' personal background, familiarity with literature, and aesthetic likes and dislikes will also have a bearing on how texts are narrativized. At the least, readers with little or no exposure to modern texts will perhaps already find it hard to narrativize Virginia Woolf, just as twentieth-century readers find some fifteenth- or seventeenth-century texts unreadable because they lack argumentative consistency and teleological structuring. The concern for subjective difference clearly relates to a competence/performance understanding of narrative processing. Along these lines one can argue that readers try to narrativize texts that they intuit to be 'narrative', and that they are competent to do so since they can access familiar cognitive structures. Performatively, though, their readings will be contextually, historically, and subjectively situated and perhaps depend on talent and intuition as much as does story production: after all, few of us are born storytellers, and even fewer excel in this activity.

Having arrived at the issue of aesthetics and contextual grounding, one needs to go on to question how far narrative theory is merely a child of its own time and—just by having recourse to the cognitive sciences—reveals its situatedness within the current critical climate. There is an easy answer to that question which simply says that narratology has moved from Saussurian structuralism to Chomsky-inspired text grammars and from there to pragmatics, discourse analysis, and cognitive linguistics. The emphasis on basic cognitive categories in Natural Narratology would then strongly reflect the most recent linguistic paradigms of typology, grammaticalization, and prototype theory. According to that viewpoint, any theory is provisional and bound up with its historical context. From that perspective, perhaps, a more poststructuralist narratology that reinterprets *all* narratives from a poststructuralist framework could still be in the offing, although in the current climate it is unlikely to be a popular effort.

The more sophisticated answer to the situatedness of narratology would agree with the contention that classical narratology was realist in orientation since its primary focus was the novel between Defoe and Virginia Woolf. I wonder whether that really does make *Towards a 'Natural' Narratology* a modernist version of narratology (Alber 2002), or whether Marie-Laure Ryan's recent work on computer narratives (Ryan 1999, 2001) would then be an instance of a postmodernist or 'post-medial' narrative theory. (Note that Ryan is a resolute dichotomist in the structuralist sense and that the term postmodernist therefore does not imply poststructuralist stances.) *Towards a 'Natural' Narratology* certainly sees the modernist concentration on the representation of consciousness as a point of the maximal deployment of the EXPERIENCING pattern, 'narrative coming into its own', as I have called it (1996: 317). However, since—according to my analyses—this emphasis on consciousness can be preserved in quite different form in self-reflexive fiction, this is less a modernist bias than a bias *against* radically experimental techniques which, precisely, deconstruct the centrality of consciousness in the fragmentation of identity and the destruction of language.

Interestingly, I believe that Gibson and Alber would agree that this type of experimental 'fiction' (which is in fact no longer 'fictional' in my own terms) is a creature in its own right, separate from the rest of narrative zoology. Personally, I feel more comfortable with a less exclusionist model in which the frames that I use have been inspired both by conversational narrative and by the achievements of modernist and some (though not all) postmodernist writings. As I suggested, the feminist novel, ethnic fiction, and postcolonial literatures have definitely shifted the emphasis back to a resuscitated modernist aesthetics interlaced with postmodern anxieties and ambivalences.

Last, but not least, this poses the question of empiricism versus cognitivism — a seeming contradiction. The cognitive sciences employ constructivist models, yet they are also dedicated to an empiricist reliance on observable facts and to a search for truth, however tentative and provisional. Perhaps it is in this respect that *Towards a 'Natural' Narratology* is, after all, 'modernist' since its basic paradigms are linguistic paradigms: pragmatic and cognitive ones, it is true, but still linguistic paradigms. Natural Narratology's relationship with poststructuralism is not an 'ambivalent' one, as Gibson surmises (Gibson 1997: 238); that is to say, not in the classic sense of ambivalence. Poststructuralism provides interesting insights into the complexity and inexhaustibility of literary narrative. Narratology has to take account of these factors, but as a scholarly discipline with an empirical interest, it needs to remain aloof. The cognitive framework of Natural Narratology is sufficiently expansive to engage creatively with postmodernism and poststructuralism, but its main advantage lies in its general applicability. Cognitive narratology, in the shape of Natural Narratology, holds out the promise of having your cake and eating it too—of being able to describe what is going on in narrative and in the reading process without needing to be essentialist, realist, modernist, or, more generally, old-fashioned. So much for squaring the circle after all.

References

Alber, J. 2002. The 'Moreness' of 'Lessness' of 'Natural' Narratology: Samuel Beckett's 'Lessness' Reconsidered. *Style* 36.1: 54-75.

Banfield, A. 1982. *Unspeakable Sentences. Narration and Representation in the Language of Fiction*. Boston: Routledge and Kegan Paul.

Banfield, A. 1987. Describing the Unobserved: Events Grouped Around an Empty Centre. *The Linguistics of Writing. Arguments Between Language and Literature*, eds. N. Fabb, D. Attridge, A. Durant, and C. MaCabe, 265-85. New York: Methuen.

Culler, J. 1975. *Structuralist Poetics. Structuralism, Linguistics and the Study of Literature*. London: Routledge & Kegan Paul.

Dressler, W. U. 1989. *Semiotische Parameter einer textlinguistischen Natürlichkeitstheorie*. Österreichische Akademie der Wissenschaften. Philosophisch-Historische Klasse. Sitzungsberichte, 529. Vienna: Verlag der ÖAW.

Dressler, W. U. 1990. The Cognitive Perspective of 'Naturalist' Linguistic Models. *Cognitive Linguistics* 1.1: 75-98.

Dressler, W. U., W. Mayerthaler, O. Panagl, and W. U. Wurzel. 1987. *Leitmotifs in Natural Morphology*. Studies in Language Companion Series (SLCS), 10. Amsterdam: John Benjamins.

Feldmann, D. 1999. Review of *Towards a 'Natural' Narratology*, by M. Fludernik. *Anglia* 117.3: 450-53.

Fludernik, M. 1993. *The Fictions of Language and the Languages of Fiction: The Linguistic Representation of Speech and Consciousness*. London: Routledge.

Fludernik, M. 1994a. Introduction: Second-Person Narrative and Related Issues. *Style* 28.3: 281-311.

Fludernik, M. 1994b. Second-Person Narrative as a Test Case for Narratology: The Limits of Realism. *Style* 28.3: 445-79.

Fludernik, M. 1996. *Towards a 'Natural' Narratology*. London: Routledge.

Fludernik, M. 2000. Genres, Text Types, or Discourse Modes—Narrative Modalities and Generic Categorization. *Style* 34.2: 274-92.

Fludernik, M. 2001. New Wine in Old Bottles? Voice, Focalization and New Writing. *New Literary History* 32.3: 619-38.

Fludernik, M. 2003. Metanarrative and Metafictional Commentary. *Poetica* 35: 1-39.

Gibson, A. 1996. *Towards a Postmodern Theory of Narrative*. Edinburgh: Edinburgh University Press.

Gibson, A. 1997. Review of *Towards a 'Natural' Narratology*, by M. Fludernik. *Journal of Literary Semantics* 26.3: 234-38.

Hamburger, K. 1968. *Die Logik der Dichtung* [1957]. 2nd ed. Stuttgart: Klett.

Hamburger, K. 1993. *The Logic of Literature*. 2nd, rev. ed., trans. M. J. Rose. Bloomington, IN: Indiana University Press.

Ishiguro, K. 1990 [1989]. *The Remains of the Day*. London: Faber and Faber.

Labov, W., and J. Waletzky. 1967. Narrative Analysis: Oral Versions of Personal Experience. *Essays on the Verbal and Visual Arts*, ed. J. Helm, 12-44. Seattle: University of Washington Press.

Lieske, S. 1998. Review of *Towards a 'Natural' Narratology*, by M. Fludernik. *ZAA* 46.4: 373-75.

Longacre, R.E. 1983. *The Grammar of Discourse*. New York: Plenum Press.

Mansfield, K. 1984 [1912]. At the Bay. *The Stories of Katherine Mansfield*, ed. Antony Alpers, 441-69. Auckland: Oxford University Press.

Minami, M. 1998. Review of *Towards a 'Natural' Narratology*, by M. Fludernik. *Narrative Inquiry* 8.2: 467-72.

Norrick, N. 2000. *Conversational Narrative: Storytelling in Everyday Talk.* Amsterdam: John Benjamins.

Nünning, A. (ed.) 1998a. *'Unreliable Narration': Studien zur Theorie und Praxis unglaubwürdigen Erzählens in der englischsprachigen Erzählliteratur.* Trier: Wissenschaftlicher Verlag Trier.

Nünning, A. 1998b. Review of *Towards a 'Natural' Narratology*, by M. Fludernik. *EJES* 2.2: 259-61.

Nünning, A. 2001. Mimesis des Erzählens: Prolegomena zu einer Wirkungsästhetik, Typologie und Funktionsgeschichte des Akts des Erzählens und der Metanarration. *Erzählen und Erzähltheorie im 20. Jahrhundert. Festschrift für Wilhelm Füger*, ed. J. Helbig, 13-48. Heidelberg: Winter.

Petrey, S. 1990. *Speech Acts and Literary Theory.* Lonndon/New York: Routledge, 1990.

Phelan, J., and M. P. Martin. 1999. The Lessons of 'Weymouth': Homodiegesis, Unreliability, Ethics, and *The Remains of the Day. Narratologies: New Perspectives on Narrative Analysis*, ed. D. Herman, 88-109. Columbus, OH: Ohio State University Press.

Pier, J. 1997. Review of *Towards a 'Natural' Narratology*, by M. Fludernik. *Style* 21.3: 555-60.

Quasthoff, U.M. 1980. *Erzählen in Gesprächen. Linguistische Untersuchungen zu Strukturen und Funktionen am Beispiel einer Kommunikationsform des Alltags.* Kommunikation und Institution, 1. Tübingen: Narr.

Ricoeur, P. 1984. *Time and Narrative*, vol. 1, trans. K. McLaughlin and D. Pellauer. Chicago, IL: University of Chicago Press.

Ronen, R. 1997. Review of *Towards a 'Natural' Narratology*, by M. Fludernik. *Journal of Pragmatics* 28: 646-48.

Ryan, M.-L. (ed.) 1999. *Cyberspace Textuality. Computer Technology and Literary Theory.* Bloomington, IN: Indiana University Press.

Ryan, M.-L. 2001. *Narrative as Virtual Reality: Immersion and Interactivity in Literature and Electronic Media.* Baltimore: Johns Hopkins University Press.

Schaner-Wolles, C., J. Rennison, and F. Neubart, eds. 2001. *Naturally! Linguistic Studies in Honour of Wolfgang Ulrich Dressler Presented on the Occasion of His 60th Birthday.* Turin: Rosenberg and Sellier.

Sell, R. 2000. *Literature as Communication.* Amsterdam: John Benjamins.

Stanzel, F.K. 1984. *A Theory of Narrative.* Cambridge: Cambridge University Press.

Surkamp, C. 1998. Review of *Towards a 'Natural' Narratology*, by M. Fludernik. *Referatedienst zur Literaturwissenschaft* 30.1: 81-82.

Wall, K. 1994. *The Remains of the Day* and Its Challenges to Theories of Unreliable Narration. *Journal of Narrative Technique* 24: 18-24.

Wierzbicka, A. 1990. The Meaning of Color Terms: Semantic, Culture, and Cognition. *Cognitive Linguistics* 1.1: 99-150.

Witt, T. 1998. Review of *Towards a 'Natural' Narratology*, by M. Fludernik. *LWU* 31.3: 293-94.

Wittchow, F. 2001. *Exemplarisches Erzählen bei Ammianus Marcellinus: Episode, Exemplum, Anekdote.* Munich: Saur.

Wolf, W. 1993. *Ästhetische Illusion und Illusionsdurchbrechung in der Erzählkunst: Theorie und Geschichte mit Schwerpunkt auf englischem illusionsstörenden Erzählen.* Tübingen: Niemeyer.

Wolf, W. 1998. Aesthetic Illusion in Lyric Poetry? *Poetica* 30.3-4: 251-89.

Yacobi, T. 1987. Narrative and Normative Patterns: On Interpreting Fiction. *Journal of Literary Studies* [Pretoria] 3: 18-41.

Zerweck, B. 2000. Review of *Towards a 'Natural' Narratology*, by M. Fludernik. *GRM* 50.1: 123-28.

Zerweck, B. 2001. Historicizing Unreliable Narration: Unreliability and Cultural Discourse in Narrative Fiction. *Style* 35.1: 151-78.

Part IV

Fictional Minds

11

Cognitive Science, the Thinking Mind, and Literary Narrative

URI MARGOLIN

1 Introduction: The Thinking Mind and Levels of Narrative Communication

The cluster of disciplines or disciplinary areas known collectively as the cognitive sciences forms one of the central areas of inquiry in the human sciences and beyond. In a way, it is a super-discipline—on a par with semiotics, system theory, and information and communication theories—in that its concepts and models can be interpreted in terms of diverse domains of phenomena consisting of humans, animals, and machines. As such it constitutes a high-level tool of inquiry which may serve to integrate findings from diverse domains.

Loosely defined, the cognitive sciences consist of the systematic study of information processing: its acquisition (intake), internal representation in a mind or machine, storage and retrieval, and transformation, leading ultimately to some behavioral or symbolic output. The sources of information may be perceptual, especially visual, or symbolic (linguistic, propositional), internal or external, and its objects are some aspect(s) of the world, including the processor itself (in the case of humans one's own body and mind). Perception involves feature and object recognition, as well as selective attention. The internal representation of information includes at least

Narrative Theory and the Cognitive Sciences.
David Herman (ed.).
Copyright © 2003, CSLI Publications.

typification, hence concepts and categories, frames and scripts, semantic networks and propositions, as well as design and organization features, that is, an architecture. Storage and retrieval, or memory and remembering, includes, among other cognitive capacities, long and short term memory and routines for the retrieval of stored information. Transformation includes procedures for utilizing and modifying the stored information, such as category and concept formation, belief formation, judgment, inference, reasoning, problem solving, and decision making.

As far as humans are concerned, cognitive science is one of the main areas of the theory of mind—together with theories of emotion, motivation, and possibly personality—and can be viewed as basically the study of the thinking mind, its structures, and its activities. Most scholars would also include here theorizing about the nature of consciousness and experientiality. In addition to formulating models and hypotheses about cognitive processes in individuals, cognitive science is also interested in cognition involving interacting individuals and group settings (and hence in the transfer of mental contents and distributed cognition), as well as in cognition as related to its broader social and cultural setting.

We have just asserted that in the human or humanoid (human-like) sphere, cognitive science is concerned first and foremost with the thinking mind. Seen from a functionalist perspective, the human mind is the totality of an individual's mental life, that is, his or her psychological states, episodes, events, activities, and processes. The thinking mind could be defined, again informally, as that subsystem of the individual's mental life concerned with the processing of information, and its essentially dynamic nature is best captured in Alan Palmer's apt term cognitive mental functioning (CMF) (see Palmer's contribution to this volume). It goes without saying that the totality of an individual's mental life, be it actual or created by a literary text, also includes affects and desires or volitions and that the cognitive component is intimately interrelated with both. A desire, for example, may act as a motive for a reasoning process and the consequent formation of intentions. Cognitive processing may be accompanied by an emotional aura or give rise to emotional states. A comprehensive description of any individual's mental functioning must hence go beyond the purely cognitive activity, account for the affective and volitional sides as well, and interrelate them with the cognitive one. In addition, it needs to take account of the relevant sociocultural context, providing the full picture of the social mind in action (once again, Palmer's term). But, as in all areas of inquiry, here too it is methodologically warranted, sometime even necessary, to concentrate initially on one major component in isolation for the closer study of its specifics, as long as we bear in mind that the only natural unit is indeed the social mind in action.

The notion of a human or human-like thinking mind or of cognitive mental functioning is intuitively of great significance to all four levels or circuits of narrative communication as defined in classical, structuralist narratology. The first circuit is that of actual author and reader. The *author*'s cognitive activity consists primarily of processing information of various sorts, factual and fictional, specific and general, textual and perceptual, and producing as an end result a verbal text and its correlated story or text world. The *reader*, starting with the perception of verbal signs, subjects the textual information encoded in them to a multistage, probably cyclical, processing activity whose final product is a complex mental representation or image of the text's storyworld (Werth 1999). On the second, intermediate level, one encounters the author's second self or implied author (Booth 1983) and the implied reader (Iser 1974). The *implied author* is supposed to manipulate the information concerning the text world in particular ways, both semantic and compositional, so as to create certain attitudes and judgments in the reader with respect to storyworld participants (for an account of participants in storyworlds, see Herman 2002: 115-69). Inside the text proper, a textually inscribed narrator and his or her narratee (Prince 1980) define the third circuit of communication. The *narrator* is understood as an individual reporting, and often commenting, with a particular slant, cognitive and emotive, on individuals, states, actions, and events in one or more domains. The fourth, innermost level consists of the *storyworld participants*, i.e., interacting individuals who perceive the world around them, construct mental representations of it, form intentions (that is, goals plus plans), construct in their minds theories about their co-agents, draw inferences, solve problems, formulate generalizations, recollect past episodes and, in fact, engage in any conceivable cognitive activity.

Let me admit right away that only in the case of actual human beings can cognitive-science concepts, models, and claims apply quite literally, and that only with respect to them can claims couched in cognitivist terms be empirically tested, be it directly or indirectly. On all other levels we are operating within the confines of a make-believe world, pretending that narrators and storyworld participants exist independently of the text which actually creates them via semiotic means, and that they are sufficiently human-like so that concepts developed in cognitive science to model the activities of actual minds are applicable to them, even if only through analogical transfer. Similarly, reader- or scholar-formulated claims about the cognitive mental functioning of narrators and storyworld participants can only be assessed by means of semi-intuitive criteria, such as the ability of these claims to illuminate our pre-theoretical insights about this functioning, to make us see new aspects in the CMF of a character, view familiar aspects in a new light, and so on. And, of course, what is illuminating or insightful is culturally negotiated and consensual rather than independently and constantly defined. But this is equally true about the application of *any* representational kind of vocabulary to semiotically generated domains and their denizens. In short, as soon as we are ready to apply concepts from action theory to storyworld participants, we should be as ready to apply to them concepts and models concerning CMF. By the same token, once we are ready to ascribe actions to fictional storyworld participants, we should be as ready to ascribe to them minds, and especially cognitive activities. A refusal to do so in the name of philosophical purism runs counter to every single readerly experience and deprives narratology of the ability to handle a major component of all storyworlds, essential for making sense of any action sequence.

While the CMF of individuals on all four levels of narrative communication has long been recognized by readers and scholars alike to be of great importance, it is the rise of cognitive science in the last twenty years or so that provides the literary scholar with what I believe to be the richest and most powerful framework yet for its systematic description. There is no guarantee that individual CMF as portrayed in a given fictional narrative will possess any psychological reality, nor is it required to do so. Nonetheless, cognitive-science concepts and categories, including the overall scheme of the basic areas of information processing and their sequence, will in all probability be applicable to the fictional individuals portrayed in literary narratives. Besides, since the cognitivist arsenal is the best we have, the narratologist concerned with CMF as portrayed in literature has no choice but to begin with it and see how far he or she can get employing it. My own view, which I shall seek to support through examples drawn from all four levels, is that employing cognitive-science discriminations and models will greatly advance current attempts to construct theories of authoring and reading or reception, as well as theories dealing with the content aspect of narrative.

I base my claim in large part on a cognitive procedure known as analogical reasoning. One other major component of narrative content, namely the fictional world or universe as a whole, has undergone a major theoretization in the last two decades due to parallel analogical transfer. At issue is the introduction, adoption, and adaptation of concepts and models from possible-worlds semantics and modal logic. The differences between possible and fictional worlds having been duly noted, scholars like Doležel (1998), Pavel (1986), and Ryan (1991), using the philosophical and logical mechanisms mentioned above, have nonetheless been successful in constructing a rich theory of the nature, regularities, major constraints, and varieties of fictional worlds, which constitutes a major improvement over previous semi-intuitive theories.

Using cognitive-science theories promises to advance narratology's treatment of CMF in a number of ways. These include rendering explicit readerly intuitions and interconnecting them to form a whole semantic network; providing an economical and systematic way of identifying, describing, and categorizing phenomena; and reconceptualizing terms coined in narratology and integrating them into a wider theoretical framework, thereby furnishing a deeper level of analysis and suggesting new insights—that is, providing an optics through which one can distinguish cognitive functions or acts which could not have been identified otherwise. In the rest of this chapter, I shall try to demonstrate some of these benefits of an explicitly cognitivist approach to fictional minds.

2 Storyworld Production and Comprehension

The cognitive modeling of story production (generation) and comprehension by means of conceptual analysis, empirical methods, and computer simulation is a vast field which falls outside the purview of this chapter, being a domain of expertise in its own right, and a multidisciplinary one to boot, in which a huge amount of work has been done for the last 30 years by psychologists, computer experts, linguists, and literary scholars. In our current context, one especially pertinent aspect of storyworld (re)construction by the reader would encompass the activities and kinds of reasoning involved in the attribution by the reader of CMF to a narrator or storyworld participant.

This problem is related to the study of the ways in which character features and a personality model are ascribed by readers to narrators and narrative agents. The information-processing activities that go into the authorial creation of storyworlds are numerous, diverse, and in part intractable to systematic description or formalization. But one specific area of narrative studies, that of intertextuality (i.e., the network of relationships linking a given narrative text with other narratives), could probably gain considerably from reformulating its questions in cognitive terms. The creation of a text world on the basis of specific antecedent text worlds encoded in specific identifiable texts is ultimately one of transforming incoming information into a new information structure. Once the shape of the antecedent and the resultant text worlds is described, one could regard the transformation as a complex activity employing reasoning processes of various kinds as well as preference rules in order to effect decisions and choices which are all means to achieving an overriding artistic goal. The scholar's task would consist accordingly of formulating hypotheses about the specific nature of all of these factors in each case.

3 The Implied Author and Defamiliarization: Cognitive Style and Frame Blocking

While narratology as a field of inquiry should certainly include issues of storyworld production and of narrative comprehension, the narratologist must share work in this area with cognitive psychologists and computer science experts. Narratology's special brief commences with the next level or presumed level, that of the implied author, a postulated level meant to define both a transition and a link between actual author and fictional sphere, based on particular choices made concerning the overall mode of presentation of the storyworld and of its inner-textual narrator alike. Each mode of presentation can be characterized according to the categories of items selected (physical or mental) and the proportions between them, degree of detail of each (attention to minutiae or schematic patterns) and preference for direct scenic presentation and momentary sense impressions or for summary and generalization.

A second major dimension has to do with the mode of combination of the selected items: simple array or complex hierarchy; fragmentary or coherent; proceeding by contiguity or similarity; topic-preserving or digressive; chronological or scrambled. And then there is the attendant epistemic stance: (in)tolerance of ambiguity and uncertainty; employment of the hypothetical, conjectural mode or its avoidance, and so on. All of these factors are gleaned from the text in its entirety and are clearly cognitive or discursive, being well-preserved in translation. But whose cognition should they be ascribed to? Traditional narratology has noted correctly that there are many such modes of presentation, that widely different ones can often be identified in different works by the same author, and that, conversely, the same method of presentation can be identified in narratives by different authors. Consequently, no method of this sort can be ascribed directly to an author as a unique biographical entity as 'his' or 'her' specific way of doing things. Instead, each such mode of presentation was attributed to a text-specific author's second self, creative personality, or implied author.

But this supposed shaper of the discourse is nowhere to be found as a speech position, and remains an unanchored, elusive entity hovering above the text. I believe recourse to a cognitive-science perspective could shed some much-needed light on this vexed issue. We could well assume that writing a literary work is like a problem-solving or goal-directed activity. The author as an actual person sets himself or herself the goal of creating a certain epistemic and aesthetic (that is, artistic and cognitive) impact on his or her readers and providing them with a certain 'vision'. He or she has next to choose a strategy that will be effective in this respect, and, in the case of literary creation, the mode of presentation of the narrated is the crucial part of this strategy. Each mode of presentation, though, is in its turn a manifestation of a specific *cognitive style*, a tendency to process information in a particular way which constitutes an interface between cognition and personality.

The same actual author thus chooses for each intended readerly effect that particular cognitive style which, in his or her opinion, will be the most effective in achieving it. The cognitive style in question is knowingly adopted and influences the text's shape and mode of presentation throughout. I believe that the triple categories of authorial problem-solving intentions, a particular cognitive style selected as a means of problem solving, and method of presentation as its discursive manifestation or embodiment go a long way towards offering a better link or transition between the actual and the fictional than any putative authorial second self. If I am correct in my assumption, then the use of cognitive concepts in this case has brought about the subsumption of a supposedly specifically literary and verbal issue under a broader cognitive one (cognitive style is manifested in all kinds of symbolic behavior); an explication of a vague term by a more precise one; and a major modification of a controversial narratological claim. These are some of the payoffs one hopes to achieve by adopting a cognitivist approach to key narratological issues.

If the author's second self can be explicated through the notion of cognitive style, the author's 'freshness of sensation' or presentation of the familiar as if encountered for the first time, often called 'defamiliarization' and claimed to be the essence of the artistic vision of the world, can also be rendered more explicit through *schema theory* (for a detailed presentation see Semino 1997). The purpose of the defamiliarization technique is to render unfamiliar that which is already familiar to a certain actual readership possessing, together with the author himself or herself, a set of culturally established and shared schemata (frames, scripts, scenarios) adequate for the mental categorization and representation of the phenomenon in question. To achieve this, the author has *to prevent (block) the reader from activating his or her pertinent categories of world or literary knowledge* and applying them to the textual fragment in question in order to identify the persons, situations, or events portrayed in it. The resultant (at least initial) lack of recognition or understanding on the part of the reader is created by the author's avoiding or refusing to use the linguistic label or header or category term by which the phenomenon in question is standardly referred to, and whose occurrence triggers or activates the corresponding semantic category. What the author does instead in some cases is provide a hyper-detailed description or an array of details without their superordinate category, for example, 'an unfamiliar level of detail for telling an event sequence...dissolving both human and animal behaviour into micro sequences of atomistic gestures' (Herman 2002: 113).

Another procedure of the same nature would be the presentation of human behavior in terms of surface physical doings instead of intentional meaningful human action, or the application to the details in question of unfamiliar frames and categories, such as highly technical or scientific ones, or ones originating with an entirely different culture. Now all speech and vision in a literary text stems from its author; yet, in the case of defamiliarization originating with a textually inscribed and individuated narrator or with a character, it is conventional to speak in the mimetic mode not of the author refusing to employ standard familiar categories as an artistic ploy, but rather of the narrator's or characters' actually lacking them in their mental make-up. This, in turn, is motivated by making these narrators or characters themselves 'nonstandard', e.g., strangers, children, or individuals limited or distorted in their mental capacity for some reason. But the readerly effect of slowing perception, making it more difficult, and forcing on us, at least momentarily, perceptions without concepts which, as we know from Kant, are blind, remains the same. The vital role of appropriate mental categories and prototypes in making sense of incoming data and in enabling us to orient ourselves in our life world is powerfully impressed upon us in all such cases, even if the initial lack of identification ends up creating a comic effect. The fictional presentation of cognitive mechanisms in action, especially of their breakdown or failure, is itself a powerful cognitive tool which may make us aware of actual cognitive mechanisms, and, more specifically, of our own mental functioning.

4 Narrators as Information Processors: Selection to Metacognition

Many if not most narratologists would argue that for a variety of logical reasons one needs to attribute the totality of any fictional narrative to a narrating voice or speech position which is different from that of the biographical author. But if this voice remains covert, if there is no textually indicated situation of enunciation, and if one cannot recuperate from the text an image of a specific speech situation and of an individuated teller with whom the current reporting activity originates, it is difficult to speak meaningfully of any individuated cognitive mental functioning as distinct from general logical factors. Once such an image begins to emerge, though, we may treat the what and the how, the matter and the manner of the narrator's discourse, as indicators of his or her cognitive mental functioning, all the more so since reporting consists by definition of processing and judging information (by judging I mean here drawing conclusions from the evidence). Ontologically, an individuated narrator of a fictional narrative is as much of a fictional individual as the storyworld participants whose actions he or she reports and comments upon. But his or her only activity *qua* narrator is that of verbal reporting and commenting, and, in contrast to those of his or her characters, there can be no direct access to the narrator's mental activities and states, which need be inferred from the narrator's verbal activity. Like all speakers, actual or fictional, a narrator may comment on his or her own past or present mental functioning, but such comments are themselves the object of readerly analysis and assessment.

In a classical article, Jahn and Nünning (1994: 291) have adopted a Jakobsonian, communicative model to describe the diverse functions of narratorial discourse. An alternative, cognitive (information-processing) model could also be formulated, with the proviso that the functions in question are general and not specific to fictional discourse. In logical sequence, such underlying cognitive functions or acts would consist of *selection, chunking of the available information, its categorization, the use of prototypes or exemplars for sense-making of the category members, temporal and causal sequencing, inferencing, judgment, and generalization.* In his contribution to this volume, David Herman lists the first five as cognitive capabilities one can acquire or enhance by being a reader of narrative, and then goes on to say that they are also indispensable for the very telling of narrative. In other words, the very act of narration as meaningful information transmission requires the exercise of these functions. Their indispensability is illustrated in all cases of experimental writing where the author ascribes to a narrator a manner of narration which is deficient with respect to one or more of them, and there is a resultant upset of reader expectations and attendant difficulties when it comes to comprehension. Through its use of nonstandard, often strongly deviant or deficient manners of narration, literature makes us aware *ex negativo* of the default clause, the standard or normal mechanisms and patterns of information processing which are at the center of all cognitive-science theorizing and model building, but of which we are not usually aware as laypersons. The high number of such experiments with 'deficient' cognitive processing and reporting is part of the tendency of modern literature to test the limits of comprehensibility, and what better way of doing so than by omitting or inverting what writers feel instinctively are the basic steps of making mental sense of incoming raw data?

Judgment and generalization are major, yet optional, cognitive operations associated with narration. Two further significant optional operations in this domain are *recall* and *metacognition.* Whenever the narrator is also a participant, no matter how minor, in the events and states being recounted by him or her, and whenever these events took place prior to the time of narration, the nature of the teller's current mental activity in retrieving stored information about the events and in (re)configuring it may be highly significant. The narrator may of course recall not only past external events but also internal episodes of his or her own mind, from perception to complex conceptual activity, including past acts of recollection. The latter case is obviously an instance of metacognition, that is, 'knowledge or cognitive process that refers to...an aspect of cognition' (Moses and Baird 1999: 533). But metacognition in narrative can, and does, include also instances where the cognitive process being referred to is the current activity of recollecting and/or recounting, in which case metacognition may also involve monitoring or controlling this activity. This clearly covers the celebrated self-awareness and self-reflexivity of modern and postmodern narration. The more self-aware, self-conscious, and self-referring a narrator becomes with respect to his or her current activity, the more we can infer about current cognitive processes, both first- and second-order, relating to this narrating activity. At the limit, metacognition occupies almost all of the narrator's discourse, impeding both the cognitive processing and the verbalization of information about the narrated domain. Once again, this is traditionally referred to as a story becoming its own meta-story, and one could of course describe this phenomenon in the purely logical terms of textual self-referentiality, or discourse and meta-discourse. But insofar as we postulate an individual fictional mind and its activity as the origin of the narration, it behooves us to adopt the appropriate cognitive perspective for describing the process at work.

In contrast with the case of cognitive style and the implied author, it would be difficult to argue that a cognitive-science perspective introduces a major change or improvement into the current narratological discussion of narration. Nor could one speak here of explication and clarification as in the case of defamiliarization. Concerning the cognitive modeling of narration, it seems more appropriate to think of it as reconceptualization: the introduction of an alternative perspective and theoretical vocabulary, both of which tend to integrate the listed operations into a cognitive rather than logical, linguistic, or discursive framework. The choice between such alternative conceptual frameworks is case-specific but, as I have just said, if we wish to personalize the narrating activity and anchor it in a mind, then cognitivism would naturally tend to occupy a central position.

Another fundamental consideration involves the difference between the possible-worlds and cognitivist paradigms in the study of fiction. The sequence of information-processing activities I have attributed to the textually inscribed narrator is no different from the one we as actual readers undertake when we read the narrative ostensibly produced by this fictional mind. This should not come as a surprise, since, when reading a fictional narrative, we are ultimately processing external verbal information produced by this narrator as a result of his or her own processing of information of all sorts: verbal, symbolic and/or perceptual, external, and internal. Possible-worlds approaches to the study of literary narrative, such as that developed by Ryan (Ryan 1991), are truth-functional or semantic in nature and stress the gap between fictional and actual, based on the different ontological status of the two domains. (For the philosophical, especially model-theoretic, background of fictional-worlds semantics, see the definitive study by Hodges [1993].) The cognitive approach, on the other hand, focuses on mental constructs and the internal representation of content or information. In this area our cognitive processing of a fictional narrative may not be all that different in its fundamentals from our processing of a fact-based one.

Secondly, but this is sheer speculation, while we may be able to imagine worlds with objects and regularities which are vastly different from our own, it may be far more difficult to portray the functioning of a mind of an entirely different sort, or to describe any mind in terms which are totally different from those we use for the human one. This applies respectively to the author, who, after all, creates the textual narrator and his or her mental functioning, and to the reader who seeks to recreate it in the course of the reading and interpretation process. For all of these reasons, a cognitivist approach, assuming a basic affinity between actual and fictional minds when it comes to information processing, seems to be far more integrative than the possible-worlds one.

5 Storyworld Participants as Minds in Action

5.1 Focalizers: Perception, Attention, Mental Representation

No matter how varied and interesting the CMF attributable to a narrator, we should not forget that a personalized narrator is not a universal component of narrative, that there is no direct access to his or her mind, and that the activity of any narrator is limited to verbal reporting on actions and events, sometimes with a personal slant. It is only in the narrated domain that the full range of human cognitive activities can be portrayed or represented. Let me begin with one such activity which, once again, forms a transition link, this time between the teller and the told.

One of the fundamental distinctions of classical narratology is that between seer and sayer, based on the general ability of any narrator, or speaker in general, to take the point of view of someone else with respect to any phenomenon, to see it through someone else's eyes so to speak. But while in actuality a speaker can only assume how things will be seen, literally or metaphorically, through someone else's eyes, the narrator in a fictional narrative can present us with information about an object or event as filtered through another mind. More specifically, only fictional narrative can present us with a storyworld participant's mind in action, as it perceives, categorizes, represents internally (creates a 'mental image'), and judges any object in the storyworld. This unique ability is part of the postulate of unrestricted mental access to the minds of characters, which is in its turn one of the constitutive conventions of literary narrative. A focalizer can be defined as an individual storyworld participant whose mental activity in constructing an internal representation of some object or event in his or her world and the resultant product of this activity are both displayed in the narrative. The agent, the activity, and the product have all been the subject of enormous debate in narratolgy. Let us now see whether the utilization of a cognitive perspective may make things a bit clearer. To simplify matters, I will limit the objects and events in the focalizer's world to external ones which are the source of immediate sense perceptions for this individual's mind.

The focalizer is a human or human-like storyworld participant who concentrates or focuses selectively on a portion of the available sensory information (an act defined by William James interestingly enough as 'focalization or concentration'; see Duncan 1999: 39). This selected information is next interpreted in the focalizer's mind, yielding a mental image, sometimes quite literally, or a propositional representation of a segment of the storyworld, which world is supposed to exist independently in the outside, inter-subjective domain. As we know from cognitive studies, perception, the first stage of this process, is far from being an innocent, simple recording of external input stimuli. It involves rather active selection, organization, and interpretation of data. In addition, each act of perception is carried out by a mind which has previous knowledge, memories, and expectations, all of which play a decisive role in shaping the inner representation of the input data. The unique 'take' of each storyworld participant on the same storyworld segment is hence not only a function of a different spatial position and of the need for epistemic and artistic variety, but an inevitable psychological given. The focalized is that externally existing storyworld segment which is the object of the focalizer's attention and subsequent internal processing.

Focalization as a whole thus involves an external object to be attended to, an associated act of individual perception followed by internal information processing, and its product: an individual perspectival projection of part of a shared phenomenal world. As a mental activity, focalization is clearly intentional in the technical sense of being directed at some object or state of affairs. Each act of focusing one's attention on some external sensory data is also deictically anchored in a unique way, being indexed to a particular embodied mind, that is, an individual space, time, and person combination. When a narrative has an overall impersonal and omniscient narrating voice, a report by this voice about any part of the narrated domain serves as the standard of factual truth against which individual perspectival visions as psychological facts are compared for their specific bias. Modern psychologism in the novel avoids such a voice-of-truth technique and tends instead to provide most of the information about the narrated domain through individual character 'takes', assuming that any information we can possess about external reality is of necessity focalized through some individual mind, that each focalization on a given domain is partial only, that different minds inevitably have different 'takes' on the same domain, and that there cannot be any absolute perspective on any state of affairs. Understood in terms of *deictic anchoring, intentionality, attention and perception, cognitive processing and resultant mental representation of a domain* (which can of course be verbalized), focalization can be integrated into the general cognitivist view on perception and its products. While direct access to process and product, independently of the focalizer's verbal reporting, is of course a purely literary technique, the process itself forms part and parcel of human cognition as a whole, and in this sense definitely possesses psychological reality.

5.2 Cognizers and Related Concepts

As already indicated, there is no cognitive process, or mental activity in general, which cannot be portrayed with respect to a storyworld participant. This enormous variety of possible activities has given rise to several terms, all focusing on the activity or quality of the mind of storyworld participants. The resulting proliferation of terms justifies an attempt, based on actual usage rather than conceptual essentialism, to delimit the terms mutually.

A storyworld participant, when conceived of as a thinking agent, a processor of information, could be termed 'cognizer' and placed in a relative-contrastive position vis-à-vis other theoretical modelings of the mental dimension or interiority of such participants. 'Narrative agent' emphasizes those mental factors and activities related to external action, such as acts of intending (design, plan, goal) and choice- and decision-making operations. 'Character', when not used as synonymous with storyworld participant, is more or less synonymous with 'individual personality' as defined in psychology: a complex of enduring traits, attitudes, and dispositions. While mental information-processing operations, being internal actions, can be directly presented in literature, character features cannot, and must therefore either be explicitly attributed to a storyworld participant by others or by a narrator, or inferred by the reader from details of behavior and setting. Issues of the 'self' (or 'I', or 'ego') concern the self-reflexive capacities of the person as revealed in specific modes of self-awareness versus awareness of others, embodied in an exemplary fashion in spiritual autobiographies. 'The subject', as the term is currently being used in literary theory, is the locus of one's construction of one's individual identity or self-image, for answering questions such as 'Who am I?' racially, sexually, socially, ethnically, and so on. Since all these concepts, and the respective theories about each of them, are concerned with mental activities which are themselves ultimately united in the social mind in action, the demarcation itself is less a matter of the ontology of storyworlds than a reflection of a different theoretical focus and perspective in each case.

5.3 Fictional Minds in Action and Their Actual Readers

If narrative is essentially a verbal representation of things in time, and more specifically of changes of state caused by physical events, how important to it then is the cognitive dimension of agents? It turns out that even if very little of the cognitive functioning of agents is explicitly provided by the story text, narratives must nonetheless 'allow the reconstruction of an interpretive network of goals, plans, and psychological motivations [i. e., mental causation] around the narrated events to give intelligibility to the physical events' (Ryan forthcoming). Once again, since we cannot but conceive of narrative agents as human or human-like, it is a basic cognitive requirement of ours that we attribute to them information-processing activities and internal knowledge representations. In other words, even if the story is behavioristic in its manner of portrayal and provides no information about the cognitive functioning of storyworld participants, readers need to formulate hypotheses about the minds of agents and ascribe to them mental functioning in order to make sense of their doings in terms of human actions and interactions.

Reading Hemingway's 'The Killers' (Hemingway 1978), for example, we must assume that Nick, by activating knowledge frames acquired from his life world or his encounters with literature and cinema, identifies the strangers looking for Ole as professional killers. It is equally necessary for us to assume next that he forms the intention to go and warn Ole, and that Nick seeks in vain to form a hypothesis about the reasons for Ole's indifference to the news. Not only the working of the individual mind in isolation, but also its working as influenced by its internal image of the working of other minds appear to be necessary to make human sense of a narrative.

A related question concerns the possible cognitive benefits to the reader from descriptions of the working of fictional minds in all their complexity and variety, be they in a reported or scenic mode. Because mental functioning is essential to being human, the wide array of kinds and types of mental functioning displayed in narrative fiction enriches our store of conceivable models of human experientiality, suggests various views about its underlying features and regularities, and enlarges, through example rather than theory, our sense of what it may mean to be human. It is clear that no instance of the mental functioning of a nonactual individual can provide us with singular truths about actuality. Yet, through a process of abstraction and generalization, such instances can and do serve for readers as a major factor in organizing and interpreting their beliefs about key aspects of actual human interiority, and in this way they can and do contribute at least to 'folk psychology', if not to cognitive science.

Further, let us not forget that folk psychology itself *is* part of psychological reality! On occasion, upon reading a literary representation of some aspect of cognitive mental functioning, a reader may also feel something akin to Bühler's *Aha-Erlebnis* ('Aha! experience') (Bühler 1982: 311), realizing all of a sudden that this is how she herself perceives, categorizes, or recalls, that the fictional representation has made her aware of the very nature of a mental activity in which she constantly engages, but of which she had not been as aware ever before, or which she had been unable to describe so effectively. This point is reinforced by the claim of cognitive science that many of our cognitive processing activities are indeed 'unconscious', not being accompanied by any self-awareness or self-consciousness. The reading of literary representations of mental functioning is also a major source of another undeniable common psychological fact, namely, readerly engagement with fictional figures, caring for their fortunes, and sometimes empathizing with their mental states and episodes.

5.4 Discourses of Minds in Action: Fiction and Cognitive Science

We have just looked briefly at some of the interrelations between portrayals of mental functioning in fiction and the cognitive mental functioning of the readers of these descriptions. A parallel question concerns the relations between the basic assumptions underlying the representation of CMF in fiction and in the discourse of cognitive science. The two would be incommensurable if they did not share some assumptions, such that there is a mind, that it performs a variety of information processing functions, that these are knowable and expressible in language and so on. But beyond this, some fundamental differences do exist. Note, though, that these differences themselves can be identified and described only by using the theoretical vocabulary of cognitive science.

The first is the possibility or impossibility of direct (unmediated), reliable, and full access to the contents and workings of other minds. In cognitive science, the investigator typically attributes mental states and operations to the subjects of his or her research on the basis of pertinent evidence, seeks to represent cognitive functioning through various computational procedures, and simulates this functioning through corresponding computer programs. In fiction, all of this is directly open to our inspection (as and when it occurs) with respect to one or more storyworld participants, but obviously on the assumption that all these operations involve the use of a natural language—an assumption not generally held in cognitive science. Direct access to other minds at work has been described as rendering them transparent (Cohn 1978) or as assuming a first-person perspective with respect to a third person (Hamburger 1968). As a result, the difference between first-person and third-person perspectives (i. e., unmediated versus mediated and inferred ones) is sometimes obliterated in fiction, and this on two levels: narrator versus characters (as in Proust for example), and reader versus characters. What this means quite simply is that a narrator can access and know about the mental functioning of one or more of the storyworld participants in the same way and to the same extent as the participants themselves do, and share this knowledge with his or her addressees.

A second major difference concerns consciousness. In the portrayal of mental functioning in fiction, great importance is often attributed to the character's accompanying consciousness of the relevant states and operations, whether they involve sensations, perceptual experiences (sentience), or thoughts and propositional attitudes (awareness). A huge debate is currently raging in cognitive science and the philosophy of mind concerning the nature of consciousness, but most scholars would agree that consciousness has something to do with the first-person perspective or the subjective character of experience. At issue is the sense that an experience is uniquely mine rather than someone else's (the indexicality of conscious mental states or *Jemeinigkeit der Erfahrung* in phenomenological terminology), with its unique qualitative feel. It is this elusive feel or quality that Proust for example is so concerned with, that his personalized narrator can portray with respect to others, and not just himself, and that in general is much easier for writers to embody through individual instances than for philosophers to define in general conceptual, categorial terms.

Closely associated with consciousness and sometimes identified with it is the issue of qualia or what-it's-like to be in a certain mental state. According to Keenan (1999: 693), the term *qualia* '[c]haracterizes the qualitative, experiential or felt properties of mental states', either all of them or at least sensations (internally generated) and perceptions (originating with external stimuli). Again, one could detect in the novels of Virginia Woolf and in James Joyce's *Ulysses* (Joyce 1961), for example, a concern precisely with this accompanying aspect of perception and an attempt to render it for their characters. This is sometimes done through a direct presentation of introspective acts of these characters, portraying their attentive, focused awareness of a concurrent mental state, especially a sensation or perception. But whether it is another person's subjectively felt experience or introspective awareness of that experience, neither can be directly accessed by any cognitive scientist.

While science uses individual features as a mere source of data for constructing prototypes, and individual behavior as information for formulating regularities of some kind, fiction, by its very nature, must provide the reader with individual, differentiated story participants and their specific cognitive features and acts, and only as a second, optional step, formulate some general statements about aspects of cognitive functioning, apparently based on extrapolation from the presented individual cases. The uniformity and generality of the scientific exemplar or prototype is thus replaced by individual cases, and by the stress on individual differences of mental behavior in the performance of cognitive functions. What is probably even more significant is the preference of much literature for nonstandard forms of cognitive functioning, be they rare and marginal, deviant, or involving a failure, breakdown, or lack of standard patterns. We have already seen that this sort of artistic procedure stems from a desire to explore new possibilities, and, in some cases such as that of Samuel Beckett (e.g., Beckett 1980), the very limits or minimal conditions of cognitive activity as such. This procedure provides the reader with novelty and an intellectual challenge to make sense of the unfamiliar and exceptional and, in addition, makes him or her aware *ex negativo* of the presumed standard case.

But standard case or deviation according to whom? As it turns out, (almost) all writers of fiction base their portrayal of mental functioning on one version or another of what cognitivists term 'folk psychology', that is, a socially constructed and shared everyday common-sense set of general views or a theory that 'explains human behavior in terms of beliefs,...intentions, expectations, preferences,...and so on' (Baker 1999: 319). It is a shared model of this kind that enables the artist to portray the mental functioning of a character in a way which would make that character be considered standard or exceptional by a readership. However, whereas cognitive science seeks the broadest and longest- lasting generalizations about human mental functioning, the details of folk psychologies are obviously period- and culture-dependent. Can then the literary portrayal of individual cases of mental functioning and the generalizations about them made by a character, narrator, or impersonal narrating voice be of any use to cognitive science?

Two uses are conceivable. First, if we assume that many authors have an exceptional insight into the human mind, mental functioning as portrayed by them may be suggestive for scholars as a source of hypotheses to be tested on actual human beings: Do at least some people process information, retrieve it, and draw inferences from it the way character X does in a given work of fiction? Narrative fiction, portraying collectively a vast array of cognitive activities, may also suggest to the investigator new aspects and issues for scrutiny, from the relation between perception, optical illusion, and hallucination, through visual knowledge and explicit and implicit memory, to various forms of cognitive dissonance. In fact, many complex phenomena acknowledged by but not yet amenable to explicit scientific theorizing are enacted in literary narrative, which thus serves as a reservoir of potential insights, literature being probably the most eloquent and differentiated non-scientific mode of describing specific instances of the mind in action.

Second, on a meta-level, researchers may be interested in how authors' actual-world mental functioning enables them to portray fictional mental functioning of any kind or of specific kinds, in one manner or in another. At this point we are back to the cognitive component of literary creativity.

5.5 Characters' Acts of Perception: A Cognitivist Perspective

To summarize: at the very beginning of this chapter I cited the four major components of information processing as it is currently modeled in cognitive science: intake, internal representation, storage and retrieval, and transformation. We noted that a whole range of activities is subsumed under each of them. I have also claimed in passing that instances of cognitive functioning portrayed in fiction will fall under one or another of these categories or activity types. Yet literary narrative, in portraying storyworld participants, does pay disproportionate attention to marginal/exceptional cases, to unusual varieties, to breakdowns or failures of one or more of these categories, and to components, such as qualia, which have not yet been successfully handled by a set of rigorous theoretical concepts and claims. Nevertheless, the very utilization of the four basic categories still enables us, probably for the first time, to begin to map out systematically and coherently the myriad kinds of cognitive mental functioning encountered in narrative fiction, and the kind of cognitive activities dominant in a particular narrative. Further, when sufficiently developed, cognitive concepts and categories will greatly increase our ability to identify, define, and describe individual mental states and episodes in storyworlds, whether we are interested in them per se, or for the degree of psychological reality they possess.

I would accordingly like to conclude this exploratory account with a brief presentation in cognitive-science terms of some salient literary phenomena pertaining to just one sector of one major category: visual perception as a key mode of information intake. This should also serve as a test case, in that my readers can then judge for themselves how much, or how little, of a conceptual advance for narratology is effected by importing the cognitive conceptual framework. But let us not forget that even if a particular literary variety of cognitive processing does not correspond to any variety observed in actuality, our ability to describe its nature and working could still be greatly enhanced by employing the cognitive-science framework, in the same way that the concepts of physics help us describe the very different worlds or universes of radical science fiction.

As we know, in our wakeful state we are constantly exposed to a flow of external sensory stimuli, with the visual ones taking pride of place. Perception proper starts with the active mind making discriminations among the registered stimuli and recognizing objects or patterns through the use of templates, prototypes, or features stored in the mind. But authors may want to portray the raw sensory experience that precedes all such *perceptual discriminations*—the 'blooming, buzzing confusion' William James spoke of (as quoted in Gibson, Eppler, and Adolph 1999: 632)—i.e., to record 'the myriad atoms as they impinge upon the mind', in the way Joyce sometimes does in his portrayal of Bloom's mind as he wonders around Dublin in *Ulysses* (Joyce 1961). Since our sensory apparatus is multi-channel, a rapid alternation of unprocessed sights, sounds, and smells could be even more effective for this purpose. Or authors might choose situations where the mind fails to cope with the normal data stream and master it due to, say, extreme illness or weakness, as in scenes of near death.

A similar case would be perceptual system shutdown or crash, where the mind is overwhelmed by too many sense impressions all at once, as in scenes where a child or an outsider faces a riot of sights and sounds in a big city, and is unable to process them in terms of selection and coordination. Reduced ability to decode visual stimuli is obviously associated with deficient or failing eyesight, and when a whole narrative is literally focalized through a half-blind observer, the result is a radical undermining of the traditional reliable eyewitness account. A paradigm example is Mario Vargas Llosa's *La guerra del fin del mundo* (Vargas Llosa 1981), where the main events of the war are reported as seen by an extremely near-sighted journalist who loses his glasses shortly after arriving on the scene.

The emergence and waning of our registering and decoding of external stimuli is a daily event, associated with waking up and falling asleep. This is so familiar that we hardly take notice of how radical the transformation really is. But authors often explore this process, Proust being probably the most striking example (Proust 1954). Regaining one's consciousness, hence ability to perceive, after a trauma or anaesthesia is another favorite literary topos, but in this case awareness of self, of world, and of self as defined relative to world are concurrently restored. The opening of John Fowles' short novel *Mantissa* (Fowles 1982) is a case in point. In all these cases of perception lost and regained we notice once again the literary preference for borderlines and radical border crossings.

One form of perception is pattern recognition, finding a figure in the carpet, in Henry James' words (James 1986). But can one always be sure of one's recognition, and will it be shared by everybody looking at the same set of data? Obviously not, as James' eponymous story indicates. And then there is the case of ambiguous or undecidable categorization. Is it X I see before my eyes or is it rather Y? Individual features are indeed discriminated, but not a unique overall Gestalt. A humorous example occurs in Gogol's *Dead Souls* (Gogol 1961), where the main character, Chichikov, first sets his eyes from a distance on the miserly landlord Pliushkin standing in the middle of a field. In a hierarchy of binary choices he needs to decide whether what he sees is a scarecrow or a live person, a man or a woman, young or old.

Perceptual discrimination and recognition require *attention*, that is, *selectivity* in (sensory) information-processing operations—what William James described as '[w]ithdrawal from some things [data] in order to deal effectively with others' (quoted in Duncan 1999: 41). Literature abounds in episodes embodying numerous varieties of attention and attention failure with respect to visual and auditory data, especially the sight and speech of other human beings.

There is first of all wandering or roaming attention, the ability and readiness to focus on some object or occurrence, but with none having been fixed upon as yet. Next is the searchlight beam of attention: purposefully scanning the visual field, anticipating someone, looking for a particular individual or for one fulfilling certain conditions, like the generic young officer in a party looking the women over in search of a beauty. Another aspect of perceptual attention common in narrative is that of rapt attention or attention capture, the character being transfixed by some object or person, it being for him or her a most powerful signal from which he or she is unable to deflect his attention. The first sight of the beloved is of course the classical case. At the other extreme stand cases of deficient attention, of someone skipping too freely and too often distracted to establish or sustain a cognitive fix on any object in his or her field of awareness.

Closely related, and common in humorous narrative, are characters suffering from absent mindedness, better defined as inattentional blindness:
being too preoccupied with internal objects of thought, the characters miss
out on or skip over objects in front of their eyes, with the obvious comic
disaster following suit. Characters may also be distracted, with their goal
control being overcome by novel perceptual input, or because they are di-
viding their attention between two ongoing sets of data, visual or conversational. In the literary portrayal of parties, receptions, dinners, and the like
one encounters the related, so-called cocktail party effect: the character concentrates on his conversation with his interlocutor, perceiving some other
surrounding speech but relegating it to the background, until a word or
name occurring in one of these surrounding conversations catches his attention. Then one of two things happens: he either begins to focus on this
overheard exchange, relegating the speech of his current conversation partner
to the background, or, even more radically, abandons the current exchange
and cuts into the other, hitherto peripheral one. Once again, Proust's Baron
de Charlus readily comes to mind (Proust 1954, II, 633-781). And, finally,
when the mind is exposed to too many attentive tasks at once, its attentive
capability just gives out and the character ends up in a state of total confusion, withdrawal, or panic.

Both science and common sense distinguish between standard and nonstandard modes of perception and resultant *mental images*. Nonstandard
modes, resulting in a disproportionate or distorted visual image, are associated in literature with the defamiliarization effect on the reader, and are realistically motivated by the perception of an infant or small child (compare
the opening of Joyce's *Portrait of the Artist as a Young Man* [Joyce
1969]), or the use of hallucinogenic drugs and alcohol (as in William Burroughs *Naked Lunch* [Burroughs 1992]). A more radical departure can be
found in the early work of Alain Robbe-Grillet, who employs a technique
sometimes referred to as *ecole du regard* (roughly, 'the school of the gaze
or look'). The strangeness of the descriptions of objects one encounters in
La Jalousie (Robbe-Grillet 1957), for example, is caused by this author's
adherence to the retinal image as contrasted with the mental one. Retinal
images are two dimensional, while their cognitive counterparts are of course
three dimensional. With no third dimension admitted, seen objects are inevitably mere collections of lines and surfaces, light and dark patches. And
a mere flat image has no depth and direction associated with it, since both
presuppose placement relative to a perceiver in a three-dimensional space.
This is quite literally a camera-eye view of the world, with the human decoding operations bracketed out.

Cognitive science distinguishes between correct perception, erroneous
perception (where there is an independent object, but it is not the way it is

perceived by this individual on this occasion), and hallucination (an internally generated image without any corresponding external object, mistakenly believed by the subject to be a true representation of an external object). But can one unequivocally decide for each image, individual, and occasion what is the status of the image in focus? Many of E. T. A. Hoffmann's (Hoffman 1964) and Dostoevsky's (Dostoevsky 1960) characters, for example, are wracked by doubts as to which is which and, since these authors often employ extensive focalization through such characters, the reader is made to share this undecided picture of the character's life world. And the same goes for the hesitation between an externally originating image resulting from current perception, a memory image stemming from a past perception, and an internally generated image (dream, creative imagination).

As we have just seen, perception is often tied to other cognitive functions, of which memory and metacognition will provide our final illustrations. Face recognition is apparently a distinctly human (or perhaps human-plus-primate) capability, and an attempt at reidentification of a long-lost person (relative, spouse) performed by an observer comparing a current visual image with a facial image stored in long-term memory is often a climactic scene in a narrative. Sometimes the issue at hand is rather reidentification of a person or object through comparing a visual image in memory with a graphic representation of this person or object as in a photograph or painting. A desperate attempt at such reidentification, coupled with an attempt to obtain additional situational information from the photograph, is the subject of Julio Cortázar's celebrated short story 'Blowup' (Cortázar 1963). Sometimes the process is multi-staged and multi-level. In Proust, for example, a current sensation or perception (smell, taste) helps retrieve first a memory of a similar sensation from the past, which, in its turn, activates an extensive related store of associated visual and propositional information hidden in implicit memory (Proust 1954). The retrieved information then serves as material for an extensive transformation through mental elaboration, leading to the formulation of an intention, namely, the writing down of one's memories. Proust's quest for lost time thus encompasses all four major components of information processing.

As for metacognition in this context, Max Frisch's Gantenbein is a prime example (Frisch 1964). This character decides one day to pretend being a blind man. To succeed, he must create erroneous perceptions in the minds of his co-agents. And to do this, he must employ folk psychology: either put himself in the place of some specific other person and his image of a blind man (mental simulation), or formulate a general belief about the cognitive stereotype of a blind person that people in his environment possess. Either way, Gantenbein is forming a mental representation of a mental representation in the mind of another, or others. Moreover, while acting the blind man, he must constantly monitor his behavior online, making sure it conforms to the blind-man image he is attributing to others. Ruse or deception is indeed a very old plot device, but I think that, here as in many other cases, it is the very modern cognitive framework that helps us greatly in clarifying its mechanisms and modes of generation.

References

Booth, W. 1983. *The Rhetoric of Fiction*. 2nd ed. Chicago: University of Chicago Press.

Baker, L. R. 1999. Folk Psychology. *The MIT Encyclopedia of the Cognitive Sciences*, eds. R. A. Wilson and F. C. Keil, 319-20. Cambridge, MA: MIT Press.

Beckett, S. 1980. *Company*. New York: Grove Press.

Bühler, K. 1982. *Sprachtheorie*. Jena: Gustav Fischer.

Burroughs, W. 1992. *Naked Lunch*. New York: Grove Press.

Cohn, D. 1978. *Transparent Minds*. Princeton, NJ: Princeton UP.

Cortázar, J. 1963. Blow-up. *Blow-Up and Other Stories*, trans. P. Blackburn, 114-31. New York: Pantheon Books.

Dostoevsky, F. 1960. *The Double. Three Short Novels of Dostoevsky*, trans. C. Garnett, 3-176. Garden City: Anchor Books.

Duncan, J. 1999. Attention. *The MIT Encyclopedia of the Cognitive Sciences*, eds. R. A. Wilson and F. C. Keil, 39-41. Cambridge, MA: MIT Press.

Doležel, L. 1998. *Heterocosmica*. Baltimore: Johns Hopkins University Press.

Fowles, J. 1982. *Mantissa*. London: J. Cape.

Frisch, M. 1964. *Mein Name sei Gantenbein*. Frankfurt: Suhrkamp.

Gibson, E. J., M. Eppler, and K. Adolph. 1999. Perceptual Development. *The MIT Encyclopedia of the Cognitive Sciences*, eds. R. A. Wilson and F. C. Keil, 632-35. Cambridge, MA: MIT Press.

Gogol, N. 1961. *Dead Souls,* trans. D. Magarshack. Harmondsworth: Penguin.

Hamburger, K, 1968. *Die Logik der Dichtung*, 2nd ed. Stuttgart: Klett.

Hemingway, E. 1978. The Killers. *Fiction 100*, ed. J. Pickering, 459-63. New York: Macmillan.

Herman, D. 2002. *Story Logic: Problems and Possibilities of Narrative*. Lincoln: University of Nebraska Press.

Hodges, W. 1993. *Model Theory*. Cambridge: Cambridge University Press.

Hoffman, E. T. A. 1966. Der Sandmannn. *Spukgeschichten und Märchen*, 109-39. München: Wilhelm Goldman.

Iser, W. 1974. *The Implied Reader*. Baltimore: Johns Hopkins UP.

Jahn, M., and A. Nünning. 1994. A Survey of Narratological Models. *Literatur in Wissenschaft und Unterricht* 27.4: 283-303.

James, H. 1986. The Figure in the Carpet. *The Figure in the Carpet and other Stories*, ed. Frank Kermode, 357-400. Harmondsworth: Penguin

Joyce, J. 1969. *A Portrait of the Artist as a Young Man*. New York: The Viking Press.

Joyce, J. 1961. *Ulysses*. New York: The Modern Library.

Keenan, E. L. 1999. Qualia. *The MIT Encyclopedia of the Cognitive Sciences*, eds. R. A. Wilson and F. C. Keil, 693-96. Cambridge, MA: MIT Press.

Moses, L. J., and J. A. Baird. 1999. Metacognition. *The MIT Encyclopedia of the Cognitive Sciences*, eds. R. A. Wilson and F. C. Keil, 533-35. Cambridge, MA: MIT Press.

Pavel, T. G. 1986. *Fictional Worlds*. Cambridge, MA: Harvard University Press.

Prince, G. 1980. Introduction to the Study of the Narratee. *Reader-Response Criticism*, ed. J. Tompkins, 7-25. Baltimore: Johns Hopkins UP.

Proust, M. 1954. *A la recherche du temps perdu*. Paris: Gallimard

Robbe-Grillet, A. 1957. *La Jalousie*. Paris: Editions du minuit.

Ryan, M.-L. 1991. *Possible Worlds, Artificial Intelligence and Narrative Theory*. Bloomington: Indiana University Press.

Ryan, M.-L. Forthcoming. Introduction. *Narrative Across Media: The Languages of Storytelling*. Lincoln: University of Nebraska Press.

Semino, E. 1997. *Language and World Creation in Poems and Other Texts*. London and New York: Longman.

Vargas Llosa, M. 1981. *La guerra del fin del mundo*. Barcelona: Seix Barral.

Werth., P. 1999. *Text Worlds*. London and New York: Longman.

12

Constructing Social Space: Sociocognitive Factors in the Interpretation of Character Relations

CATHERINE EMMOTT

1 Introduction

Cognitive researchers have generally tended to place little emphasis on the social relations between characters in narratives. This is perhaps not surprising when we consider the origins of cognitive approaches. Much of the classic work in cognitive science[1] (in areas such as psychology and artificial intelligence) and cognitive linguistics[2] has examined small fragments of artificially constructed materials that often do not contain developed characters and consist of event sequences that are too short for there to be any complex social relations. Although these disciplines have, in the last few years, been moving increasingly towards analysing more natural narratives,[3] such as short stories and novels, much of the work still focuses on solving philosophical and information-processing problems. For narratologists, however, it is crucial to understand how characters relate to each other in temporal-spatial settings. In this chapter, I select a number of cognitive theories and show how they can be used and adapted to explore how 'social space' is constructed in the mind of the reader.

---

[1] For example, Schank and Abelson (1977a/b) and Sanford and Garrod (1981).
[2] For example, Fauconnier (1994).
[3] For example, Sanders (1994), Duchan et al. (1995) and Oakley (1998).

Narrative Theory and the Cognitive Sciences.
David Herman (ed.).
Copyright © 2003, CSLI Publications.

I use the term 'social space' here both as a metaphor for social relations between characters who are within narrative contexts and also for cases where these relations cross spatio-temporal boundaries. My objective in this article is an initial exploration of the concept of social space through narrative examples. The narratives I examine are mainly popular fiction and literary works, although I also apply the same techniques in examining the relations between individuals in a medical biography and a travel autobiography.

I will look at three separate topics in order to study how 'social space' is constructed by readers. In Section 2, I examine how 'cognitive status' models from linguistic work on reference theory (e.g. Gundel et al. 1993; Ariel 1990, 2001) need to take account of stylistically unusual references to characters, since these references can sometimes be interpreted as reflecting social perspectives that are central to the themes of narratives. In Section 3, I use my own 'contextual frame theory' (Emmott 1997) to highlight how story comprehension generally relies on assumptions of co-presence in a physical context and also on inferencing about the social consequences of proximity. I also look at examples where these normal social assumptions about co-presence are overridden. In Section 4, I turn from the main characters in stories to the minor ones. Classic 'schema theory' (e.g. the scripts of Schank and Abelson's 1977a/b) deals with information about minor characters that is so predictable that it can be elided in the text and left for the reader to infer. By contrast, I show how in some narratives we sometimes need to consider minor characters when they are brought from the background into the forefront of our attention as representatives of social institutions or the general public.

In Section 5, I examine some of the main points that come out of the analysis of the examples in Sections 2 to 4. I look at how social relations in a story can be based on metaphors of physical space. Also I discuss how social relations can sometimes be rooted in physical proximity and sometimes stand in ironic juxtaposition to physical space. I also show how social attitudes can be represented as being reflected in and generated from individual encounters in specific settings. Finally, I discuss cases where physical space is sub-divided to reflect social power and exclusion.

Throughout the article I use a mix of different methodologies. In Section 2, I look at how linguistic theories need to take adequate account of stylistic factors. In Section 3, I use 'cognitive discourse analysis' techniques which highlight the balance of textually-presented and cognitively-inferred information that a reader uses to construct narrative contexts. In Section 4, I use a more literary approach and suggest that the forefronting of background information serves the function of highlighting key social themes. In the essay as a whole, my main objective is to show how social relations are linked to physical space, but I also use this topic to show how social and cognitive observations can be combined in narrative analysis.

2 Beyond 'Cognitive Status' Theories: Narrative Perspectives and Social Proximity/Distance

In this section I look at certain linguistic theories that I will refer to as 'cognitive status' theories. The 'cognitive status' of a character is a hypothesis about the degree of prominence that a character has in a reader's mind when a referring expression is used. Generally, such theories focus on textual reasons why a character might be prominent (primarily whether the character has been recently mentioned) and they have not tended to look in any detail at social factors, such as the relationship between the focalized and the focalizer.

The term 'cognitive status' comes specifically from the work of Gundel et al. (1993), but the idea is found elsewhere, most notably in Ariel's 'accessibility theory' (1990, 2001) and in 'centering theory' (e.g. Walker et al. 1998). As a general principle, there is seen to be an inverse relationship between cognitive status and referential form. According to these 'cognitive status' theories, the greater the prominence of an individual in the mind, the less explicit is the linguistic form needed to refer to him/her, and vice versa. In practical terms, this means that in a narrative, we would generally expect a character who is at the forefront of attention to be identified by a pronoun and, conversely, a character who is not currently cognitively prominent, to require a name or some other full noun phrase (e.g. 'the man/woman') to reintroduce him/her.

Such linguistic theories deal with general tendencies in language and the emphasis is on the amount of linguistic information needed to identify a referent rather than on how special uses of a linguistic form can create particular stylistic effects in relation to narrative worlds. In this study, I place more emphasis on stylistic factors, looking first at how such effects can be created in a popular fiction text, then moving on to similar but more subtle effects in literary texts. In Nicci French's popular fiction story *Killing Me Softly*, an unusual use of pronouns has a straightforward interpretation, particularly after the device has been used repeatedly. Towards the start of this novel, Alice Loudon is walking across a pedestrian crossing on her way to work and inadvertently catches the eye of a stranger, stops still, and is overcome by desire for him. Later that day, she has the following encounter:

Example 1

> Just before one I picked up my coat, left a message for my assistant that I would be out for an hour or so, then clattered down the stairs and into the street. It was just beginning to drizzle, and I hadn't got an umbrella. I looked up at the clouds, shrugged, and started to walk quickly along Cardamom Street where I could pick up a taxi to the hairdresser's. I

stopped dead in my tracks and the world blurred. My stomach gave a
lurch. I felt as if I was about to double up.
      <u>He</u> was there, a few feet from me. (French 2000: 19-20)

Normally, we would expect that as a character is introduced into a particular physical space, a full noun phrase is used, since a character who has
been 'off scene' is not normally cognitively prominent. Here, the character's
name is so far unknown, but a phrase like 'the man on the [pedestrian]
crossing' or 'the man I had seen earlier' would give the relevant amount of
information. The use of the pronoun, nevertheless, suggests that the character is so prominent in Alice's thoughts (and hence also the reader's
thoughts) that the normal form of re-introduction is unnecessary. Thus, cognitive status here is a matter not of the usual considerations of linguistic
theory (i.e. recency of mention, episode shifts, etc.) but of social relations in
the narrative world, as mediated through the perceptions of the focalizer.
This is the case even when there is a competing male referent for the pronoun, a factor which would also normally lead to the use of a full linguistic
form:

Example 2

I went to bed early ... When *Jake* climbed in beside me later, I pretended to
be asleep, though I lay awake for hours in the dark. I planned what I would
wear. I thought about how I would hold **him** [Adam], learn his body, trace
his ribs and his vertebrae... (French 2000: 37, my italics)

Here, Jake is Alice's partner, so he might be expected to be central to her
thoughts, but the stranger from the pedestrian crossing (now known to her as
Adam) is so prominent that male pronouns can be assumed to refer to him.
We might expect the male character who is physically present to have predominance, but here Adam fills the focalizer's imagination, so that her plans
and desires partially over-ride physical actuality. The effects shown in Examples 1 and 2 occur repeatedly in the initial chapters of this novel. What is
being presented here is a 'mind-style' (Fowler 1996) that shows a disjunction between the main narrative scene and the character's 'sub-world'
(Werth 1999), the referring expressions mirroring the main concerns of the
focalizer.[4]
      In Tracy Chevalier's *Girl With a Pearl Earring*, the same device is also
used repeatedly throughout the novel and reflects a more subtle and ambiguous relationship between the focalizing female protagonist and the focalized male. This story is set in The Netherlands in the seventeenth century
and provides a fictionalized view of life in the household of the Dutch
painter, Johannes Vermeer. The events are seen from the perspective of the

---

[4] See Emmott (1999) for a discussion of similar examples in a detective story by Ruth Rendell.

subject of his famous painting of a servant girl wearing a pearl earring. In the story, the servant girl has been obliged to enter Vermeer's household at a young age in order to provide for her family after her father suffers a disabling accident. As her master, Vermeer therefore has considerable power over this girl, as he also does over his whole household.

Throughout the story, Vermeer, as seen through the girl's eyes, is rarely named and only occasionally referred to in her thoughts as 'the master'. Repeatedly, pronouns are used when nouns might normally be anticipated by standard linguistic theories. In Example 3 (a), Vermeer is introduced into a particular physical space with pronouns that have the effect of suggesting that he needs no proper introduction. In Example 3 (b), Vermeer is again referred to by pronouns, even though he is not even present in the scene.

Examples 3 (a) and (b)

(a) Catharina was combing through Cornelia's hair when we returned. They paid no attention to me. I helped Tanneke with dinner, turning the meat on the grill, fetching things for the table in the great hall, cutting the bread.

When the meal was ready the girls came in, Maertge joining Tanneke in the cooking kitchen while the others sat down in the great hall. I had just placed the tongue in the meat barrel in one of the storage rooms - Tanneke had left it out and the cat had almost got to it - when **he** appeared from outside, standing in the doorway at the end of the long hall, wearing **his** hat and cloak. I stood still and **he** paused, the light behind **him** so that I could not see **his** face. I did not know if **he** was looking down the hallway at me. After a moment **he** disappeared into the great hall. (Chevalier 1999: 29-30)

(b) It had begun two months before, one afternoon in January not long after Franciscus was born. It was very cold. Franciscus and Johannes [Vermeer's sons] were both poorly, with chesty coughs and trouble breathing. Catharina and the nurse were tending them by the fire in the washing kitchen while the rest of us sat close to the fire in the cooking kitchen.

Only **he** was not there. **He** was upstairs. The cold did not seem to affect **him**. (Chevalier 1999: 99)

There are many similar examples of this unusual use of pronouns throughout the book, so each example can only be interpreted as part of this cumulative effect. There may be different interpretations, depending on whether these linguistic forms are seen as reflecting the general view of Vermeer by his household or a special perspective of the focalizing girl.

At a general level, the lack of naming may serve to reinforce how central Vermeer is to this household. It may also reflect his ability to move easily between physical spaces in a way that is not possible for the women. Even when he is not physically present, as in Example 3 (b), he may still be able to dominate their social space. The lack of a name could also be a taboo about naming an individual who is powerful and respected (Saville-Troike 1989). Throughout the book, the direct speech of the women in Vermeer's household often uses just pronouns to denote him (e.g. 37-9), so this referring style is not specific to the girl's thoughts.

There is also, nevertheless, a possibility that the girl could be preoccupied with Vermeer at a more personal level. In the following example, the girl's future partner, Pieter, is dismissed in a single sentence and the pronouns denoting Vermeer resume without Vermeer's being named.

Example 4

> I looked down, stung by her words. They were a Mother's words, words I would say to my own daughter if I were concerned for her. Although I resented her speaking them, as I resented her questioning the value of **his** painting, I knew they held truth.
> *Pieter* did not spend so long with me in the alley that Sunday.
> The next morning it was painful to look at the painting. The blocks of false colours had been painted, and **he** had built up her eyes, and the high dome of her forehead ... (Chevalier 1999: 146, my italics)

There is sufficient information here to make these pronouns interpretable since Vermeer is the only character likely to be painting. Also, the episode shift[5] ('The next morning') may turn our attention away from Pieter. Nevertheless, the sudden shift of referent without renaming is odd. This hints at Vermeer's centrality in the girl's thoughts, without committing her to anything specific. In the story as a whole, we know that the girl feels some initial physical distaste for Pieter (e.g. 169-70), but she accepts the relationship as an inevitability in view of the social expectations for someone of her class. Conversely, although there are suggestions that she is interested in Vermeer (e.g. 177), any real alliance threatens to destroy her and may therefore be largely unthinkable to someone in her situation.

Generally, in Examples 1 to 4 the referring expressions seem, in certain respects, to bring the relevant male characters 'closer', since they allow them to be prominent irrespective of spatio-temporal boundaries. By contrast, in the following examples a distancing effect is achieved through the use of indefinite referring forms. In William Golding's *Darkness Visible,* Matty is being taunted by the other schoolboys and has been persuaded by them to perform an embarrassing act of a private nature. The other boys move across physical space to a viewing place that allows them to gaze

---

[5] The psychologists Sanford and Garrod (1981) and Anderson et al. (1983) use the term 'episode shift'. Their empirical work suggests that major characters can sometimes still be cognitively 'in focus' after an episode shift because of their overall prominence in a text. However, in this case, Pieter is less prominent than Vermeer in the story as a whole, so the episode shift might facilitate a shift of assumptions here.

from a high angle at what becomes a public spectacle. As the viewpoint becomes distant, the use of the indefinite noun phrase, 'a boy', may be taken to signal that the character is less visually identifiable at a distance, but it also reflects the social alienation he is experiencing.

Example 5

He [Matty] thrust his books into their hands and limped quickly away. They held on to each other, laughing like apes. They broke apart, clamorously collected their fellows. The whole troupe clattered up the stone stairs, up, up, one, two, three storeys to the landing by the great window. They pushed and shoved against the great bar that ran from one end to the other at boy-height, and held the verticals that were less than a boy's width apart. Fifty yards away and fifty feet down **a boy** limped quickly towards the forbidden tree. (Golding 1980: 24)

In its prototypical role, the indefinite article provides a signal that an individual lacks 'identifiability' (Chafe 1980, 1994). Du Bois (1980) uses the term 'late indefinite' for indefinite referring expressions that occur when a character is well-established in a story and so they would be expected to be 'identifiable'. Using a cognitive linguistic framework, Sanders (1994) suggests that these forms can occur when a character is known to the reader but unknown to a focalizing character.[6] Sanders also provides an example in which a focalizing character temporarily fails to recognize a woman even though she is actually well-known to him. This is because he has been asleep and the woman has appeared unexpectedly by his side during the night (98). Hence a familiar character is seen for a moment as a stranger.

A related but subtly different effect can be seen in the following example from Doris Lessing's *The Four-Gated City*:

Example 6

Mark made a visit to **Martha's** room. When he did this it meant something of importance, something he found hard to talk about ...

She had been sitting in the dark, looking out of the window at the ragged sycamore tree, thinned by late autumn. The knock on the door was abrupt, but soft.

'Do you mind if I come in?' he switched on the light, and saw, as he always did, a succession of rooms in this one, back to where young children played in it, he among them.

He took hold of the present, where **a woman in a red housecoat, with untidy hair**, sat by a dark window, looking out...(Lessing 1972: 202-3)

---

[6] See also Sanders and Redeker (1996) for a discussion of this work.

Here, there is no question of either the reader's or Mark's not recognizing Martha. She is central to the novel and this example occurs late in the story (and the text is the last book in a five-volume series about Martha). Mark knows Martha well, since they share a house, and he has gone to her room with the specific intention of finding her there, so there is no real sense in which she is 'unidentifiable'. This distancing effect is also very short-lived since in the paragraph after this example Mark and Martha are described as being 'like an old married couple, or a brother and sister' (203).

This example is only interpretable in the context of a novel that continually questions identity and repeatedly uses late indefinites to present a distancing perspective on familiar characters. In the example above, the entry into a new room may be significant in providing this different perspective. Elsewhere in the novel, passing through a door is viewed as providing multiple alternative possibilities (e.g. 34) and gates symbolize the passage of time (66). Here the doorway allows Mark an awareness of multiple past versions of this room into which Martha intrudes in the present.

The indefinite noun phrase combines the distancing effect of the indefinite article with the use of a common noun such as 'woman' rather than a name. This may also have the effect of providing an emphasis on gender and social role. In the following example, from the same novel, the mention of 'a ... woman' comes straight after Mark has been characterized as 'the man', emphasizing the sense of gender conflict in the previous scene:

Example 7

> Next door Martha sat by **Dorothy** ... **Dorothy** now stacked balls of blue wool in to a raffia basket, made by herself. [Half a page omitted]
>   Martha said, 'Yes,' and **Dorothy** nodded. It was a placid domestic sort of nod. Now the man had gone, all drama had ebbed. **A large, sad soft woman** sat sorting balls of wool, chatting ordinarily... (Lessing 1972: 235-6)

Since the use of indefinite noun phrases is quite subtle, some narratologists might question whether these linguistic expressions actually do play a major role in this novel's interpretation. One argument for viewing this device as significant is that it is used repeatedly throughout the novel and is sometimes coupled with other stylistic features that place particular emphasis on it. So after a sex scene between Martha and Jack, these named characters suddenly become 'A tall thin man—a body. A woman lying on the bed, a body' (74). These two elliptical pseudo-sentences and the repeated appended apposition of 'a body' suggest that this is a deliberate stylistic pattern. Moreover, this novel contains some particularly clear narratorial statements about the significance of names and descriptions in relation to the book's core themes:

Examples 8 (a), (b) and (c)

(a) ... **she was a 'young woman', category 'young woman'**—yes, she must remember that she was, and that along these pavements, a category of being, 'man' prowled beside or behind her. That was what she must be for a few minutes, not Martha or 'Matty', only 'young woman'. (Lessing 1972: 45)

(b) Sometimes she felt like a person who wakes up in a strange city, not knowing who he, she is. There she sat, herself. **Her name was Martha—a convenient label to attach to her sense of herself**... (Lessing 1972: 236)

(c) The word 'tree' was alien to the being on the pavement. Tree, tree, she kept saying, as she said **Martha, Martha, feeling the irrelevance of these syllables, which usurped the reality of the living structure.** (Lessing 1972: 237)

My discussion of the above examples does not view linguistic forms as just being a convenient means of referring to characters who are more or less prominent in the mind, as suggested by the 'cognitive status' theories outlined at the beginning of this section. The pronouns in Examples 1-4, and the indefinite noun phrases in Examples 5-7, shift from the core function of these linguistic forms (signalling accessibility, unidentifiability, etc.) to offering interpretations that would require a broadening of the notion of cognitive status (e.g. to signal characters who are prominent in the thoughts of the focalizer or to indicate distancing). In addition, cognitive status is coupled with an awareness of other functions of linguistic forms, such as their use to signal role or identity.

3 Contextual Frame Theory: Co-Present Characters and Social Proximity

One of the most basic aspects of social relations is the way in which individuals who are present together in a physical context are aware of their social proximity to each other. In comprehending narratives, readers have to construct these co-presence relations and make inferences about the social consequences of proximity. Elsewhere (e.g. Emmott 1994, 1997), I have put forward detailed arguments for a 'contextual frame theory', which points to the fact that the linguistic medium of stories only usually presents fragments of a context in any particular sentence and hence the reader has to 'fill in' the remaining details by means of a cognitive representation termed a 'contextual frame'.[7] The 'contextual frame' stores information about which characters are co-present in which location at which time. Usually a text focuses on particular characters (from the set of co-present characters) in any particular sentence and these I refer to as being 'overt' participants for the duration of that sentence. Those that are assumed to be present but are not mentioned in a particular sentence are 'covert' participants for that sentence. This is a dynamic model, so, as each new sentence is read, characters are sometimes overt and sometimes covert.

The cognitive significance of this is that as we read each sentence we are using our memory and making inferences in order to transform the fragment of contextual information that is explictly mentioned in each sentence (i.e. 'overt') into a fuller construction of a context built from both the current 'overt' information and our current contextual frame knowledge of the 'covert' participants. From a social point of view, we are constantly making assumptions about how the actions of characters affect the other characters who are co-present. These inferences will vary from those that are mundane but essential aspects of context building to those that are of major plot significance or thematic significance. Overall, this model describes a part of the core fabric of reading narratives of all types since it provides a model of how we construct scenes from words. Also, as I will show later in this section, our normal contextual assumptions can help to explain special types of presentation of contextual information for stylistic and rhetorical effect.

The way that contextual frames can account for reading is best illustrated with a simple example. Every action and speech utterance by characters in a context can generally be inferred to have an effect on the co-present participants. Most commonly, we infer acts of witnessing and hearing/overhearing[8] that affect the knowledge states of characters. Here, I present a small part of a text (Tracy Chevalier's *Girl with a Pearl Earring*) to show how much we need to bring to bear from our contextual knowledge (assembled from the earlier text and stored cognitively) as we read each small portion of a text.

Example 9

'And then there were the children. Do **you** know how much bread eleven children eat?' **She** looked up at **me** briefly, then back down at the powderbrush. (Chevalier 1999: 245)

In this extract, both the speaker and addressee ('She' and 'you'/'me') are mentioned (i.e. overt), so there is no need here to draw on our contextual

---

[7] The same type of 'filling in' process also occurs in other media, such as film (Anderson 1996).
[8] See Clark (1992) for a psycholinguistic framework for studying overhearing.

frame knowledge to infer the addressee's presence (although this would often be the case). Nevertheless, we still need to use our contextual knowledge to work out that 'She' and 'you'/'me' are Catharina and Griet (the girl with the pearl earring). Also we need to make the obvious inference that Catharina utters this direct speech and that Griet hears what is said. In addition, we need to be aware of information about co-presence presented at earlier stages in the scene, so that we take account of characters who are 'covert' at this point in the text. In Example 9, a reader of the full text will know that van Leeuwenhoek, Catharina's lawyer, is also present and so presumably also hears what is said. Moreover, Griet, as focalizer, believes that one of Catharina's children, Cornelia, is spying on the scene and hence overhearing (although we only learn this after this particular utterance, and so have to infer this retrospectively).

Obviously, my discussion of Example 9 only accounts for what is happening for this small portion of text, but to explain the amount of cognitive work that has to be done would require the same type of analysis for every sentence. Overall, when we read a scene, we are doing the following cognitive work:

(1) Establishing who is present in the context.
(2) Monitoring the presence of characters during the scene, using contextual frames.
(3) Filling in the 'covert' characters as each sentence is read.
(4) Interpreting 'overt' references made by pronouns.
(5) Adjusting our monitoring to take account of any characters who enter or leave the context during the scene.
(6) Assuming that characters have a social awareness of co-present characters.
(7) Making assumptions that the speech and actions of characters have a social effect on co-present characters (e.g. that they hear and see speech and actions).
(8) Being aware of changes in the temporal and/or spatial location that can cancel the current assumptions of co-presence and can introduce new assumptions.

There are, of course, some exceptions to the normal assumptions described above, for example:

(1) Some characters may be judged not to have full awareness or any awareness of the actions or may be oblivious to the social implications of actions (e.g. someone who is too ill to notice or a child who is too young to understand).
(2) In certain types of text, such as Science Fiction and Fantasy, the normal social assumptions may, of course, be over-ridden. Sometimes, too, assumptions about the continuity of co-presence may be over-ridden (Stockwell 2000 discusses examples of such texts in relation to my contextual frame theory).

In Example 9, I illustrated the assumed listening and overhearing of co-present characters. Sometimes the effect of proximity is that of ironic juxtaposition which can create an emotional response in the reader. This can be seen in the following example from Paul Theroux's travel autobiography, *The Great Railway Bazaar: By Train Through Asia.* In the final sentence, the young man is mentioned (i.e. 'overt') but the old man and the narrator (Theroux) are unmentioned at that point (i.e. 'covert'). The reader will be aware that Theroux (and the old man, if he is capable) witness the young man's champagne drinking. The reader may also perceive the action of champagne drinking to be inappropriate in the presence of the dying father:[9]

Example 10

> The young man bought a bottle of champagne and took it back to his compartment, which was in my sleeping car. He offered me a drink. We sat down; in the berth opposite the old man lay sleeping, the blankets drawn up to his chin. His face was grey, waxen with illness, and strained; he looked as if he were painfully swallowing the toad of death, and certainly the compartment had the dull underground smell of death about it, a clammy tomb here on the train. **The young man clucked, poured himself more champagne, and drank it.** (Theroux 1977: 366)

In general, narrative texts will either keep re-focusing on different aspects of scenes in turn (e.g. as we hear each turn in a conversation) or will focus for longer periods on particular characters. In the following example, from Doris Lessing's 'The Real Thing', this has a 'spotlight effect'. Henry and Angela are temporarily at the centre of attention as they express their enjoyment, to the extent that they almost seem to be 'taking over' the social space of the kitchen.

Example 11

> When the outer door, and then the door into this kitchen slammed open, and Henry and Angela stood there, they were sparkling with the run across from the other house in the half dark of the lanes and paths, and then under the great arch and across this court. It was raining, they exclaimed, no, just a little, great big drops, they said. It was like a showerbath. They stood exclaiming and explaining, taking over the kitchen with their vitality. (Lessing 1993: 207)

The reader knows that Sebastian and Jody are present, although they are 'covert' here, and that their gaze is presumably falling on the 'overt' characters, Henry and Angela. The whole point of the story is that Henry and

---

[9] However, this may depend on the cultural schema of the reader. This is my interpretation of the text as a British reader, since I associate champagne with celebrations. However, when I presented this example at a conference in Hungary (PALA, Budapest, 2001), a number of Eastern European participants pointed out that they would hold the opposite view, presumably regarding champagne as a suitable drink for 'drowning one's sorrows'.

Angela are ex-husband and wife, and that Jody and Sebastian, as Henry and Angela's current partners, feel excluded by their closeness. The 'spotlight effect' makes what might be a private moment between Henry and Angela into a more public occasion, ironically focusing on the togetherness of the two in the context of the gaze of their current partners.

Narrative texts can sometimes break the normal patterns described above. The sentence below comes immediately after Example 10. This sentence is not typical, but has an obvious rhetorical effect. It is unusual for all the key contextual information to be stated in a single sentence, particularly after the context has been set up.

Example 12

> He tried to give me more, but I found the whole affair appalling—the dying man in the narrow berth, his son beside him steadily drinking champagne, and at the window the snowy forests of Central Russia. (Theroux 1977: 366)

By this stage, the information is already known to the reader and the text would normally focus on specific aspects of the scene, such as the individuals in the context and the actions they perform. This example is, therefore, a 'contextual recapitulation'. Here, this has the effect of stressing the narrator's attitude to these juxtaposed elements and explains his refusal to participate in the drinking episode and his subsequent departure from the scene. This confirms the response that we may have already had to the scene and allows the narrator an explicit commentating and evaluating role which is a feature of Theroux's real-life travel narratives.

Another way that texts can break our expectations is for our assumptions of co-presence to be challenged, as shown in the following example from Tracy Chevalier's *Girl with a Pearl Earring*:

Example 13

> At last she waved the powderbrush at Tanneke. 'Stop!' she [Catharina] cried with a laugh. 'We need the nurse and she must sleep near me. There's no space in the girls' room, but there is in yours, so she is there. There's nothing to be done. Why do you bother me about it?'
> 'Perhaps there is one thing that may be done,' **he** said. I glanced up from the cupboard where I was searching for an apron for Lisbeth. **He was standing in the doorway**. (Chevalier 1999: 112)

As a reader of the novel reads the first sentence of this example, he/she would only be aware of the characters so far introduced into the scene, Tanneke, Catharina and Griet. Suddenly, at the start of the second paragraph of the example, Vermeer, who has not been present so far, contributes to the conversation. Even the ubiquitous Vermeer (who, as we have seen in Section 2, is able to enter scenes without being named) is not able to speak when he is not present in a scene. We therefore have to perform a 'cognitive repair' (Emmott 1997: 160-63). As we read that Vermeer is standing in the doorway, we retrospectively add him into the context, making him present as a covert overhearer when Catharina speaks to Tanneke.

Whilst reading about a scene we can also occasionally see a whole context apparently disintegrate, as can be seen in the following example from Flora Rheta Schreiber's *Sybil: The True Story of a Woman Possessed by Sixteen Separate Personalities*. This type of effect might be acceptable within certain types of science fiction, but is rather unusual in what is supposed to be a 'true story'.

Example 14

Sybil Isabel Dorsett hastily flung her chemistry notes into her brown zipper folder and rushed to the door ...
The door closed behind her. She was in the long, dusky hall on the third floor of Columbia University's Havemeyer Hall. Then she was waiting at the elevator, the only person there.
'Too long, too long.' Her thoughts spun round. She had waited too long before leaving the lab. She might have prevented what happened by leaving the very moment that she heard the crash.
Too long. The elevator, too, was taking too long.

Sybil clutched for her zipper folder. **It wasn't there. The elevator wasn't there, either, or the long, dusky hall.** She was standing on a long, narrow street covered with snow. The elevator hadn't come for her, but instead of waiting, she was walking.
A sharp, pungent wind whipped her. Snow, white, crackling, and swirling, was underfoot. (Schreiber 1974: 19)

This example is taken from the first page of the story and we have been given no information to explain the sudden disappearance of objects and of the location. In fact, the normal temporal-spatial rules apply here, but it is the character's perception that is faulty (as we might guess from the title of the book and, perhaps, from the general information about Sybil's medical condition in the preface). As we later find out, Sybil experiences time lapses (sometimes involving moves to new locations), since she has no memory of the periods when she is taken over by one of her other personalities. Hence we see her here switching personalities as she waits for the elevator and then recovering her original personality on the long, narrow street (in fact, five days later in a different city, to which one of her other personalities has travelled). She is unaware of the change of personality and unaware at this stage that she even has multiple personalities. For Sybil, this type of occur-

rence is particularly disorientating and threatens her social relations and
sense of identity. She finds that 'People she had never seen before would
insist that they knew her' (51). In fact, these people are correct and it is she
who has no memory of the original context of meeting since the meeting
was with one of her other personalities. For the reader, this particular example may be puzzling because we are still awaiting an explanation of this odd
spatial shift. However, the context change itself does not seem to be particularly cognitively challenging since we are explicitly told to cancel our
normal assumptions of continued presence and we do so. In some respects,
it perhaps requires less cognitive work to read this passage than to read Example 13. In Example 13, the cognitive repair means that we have to re-
evaluate a stretch of text that we have already read and interpreted (i.e. first
assuming that Vermeer is not present and then assuming that he is present).

Another example which forces us to handle a context in a rather different way than usual is taken from the final chapter of Michael Ondaatje's *The
English Patient*. By this stage in the novel, Kirpal is physically separated
from Hana. He has left her immediately after the bombings of Hiroshima
and Nagasaki. This is because he believes that these political events are an
affront to non-Western races and that they have an impact on private relationships, particularly mixed-race relationships (282-7). He is now married
to another woman, with children, but he still feels as if he can sometimes see
Hana:

Example 15

Now where does he sit as he thinks of her? These years later ... [One page
omitted.]
  He sits in the garden. And he watches Hana, her hair longer, in her own
country. And what does she do? He sees her always, her face and body, but
he doesn't know what her profession is or what her circumstances are, although he sees her reactions to people around her, her bending down to
children, a white fridge door behind her, a background of noiseless tram
cars. This is a limited gift he has somehow been given, as if a camera's
film reveals her, but only her, in silence ... [One and a half pages omitted.]
  And so Hana moves and her face turns and in a regret she lowers her
hair. Her shoulder touches the edge of a cupboard and a glass dislodges.
Kirpal's left hand swoops down and catches the dropped fork an inch from
the floor and gently passes it into the fingers of his daughter, a wrinkle at
the edge of his eyes behind his spectacles. (Ondaatje 1993: 299-302)

In the final paragraph of this example, Kirpal's action almost seems to
be a response to Hana's ('a glass dislodges', 'Kirpal's left hand swoops
down'), although it is clear as we read on that it is in fact a different object
being passed to a different person ('[He] catches the dropped fork', 'passes
it into the fingers of his daughter'). Normally, we would integrate this type

of text into a single contextual frame in which the characters are all co-present and respond socially to each others' actions. Here, our knowledge that Hana and Kirpal are apart and that he is simply imagining her forces us to read 'against the grain' of the text.[10] Nevertheless, the normal method of reading is not irrelevant since it gives the impression of desired proximity even when we know that the characters are not physically close. The effect of this passage and of the text as a whole also comes from Kirpal's name. Hana has always known him as 'Kip', the nickname he has been given in the English army (87). When he leaves her he re-discovers his full name 'Kirpal Singh' (287). Here, the use of the name 'Kirpal' highlights the fact that he and Hana are not really together (for she would have called him 'Kip') and stresses his non-western identity.

4 Bringing Background Characters into the Foreground: Minor Characters as Representatives of Social Institutions and the General Public

So far this discussion has focused mainly on the central characters in stories, looking particularly at the relationship between focalizer and focalized (Section 2) and how key characters are placed together in contexts (Section 3). In this section, I examine cases in which the background characters become prominent in a way that would not normally be predicted from their minor status in the plot, but which can be interpreted as a form of social comment.

Within cognitive science, the most obvious framework for studying background detail is schema theory, which seeks to outline our general knowledge of the world, including stereotypical scenes, termed 'scenarios' (Sanford and Garrod 1981, Anderson et al. 1983), and stereotypical action sequences, termed 'scripts'. Schank and Abelson's classic (1977a/b) work on restaurant scripts is particularly well-known.[11] This assumes that certain aspects of restaurant visits are so predictable that there is sometimes no need explicitly to state information, for it can be inferred from the script.

Schank and Abelson's observations are based on artificially constructed stories, but their work does, nevertheless, have some relevance to real narrative texts, including literary narratives. Doris Lessing's *The Four-Gated City* contains a scene set in a high-class restaurant in London, shortly after the end of the Second World War. In this scene, the restaurant itself becomes a locus for the main character, Martha, to express, in her speech and thoughts, her anger at gender and social class inequalities. Although this

---

[10] See Ireland (2002) for a discussion of similar examples that interleave sentences of different scenes and thereby convey social themes.
[11] See Cook (1994) and Semino (1997) for surveys of schema theory in relation to literary texts.

scene is unusual because, at key points, it makes the background central to the narrative, certain aspects of the presentation conform entirely with classic schema theory. Hence, for example, when the focus of attention is on the main characters and the meal, the source of the food can be elided, as in the sentence, 'Here came the scallop shells filled with lumps of cod covered with a cheese-coloured white sauce' (38). In this passage, readers can infer that the scallop shells are brought by a waiter rather than arriving of their own accord.

Nevertheless, certain details that could be elided in this scene are not only included but highlighted, in a way that would not be seen in the artificial stories often studied in cognitive science but has significance for a social interpretation. At the end of the restaurant scene is the short sentence, 'The bill was for six pounds' (43), set prominently as a paragraph in its own right. In classic schema theory, the bill-paying would be simply a predictable stage before the main characters leave the restaurant, but here it can be assumed to be significant because Martha has earlier pointed out to her dining partner, Henry, that the meal will cost over £5 and that that is more than the working-class people she has been staying with spend on food in a week. The main theme of this episode is, however, the way in which Martha herself feels socially constrained by the restaurant and her reaction to this sense of constraint. The conflict in this scene is between both the major and minor characters, the minor characters appearing to represent the social values mediated through the institution of the restaurant. Martha tries to order, but Henry repeatedly intervenes to force her to change her choice of food or simply to order on her behalf. The waiter does not challenge Martha so directly, but simply ignores her orders or automatically brings the socially accepted choices:

Examples 16 (a) and (b)

(a) [Martha] asked for a dry sherry. The wine waiter brought a bottle of semi-sweet sherry, because in such places **a lady** would be expected to drink sweet sherry. (Lessing 1972: 37)

(b) They had finished their fish. Henry had ordered some blanquette of veal for both of them. It wasn't bad. The wine, however, was very good indeed, marvellous; and Martha was drinking it, although she knew that drinking it might lead to an exchange every word of which she could recite even before it happened ... [2 pages of conversation omitted.]
[Martha said] 'No, no, if you were hypocrites that would be something. A hypocrite is somebody who maintains a virtuous position knowing it to be false. You all seem to me to be—you're drugged, you're hypnotized, you don't seem to be able to see facts when they're in front of you—you're the victim of a lot of slogans.'

Here the wine waiter offered **the lady** a sweet liqueur and Henry brandy. **The lady** insisted on asking for brandy. The wine waiter offered Henry a look of commiseration, so far had complicity grown between them. But Henry frowned at him and told him to bring brandy. Martha and the brandy changed the note or current: Henry was able to let slide away any chance there was of their meeting on at least the possibility of there being something in what she said: Martha, gay buccaneer, adventuress, warmed by wine, enabled him to wave over his partner [from another table to join them]. (Lessing 1972: 38-41)

In Example 16 (b), the definite noun phrases 'the lady' echo the earlier indefinite 'a lady' of Example 16 (a). Nevertheless, the indefinite noun phrase is a generalisation providing the yardstick by which Martha is to be judged, whereas the definite noun phrase specifically describes Martha, placing her in this role. This comes at an opportune moment for Henry, because, even though Martha insists on her order, the incident serves to silence Martha's socio-political outburst. This technique might be argued to show the waiter's point of view, but, since Martha is the major focalizer in the novel, an alternative interpretation is that this is her ironic awareness of the waiter's attitude and the pervading social perspective. She is positioned against the male participants, who are metaphorically grouped together and ranked against her in social space.

Example 17

For a moment the two men [Henry and his friend] sat, united, opposite Martha, eyeing her. It was ugly: behind them, the waiter, and behind him the head waiter: very ugly ... They were savages, masters and servants both. (Lessing 1972: 41)

It could be argued that in this episode the wine waiter steps out of his schema role since one of a waiter's key functions is to take orders. Nevertheless, by the standards of the time he seems to be conforming to the social schema for handling women. This seems to be the general model of behavior for the restaurant staff since in relation to the doorman in the restaurant, Martha feels that 'this man's automatic bad manners ... were the stuff of his life and what he earned his wages for' (34-5). Throughout the episode, references to physical and metaphorical space serve to emphasize that it is Martha who, in this setting, is beyond the normal boundaries, not the waiters. She knows that without Henry's invitation she would never have been admitted to the restaurant and that it is a place where her working-class friends would always be excluded (40). Once admitted, her supposedly inappropriate dress leads to her being placed facing a wall (35), symbolizing an attempt to separate her from the other diners. The discussion during dinner centers on Henry's concern that she does not currently fit into a suitable 'slot' in society (36). Within the restaurant itself, she feels that for Henry's friend (who joins them at the end of the meal) she is 'outside the rules of ordinary politeness ... outside [his] circle of humanity' (41). Indeed when Henry and his friend exchange glances in response to one of Martha's comments, she finds it incredible that they are behaving as if they are invisible to her, another indicator that Martha and all the other characters in the restaurant, major and minor alike, seem to exist in different spheres in terms of their notions of politeness.

This Doris Lessing scene includes the type of character that has been most studied in schema theory, the waiter in the restaurant. Normally, a waiter's role in the script mirrors his professional role, creating specific expectations for readers. Everyday scenes can also, however, include members of the public who are minor background characters, but whose actions are less predictable than those having a professional role. Although insignificant in a plot as individuals, these everyday members of the public can play an important group role, particularly at moments of crisis. Goffman (1971) has shown that events such as a loud argument or an accident can sometimes be regarded as a public spectacle in which it becomes socially acceptable for those around to listen, watch, and report what is witnessed, since private matters have by then already moved into the public sphere. In Sue Townsend's *Rebuilding Coventry*, for example, we see a rumor circulating in private conversations round a specific place, then escalating in response to a public argument in that place, then circulating further within the whole community as gossip.[12] The relevant episode is set in a bar in which the main character, Coventry Dakin, is present with her friends. Some named local men and women are also present, positioned around the bar. During the evening, Gerald Fox privately boasts to Norman Parker that he has been having an affair with Coventry, this being described by the narrator as a *'terrible lie'* (15, Townsend's italics). This lie later erupts publicly, as follows:

Example 18

    Coventry protested, 'But I'm not involved with either of them.'
    Norman shouted, 'Oh yes you are, you lying cow ... *you're Gerald Fox's mistress, and have been for the past year.*'
    They haven't been mentioned earlier, being unimportant until now, but there were other people sitting in the Astaire's bar that night and all of them heard Norman's allegation clearly. Thirty per cent of them had problems and didn't retain the information. However, seventy per cent not only retained it but relished it and told other people. And so it became

---

[12] See Fine (1985) and Hess-Lüttich (2002) for useful summaries of work on gossip in discourse analysis and literary criticism respectively.

widely known on the Grey Paths Council [Housing] Estate that Coventry Dakin and Gerald Fox were lovers and had been brawling in Astaire's and wasn't it awful and her with two children and a respectable husband and him with four lovely little girls and a wife who had a nervous disposition and couldn't watch horror films on the television. (Townsend 1989: 17, Townsend's italics)

Here, the public are suddenly brought into the foreground by the unusual metatextual device of signalling the fact that they have not so far been mentioned. This raises questions about the cognitive processes involved in scene construction. A reader might perhaps have already inferred characters to be present in a bar that is typically busy, even though these characters have not been mentioned until this point. The alternative to this would be to imagine that the bar is empty except for those explicitly mentioned, but then we might expect an explicit comment on the bar's emptiness. In this case, the impression of a crowded bar is achieved by earlier describing the bar in general terms. The mention of 'the clientele' gives the general impression of other drinkers without the text's having actually specified who is present on this occasion:

Example 19

The pub Coventry and her friends were sitting in was called Astaire's. It was a theme pub. The theme being the cinematic persona of Fred Astaire. The brewery's designer had razed the old name, the Black Pig, from the exterior and the sturdy wooden tables and comfortable bench seating from the interior. **Drinkers** were now forced to crouch over pink and chromium coffee-tables. Their large bums lapped over the edges of tiny, pink Dralon stools. The refurbishment was meant to represent a nineteen-thirties Hollywood night-club, but **the clientele** remained stubbornly unsophisticated... (Townsend 1989: 12)

The response of the minor characters in Example 18 adds to the sense of inevitability of the spread of the rumor, since simply being in a public place allows gossip to circulate, regardless of who is actually there. The 'allegation' changes to 'information' that is 'widely known' during the course of Example 18. The final sentence of Example 18 includes what is apparently free indirect speech/discourse (e.g. Leech and Short 1981; Fludernik 1993), although this perhaps includes typical fragments conflated from numerous conversations as the gossip circulates beyond the immediate physical location of the bar. The gossip also spreads to the policemen called to resolve the argument. They are supposed to represent an impartial public institution, but in fact they 'discussed Coventry Dakin in the police car and decided that Gerald Fox was a lucky man' (17). Overall, the effect of this gossip is also reflected in the strategic placing in Example 18 of the paragraph about the 'other people [in the bar]' in such a position that Coventry is silenced, leaving no opportunity for her to counter this lie. Each unnamed individual in the bar is minor, but cumulatively they act together to create a weight of public opinion. These minor characters, who would normally be totally in the background, provide a means by which the lie circles round the social space of the bar, becomes amplified within the bar, then leaks out into the wider community.

5 Physical Space and Types of Social Space

In this section, I review some of the different notions of social space that have been illustrated in the examples in Sections 2 to 4.

5.1 Distance and Closeness in Physical and Social Space

It is not surprising that the term 'social space' is sometimes used to describe social relations, since social relations are often viewed in spatial terms. Most obviously, words like 'distant' and 'close' can have both physical and social meanings. This is explained by cognitive linguistic theories of metaphor, since cognitive linguists suggest that abstract notions are often viewed using metaphors from physical domains (e.g. Lakoff and Johnson 1980).

In certain cases, the texts examined in Sections 2 to 4 show this link between social distance and physical distance. The Tracy Chevalier novel discussed earlier portrays how 'the girl with the pearl earring' feels distanced from Vermeer as he paints her and shows her perceiving this social alienation using a metaphor of physical space.

Example 20

He looked at me as if he were not seeing me, but someone else, or something else ...
It was almost as if I were not there ... I viewed his movements as if I were standing in the street, looking in through the window. (Chevalier 1999: 190-1)

Here, the girl remains static, simply imagining herself to be at a distance. In other cases, actual physical movement can symbolize social distance. In Golding's *Darkness Visible* (Example 5) the schoolboys move away from Matty at the point that he is about to become most alienated, the indefinite article hence reflecting a distant emotional and spatial point of view (Uspensky 1973; Fowler 1996).

Although physical distance can mirror social distance, the strength of social relations can, conversely, over-ride physical distance. In a number of other examples in Section 2 (Examples 1 to 4 and 6, from Chevalier's novel and Lessing's *The Four-Gated City*) the texts over-ride our expectations about how characters entering a physical space would normally be referred to in order to create unusual stylistic effects. Examples 1 to 4 show characters who are either not in the current physical space or are just entering the physical space. They are nevertheless referred to as if they are already in the forefront of our attention, in order to reflect their predominance in the mind of the focalizer. In certain respects, this could be argued to bring the characters 'closer' to their focalizers (in their minds, at least) and to the reader. However, 'closer' would have connotations of intimacy which are not appropriate for these texts, particularly Chevalier's characterisation of Vermeer.[13] Hence, it may be more accurate to describe these as 'mind-styles' in which the focalized males have 'centrality' in the focalizers' perceptions.

This type of effect can work in two directions. Example 1, from Nicci French's *Killing Me Softly*, illustrates a stranger being treated as highly familiar. By contrast, Examples 6 and 7, from Lessing's *The Four-Gated City*, show familiar characters being viewed as strangers. The effect is like suddenly zooming out a camera lens. In Examples 6 and 7 the entry and exit to and from a room provide the points at which this distancing effect occurs, but this may be partly because the theme of gates and doors is significant in Lessing's *The Four-Gated City*.

5.2 Contextual Frames: Arenas for Social Relations

Some of the examples mentioned in sub-section 5.1 show how the effects of social relations can transcend spatial boundaries, in terms of making characters prominent in the minds of focalizers. In Section 3 (Examples 9-15), I used 'contextual frame theory' to highlight certain aspects of social relations that are rooted in physical co-presence, although literary texts can nevertheless manipulate these temporal-spatial boundaries. Generally, we have an awareness of who is around us and we view it as important to know whether we are in public or private. We judge the effect of our words and actions on others (whether as direct participants or on-lookers/overhearers). In some respects, this might be argued to be more basic than our awareness of the weight of public opinion and gender/class divisions (see sub-section 5.3 below). Without an awareness of those around us and the impact of our actions on them we become fundamentally asocial. Also, our ability to keep track of encounters in physical space provides the basis for our feeling of orientation, our assessment of the role of others in our lives and our sense of identity (as shown by the disintegration of these aspects of Sybil's life in Schreiber's account (Example 14)). Contextual frames provide a cognitive

---

[13] There are some moments of intimacy in this story, but overall we see Vermeer's powerful control over the girl. See Bridgeman (2001) for a discussion of the complex, shifting nature of factors such as distance, power, etc. in many literary texts.

store of information (from the previous text and general knowledge) that enable us to construct scenes from the fragmentary contextual information provided by the individual sentences being read at any one moment.

5.3 Social Settings: Sites for Transmitting Social Attitudes and Opinions

The artificial intelligence and psychology research has generally made straightforward divisions between major and minor characters in stories. Sanford and Garrod (1981) and Anderson et al. (1983), for example, have distinguished between major characters and scenario-dependent characters. Scenario-dependent characters, such as waiters, are regarded as being tied to the setting, so that a switch to a new episode is more likely to involve the major characters than the scenario-dependent ones. This is the case here, since characters such as Lessing's waiter (Examples 16 and 17) and Townsend's 'the other people sitting in the Astaire's bar' (Example 18) are specific to that scene. Nevertheless, the distinction between major and minor characters is not always clear-cut in natural narratives, particularly literary texts. There is a sense in which in these scenes the scenario-dependent characters and the settings themselves become extremely prominent.[14] The restaurant becomes a site for observing social divisions. The restaurant staff are a 'social conduit'[15] for general social attitudes to surface in individual encounters. In many respects, Martha's encounter with the restaurant is more important in this scene than her encounter with Henry. In the Townsend example, the minor characters, such as Norman Parker, become the means by which a lie is circulated around the bar and the unidentified 'other people' in the bar are again a 'social conduit', allowing this lie to permeate into the outer community as gossip. The minor characters here are of little significance to the plot as individuals, but as a group they embody public opinion.

5.4 Physical Divisions and Social Divisions

In addition to the main topics in Sections 2 to 4, some of the examples used in this chapter reflect the way in which space can be divided up in order to reflect social power and exclusion.[16] In Tracy Chevalier's *Girl with a Pearl*

---

[14] See also Emmott (2003) for a discussion of how a scenario-dependent character becomes central to the plot in one of Roald Dahl's *Tales of the Unexpected*.

[15] Cognitive linguists (e.g. Lakoff and Johnson 1980) discuss the 'conduit metaphor' (based on Reddy 1979) as a general metaphor for communication (although there are arguments about how appropriate it is). In this section, I am referring specifically to the way in which individuals act as channels for social attitudes to surface in specific situations or, conversely, as channels for rumor and gossip originating in specific conversations to spread to the wider community.

[16] See Lefebvre (1991) for a discussion of this type of social space.

Earring, Vermeer is able to move easily between locations (Examples 3 (a) and 13), reflecting his social power. Also, he has his own working area, the studio, whereas the women generally work together and have little privacy. In Example 13, he is able to intrude across space into conversations, offering a 'solution' to the problem of the cramped sleeping quarters of the women. His solution is to move Griet to the attic[17] above his studio, turning her into a virtual slave since she is locked in there at night and secretly works there for him, unpaid and unacknowledged, in the evenings (113-18).

In Lessing's *The Four-Gated City* (Examples 16 and 17), the restaurant itself serves as a means of excluding Martha's working-class acquaintances (40), but it also provides a social threshold over which Martha seems to wish she had not stepped and, when inside, the waiters place her on the periphery of the social space. In addition, her angle of view groups the male characters (diners and waiters) together, allowing gender divisions to override the class divisions between 'masters and servants' (41).

In a rather different way, social space can also be divided up by 'spotlighting' certain characters by focusing on a subgroup of characters over a stretch of text and leaving the other co-present characters unmentioned. This can create an impression of intimacy between the subgroup and/or distance from the other characters, as in the presentation of Henry and Angela in Lessing's 'The Real Thing' (Example 11).

6 Conclusion

Narratives describe people in social settings, so methods of analysis need to take account of social factors. At the same time, cognitive factors are also important since written narrative is a medium which demands cognitive input from the reader in order to construct the text into a 'text world' (Werth 1999). In this chapter, I have tried to combine these different factors in order to perform a socio-cognitive analysis. When all the topics of Sections 2 to 4 are assessed together, this provides challenges for future cognitive models. Specifically, each of these sections has presented a different notion of prominence.

In Section 2, 'cognitive status' normally suggests local discourse prominence, although I have argued for a broader notion including centrality in the mind of the focalizer. Section 3 distinguishes between the prominence of contextual information which is 'overtly' presented in the current sentence being read and other 'covert' contextual information that the reader is aware of. In the classic scenario/schema theory discussed in Section 4, it is normally the major characters who are prominent, rather than the minor ones.

---

[17] This is a common theme in women's literature, as in Charlotte Brontë's *Jane Eyre* (see Gilbert and Gubar 1979).

The narrative examples in this article show that there are plenty of exceptions to the general theories provided by linguists and cognitive scientists. More fundamentally, they point to the need for a complex overarching model of narrative processing that takes into account the range of different ways in which characters can be cognitively prominent and recognizes the complexity of social situations in narrative texts. Cognitive science can provide new technical tools for narratologists, but, conversely, narratology has a wealth of understanding of complex narrative texts to offer cognitive science.[18]

References

Anderson A., S. Garrod, and A. Sanford. 1983. The Accessibility of Pronominal Antecedents as a Function of Episode Shifts. *Quarterly Journal of Experimental Psychology* 35A: 427-40.

Anderson, J. 1996. *The Reality of Illusion: An Ecological Approach to Cognitive Film Theory*. Carbondale and Edwardsville: Southern Illinois University Press.

Ariel, M. 1990. *Accessing Noun-Phrase Antecedents*. London: Routledge.

Ariel, M. 2001. Accessibility Theory: An Overview. *Text Representation: Linguistic and Psycholinguistic Aspects*, eds. T. Sanders, J. Schilperoord, and W. Spooren, 29-87. Amsterdam: Benjamins.

Bridgeman, T. 2001. Making Worlds Move: Re-ranking Contextual Parameters in Flaubert's *Madame Bovary* and Céline's *Voyage au bout de la Nuit*. *Language and Literature* 10: 41-60.

Chafe, W., ed. 1980. *The Pear Stories: Cognitive, Cultural and Linguistic Aspects of Narrative Production*. Norwood, NJ: Ablex.

Chafe, W. 1994. *Discourse, Consciousness and Time: The Flow and Displacement of Conscious Experience in Speaking and Writing*. Chicago: University of Chicago Press.

Chevalier, T. 1999. *Girl With a Pearl Earring*. London: HarperCollins.

Clark, H. 1992. *Arenas of Language Use*. Chicago: University of Chicago Press and Center for the Study of Language and Information.

Cook, G. 1994. *Discourse and Literature: The Interplay of Form and Mind*. Oxford: Oxford University Press.

Du Bois, J. 1980. The Trace of Identifiability in Discourse, in Chafe 1980: 203-74.

Duchan, J., G. Bruder, and L. Hewitt. 1995. *Deixis in Narrative: A Cognitive Science Perspective*. Hillsdale, N.J.: Lawrence Erlbaum.

Emmott, C. 1994. Frames of Reference: Contextual Monitoring and Narrative Discourse. *Advances in Written Text Analysis*, ed. M. Coulthard, 157-66. London: Routledge.

Emmott, C. 1997. *Narrative Comprehension: A Discourse Perspective*. Oxford: Clarendon Press (Oxford University Press).

Emmott, C. 1999. Embodied in a Constructed World: Narrative Processing, Knowledge Representation, and Indirect Anaphora. *Discourse Studies in Cogni-*

---

[18] I am grateful to the Royal Society of Edinburgh and the Caledonian Research Foundation for providing funding to support this research.

tive Linguistics, eds. K. van Hoek, L. Noordman, and A. Kibrik, 5-27. Amsterdam: Benjamins.

Emmott, C. 2003. Reading for Pleasure: A Cognitive Poetic Analysis of 'Twists in the Tale' and Other Plot Reversals in Narrative Texts. *Cognitive Poetics: A Reader*, eds. G. Steen and J. Gavins, 145-59. London: Routledge.

Fauconnier, G. 1994. *Mental Spaces*. Cambridge: Cambridge University Press.

Fine, G. 1985. Rumors and Gossiping. *Handbook of Discourse Analysis, Volume 3: Discourse and Dialogue*, ed. T. van Dijk, 223-37. London: Academic Press.

Fludernik, M. 1993. *The Fictions of Language and the Languages of Fiction: The Linguistic Representation of Speech and Consciousness*. London: Routledge.

Fowler, R. 1996. *Linguistic Criticism*, 2nd ed. Oxford: Oxford University Press.

French, N. 2000. *Killing Me Softly*. London: Penguin.

Gilbert, S., and S. Gubar. 1979. *The Madwoman in the Attic: The Woman Writer and the Nineteenth-Century Literary Imagination*. New Haven and London: Yale University Press.

Goffman, E. 1971. *Relations in Public: Microstudies of the Public Order*. New York: Harper and Row.

Golding, W. 1980. *Darkness Visible*. London: Faber and Faber.

Gundel, J., N. Hedberg, and R. Zacharski. 1993. Cognitive Status and the Form of Referring Expressions in Discourse. *Language* 69: 274-307.

Hess-Lüttich, E. 2002. 'Evil Tongues': The Rhetoric of Discreet Indiscretion in Fontane's *L'Adultera*. *Language and Literature* 11: 217-30.

Ireland, K. 2002. Temporal Traps: Simultaneous Phase and Narrative Transitions in Conrad. *Language and Literature* 11: 231-42.

Lakoff, G., and M. Johnson. 1980. *Metaphors We Live by*. Chicago and London: University of Chicago Press.

Leech, G., and M. Short. 1981. *Style in Fiction: A Linguistic Introduction to English Fictional Prose*. London: Longman.

Lefebvre, H. 1991. *The Production of Space*, trans. by D. Nicholson-Smith. Oxford: Blackwell.

Lessing, D. 1972. *The Four-Gated City*. London: Grafton.

Lessing, D. 1993. 'The Real Thing', in *London Observed: Stories and Sketches*. London: HarperCollins.

Oakley, T. 1998. Conceptual Blending, Narrative Discourse, and Rhetoric. *Cognitive Linguistics* 9.4: 321-60.

Ondaatje, M. 1993. *The English Patient*. London: Picador.

Reddy, M. 1979. The Conduit Metaphor—A Case of Frame Conflict in Our Language about Language. *Metaphor and Thought*, ed. A. Ortony, 284-324. Cambridge: Cambridge University Press.

Sanders, J. 1994. *Perspective in Narrative Discourse*. Doctoral dissertation, Katholieke Universiteit Brabant, Tilburg.

Sanders, J., and G. Redeker. 1996. Perspective and the Representation of Speech and Thought in Narrative Discourse. *Spaces, Worlds and Grammar*, eds. G. Fauconnier and E. Sweetser, 290-317. Chicago: University of Chicago Press.

Sanford, A., and S. Garrod. 1981. *Understanding Written Language: Explorations in Comprehension Beyond the Sentence*. Chichester: John Wiley and Sons.

Saville-Troike, M. 1989. *The Ethnography of Communication: An Introduction*, 2nd ed. Oxford: Basil Blackwell.

Schank, R., and R. Abelson. 1977a. *Scripts, Plans, Goals and Understanding: An Inquiry into Human Knowledge*. Hillsdale, NJ: Lawrence Erlbaum.

Schank, R., and R. Abelson. 1977b. Scripts, Plans, and Knowledge. *Thinking: Readings in Cognitive Science*, eds. P. Johnson-Laird and P. Wason, 421-32. Cambridge: Cambridge University Press.

Schreiber, F. 1974. *Sybil: The True Story of a Woman Possessed by Sixteen Separate Personalities*. Harmondsworth: Penguin.

Semino, E. 1997. *Language and World Creation in Poems and Other Texts*. London: Longman.

Stockwell, P. 2000. *The Poetics of Science Fiction*. London: Longman.

Theroux, P. 1977. *The Great Railway Bazaar: By Train Through Asia*. London: Penguin.

Townsend, S. 1989. *Rebuilding Coventry*. London: Methuen.

Uspensky, B. 1973. *A Poetics of Composition: The Structure of the Artistic Text and the Typology of a Compositional Form*, trans. V. Zavarin and S. Wittig. Berkeley: University of California Press.

Walker, M., A. Joshi, and E. Prince, eds. 1998. *Centering Theory in Discourse*. Oxford: Clarendon Press.

Werth, P. 1999. *Text Worlds: Representing Conceptual Space in Discourse*. London: Longman.

13

The Mind Beyond the Skin

ALAN PALMER

1 Introduction

What do we mean when we talk about the presentation of consciousness in fiction? It is clear what Dorrit Cohn has in mind when she refers to her 'predilection for novels with thoughtful characters and scenes of self-communion' (1978: v), and her interest in 'moments of lonely self-communion minutely tracing spiritual and emotional conflicts' (1999: 84). And I would guess that her liking for private and heavily introspective thinking is shared by other narrative theorists. However, if we apply to fictional minds some of the various discourses on real minds, then things start to look very different. For example, the philosopher Gilbert Ryle suggests that to

> talk of a person's mind is ... to talk of the person's abilities, liabilities, and inclinations to do and undergo certain sorts of things, and of the doing and undergoing of these things in the ordinary world. (1963: 190)

This is an alternative picture which consists of the social mind in action while engaged in purposive mental functioning in a physical context. Other disciplines share this view of the mind. Within anthropology, Clifford Geertz argues that

> thought is consummately social: social in its origins, social in its functions, social in its forms, social in its applications. At base, think-

Narrative Theory and the Cognitive Sciences.
David Herman (ed.).
Copyright © 2003, CSLI Publications.

ing is a public activity – its natural habitat is the houseyard, the marketplace, and the town square. (1993: 360)

Another anthropologist, Gregory Bateson, discusses the extent of the
individual mind in this way:

> Suppose I am a blind man, and I use a stick. I go tap, tap, tap. Where do
> I start? Is my mental system bounded at the handle of the stick? Is it
> bounded by my skin? Does it start halfway up the stick? Does it start
> at the tip of the stick? But these are nonsense questions. The stick is a
> pathway along which transforms of difference are being transmitted.
> The way to delineate the system is to draw the limiting line in such a
> way that you do not cut any of these pathways in ways which leave
> things inexplicable. (1972: 465)

These views lead the psycholinguist James Wertsch to remark that, 'to bor-
row from theorists such as Gregory Bateson (1972) and Clifford Geertz
(1973), mind is viewed here as something that "extends beyond the skin"'
(1991: 14). Hence my rather strange sounding title.

The dominant discourse within narrative theory on the presentation of
the consciousnesses of fictional characters is what I shall call *the speech
category approach*. I use this term because it is based on the assumption
that the categories that are applied to fictional speech can be unproblemati-
cally applied to fictional thought. The main categories are these:

- *direct thought*. This is the narrative convention that allows the narrator to present a verbal transcription that passes as the reproduction
  of the actual thoughts of a character. For example: 'The train pulled
  away. He thought, "Why the hell am I still waiting for her?"'
- *thought report*. This is the equivalent of indirect speech, in which
  the narrator describes characters' thoughts in the narrative. For example: 'The train pulled away. He wondered why he was still waiting for her.'
- *free indirect thought*. This is, to put it crudely, a combination of
  the other two categories. It combines the subjectivity and language
  of the character, as in direct thought, with the third person and past
  tense of the narrator's discourse. For example: 'The train pulled
  away. Why the hell was he still waiting for her?'

The speech category approach does not give an adequate account of the
form or the function of presentations by narrators to readers of fictional
characters' minds. In summary, the following problems occur. It:

- privileges the apparently mimetic categories of direct thought and
  free indirect thought over the diegetic category of thought report;
- views characters' minds as consisting primarily of a private, passive flow of consciousness, because of its overestimation of the

324 / ALAN PALMER

importance of *inner speech* – the highly verbalized flow of self-
conscious mental events; and
-   neglects the thought report of such states of mind as emotions,
    sensations, dispositions, beliefs, attitudes, intentions, motives, and
    reasons for action.

This chapter suggests that narrative theory has been concerned for too
long primarily with the privacy of consciousness, and that an emphasis on
the social nature of thought might form an informative and suggestive perspective on fictional minds. This argument is pursued in more detail in
Palmer (2002) and (2004). Reduced to the very minimum, a character is
simply a collection of the words which relate to a particular proper name
occurring at intervals within the long series of words that makes up a narrative. The perspective that I am advocating might help provide the beginning
of an answer to questions like these: How precisely do these groups of
words become the recognizable fictional minds that are clearly contained in
a text such as Evelyn Waugh's *Vile Bodies* (which I will discuss in detail
later in the chapter)? This narrative is about the vile minds that are contained within, and expressed through, the vile bodies of the characters, but
how are they constructed by the narrator and reconstructed by the reader of
the text? Obviously these are huge questions that one short chapter cannot
hope to answer. Instead, I will use a discussion of *Vile Bodies* to try to
identify a few of the areas of fictional mental functioning that have hitherto
been neglected within narratology. In doing so, I will work within the possible worlds framework established by Doležel (1998), Pavel (1986), Ryan
(1991), and Margolin (1990). Doležel suggests that, from 'the viewpoint of
the reader, the fictional text can be characterized as a set of instructions according to which the fictional world is to be recovered and reassembled'
(1988: 489). My argument is that we need to look again at the sets of instructions that relate to fictional minds.

What I envisage is a holistic view of the whole of the social mind in action in the novel which avoids the fragmentation of previous approaches
such as those which focus on the speech categories, characterization, actants
and so on. It is a functional and teleological perspective which considers the
purposive nature of characters' thought in terms of their motives, intentions, and resulting behavior and action. This will involve some provisional and tentative typology, but, as Brian McHale remarks,

> we should not underestimate the usefulness of 'mere' typology. Before
> a phenomenon can be explained it must first exist for those who would
> explain it, which means that it must be constituted as a category with
> boundaries and a name. (1981: 185)

This discussion will take us a long way from analyses of lonely, introspective self-communings in terms of the speech categories. But this is just

as well perhaps, as the characters in *Vile Bodies* are not given to intense introspection, and the narrator of the novel makes little use of free indirect thought and even less of direct thought.

2 Cognitive Science and Fictional Minds

Cognitive science is another discourse on real minds that can, like philosophy, anthropology, and psycholinguistics, be applied to the construction of fictional minds. It can help narrative theory to analyze the cues that enable readers to create the effect of characters' mental functioning. Readers use cognitive frames and scripts to interpret texts. In particular, they apply the key frame of the continuing consciousness of narrative agents. In real life we construct narratives for the minds of people we know partially by acknowledging that their minds continue to function when they are not with us. When we see them again after an absence, we have to fill in the gaps in our knowledge of what has happened to them in the meantime if we want to make sense of their current behavior. We can then, as readers, utilize this existing or prestored knowledge of other minds in order to process the emergent knowledge that is supplied by fictional mind presentations. The work that we put into constructing other real minds prepares us, as readers, for the work of constructing fictional minds. The processing strategies that are used by readers to infer characters' inner lives are a central way in which structure is imputed to strings of events. Because fictional beings are necessarily incomplete, frames, scripts, and preference rules are required to supply the defaults that fill the gaps in the discourse and provide the presuppositions that enable the reader to construct minds from the text. The reader strategy of 'joining up the dots' is particularly important in the case of a 'behaviorist' narrative such as *Vile Bodies*, where the reading process has to be very creative in constructing fictional minds from less information than is available in other types of narrative.

An example that is used by Roger Schank and Robert Abelson illustrates the centrality of the continuing consciousness frame. They argue that

> there has been increasing recognition that context is of overwhelming importance in the interpretation of text. Implicit real-world knowledge is very often applied by the understander, and this knowledge can be very highly structured. The appropriate ingredients for extracting the meaning of a sentence, therefore, are often nowhere to be found within the sentence. (1977: 9)

They then illustrate the last point with the following example:

> The policeman held up his hand and stopped the car.

Somehow in understanding this sentence we effortlessly create a driver who steps on a brake in response to seeing the policeman's hand. None of the intermediate links are mentioned in [the] sentence. (1977: 9)

However, it seems to me that we can go further than Schank and Abelson do in revealing the basis of our understanding of the sentence. This basis is that the reader has to use the available information to try to create the consciousnesses of both the policeman and the driver. This inferential process might, perhaps, proceed along the following lines:

the policeman perceived the car

the policeman came to the belief that he should stop the car

the policeman took the decision to stop the car

the policeman then undertook the action of holding up his hand

the driver perceived the policeman holding up his hand

the driver understood the meaning of this sign

the driver came to the belief that he should comply with the sign

the driver took the decision to put on the brakes

the driver then undertook the action of putting on the brakes

Somehow, to use Schank's and Abelson's words, in understanding this sentence, we effortlessly create the supposed mental functioning of the policeman and the driver. Comprehension is simply not possible unless we have available to us hypothetical versions of the minds of the actors that appear to account for the events described. (We may be wrong, of course, but that is another issue.) We do not just create the driver: we create the driver's mind and the policeman's mind. Narrative is, in essence, the description of fictional mental functioning.

Of course, it is not necessary to make these steps explicit in such laborious detail during actual reading conditions. Because the process is usually automatic, Schank and Abelson point out that frames and scripts 'let you leave out the boring details when you are talking or writing, and fill them in when you are listening or reading' (1977: 41). The task of the analyst who wishes to add back in the boring details is to 'break down a sentence into its minimal meaning units' (1977: 16). I will be attempting to break down a number of the sentences in *Vile Bodies* into some of the minimal meaning units that relate to the maintenance of characters' consciousnesses. I will explain this process, which I refer to as decoding action statements into consciousness statements, more fully below.

Schank and Abelson explain that their approach

is oriented towards handling actions by goal-oriented humans. Problems in representing inner affective life ... are issues still to be dealt with as well. We are not ready to handle novels, in other words. (1977: 167-68)

I believe that there are ways of bridging the gap between the two discourses of cognitive science and narrative fiction and that, if not cognitive scientists, then at the very least narratologists using the techniques of cognitive science, *are* ready to handle novels. However, if cognitive science terminology is to be integrated successfully into narrative theory, it will be necessary first to deepen and enlarge our understanding of the central role that fictional minds play in the functioning of narrative. Manfred Jahn (1997) successfully integrates the cognitive science terminology of frames and slots with Franz Stanzel's three narrative situations (1984), but the other frames that can be applied during the reading process should not be forgotten. In this chapter I attempt to expand our notion of fictional minds by exploring two major subframes of the main consciousness frame: the relationship between thought and action, and group or shared thinking.

Both of these subframes utilize fundamental aspects of our real-world knowledge of the mental functioning both of ourselves and of others. These are certainly not the only subframes, but I have chosen them because they show the mind beyond the skin in action. Both contain a number of areas of interest that, although the terminology is now becoming very cumbersome, one might label *sub-subframes*. Within the thought and action subframe I discuss the decoding of action statements, indicative description, causation, and local and teleological motivation. Within the group thinking subframe I discuss norm establishment and maintenance, group conflict, and intramental assent and dissent. These unfamiliar terms are explained below.

As the policeman example showed, the attempt to isolate the basic elements of fictional mind construction is similar to the need to make as explicit as possible every step of an artificial intelligence programme. Computers are completely literal machines that do only what they are explicitly asked to do and do not use their own initiative. This is why AI programmes look so odd to readers who use a good deal of initiative and creativity in joining up the dots without conscious thought. The decoding of action statements into consciousness statements is almost like writing an AI programme on how to read a narrative. When all the immensely sophisticated work that the reader does in constructing mental processes from surface descriptions is made as explicit as possible, the results necessarily appear very strange. To the real reader, the implied reader, and the model reader should now, perhaps, be added 'the robot reader'!

3 Behaviorist Narrative

In his *Dictionary of Narratology*, Gerald Prince defines *behaviorist narrative* as an:

> objective narrative; a narrative characterized by external focalization and thus limited to the conveyance of the characters' behavior (words and actions but not thoughts and feelings), their appearance, and the setting against which they come to the fore ('The Killers'). In this type of narrative, the narrator tells less than one or several characters know and abstains from direct commentary and interpretation. (1987: 10)

It is well known that 'pure' behaviorist narrative is difficult, if not impossible, to find. There are even different views on the extent to which Ernest Hemingway's self-conscious experiments in this mode, such as the short stories 'The Killers' and 'Hills Like White Elephants', are purely behaviorist. This is an argument that I would prefer to avoid. I will simply suggest that behaviorism in narrative is a tendency towards the features described by Prince and that *Vile Bodies* is an illustration of that tendency. The novel is about a group of 'Bright Young People' who attend an endless round of parties in London in 1930. The main character is Adam, whose fiancée, Nina, calls off their engagement because she meets someone else with more money. The novel ends with a shocking change of tone: global war is announced and we last see Adam wandering around a desolate battlefield.

My guess is that most readers of the novel would say that they were struck by how little direct access was given to characters' minds. What little there is tends to consist of a few words of thought report discreetly inserted into accounts of the happenings in the storyworld:

> (1)... he told her that she looked like a fashion drawing without the clothes. Nina was rather pleased about that .... (68)

In fact, this is the only direct access given to Nina's mind, which is significant as she is an important character in the novel. We see a little of Adam's inner life, but very little of the other characters', and this lack of access creates a faintly disturbing impression. The novel has become associated with its famous chapter eleven which, apart from 'Adam rang up Nina' and 'Later Nina rang up Adam', consists in its entirety of forty-three very short episodes of untagged speech.

I am not questioning the general validity of the behaviorist label. Neither, in view of the narrative's distinctive features of pure dialogue, attenuated characterization, and minimal motivation, am I questioning the application of the label to *Vile Bodies*. My point is merely that behaviorist narratives contain a good deal more information about fictional minds than has generally been appreciated. Specifically, I hope to show that this particular discourse is saturated with meanings that are closely related to the inner lives of characters. A character's name is a space or a vacuum into which readers feel compelled to pour meaning: characteristics, dispositions, states of mind, causations. Readers take even the most apparently uninformative references to characters as cues to construct attributes. However, much of this process can only be theorized by defamiliarizing, labeling, and so making visible some of the hitherto neglected devices that enable readers to understand how fictional minds function within the context of their story-worlds.

4 The Speech Categories

4.1 Inner Speech, Direct Thought, and Free Indirect Thought

I will say a little about inner speech and the speech categories at this point before discussing the two subframes. There is very little evidence in *Vile Bodies* of the presence in characters' minds of inner speech. One reason for this is that the use of direct thought necessarily entails inner speech and there is very little direct thought in the novel. What little there is consists of just a few, rather inconsequential and uninformative words such as these: "'More trouble for Simon'", thought Adam' (76); "'Has he given all to his daughters?'" thought Adam' (118); and '("What, indeed?" thought Adam)' (165). Of course, the other two modes of thought report and free indirect thought can also be used to represent inner speech. In the case of the relatively small number of episodes of free indirect thought, some appear to represent inner speech and some do not. Some theorists such as Gérard Genette (see 1980: 171) appear to regard thought report primarily as *narrativized* inner speech, and it is true that this is one, though only one, of its many functions. Nevertheless, I quote a large number of episodes of thought report below and almost all of them appear to me to describe states of mind such as desires, emotions, dispositions, beliefs, and attitudes rather than inner speech.

The following discussion of free indirect thought anticipates some of my main argument, but it is placed here because of the intense interest in this particular speech category. There are two aspects to the use of free indirect thought in *Vile Bodies* that are concerned with the mind beyond the skin. Firstly, the following grammatical form occurs on no less than nine occasions:

(2) (a) It was awful when Mrs. Ape was like this. (8)

(b) It was so difficult. (40)

330 / ALAN PALMER

(c) It had been an awkward moment. (85)

(d) It would be awkward ... (113)

(e) It seemed odd ... (119)

(f) It was all like one of those cabinet meetings ... (87)

(g) It was clearly going to be a bad crossing. (7)

(h) It seemed odd that a man so bulky could be so elusive. (98)

(i) It was clearly suitable that he should marry before he was thirty. (108)

Although it is not apparent from this heavily truncated presentation, these sentences, with the exception of (g), occur in the context of some form of social awkwardness. The character has internalized the social norms that he or she perceives to be appropriate to the occasion and is embarrassed by the danger that they might be transgressed. The intimate link between social norm and individual consciousness is particularly well-illustrated by example (2) (i), a sentence of free indirect thought that occurs in a passage of thought report of Edward Throbbing's mind. It takes place two paragraphs after this description of the social context in which the character is thinking:

(3) It was generally understood that now Edward Throbbing was back these two would become engaged to be married. (108)

The statement of reinforcement of the social norm of marriage in (3) is unmistakably echoed in the free indirect thought in (2) (i). It is clear that the norms of the social consensus have been very efficiently internalized, and that Throbbing's mental functioning has been severely constrained by the public context within which it occurs.

Secondly, the text contains some examples of joint, group, or shared free indirect thought. I will start with some marginal cases and go onto some more definite examples. In (4), the second sentence could be a comment by the narrator:

(4) A profusion of men in plus-fours were having 'quick-ones' before the start. There was no nonsense about not smoking. (141)

It could, however, also be a free indirect rendering of the collective consciousnesses of the users of the bar. In the next example, a long list of various features of the physical context, clearly focalized through a group of people, is followed by this statement:

(5) There was nothing for it but to go back to the bar. (148)

Again, it is possible to interpret this statement as a narratorial judgment on the situation, but equally possible to regard it as the collective decision of the group, expressed in free indirect thought. The following three examples are made less ambiguous by the use of expressive devices:

(6) (No one had warned them that there was a motor race on; their hotel bill *was* a shock.) (133)

(7) ... and at last they all went to bed, very tired, but fairly contented, and oh, how they were bitten by bugs all that night. (132)

(8) The angels crowded together disconsolately. It was awful when Mrs Ape was like this. My, how they would pinch Chastity ... (8)

The expressive emphasis on the italicized '*was*' allows (6) to be plausibly interpreted as free indirect thought rather than thought report. The same goes for 'oh how ...' in (7) which is, perhaps, indeterminate between thought and speech. In (8), the collective action (crowding) and the collective feeling or sensation (being disconsolate) is followed firstly by a free indirect presentation of their awareness of the reason (Mrs. Ape's behavior) for the action and the accompanying state of mind (see (2) (a) above), and secondly by a free indirect presentation of their intention to act in response to the above by pinching Chastity.

The final example is particularly interesting for the skilful way in which the narrator alternates within a single sentence between collective thought report in (a) and (c), collective free indirect speech in (b), and collective free indirect thought in (d):

(9) (a) Their flashes and bangs had rather a disquieting effect on the party, causing a feeling of tension, because everybody looked negligent (b) and said what a bore the papers were, and how *too* like Archie to let the photographers come, (c) but most of them, as a matter of fact, wanted dreadfully to be photographed and the others were frozen with unaffected terror that they might be taken unawares (d) and then their mamas would know where they had been when they said they were at the Bicesters' dance, and then there would be a row again, which was so *exhausting*, if nothing else. (45)

4.2 Contextual Thought Report

Almost all of the direct access with which I am concerned for the rest of this chapter consists of *contextual thought report*. I am using this term for the short, unobtrusive sentences, phrases, or even single words which describe an aspect of a character's mind and which are often combined with descriptions of action or context. This device often refers to intentions to act or motives for action and is, therefore, purposive and explanatory in nature. In discussing a story from *The Decameron*, Wayne C. Booth describes it as 'frequent – though by modern standards certainly shallow – inside views' of characters' thoughts (1983: 12).

Most of the examples discussed below illustrate the complexity of the relationships between contextual thought report, action, and context. The three are often inextricably linked and so it can be a very artificial operation to lift contextual thought report out of the sentence that contains it. This inseparability is an illustration of the centrality of consciousness to narrative which Monika Fludernik (1996) stresses so persuasively. Specifically, many of the following examples contain a reference to the social and physical context within which the mental functioning takes place, although a number have been cut for reasons of space. The following sentence uses twenty two words to describe, not just mental states, but also several facts about the physical environment: how the members of the group are positioned, the fact that they have a book in front of them, and the movement of Mrs. Ape:

> (10) Their heads were close together and they were so deeply engrossed in the story that they did not hear Mrs. Ape's entry. (80)

Sometimes the reference to the context accompanies the action or consciousness description:

> (11) Adam sat in the back of the car with Miles, who was clearly put out about his friend's lack of cordiality. (138)

At other times, the context is contained within the description:

> (12) They went down the hill feeling buoyant and detached... (145)

Contextual thought report plays an important role in the process of characterization. This may sound a little odd, as the use of the term *characterization* implies the presence of long and ponderous passages in Victorian novels which appear to tell the reader everything there is to know about a character. But one should not lose sight of the characterization illustrated in (13), which occurs when Adam tells Lottie, his landlady, that he now has money:

> (13) 'Have you now' said Lottie indifferently. She lived on the assumption that everyone she knew always had several thousand pounds. (64)

In only fourteen words, the reader has learnt a good deal about Lottie.

5 Thought and Action

5.1 The Decoding of Action

The first subframe that I wish to discuss is the relationship between thought and action. The following comments attempt to build on the stimulating work done by van Dijk (1976), Margolin (1986), and Doležel (1998, chapters two and four) on the philosophy of action and narrative. Constructions of fictional minds are inextricably bound up with presentations of action. Direct access to inner speech and states of mind is only a small part of the process of building up the sense of a mind in action. This centrality of consciousness to narrative can be demonstrated by asking readers to retell the plot of a novel. My guess is that most would not be content to respond by saying: X did A; Y did B; Z did C. They would be more likely to describe characters' actions in terms of mental functioning such as: X decided to do A, Y wanted to do B, Z regretted doing C. Deciding, wanting, and regretting are the mental events and states that provide the causal network behind the physical events, and they are just as much a part of the storyworld as the physical environment, events, and happenings. *Vile Bodies* contains very few action descriptions that simply describe only the surface of physical behavior. The mental event that necessarily accompanies an action is often made part of the action description or is added in an adverb, rather than left implicit. Take this simple statement:

(14) The three statesmen hid themselves. (86)

This is a description of an action, but it goes further in identifying the accompanying mental processes than a statement such as: 'They stood behind the curtain', which leaves more work for the reader to do in deciding why they are standing there. (14) can be decoded in consciousness terms as follows: the three agreed that it was in their interest to conceal themselves from someone, realized that it was possible for them to do so, and decided together to take the action of hiding. In this way, the reader, as part of the process of understanding narratives, has to translate passages of action description into mind description in the manner of a 'psychological' novel. It is significant that philosophers often discuss action in terms of how onlookers to an action would reasonably interpret it (for example, O' Shaughnessy 1997: 56). This perspective is very similar to the role of the reader in considering the motives behind, and the reasons for, a character's actions.

When we explain an action by giving the reason for it, we often redescribe the action by placing it in its context. The descriptions of the physical context and the causal network behind the fictional behavior are sometimes identical:

(15) People had crowded into the Underground station for shelter from the rain ... (29)

In just twelve words, the narrator describes the action, the physical context in detail (the rain, the station, and the crowd), and the fact that this context is the reason for the action of sheltering. However, many narrative statements require a good deal more decoding than (14) and (15). For example, some convey information about more than one consciousness:

(16) Here an atmosphere of greater geniality prevailed. (141)

Decoded, this might mean that the consciousnesses of the individuals in the group are open and welcoming, and are enjoying the atmosphere. To go further, it might also mean that the consciousness of anyone coming in would feel welcome and at home.

Many narratorial statements such as (16) above and (17) below might seem a long way from a study of the presentation of consciousness:

(17) You see, that was the kind of party Archie Schwert's party was. (43)

But, as with (16), when (17) is decoded, we find that that it is precisely about consciousness. It is saying that, within the storyworld of the narrative, this is what the fictional minds of the group of characters that comprised the party thought, felt, perceived, experienced when they were present in the social and physical context of the party. Mental functioning is always present, however oblique the explicit reference to it.

The distinction between action and nonaction is frequently not clear, illustrating the point that it is the mental process, not the physical movement, that is the significant issue:

(18) This time no-one troubled to pick them up. (15)

The absence of action, such as not picking something up, can be as much of an action as a physical movement, particularly when the nature of the intention is specified, as in this case. When nonaction is deliberate, it is an action.

(19) They were very late for the film Nina wanted to see, and that set them back again. They didn't speak for a long time. (76)

Not speaking is a nonaction that amounts, in a context such as this, to a very significant action.

5.2 The Thought-Action Continuum

Talk of decoding action statements into consciousness statements can, however, be misleading if it gives the impression that, notwithstanding the intimate and complex connections between the two, thought and action are easily separable. They are not, and many of the statements in fictional narratives inhabit the large gray area between the two. I shall refer to this phenomenon as the *thought-action continuum*, and it is one of the key senses in which the mind extends beyond the skin. It is a serious drawback of the speech category account that it assumes that the separation of thought and action is unproblematical. In the *Philosophical Investigations*, Wittgenstein considers the statement, 'I noticed that he was out of humour', and asks: 'Is this a report about his behaviour or his state of mind?' (1958: 179). I will refer to this as *Wittgenstein's question* and it is one that can usefully be asked of many statements in novels.

Consider the following passage:

> (20) Adam undressed very quickly and got into bed; Nina more slowly arranging her clothes on the chair and fingering the ornaments on the chimney piece with less than her usual self-possession. At last she put out the light. (68)

This passage, with the exception of the phrase 'with less than her usual self-possession', consists of what might be called *significant action*: the reader is provided with enough contextual information to appreciate the significance of Adam acting very quickly and Nina acting more slowly. The reader can speculate with assurance about what mental events accompany these two actions because he or she knows that they are about to go to bed together for the first time: Adam is eager and Nina is nervous. However, the phrase 'with less than her usual self-possession' is in the gray area between thought and action. Wittgenstein's question is appropriate because the words appear to be a description both of Nina's behavior and of her state of mind.

I will illustrate the thought-action continuum with a study of the speech tag adverbs in *Vile Bodies*. In his *Dictionary of Narratology*, Gerard Prince defines words such as these as 'attributive discourse': 'The discourse accompanying a character's (direct) discourse and specifying the act of the speaker or thinker … and (sometimes) indicating various dimensions or features of the act, the character, the setting in which they appear etc' (1987: 7). The purpose of this discussion is to apply a cognitive perspective to the question: What precisely is being attributed? The adverbs listed below are descriptions of actions in the sense that they describe the manner in which speech acts are performed, but they can also be regarded as contextual thought report as they provide important information about the functioning of characters' minds. The descriptions can be placed at various points along the thought-action continuum (and readers may well disagree with the placings suggested below). In some cases, at the thought end of the spectrum, a state of mind is directly and obviously indicated. Subject to the context showing that the indication is ironic and therefore misleading, these cases are obviously straightforward:

Triumph: 'said Lottie triumphantly' (34)

Desperation: 'said Jane's father desperately' (49), 'he shouted desperately' (139)

Anger or annoyance: 'said the stranger crossly' (86), 'said the Colonel crossly' (179), 'said the Colonel crossly' (126), 'said the Prime Minister sharply' (112)

Bitterness: 'said Father Rothschild bitterly' (87)

Anxiety: 'asked the barmaid anxiously' (142)

Thoughtfulness: 'repeated Mr Benfleet thoughtfully' (27)

Gentleness: 'said Father Rothschild gently' (111), 'said Adam gently' (164)

In other cases, perhaps in the middle of the spectrum, one might say that a state of mind is indirectly indicated:

Wish to give encouragement: 'said Adam encouragingly' (72)

Absentmindedness: 'said the Colonel dreamily' (184), 'said Mr Henderson mechanically' (16)

Various negative feelings: 'said Miss Runcible severely' (146), 'said the drunk Major distantly' (151), 'he said rather stiffly' (163), 'repeated Miss Runcible firmly' (146)

Lack of concern: 'said Mr. Isaacs airily' (123)

However, at the action end of the spectrum, there are some very interesting examples in which the adverb appears to relate primarily to the manner of speaking:

'said the General hospitably' (188)

'said Miss Runcible, rather faintly' (131)

'said the Matron archly' (156)

'he hinted darkly' (20)

'she asked plaintively' (79)

'said Adam in no particular manner' (27)

These examples appear to contain a larger element of narratorial judgment, and seem to require more work from the reader, than the others. In particular, although the real-world knowledge that we bring to texts tells us generally what the examples mean as action descriptions (we *kind-of* know what an 'arch' tone of voice sounds like), their significance in terms of the character's consciousness can be very unclear when taken out of context. As a consequence, the accompanying state of mind is not obvious and has to be inferred from the surrounding narrative.

5.3 Indicative Description

I will refer to statements that are in the middle of the thought-action continuum as *indicative description*. They can be identified when the answer to Wittgenstein's question is unclear. Take this example:

(21) Unsteadily, but with renewed hope, the passengers had disembarked. (19)

In the case of 'with renewed hope' and 'had disembarked', the answer to Wittgenstein's question is clear: the former is contextual thought report that refers to a state of mind and the latter is behavior. But what about 'unsteadily'? I would suggest that the answer to the question is not obvious. On the one hand, it is a description of the manner in which the action of disembarking is performed; on the other hand, it appears to indicate that the action is accompanied by a sensation or feeling of unsteadiness. It is indicative description because it indicates a particular state of mind.

One important characteristic of indicative description is that it can be misleading: it only indicates, and does not absolutely guarantee, an accompanying state of mind.

(22) ... then rose ... the despairing voices of Mrs. Ape's angels, in frequently broken unison, singing, singing, wildly, desperately, as though their hearts would break in the effort and their minds lose their reason ... (12-13)

The description of the action of unison singing is followed by indicative description: the two adverbs 'wildly' and 'desperately' describe a quality in the sound but also appear to indicate the accompanying state of mind of wild desperation. However, it is by no means certain that this state of mind does exist within the reality of the fictional storyworld. The uncertainty is reinforced by the explicitly modal nature ('as though') of the next indicative description. It seems too far-fetched to suppose that the angels really are suffering broken hearts and lost reason. It is perhaps best understood as a comment by the narrator on the general mood of the angels, which has a validity beyond their mental state at that particular time.

The ironic possibilities of misleading indicative description are extensive:

(23) ... the Café Royal was crowded and overflowing. Everyone was being thoroughly cross, but only the most sarcastic and overbearing were given tables, and only the gross and outrageous were given food. (150)

Starting with the physical context, four groups are described: 'everyone'; the 'sarcastic and overbearing'; the 'gross and outrageous'; and the staff who are putting up with this behavior. This last group is understood, like the car driver in the Schank and Abelson example. 'Cross' is usually used to refer to a state of mind, but everyone 'being' cross sounds more like a description of behavior with an element of calculation about it. This suspicion is confirmed by the rest of the sentence, where the mental states present in those getting tables and then food are not necessarily the ones indicated. Their states of mind are probably related more to a cold-blooded decision to use this sort of behavior to get what they want. This difference results in misleading indicative description.

5.4 Causation

One of the most important functions of contextual thought report is to present explanations for behavior, reasons for action, the causal networks that are present behind apparently simple action descriptions. Explicit motivations are provided by what I shall call *cue-reason* words such as 'for', 'caused', 'so', and 'to'.

In (15), the word 'for' cues the reader to read the following clause as an explicit and sufficient reason for the action. Other examples include:

> (24) It was this last movement that caused the most havoc among the passengers. (11)

> (25) So they all had another drink. (36)

> (26) Then they went away to interview some more drivers. (133)

Implied or indirect motivation is even more interesting. In (27), everyone is relieved that a punishingly boring film has finished:

> (27) When the reel came to an end everyone stirred luxuriously. (178)

The use of 'when', instead of the cue-reason word 'because', leaves the motivation for the action teasingly implicit.

Next, consider (28):

> (28) There was a hush all over the course, and the refreshment tent began to empty quickly. (141)

The first part of the sentence can be decoded as a deliberate nonaction which is caused by the race being about to start. The next action is also caused by the same reason, but it is very different because here there is a clear intention. The cue-reason phrase 'to see the race' is understood. In (29), the use of the word 'clustered' and the narratorial comment of 'predatory', together with the circumstantial evidence of the autograph albums and the pens all imply that this is not a random group and that they are gathered together for a common purpose.

> (29) Outside this ring clustered a group of predatory little boys with autograph albums and leaking fountain pens ... (135)

However, the information regarding the purpose is given by implication. It is not spelt out that the boys are waiting to collect autographs. But, because the purpose is so clear to the reader, it is easy to overlook the fact that it is merely implied and never explicitly stated.

The causal networks surrounding actions can be subject to regressive questioning. For example, in the case of (15), one can ask: 'yes, but why did they shelter?' 'Because they did not want to get wet' 'Why not?' 'Because it is uncomfortable' and so on. These motivations tend to get larger and larger but the chain is not infinite because it tends to end in a fairly unanswerable motive such as 'I want to be happy'. Even when the motivation for an action appears to be explicitly provided, the reader often still has to fill in the implicit chains in the reasoning. The characters in this novel are vague, sketchy, and attenuated because the cues for the reader tend to be short-term, specific, and localized. When, for example, a character is described as saying something 'thoughtfully', this does not necessarily imply that the reader should read that person as a thoughtful character: the word may be significant only for the effects to be obtained in that particular scene. There is a good deal of what might be called *local* motivation of this sort: explanations and reasons for actions that are specific to the particular context. There is almost none of the extended or teleological motivation that readers require in order to build up a full, detailed, and coherent sense of character. This absence means that there is more for the reader to do. It is not possible to be too dogmatic about this issue, as one reader may find contextual clues to be localized while another may be more resourceful in using them to build up a coherent account of a character. Having said that, the following sentence is clearly an unusual example of teleological or extended motivation as opposed to local motivation:

(30) It hurt Adam deeply to think much about Nina. (156)

This simple statement derives much of its power and impact from the fact that there is no other description of such deep feeling in the novel.

Strong, vivid characterization and clear teleological shape rely on big and important motivations such as love or money that can propel a whole narrative. Weak, hazy characterization tends to be associated, it seems, with local and specific motivation. It is an important characteristic of *Vile Bodies* that these larger motivations are almost never made explicit. This gives the narrative its highly distinctive quality of aimless and restless desperation.

6 Intermental Thought

6.1 Communicative Action

The second subframe that I now wish to consider more systematically is shared or group thinking. I say 'more systematically' because I have already implicitly discussed this device in some detail. A large number of the examples of thought and action given above ((3) to (10), (12), (14) to (19), and (21) to (29)) were examples of what psycholinguists refer to as *intermental* or joint, group, or shared thinking as opposed to *intramental*, or individual thinking. This type of thought is also known as *intersubjectivity*. (See Trevarthen 1999: 415, and also Margolin 1996 and 2000, on 'we' narratives.) James Wertsch explains that 'the notion of mental function can properly be applied to social as well as individual forms of activity' (1991: 27), and that 'the terms *mind* and *mental action* can appropriately be predicated of dyads [that is, pairs] and larger groups as well as of individuals' (1991: 14). A Bakhtinian emphasis on the shared, social, and dialogic nature of mental functioning is, after all, clearly suitable to a novel which is explicitly concerned with:

> (31) all that succession and repetition of massed humanity ... Those vile bodies ... (104)

For the reasons given in Section 5.2, I am not going to make a hard and fast distinction between intermental thinking and *communicative action*, which Jürgen Habermas defines as:

> the interaction of at least two subjects ... who establish interpersonal relations .... The actors seek to reach an understanding about the action situation and their plans of action in order to coordinate their actions by way of agreement. (1984: 86)

Communicative action clearly requires intermental functioning. However, although core or paradigmatic intermental thinking is joint or cooperative decision making, I have widened my use of the term to include joint states of mind and other interesting marginal cases such as what might be called *conflicted* or *competitive* actions.

(32) reflects paradigmatic functional intermental thinking:

> (32) When they reached the pits they decided they were hungry. It seemed too far to climb up to the dining tent, so they ate as much of the mechanic's lunch as Miss Runcible's cigarette had spared. (145-46)

This passage involves an initial shared decision, a joint perception (of distance), a shared judgment (regarding the distance), and, finally, a group decision to act. The cue-reason word 'so' makes explicit the communal motivation for the communicative action. Likewise, contained within the description, in (33), of a joint action of desertion is the joint decision to take that action:

> (33) Outside his door, two very limp detective sergeants had deserted their posts. (12)

'Deserted' makes the mental processes much clearer than a simple description of mere physical movement. The shared feelings or emotions (for example, sensations of tiredness and feelings of resentment) that presumably caused the decision to leave are not made explicit but can be inferred from the context. In (34), meanwhile, the adverbs used in the description emphasize that this is very conscious communicative action and that the individuals are clearly aware that it is a joint enterprise:

(34) Then they all pinched her all over, but precisely and judiciously, so as not to disturb her wings or halo ... (79)

The following passages move away from core functional intermental decision making in various ways. For example, some intermental thinking is counterfactual:

(35) The gatecrashers wondered whether it would not have been better to have stayed at home. (85)

(36) The race was not due to start until noon, but any indecision which they may have felt about the employment of the next few hours was settled for them by the local police... (136)

(36) describes a counterfactual intermental state of mind. The group might have experienced, but did not in fact experience, the state of mind of indecision. The reason why the indecision did not occur is then given.

Here are illustrations of conflicted communicative action:

(37) He and Nina were lunching at Espinoza's and quarrelling half-heartedly ... (91)

and competitive communicative action:

(38) The others were jostling one another with their luggage, trying to attract the Customs officers and longing for a cup of tea. (19)

The actions described in these passages clearly differ from the cooperative actions described in (32) to (34). In (38), the joint mental event of the attempt to attract attention makes it clear that the passengers have all taken the decision deliberately to jostle one another in order to gain an advantage. Competitive action is intermental in the sense that the individuals are united in recognizing the need to engage in this action.

Descriptions of shared perceptions and states of mind such as emotions, feelings, and sensations are very common:

(39) It was not a really good evening. The long drive ...chilled and depressed them, dissipating the gaiety which had flickered rather spasmodically over Ginger's dinner. (103)

This is a description of the thoughts and feelings of a group in very abstract terms. The word 'evening' in the first sentence functions as a metonymy for 'the group of people spending the evening together'. The passage describes shared emotions and feelings such as the sensation of being chilled, the state of mind of being depressed and the previous state of mind of gaiety. Although this sort of thinking is different from functional decision making, it is the product of a shared group dynamic. The individuals are experiencing the same states of mind because of the common situation in which they find themselves. See also (12), (16), (17) and (46).

Not all groups are intermental. It may be that individuals simply happen to share beliefs or feelings which have not been worked out together or caused by the same group dynamic. In (40) it is not clear whether there is intermental agreement between Chastity and Divine Discontent or whether they intramentally happen to think the same thing:

(40) At intervals letters arrived from Buenos Aires in which Chastity and Divine Discontent spoke rather critically of Latin American entertainment. (92)

(41) (Many doctors, thus diverted, spent an enjoyable day without apparent prejudice to their patients.) (137)

(41) refers to two groups, but as discrete individuals and not as intermental groups. Although the reason for the doctors' and patients' states of mind happens to be the same, they are not cooperatively shared.

6.2 Relationship with Intramental Thinking

In a sense, intermental thinking is simply the aggregate of the individual intramental consciousnesses that make up the group. On the other hand, intermental thinking is often more than the sum of its parts, and this difference can sometimes be quantified. My partner and I actively cooperate on the answers to a weekly quiz (every Saturday in *The Guardian* newspaper) and regularly get scores of seven or eight out of ten, compared to a probable aggregate of individual scores of about three or four. The intermental dividend is clearly substantial.

In (42), an intramental state of mind, being moved, is put in an intermental context, because all the other listeners are moved as well:

(42) The American who, like all the listeners, had been profoundly moved by the ex-King's recitation ... (33)

Sometimes, an individual description becomes intermental with the introduction of others such as, in this case, co-conspirators:

(43) Father Rothschild was conspiring with Mr. Outrage and Lord Metroland. (82)

The narrator chooses a form of words that gives the weight to Father Rothschild, rather than saying: 'The three were conspiring', thereby cueing the reader to surmise that he is the most enthusiastic conspirator. On a related point, groups are sometimes specified with a leader:

(44) The old brigade, led by Mrs Blackwater, threw themselves with relish into an orgy of litigation ... (92)

A strange kind of leadership occurs when Adam works as a gossip columnist:

(45) ... arguing that people did not really mind *whom* they read about provided that a kind of vicarious inquisitiveness into the lives of others was satisfied, Adam began to invent people. (94)

The activities of Adam's creations then begin to respond to the public's reception of them as real people. Symbiotically, the fictional creations then influence readers' actual behavior, which, in turn, modifies their actions and so on. Adam's mind is in a Bakhtinian dialogue with what he anticipates, correctly, the public mind to be. His wholly fictitious narratives take on 'a life of their own' and achieve a kind of reality within the storyworld which is based on the dialogic relationship between Adam's intramental thought processes and the public's intermental mind.

In one scene, three characters are described as:

(46) ... maintaining a moody silence. (150)

This phrase implies three separate conscious decisions to remain silent, and the resulting nonaction maintains the group dynamic. 'Moody' indicates the shared reason for the silence. The next three passages contain very complex interrelationships between inter- and intramental thinking. (47) occurs before, and (48) after, Adam and Nina make love for the first time:

(47) (a) But this raised a question in both their minds (b) that had been unobtrusively agitating them throughout the journey. (c) Neither said any more on the subject, (d) but there was a distinct air of constraint (e) in the Daimler from Pulborough onwards. (67)

An intermental event is described in (a), but (b) makes it clear that it is based on previously existing or latent states of mind (of uncertainty and apprehension regarding the possibility that they might be making love that night). 'Unobtrusive' refers to the fact that their state of mind had not made itself obvious in their behavior. (c) is nonaction that arises from a conscious intermental decision not to do anything. (d) can be decoded as: Adam is experiencing a feeling of constraint; Nina is experiencing the same feeling; and an observer could tell from their external behaviour that they were experiencing that feeling. (e) is the physical context.

(48) also involves a complex interrelationship between inter- and intra mental thinking:

(48) (a) They treated each other quite differently (b) after their night's experiences. (c) Adam was inclined to be egotistical and despondent; (d) Nina was rather grown up and disillusioned and distinctly cross. (76)

The action in (a) is intermental in the sense that their thoughts and actions have changed as a unit. The reason for the changes, given in (b), is a joint experience. However, in (c) and (d), their reactions are intramentally different. 'Despondent' is clearly a state of mind. 'Egotistical' is slightly different because it has more of the quality of a behavior description and also a judgment by the narrator. 'Inclined to be' puts these mental states in the context of Adam's whole personality. As regards Nina's reactions, Wittgenstein's question is unanswerable.

A similar sort of complexity is apparent in (49):

(49) (a) Adam and Miles and Archie Schwert (b) did not talk much. (c) The effects of their drinks had now entered on that secondary stage, vividly described in temperance handbooks, when the momentary illusion of well-being and exhilaration gives place to melancholy, indigestion and moral decay. (d) Adam tried to concentrate his thoughts upon his sudden wealth, but they seemed unable to adhere to this high pinnacle, and as often as he impelled them up, slithered back helplessly to his present physical discomfort. (149)

The listing of the individuals in (a) seems significant, paving the way for the progression in this passage from inter- to intramental thought and the eventual disintegration of the group later in the narrative. (b) is significant action: it soon becomes clear why they did not feel like talking. (c) is group thought report that describes a typical process of consciousness as it applies in this case to these three individuals. (d) is intramental thought report which is standard in most novels but comparatively rare in this one. Adam's thought processes are preoccupied, as my chapter has been, with the importance of physical context.

6.3 Group Norms

A particularly important function of intermental thinking and communicative action is the formation and maintenance of group norms and conventions, such as in this case:

(50) ... the sort of people who liked that sort of thing went there continually and said how awful it was. (71)

The language that the narrator uses here to describe this consensus creates a noticeable distance between the values of the Bright Young People and the values of the implied author, and therefore, implicitly, the implied reader. This effect is even more apparent in (51), when Lady Circumference sees:

(51) ... a great concourse of pious and honorable people ... people of decent and temperate life, uncultured, unaffected, unembarrassed, unassuming, unambitious people, that fine phalanx of the passing order ... (107)

It appears for most of the narrative that the novel does not contain an implied moral norm (that is, one established by the implied author) against which the implied reader is invited to judge the norms of the various sets such as the Bright Young People and other, older sets. However, the strength of the language used in this important passage, albeit focalized by free indirect perception through Lady Circumference, appears to suggest that it should be read as more than just the perception of one character. It reveals a bedrock of 'norm-alness' or 'norm-ality' against which the artificiality, cruelty and futility of the lives of the Bright Young People is clearly revealed. The implied author appears to intend these judgments to form the moral center of the novel.

In the same vein, consider (52):

> (52) (a) There were about a dozen people left at the party; (b) that hard kernel of gaiety that never breaks ... (c) 'Of course there's always the Ritz' said Archie ...But he said it in the tone of voice that made all the others say, (d) no, the Ritz was too, too boring at that time of night ... (e) Soon someone would say those fatal words, 'Well, I think it's time for me to go to bed ...' (f) and the party would be over. (46)

Following the narrative description in (a), (b) is a subtly worded comment or judgment by the narrator on the minds of the whole group. Superficially, they are gay but all the other words apart from 'gaiety' convey a sense of their aimlessness and desperation. This is the consensus in action. The action in (c) can be decoded as follows: he intended that his action would have an effect on their minds opposite to the surface meaning of the words and cause them to come to the same decision as he regarding an intention to act (that is, to go elsewhere). (d) is intermental free indirect speech, similar to the group free indirect thought that I referred to in Section 4.1. (e) is a statement by the narrator that one of the group will come to an intramental decision to leave and so destroy the intermental consensus. (f) describes the consequences of (e). Social norms are always liable to be transgressed by individuals and the fatal words are a potentially norm-breaking intramental action. Such dissent is characteristic of many aspects of the relationship between intermental and intramental thinking.

Indeed, dissenting action can be comically inadvertent:

> (53) Then Mrs. Melrose Ape stood up to speak. A hush fell in the gilt ballroom beginning at the back and spreading among the chairs until only Mrs Blackwater's voice was heard exquisitely articulating some details of Lady Metroland's past. (84)

But, in (54), the same act, breaking a socially agreed silence, quite deliberately defies the consensus:

> (54) But suddenly on that silence vibrant with self-accusation, broke the organ voice of England, the hunting cry of the *ancien regime* ... 'what a damned impudent woman' she said. (85)

Obviously, intramental dissent can also take place amongst the norm reinforcement of core, collaborative intermental decision making:

> (55) After further discussion the conclusion was reached that angels were nurses, and that became the official ruling of the household. But

the second footman was of the opinion that they were just 'young persons' ... (79)

Also, group conflict can arise when the social norms established by two or more groups are incompatible:

(56) They stopped for dinner at another hotel, where everyone giggled at Miss Runcible's trousers ... (129)

(57) Two little American cars had failed to start; their team worked desperately at them amid derisive comments from the crowd. (142)

The next example is representative of the social fissures that are such a marked feature of the novel:

(58) The real aristocracy ... had done nothing about [coming in fancy dress]. They had come on from a dance and stood in a little group by themselves, aloof, amused but not amusing. (44)

In describing the self-conscious conflict and hostility between the small group (the aristocrats) and the larger group (the rest of the party), the passage is an interesting example of how focalization can change in just four words: 'amused but not amusing'. 'Amused' describes the consciousness of the aristocrats: 'we are amused in a superior sort of way at the rest of the party'. 'Amusing' describes the state of mind of the rest of the party: 'they are very superior but we do not find them amusing'.

On occasions the reader can experience a bewilderingly complex melange of different intermental groups which contains very marked group conflict and hostility:

(59) (a) From the window [the angels] could see the guests arriving for the party. (b) In spite of the rain quite a large crowd had collected ... (c) to criticize the cloaks with appreciative 'oohs' and 'ahs' or contemptuous sniffs ... (d) The Bright Young People came popping all together ... (e) Some 'gatecrashers' who had made the mistake of coming in Victorian fancy dress (f) were detected and repulsed. (g) They hurried home to change for a second assault. (h) No one wanted to miss Mrs. Ape's debut. (i) But the angels were rather uneasy. (78)

(a) consists of intermental free indirect perception: the angels are watching the other groups. In (b), the crowd is a second group of whom we are told the circumstances under which they took the decision to come. (c) is communicative action and the adjectives used to describe it are indicative of the accompanying states of mind. The contempt of one group for another is an obvious manifestation of group conflict. (d) describes the action of a third group. (e) consists of a fourth group and their action of coming in Victorian dress. However, the fact that they come wrongly dressed makes it clear that there is a fifth group, understood but norm regulating, who had decided that it was the wrong dress. The norm regulating group, still unnamed, takes the action in (f) of detecting and repulsing the gatecrashers. In (g), the gatecrashers then take the decision to follow another course of action with the intention of evading the norm regulators. In (h), the reason given for the course of action in (g) gives information about the states of mind (anticipation, excitement and so on) of all the groups so far referred to. Finally, in (i), the focus is narrowed again and we are back with a very specific piece of intermental thought report related to the first group mentioned.

7 Conclusion

I have argued that one of the most important of the cognitive frames used by readers to understand texts is the continuing consciousness frame. I have focused on two neglected subframes: thought and action, and intermental thought, both of which relate to states of mind and purposive mental functioning rather than inner speech. I have also attempted to show that analysis of a number of sub-subframes can reveal how much information on fictional minds is available to the reader even within a behaviorist narrative such as *Vile Bodies*. I conclude by suggesting that what is now required is the application of this approach to a wide range of other texts. It is possible that these devices are significant constituents of all narrative discourses but further work on this point is required. When the social mind exists for those who would explain it, narrative theory will understand better how characters do and undergo things in the storyworld, and how mental processes take place in their natural habitat of the houseyard, the marketplace, and the town square, because these are the places in which the fictional mind extends beyond the fictional skin.[1]

References

Bateson, G. 1972. *Steps to an Ecology of Mind: A Revolutionary Approach to Man's Understanding of Himself.* New York: Ballantine.

Booth, W. 1983. *The Rhetoric of Fiction.* 2nd ed. Harmondsworth: Penguin.

Cohn, D. 1978. *Transparent Minds: Narrative Modes for Presenting Consciousness in Fiction.* Princeton: Princeton University Press.

Cohn, D. 1999. *The Distinction of Fiction.* Baltimore: Johns Hopkins University Press.

Doležel, L. 1988. Mimesis and Possible Worlds. *Poetics Today* 9.3: 475-96.

---

[1] I would like to thank Robert Chase, David Herman, Uri Margolin, and Marie-Laure Ryan for their helpful comments on this chapter.

Doležel, L. 1998. *Heterocosmica: Fiction and Possible Worlds*. Baltimore: Johns Hopkins University Press.

Fludernik, M. 1996. *Towards a 'Natural' Narratology*. London: Routledge.

Geertz, C. 1993. *The Interpretation of Cultures: Selected Essays*. London: Fontana.

Genette, G. 1980. *Narrative Discourse: An Essay in Method*, trans. J. E. Lewin. Ithaca: Cornell University Press.

Habermas, J. 1984. *The Theory of Communicative Action. Volume 1. Reason and the Rationalization of Society*, trans. T. McCarthy. Boston: Beacon Press.

Jahn, M. 1997. Frames, Preferences, and the Reading of Third Person Narratives: Towards a Cognitive Narratology. *Poetics Today* 18.4: 441-68.

McHale, B. 1981. Islands in the Stream of Consciousness: Dorrit Cohn's *Transparent Minds*. *Poetics Today* 2.2: 183-91.

Margolin, U. 1986. The Doer and the Deed: Action as a Basis for Characterization in Narrative. *Poetics Today* 7.2: 205-25.

Margolin, U. 1990. Individuals in Narrative Worlds: An Ontological Perspective. *Poetics Today* 11.4: 843-71.

Margolin, U. 1996. Telling Our Story: On 'We' Literary Narratives. *Language and Literature* 5.2: 115-33.

Margolin, U. 2000. Telling in the Plural: From Grammar to Ideology. *Poetics Today* 21.3: 591-618.

O' Shaughnessy, B. 1997. Trying (as the Mental 'Pineal Gland'). *The Philosophy of Action*, ed. A. R. Mele, 53-74. Oxford: Oxford University Press.

Palmer, A. 2002. The Construction of Fictional Minds. *Narrative* 10.1: 28-46.

Palmer, A. 2004. *Fictional Minds*. Lincoln: University of Nebraska Press.

Pavel, T. 1986. *Fictional Worlds*. Cambridge, MA: Harvard University Press.

Prince, G. 1987. *A Dictionary of Narratology*. London: Scolar Press.

Ryan, M-L. 1991. *Possible Worlds, Artificial Intelligence, and Narrative Theory*. Bloomington: Indiana University Press.

Ryle, G. 1963. *The Concept of Mind*. Harmondsworth: Peregrine.

Schank, R., and R. Abelson. 1977. *Scripts, Plans, Goals, and Understanding: An Inquiry into Human Knowledge Structures*. Hillsdale: Erlbaum.

Stanzel, F. 1984. *A Theory of Narrative*, trans. C. Goedsche. Cambridge: Cambridge University Press.

Trevarthen, C. 1999. Intersubjectivity. *The MIT Encyclopedia of the Cognitive Sciences*, eds. R. A. Wilson and F. C. Keil, 415-9. Cambridge, MA: MIT Press.

van Dijk, T. 1976. Philosophy of Action and Theory of Narrative. *Poetics* 5: 287-338.

Wertsch, J. 1991. *Voices of the Mind: A Sociocultural Approach to Mediated Action*. Cambridge, MA: Harvard University Press.

Waugh, E. 1996 [1930]. *Vile Bodies*. Harmondsworth: Penguin.

Wittgenstein, L. 1958. *Philosophical Investigations*. Oxford: Basil Blackwell.

Name Index

Subject Index